# GCSE OCR B
# Geography

Don't bury your head in the sand about the GCSE OCR B Geography exams...
Revise with this fantastic CGP book and you'll get your just deserts!

It's overflowing with super clear study notes, helpful diagrams and cracking case studies — plus plenty of exam-style practice to test how much you've *really* learned.

We've even included expert advice on crucial geographical skills, so there won't be any earth-shattering shocks on the day.

### How to access your free Online Edition

This book includes a free Online Edition to read on your PC, Mac or tablet.
You'll just need to go to **cgpbooks.co.uk/extras** and enter this code:

3113 6123 6806 2653

By the way, this code only works for one person. If somebody else has used this book before you, they might have already claimed the Online Edition.

# Complete
# Revision & Practice
Everything you need to pass the exams!

# Contents

## Getting Started
Structure of the Course ............................................... 1

## Component 1: Our Natural World

### Topic 1 — Global Hazards

Global Atmospheric Circulation ............................. 2
Extreme Weather ............................................................ 5
    *Worked Exam Questions*.................................. 6
    *Exam Questions* ................................................. 7
Tropical Storms............................................................... 8
El Niño and La Niña ...................................................... 9
Drought........................................................................... 10
Flash Flooding — Case Study ................................. 11
Tropical Storm — Case Study ................................. 12
Heat Wave — Case Study .......................................... 13
Drought — Case Study ............................................... 14
    *Worked Exam Questions*................................. 15
    *Exam Questions* ................................................ 16
Tectonic Plates ............................................................. 17
Plate Boundaries .......................................................... 18
Earthquakes................................................................... 19
Volcanoes ...................................................................... 20
Tectonic Hazards — Case Study ............................ 21
Managing the Impacts of Tectonic Hazards............. 22
    *Worked Exam Questions*................................. 23
    *Exam Questions* ................................................ 24
Revision Summary..................................................... 25

### Topic 2 — Changing Climate

Evidence for Climate Change ................................. 26
Causes of Climate Change........................................ 28
Global Effects of Climate Change .......................... 30
Effects of Climate Change on the UK .................... 31
    *Worked Exam Questions*................................. 32
    *Exam Questions* ................................................ 33
Revision Summary..................................................... 34

### Topic 3 — Distinctive Landscapes

The UK Landscape ......................................................35
Weathering and Erosion ............................................36
Transportation and Deposition................................37
Coastal Landforms .....................................................38
UK Coastal Landscape — Case Study ..................40
    *Worked Exam Questions*..................................44
    *Exam Questions* .................................................45
River Landforms ..........................................................46
UK River Basin — Case Study ..................................50
    *Worked Exam Questions*..................................54
    *Exam Questions* .................................................55
Revision Summary......................................................56

### Topic 4 — Sustaining Ecosystems

Ecosystems .....................................................................57
Global Ecosystems ........................................................58
    *Worked Exam Questions*...................................62
    *Exam Questions* ..................................................63
Tropical Rainforests .....................................................64
Tropical Rainforests — Human Impacts ...................66
Tropical Rainforests —
Sustainable Management — Case Study ..................67
Polar Environments......................................................68
Polar Environments — Human Impacts ....................69
Managing Polar Environments — Case Studies ......70
    *Worked Exam Questions*...................................71
    *Exam Questions* ..................................................72
Revision Summary.......................................................73

## Component 2: People and Society

### Topic 5 — Urban Futures

Urban Growth................................................................. 74
Urbanisation in LIDCs .................................................. 75
Suburbanisation ............................................................ 77
Counter-Urbanisation .................................................. 78
Re-Urbanisation ............................................................ 79
    *Worked Exam Questions*................................... 80
    *Exam Questions* .................................................. 81
London — Case Study ................................................. 82
Lagos — Case Study .................................................... 85
    *Worked Exam Questions*................................... 88
    *Exam Questions* .................................................. 89
Revision Summary........................................................ 90

### Topic 6 — Dynamic Development

Measuring Development ............................................. 91
Uneven Development ................................................... 92
Factors Affecting Development ................................. 93
    *Worked Exam Questions*................................... 96
    *Exam Questions* .................................................. 97
Increasing Development — Stages and Goals .......... 98
Increasing Development — Aid.................................. 99
Increasing Development — Trade and TNCs........... 100
LIDC Development — Case Study ........................... 101
    *Worked Exam Questions*................................. 106
    *Exam Questions* ................................................ 107
Revision Summary...................................................... 108

### Topic 7 — UK in the 21st Century

Characteristics of the UK ......................... 109
The Changing Population of the UK ....................... 110
The UK's Ageing Population ................................. 113
    *Worked Exam Questions* ................................ 114
    *Exam Questions* ........................................... 115
The Changing Economy of the UK ......................... 116
UK Economic Hubs ................................................ 117
UK Economic Hubs — Example ............................. 118
The UK's Role in the World .................................... 119
UK Media Exports ................................................... 120
Multicultural UK ..................................................... 121
    *Worked Exam Questions* ................................ 122
    *Exam Questions* ........................................... 123
Revision Summary ................................................. 124

### Topic 8 — Resource Reliance

Resource Supply and Demand ............................... 125
Human Use of the Environment ............................. 126
Food Security ......................................................... 129
Access to Food ...................................................... 130
    *Worked Exam Questions* ................................ 131
    *Exam Questions* ........................................... 132
Increasing Food Production .................................. 133
Ethical Consumerism ............................................. 134
Small-Scale Food Production ................................ 135
UK Food Security — Case Study ............................ 136
    *Worked Exam Questions* ................................ 139
    *Exam Questions* ........................................... 140
Revision Summary ................................................. 141

## Component 3:
## Geographical Exploration

Geographical Exploration ...................................... 142

## Fieldwork

Fieldwork ............................................................... 143
Analysing and Concluding .................................... 144
Evaluating .............................................................. 145
    *Worked Exam Questions* ................................ 146
    *Exam Questions* ........................................... 147

## Geographical Skills

Answering Questions ............................................ 148
Labelling and Comparing ...................................... 149
Maps ...................................................................... 150
Ordnance Survey Maps ......................................... 155
Charts and Graphs ................................................ 157
Statistics ................................................................ 162

## Practice Exams

Paper 1: Our Natural World ................................... 164
Paper 2: People and Society .................................. 170
Paper 3: Geographical Exploration ........................ 176

Answers ................................................................. 182
Acknowledgements ............................................... 192
Index ..................................................................... 194

Published by CGP

*Contributor:*
Paddy Gannon.

*Editors:*
Alex Billings, Charlotte Burrows, Ellen Burton, Jack Davies, Rebecca Greaves, Charles Kitts, Nathan Mair.

*Proofreading:*
Georgina Paxman.

ISBN: 978 1 78908 090 2

*With thanks to Jan Greenway for the copyright research.*

Printed by Elanders Ltd, Newcastle upon Tyne
Clipart from Corel®

Based on the classic CGP style created by Richard Parsons.

Text, design, layout and original illustrations © Coordination Group Publications Ltd. (CGP) 2023
All rights reserved.

Photocopying more than one section of this book is not permitted, even if you have a CLA licence.
Extra copies are available from CGP with next day delivery • 0800 1712 712 • www.cgpbooks.co.uk

# Getting Started

## Structure of the Course

*'Know thy enemy', 'forewarned is forearmed'... There are many boring quotes that just mean **being prepared is a good thing**. **Don't** stumble **blindly** into a GCSE course — find out what you're facing.*

### You'll have to do **Three Exams**

GCSE OCR B Geography is divided into three components — Our Natural World, People and Society and Geographical Exploration.

See pages 148-163 for more on geographical skills.

You'll have to do three exams — one on each of the three components. Geographical skills will be assessed in all three exams, but fieldwork (see p.143) will only be assessed in Papers 1 and 2. All your exams will take place at the end of the course.

#### Paper 1: Our Natural World

Paper 1 is divided into two sections (A and B).

Section A covers four topics:
- Global Hazards
- Changing Climate
- Distinctive Landscapes
- Sustaining Ecosystems

Section B covers Physical Geography Fieldwork.

You need to answer all the questions in this paper.

 1 hour 15 minutes | 70 marks in total | 35% of your final mark

#### Paper 2: People and Society

Paper 2 is divided into two sections (A and B).

Section A covers four topics:
- Urban Futures
- Dynamic Development
- UK in the 21st Century
- Resource Reliance

Section B covers Human Geography Fieldwork.

You need to answer all the questions in this paper.

 1 hour 15 minutes | 70 marks in total | 35% of your final mark

#### Paper 3: Geographical Exploration

1) There isn't any new content to learn for Paper 3, it's all about applying what you already know.
2) In the exam, you'll get a Resource Booklet with lots of information about a specific country.
3) You could be asked about anything from 'Our Natural World' or 'People and Society'.
4) The questions will ask you to combine ideas from the different topics.
5) There will also be a decision-making exercise, where you will have to use the sources you have been given to come to a conclusion about a particular issue.

You need to answer all the questions in this paper.

 1 hour 30 minutes | 60 marks in total | 30% of your final mark

There's more information about this paper on page 142.

Each exam will have a separate Resource Booklet containing sources (e.g. photos, maps, graphs and diagrams) that you will be asked to use to answer some of the questions.

In each exam, there will be one question which has 3 extra marks available for spelling, punctuation and grammar (see p.148). These marks are included in the total marks given for each paper.

---

### Be clear on what you've got to do in your exams

It's worthwhile knowing all this stuff so nothing comes as a shock to you. It'll stop you from being the person who doesn't realise there's a Section B in the exam — there's a fine line between being relaxed and sabotaging yourself...

# Topic 1 — Global Hazards

## Global Atmospheric Circulation

*There's an overall **movement** of air between the **equator** and the **poles** that affects the Earth's **climate**.*

### Air **Circulates** between **High** and **Low Pressure Belts** as **Surface Winds**

1) Winds are large scale movements of air caused by differences in air pressure.
2) Differences in air pressure are caused by differences in temperature between the equator and the poles. Winds move FROM the areas of high pressure TO the areas of low pressure.
3) Winds are part of global atmospheric circulation loops (called cells). These loops have warm rising air which creates a low pressure belt, and cool falling air which creates a high pressure belt.
4) There are three loops in each hemisphere. Here's how it all works:

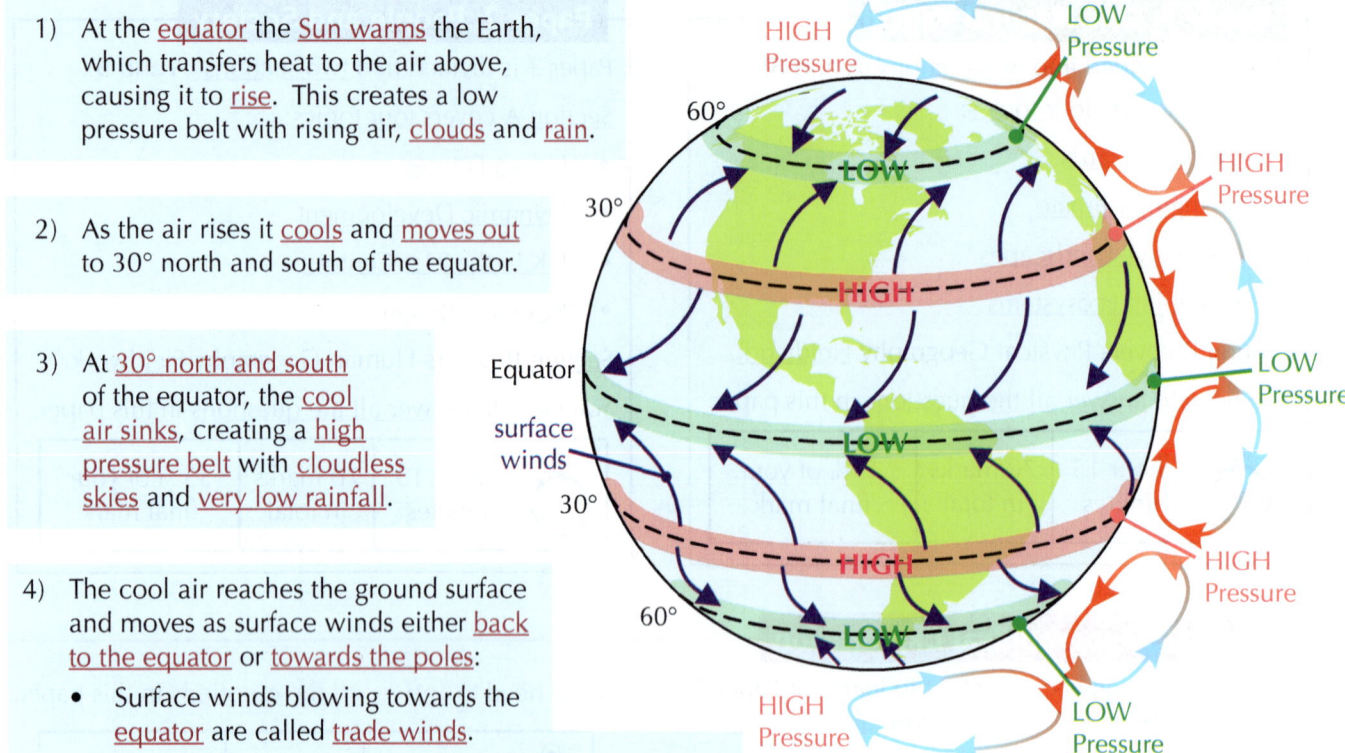

1) At the equator the Sun warms the Earth, which transfers heat to the air above, causing it to rise. This creates a low pressure belt with rising air, clouds and rain.

2) As the air rises it cools and moves out to 30° north and south of the equator.

3) At 30° north and south of the equator, the cool air sinks, creating a high pressure belt with cloudless skies and very low rainfall.

4) The cool air reaches the ground surface and moves as surface winds either back to the equator or towards the poles:
   - Surface winds blowing towards the equator are called trade winds.
   - They blow from the SE in the southern hemisphere and from the NE in the northern hemisphere. At the equator, these trade winds meet and are heated by the sun. This causes them to rise and form clouds.
   - Surface winds blowing towards the poles are called westerlies. They blow from the NW in the southern hemisphere and from the SW in the northern hemisphere.

5) At 60° north and south of the equator, the warmer surface winds meet colder air from the poles. The warmer air is less dense than the cold air so it rises, creating low pressure.

6) Some of the air moves back towards the equator, and the rest moves towards the poles.

7) At the poles the cool air sinks, creating high pressure. The high pressure air is drawn back towards the equator as surface winds.

### Pressure belts and surface winds are determined by global circulation

Air moves in loops (called cells) from the equator to the poles and back. This gives us surface winds and creates belts of high and low pressure that affect the climate, as you're about to find out on the next page...

Topic 1 — Global Hazards

# Global Atmospheric Circulation

*As you've probably noticed, **different regions** of the world have **different climates**. These differences in climate can be explained using the pattern of **global atmospheric circulation** that you met on the previous page.*

## There are Different Climate Zones Around the World

The pressure belts caused by global atmospheric circulation (see previous page) cause variations in climate.

*Different climate zones can support different types of ecosystem (see page 58).*

**Temperate**
- Moderate summers and winters.
- A low pressure belt at about 60° N/S caused by rising air from two cells meeting means rainfall is frequent.

**Polar**
Temperatures are low all year round.

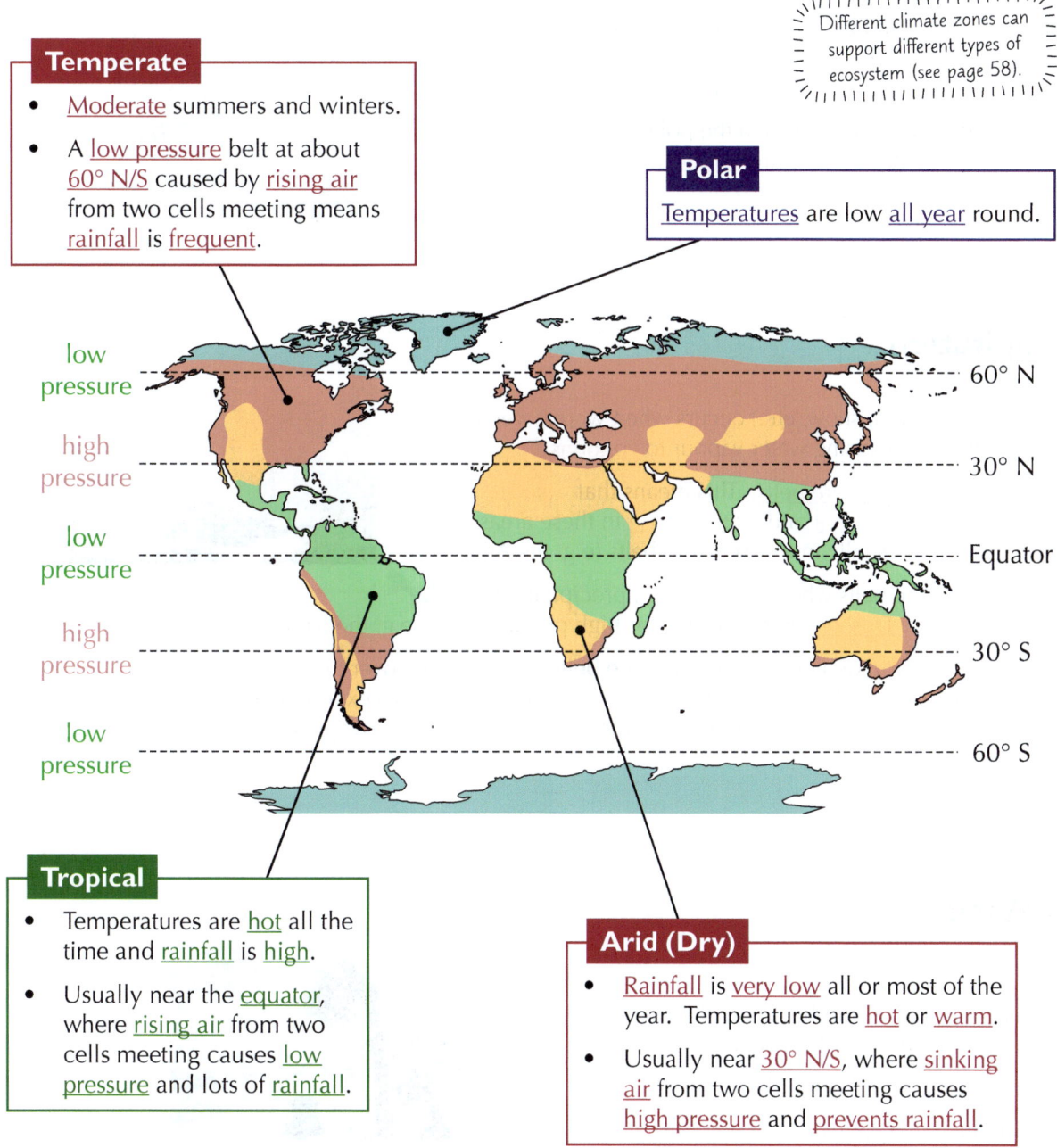

**Tropical**
- Temperatures are hot all the time and rainfall is high.
- Usually near the equator, where rising air from two cells meeting causes low pressure and lots of rainfall.

**Arid (Dry)**
- Rainfall is very low all or most of the year. Temperatures are hot or warm.
- Usually near 30° N/S, where sinking air from two cells meeting causes high pressure and prevents rainfall.

## Global atmospheric circulation is responsible for the different climate zones

Each climate zone is associated with a different low or high pressure atmospheric belt. This causes the different climate zones to be arranged in bands as you move north or south from the equator. For example, areas around the equator are likely to have a tropical climate. Then at around 30° north or south, an arid climate is most common. Moving even further out from the equator, at around 60° N/S, a temperate climate is most likely.

Topic 1 — Global Hazards

# Global Atmospheric Circulation

*Extreme weather often occurs in areas where atmospheric cells meet.*

## Global Atmospheric Circulation can lead to Extremes in Temperature...

1) The equator receives the most energy from the Sun. The poles receive the least.
2) Heat drives atmospheric circulation as warm air from the equator moves towards the poles.
3) Temperatures can be very high in high pressure areas around 30° N/S. There are few clouds due to the sinking air, so there is little to block the Sun's energy.
4) In contrast, the temperatures in the polar regions of the Arctic and Antarctic are very low.

## ...Precipitation...

1) Precipitation (rain, snow, etc.) occurs when warm, wet air rises and cools, causing water vapour to condense.
2) Air rises in low pressure belts. This means that precipitation is frequent and often intense in these areas. Rainforests are usually in low pressure belts (e.g. the Amazon).
3) In high pressure belts where the air sinks, precipitation is extremely low. Deserts are normally near high pressure belts (e.g. the Sahara).
4) The exact location of high and low pressure belts varies slightly over time. Places that normally have more moderate weather can sometimes experience extremely dry or wet weather if they find themselves in a high or low pressure belt.

## ...and Wind

1) Wind is air moving from areas of high to low pressure. This means that atmospheric circulation causes winds, making some parts of the world windier than others.
2) Winds are weak in high and low pressure belts.
3) Winds are strong between pressure belts.
4) When the difference in pressure between high and low pressure areas is large, winds can be extremely strong — e.g. the north coast of Australia.

---

 **Sinking air in high pressure belts leads to low levels of precipitation**
Remember, each of the weather conditions on this page has two extremes, e.g. extremes in temperature can mean really hot or really cold. Test yourself on this page by going through each weather condition and describing both extremes, along with a named example for each of where this extreme may occur.

Topic 1 — Global Hazards

# Extreme Weather

*The **UK** and **Australia** have **contrasting climates** — this means their climates are **really different**. You need to know about extreme weather in **contrasting countries** for the exam, but it doesn't have to be these countries.*

## Australia's Weather is **More Extreme** than the UK's

1) Extreme weather depends where you are — if a normal UK spring's amount of rain fell in the Sahara desert, it would be extremely wet for the Sahara desert. In the same way, Iceland's normal winter temperatures would be extremely cold in the UK.
2) Australia and the UK are contrasting countries which experience different weather extremes:

### Temperature

1) Australia is warmer than the UK — it has hotter summers and milder winters.
2) In Darwin, a city in northern Australia, the average maximum summer temperature is about 33 °C. Temperatures over 40 °C are considered to be extremely hot.
3) In London, the average maximum temperature in summer is about 23 °C. Temperatures over 30 °C are considered extremely hot.
4) So Australian summers are about 10 °C warmer than UK summers. For both countries, extreme temperatures in summer are about 7 °C warmer than the average temperature.

|  | Australia | UK |
|---|---|---|
| Average summer high | 33 °C | 23 °C |
| Highest extreme | 51 °C | 40.3 °C |
| Lowest extreme | −23 °C | −27.2 °C |

### Precipitation

1) Australia has much lower precipitation (rain, snow, etc.) than the UK. It is the world's driest inhabited continent.
2) The average annual rainfall in Australia is 465 mm. In the UK, average annual rainfall is over 1150 mm — more than twice as much rain as Australia gets.
3) Extremely wet years in Australia have over 550 mm of rain. In the UK, annual rainfall in extremely wet years is over 1210 mm.
4) Extremely dry years in Australia have less than 360 mm of rainfall. In the UK, extremely dry years have less than 950 mm of rain.

|  | Australia | UK |
|---|---|---|
| Average annual rainfall | 465 mm | 1154 mm |
| Annual rainfall in driest ever year | 314 mm | 835 mm |
| Annual rainfall in wettest ever year | 760 mm | 1337 mm |

### Wind

1) Australia has stronger extreme winds than the UK does.
2) Australia is affected by tropical cyclones (see page 8). Tropical cyclones cause very strong winds of over 118 km/h.
3) In the UK, gales (winds of over 62 km/h) are rare — most places only have a few days of gales each year.
4) The strongest wind recorded in Australia is over 400 km/h, recorded on Barrow Island off Australia's north-west coast during tropical cyclone Olivia in 1996.
5) The UK's strongest ever sea-level wind was over 220 km/h, recorded in Fraserburgh in Scotland in 1989.

|  | Australia | UK |
|---|---|---|
| Strongest recorded wind | 407 km/h | 229 km/h |

---

## The UK sees fewer extreme weather conditions than Australia

If you are asked to write about the differences in extreme weather conditions in contrasting countries in the exam, make sure you write about at least two countries and that they do have really different extreme weather conditions (like the UK and Australia). Then make sure you have some facts to quote to show the differences in temperature, precipitation and wind for both of these countries to gain full marks.

Topic 1 — Global Hazards

# Worked Exam Questions

Exam questions are the best way to practise what you've learnt. After all, they're exactly what you'll have to do on the big day — so work through this worked example very carefully.

1    Study **Figure 1**, which gives information about the weather conditions in a town in southern England during the first two weeks of December 2010.

**Figure 1**

| | December 2010 | | | | | | | | | | | | | |
|---|---|---|---|---|---|---|---|---|---|---|---|---|---|---|
| Day | 1 | 2 | 3 | 4 | 5 | 6 | 7 | 8 | 9 | 10 | 11 | 12 | 13 | 14 |
| Minimum temperature (°C) | −5 | −3 | −4 | 0 | −1 | 1 | −1 | −2 | −1 | 0 | −2 | −3 | 1 | 0 |
| Maximum temperature (°C) | −2 | 1 | −1 | 2 | 1 | 2 | 3 | 0 | 1 | 2 | 0 | 0 | 2 | 3 |
| Precipitation (mm) | 0 | 0 | 1 | 2 | 3 | 3 | 7 | 0 | 0 | 0 | 2 | 1 | 1 | 8 |

a)   Calculate the range of minimum temperatures shown in **Figure 1**.

*6 °C*

[1]

b)   Calculate the mean daily precipitation during the time period shown in **Figure 1**.

*2 mm*

[1]

c)   What type of extreme weather event is shown in **Figure 1**? Shade **one** oval only.

   A   Tropical storm   ○
   B   Cold snap   ●
   C   Extremely high precipitation   ○
   D   Heatwave   ○

[1]

[Total 3 marks]

2   Global atmospheric circulation leads to the formation of different climatic zones.

a)   Explain why deserts are often found around 30° from the equator.

*There is sinking air where two cells meet around 30° from the equator. This causes high pressure,*

*which limits rainfall, causing deserts to form.*

[2]

b)   Explain how global atmospheric circulation can cause extreme wind in some areas.

*Global atmospheric circulation creates high and low pressure areas. When the difference in*

*pressure between the high and low pressure areas is large, winds can be extremely strong.*

[2]

[Total 4 marks]

Topic 1 — Global Hazards

# Exam Questions

**1** Study **Figure 1**, a map of the world showing bands of high and low pressure and surface winds.

**Figure 1**

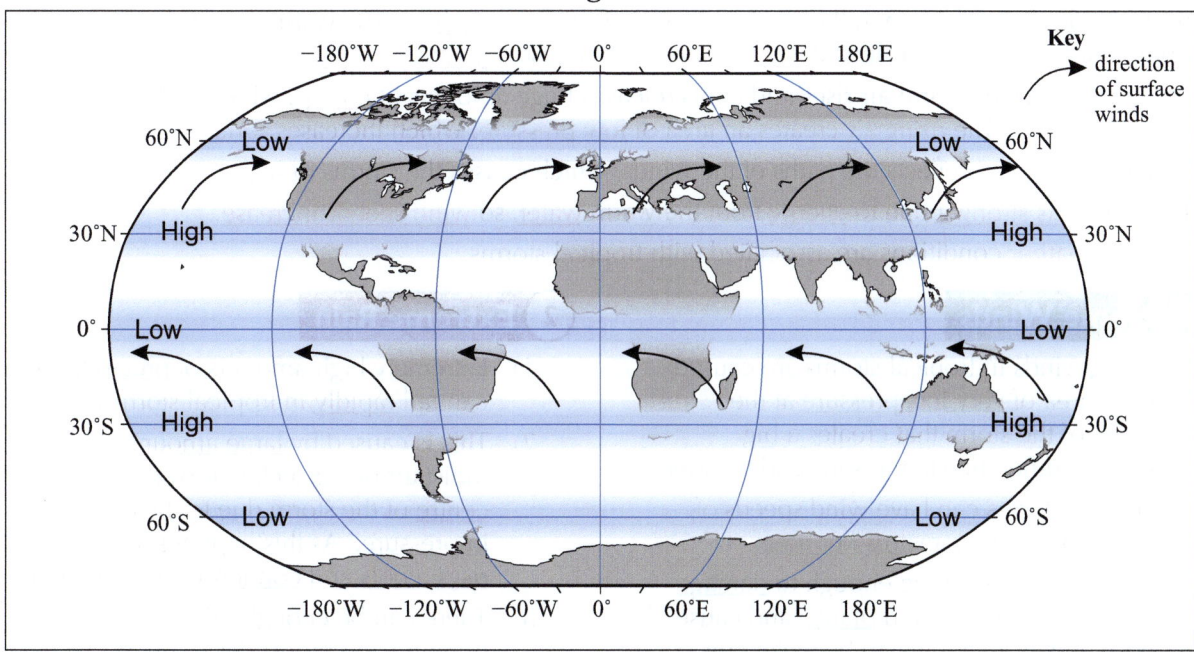

a) Mark on **Figure 1** the direction of the surface winds between 0° and 30° N.

[1]

b) Mark on **Figure 1** the direction of the surface winds between 60° S and 30° S.

[1]

c) Which of the statements below best describes the movement of air at the equator?
Shade **one** oval only.

    A    Air rises up.    ◯

    B    Air sinks down.    ⬤

    C    Air moves up and down.    ◯

    D    Air is still and does not move.    ◯

[1]

d) Which of the following descriptions matches the normal weather conditions at a high pressure belt?
Shade **one** oval only.

    A    Low rainfall, often cloudy.    ◯

    B    High rainfall, often cloudy.    ◯

    C    Low rainfall, rarely cloudy.    ◯

    D    High rainfall, rarely cloudy.    ◯

[1]

[Total 4 marks]

Topic 1 — Global Hazards

# Tropical Storms

*Tropical storms are **intense low pressure** weather systems with **heavy rain** and **strong winds** that spiral around the **centre**. They have a few names (**hurricanes, typhoons,** and **cyclones**), but they're all the **same thing**.*

## Tropical Storms **Bring Extreme Weather Conditions**

1) Tropical storms develop when the sea temperature is 27 °C or higher. The warm ocean temperature means there is lots of warm, moist air to cause extreme precipitation.
2) Condensation when warm air rises and cools releases huge amounts of energy, which makes the storms powerful. The rising air creates an area of low pressure, which increases surface winds.
3) The Earth's rotation deflects the paths of the winds, which causes the storms to spin.
4) The storm gets stronger due to energy from the warm water, so wind speeds increase.
5) Extreme weather conditions are associated with tropical storms:

### 1 Extreme Winds

1) Strong winds in tropical storms are caused by an area of very low pressure at the centre of the storm that creates a big pressure difference to the surrounding area.
2) Tropical storms can have wind speeds of more than 250 kilometres per hour.
3) These winds are strong enough to damage or destroy buildings and plants, and cause loose objects (e.g. bins) to be picked up and transported.

### 2 Extreme Rain

1) Extremely high amounts of precipitation can fall rapidly in tropical storms.
2) This is caused by large amounts of warm, moist air being sucked towards the centre of the storm due to the difference in pressure. As this happens, the air rises, cools and condenses, causing rain.
3) There can be enough rain to cause flooding and mudslides.

## The **Frequency** of Tropical Storms **Varies**, but the **Distribution Doesn't**

### Distribution

1) Most tropical storms occur between 5° and 30° north and south of the equator — any further from the equator and the water isn't warm enough.
2) The majority of storms occur in the northern hemisphere (especially over the Pacific), in late summer and autumn, when sea temperatures are highest.

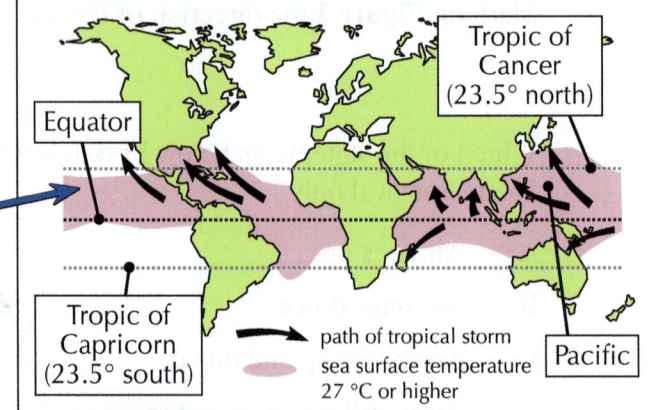

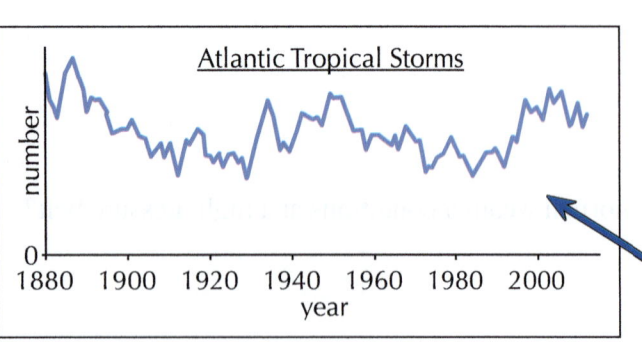

### Frequency

1) The number of tropical storms varies each year.
2) In the Atlantic, the number of tropical storms has increased since 1984 — but there is no overall trend over the last 130 years.

## Tropical storms form at low latitudes — between 5° and 30° N & S

In the exam, you might be faced with a question about the causes of the extreme weather as a result of tropical storms. In order to avoid getting the causes of the extreme wind and extreme rain mixed up, jot down the key points that you want to include before you start properly writing your answer.

Topic 1 — Global Hazards

# El Niño and La Niña

*El Niño* and *La Niña* are climatic events that happen in the Pacific Ocean. This can cause some **quite worrisome weather conditions**.

## El Niño Events are when Air and Ocean Currents Change

1) Air currents in the atmosphere and water currents in the ocean usually flow one way in the Pacific Ocean.
2) Every few years, they weaken or reverse — this is an El Niño event. Sometimes they get stronger — this is a La Niña event. Both cause changes in weather patterns in surrounding areas.

### Normal Conditions

Normally, there's low pressure over the western Pacific and high pressure over the east:

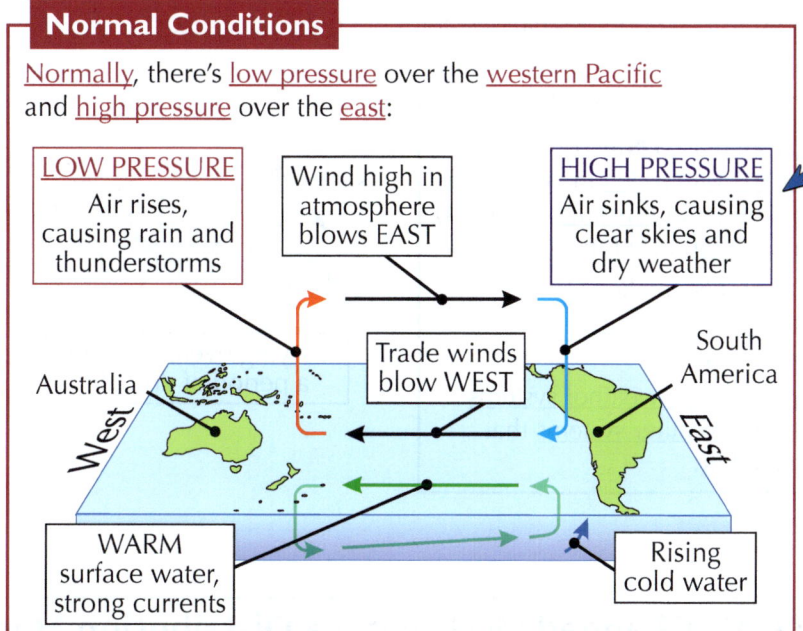

### La Niña

1) La Niña is when the NORMAL conditions become MORE EXTREME.
2) Trade winds blow to the west more strongly, and more cold water rises in the eastern Pacific.
3) It causes more heavy rainfall and floods in the west, and less rainfall and droughts in the east.
4) La Niña events occur every 2-7 years.

### El Niño Events

1) In an El Niño event, pressure rises in the western Pacific and falls in the east.
2) This causes the trade winds (which normally blow from east to west) to weaken or reverse direction.

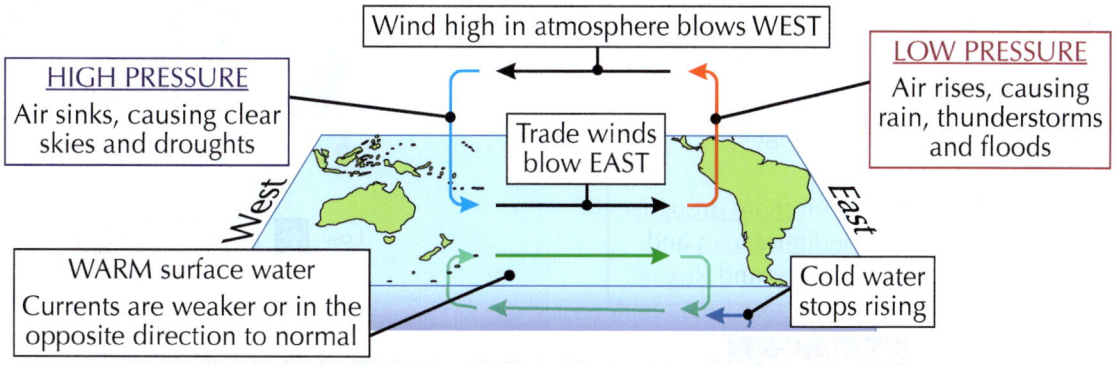

3) The sinking air in the high pressure area over the western Pacific leads to unusually dry weather. This can cause drought — there can be much less rainfall in areas like eastern Australia.
4) The rising air in the low pressure area over the eastern Pacific leads to unusually wet weather. This can cause serious floods in places that don't normally get much rain, e.g. Peru.
5) El Niño events occur every 3-4 years on average, and last for 9 to 12 months.

---

## Make sure you know the difference between El Niño and La Niña

El Niño occurs when trade winds reverse direction or weaken, whereas La Niña happens when trade winds blow West more strongly. You will also need to know the extreme weather conditions that are caused by them.

# Drought

*You **already** know a couple of causes of drought from the previous page — time to go into a bit **more detail**...*

## Drought is when Conditions are Drier than Normal

1) A drought is a long period (weeks, months or years) when rainfall is below average.
2) Water supplies, e.g. lakes and rivers, become depleted during a drought because people keep using them but they aren't replenished by rainfall. Also, droughts are often accompanied by high temperatures, which increase the rate of evaporation, so water supplies are depleted faster.
3) The length of a drought is different in different places, e.g. the worst drought in Britain since records began lasted 16 months, whilst droughts in African countries can last for more than a decade.

### Causes of Drought

1) Changes in atmospheric circulation, such as El Niño or La Niña (see previous page), can mean it doesn't rain much in an area for months or years. For example, the drought in Australia (see p.14) in the 2000s was made worse by an El Niño event in 2002.
2) Changes in atmospheric circulation can also make the annual rains fail (e.g. monsoon rains don't come when they normally do in places like India).
3) Droughts are also caused when high pressure weather systems (called anticyclones) block depressions (weather systems that cause rain), e.g. this can happen in the UK.

A drying riverbed during a period of drought

## The Frequency of Droughts Hasn't Changed Much, but the Distribution Has

### Distribution

1) The map on the right shows the distribution of severe droughts around the world.
2) Areas most at risk from drought are central and southern Africa, the Middle East, Australia, eastern South America and parts of North America.
3) The locations affected by drought vary over time.
4) Since 1950, there have been more droughts in Africa, Asia and the Mediterranean and fewer droughts in the Americas and Russia.

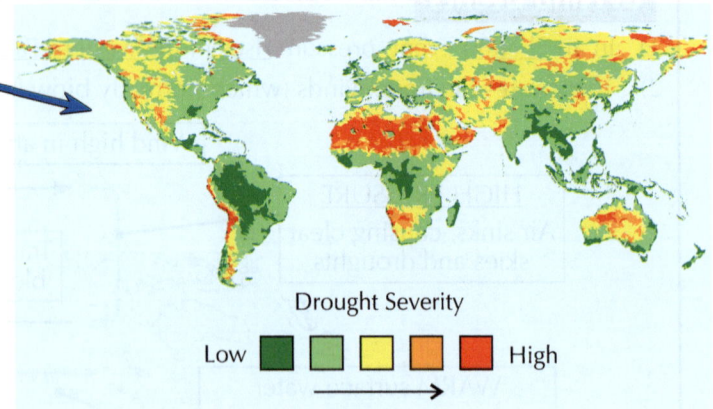

### Frequency

1) Globally, the frequency of droughts has varied from year to year but overall has not changed much since 1950.
2) Some scientists have suggested that droughts might become more frequent and more severe in future due to climate change.

## Future climate change may affect the frequency and distribution of droughts
You won't be expected to recreate the map above in the exam, but you might need to describe the pattern of global drought distribution. Make sure you understand all of this information — it'll help with the case study on p.14.

Topic 1 — Global Hazards

# Flash Flooding

*You need to learn **TWO** extreme weather case studies: either **flash flooding** OR **tropical storms**, and either **heat waves** OR **droughts**. One of these case studies MUST be from the **UK**. Take your pick...*

## There was a Flash Flood in Boscastle in August 2004

1) A flash flood is when lots of water suddenly flows into a river, causing it to overflow its banks. They're often caused by a short period of heavy rainfall.
2) The village of Boscastle on the north coast of Cornwall was devastated by a flash flood on 16th August 2004.

### 1 Causes of the Boscastle Flash Flood

1) 75 mm of rain (the amount that would normally fall in a month) fell in just two hours. A low pressure system brought warm, moist air from the Atlantic Ocean. This air mass cooled as it rose above the land, causing thunderstorms with intense rainfall.
2) Lots of rain over the previous weeks meant that the ground was wetter than normal, and could not absorb the water. So much of the rainfall simply ran off the land surface.
3) Boscastle is in a steep-sided valley close to the confluence of three rivers. The steep valley sides meant that surface water ran into the river channels very quickly, and the confluences meant that about two billion litres of water were funnelled down the river valleys into Boscastle.
4) The old bridge in the village had a low arch over a very narrow river channel. The flooding was made worse because trees and vehicles in the flood water became trapped under the bridge, forming a dam.

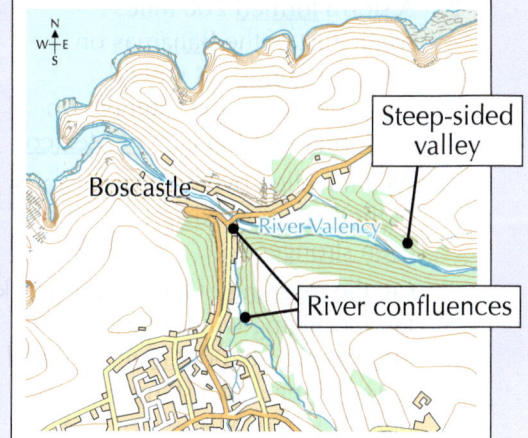

### 2 Consequences of the Boscastle Flash Flood

1) 58 properties, 4 businesses, roads and bridges were destroyed or damaged.
2) The flood was so sudden that people couldn't evacuate or move belongings to safer places.
3) About 50 cars were washed out into sea. This caused some environmental pollution.
4) After the floods, the number of tourists dropped significantly. The village is a popular tourist destination and 90% of the local economy relies on tourism.
5) One person was seriously injured. Some residents suffered mental health problems after the flood due to stress relating to the floods and insurance claims.

### 3 Responses to the Boscastle Flash Flood

1) Emergency services quickly responded to save people in Boscastle. Around 100 people had to be airlifted to safety by seven helicopters.
2) Residents and tourists that were flooded out of their accommodation were looked after in local accommodation and the village hall.
3) Homes, businesses and roads were eventually rebuilt.
4) The bridge was rebuilt with a higher arch, so that debris is less likely to dam the river.
5) A £10 million new flood defence scheme was opened in 2008, which included widening and deepening the river to improve its flow.

## The Boscastle flash flood showed the need for a flood defence scheme

Despite loads of people becoming trapped by flood water, somehow nobody died. As usual, you might have studied a different example of flash flooding. That's fine, just make sure you know the causes, consequences and responses.

Topic 1 — Global Hazards

# Tropical Storm

*Remember, you need to learn a case study for flash flooding OR tropical storms — you don't have to do both.*

## Hurricane Katrina struck Mississippi and Louisiana, USA, in August 2005

Hurricane Katrina, a tropical storm, struck the south-east USA on 29th August 2005:

### 1) Causes of Hurricane Katrina

1) Louisiana and Mississippi are in the Gulf of Mexico, where sea temperatures are often 27 °C or warmer — this means tropical storms can form.
2) A storm formed 200 miles south-east of the Bahamas on the 23rd August. It moved north-west over the southern tip of Florida into the Gulf of Mexico.
3) As it travelled over the warm water of the Gulf of Mexico it became even stronger.
4) On the morning of the 29th it struck land, bringing winds of around 200 km/h and 200-250 mm rainfall in Louisiana and a storm surge of up to 8.5 m in Mississippi.

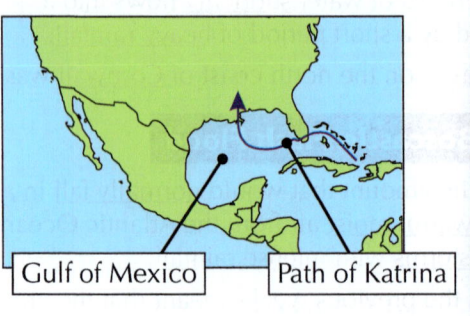
Gulf of Mexico | Path of Katrina

*Tropical storms cause storm surges as strong winds push water towards the shore, causing the water level to rise. If the storm surge coincides with a high tide, flood defences can easily be breached.*

### 2) Consequences of Hurricane Katrina

1) More than 1800 people were killed.
2) 300 000 houses were destroyed and hundreds of thousands of people were made homeless.
3) Large areas were flooded, including 80% of New Orleans.
4) 3 million people were left without electricity.
5) Roads were damaged and some bridges collapsed.
6) Coastal habitats were damaged.
7) 230 000 jobs were lost from damaged businesses.
8) Water supplies were polluted with sewage and chemicals.
9) The total cost of the damage was estimated at $150 billion.
10) Rescue and recovery efforts were hampered by disagreements between national, state and local officials.

### 3) Responses to Hurricane Katrina

1) 70-80% of New Orleans residents were evacuated before the hurricane reached land.
2) Mississippi and Louisiana declared states of emergency — they set up control centres and emergency shelters, and stockpiled supplies.
3) The coastguard, police, fire service and army rescued over 50 000 people.
4) Charities collected donations and provided aid, including millions of hot meals.
5) The US government provided over 16 billion dollars for the rebuilding of homes, and provided funds to repair other essential infrastructure.
6) The US Army recommended that buildings are rebuilt on stilts or not rebuilt at all in very low-lying areas.
7) Repaired and improved flood defences for New Orleans costing 14.5 billion dollars were completed in 2013.

---

## The facts on Katrina make for grim reading

Make sure you're clear on the causes, consequences and responses for your chosen tropical storm, if you've studied one. Try making a set of revision cards to cover each of the three boxes above.

Topic 1 — Global Hazards

# Heat Wave

*You need to know a case study about EITHER a **heat wave** OR a **drought** (see next page)...*

## A Heat Wave is when Conditions are Hotter than Normal

1) A heat wave is a long period (days or weeks) during which the temperature is much higher than normal.
2) The conditions of a heat wave are different in different places, e.g. the conditions considered a heat wave in the UK would be much cooler than in a country like Spain, where higher temperatures are expected.
3) Heat waves are caused when anticyclones (areas of high pressure) stay in the same place for some time.
4) Anticyclones can last for a long period of time, leading to heat waves, like the European Heat Wave that affected the UK (and much of Europe) in August 2003.

### 1) Causes of the 2003 Heat Wave

1) An anticyclone was situated over western Europe for most of August.
2) Air moves clockwise around an anticyclone, so hot, dry air from the centre of the continent was brought to western Europe. This meant temperatures in the UK were higher than normal and rainfall was lower than normal.
3) The anticyclone blocked low pressure systems that would normally bring cooler, rainier conditions from the Atlantic Ocean.

### 2) UK Consequences of the 2003 Heat Wave

1) People suffered from heat stroke, dehydration, sunburn and breathing problems caused by air pollution. Some people drowned when cooling off in rivers, lakes and pools.
2) Around 2000 people died in the UK from causes linked to the heatwave.
3) 20 people were injured when they were struck by lightning during thunderstorms caused by the heat wave.
4) Water levels fell in reservoirs, which threatened water supplies to houses and businesses.
5) Livestock died due to the heat, and crop yields were lower due to the lack of water.
6) Trains were disrupted by rails buckling in the heat and some roads melted, which caused delays.

Water levels in Haweswater reservoir dropped severely during the heatwave.

### 3) UK Responses to the 2003 Heat Wave

1) The NHS and the media gave guidance to the public on how to survive the heat wave — e.g. drink lots of water, have cool baths and showers, block out sunlight to keep rooms cool, etc.
2) Limitations were placed on water use, e.g. some parts of the UK had hose pipe bans.
3) A speed limit was imposed on trains because of the risk of rails buckling. Some rails were painted white to reflect heat and keep them cooler.
4) The UK created a 'heat wave plan' to minimise the consequences of future heat waves.

## The 2003 heat wave caused lots of problems in the UK

Memorising a case study can be tough, and there are four case studies on pages 11-14. But you only need to know a case study for either a tropical storm OR flash flooding event, AND either a heat wave OR a drought. Just make sure one case study is UK-based and one is non-UK-based. Then make yourself some more revision cards, like on the previous page, and use them to test yourself on the details.

Topic 1 — Global Hazards

# Drought

*Australia experienced a drought between 2001 and 2009. This had a massive impact on its inhabitants.*

## There was a Drought in Australia in the Early 21st Century

1) South-east Australia suffered from a severe, long-term drought from roughly 2001 to 2009, although scientists don't agree on exactly when it started and finished. It's known as the Millennium Drought or the "Big Dry".
2) The worst-hit area was the Murray-Darling Basin, an important agricultural region.

### 1 Causes of the Millennium Drought in Australia

1) There were several factors that may have contributed to the Millennium Drought:
2) Australia has a naturally low rainfall due to global atmospheric circulation (see p.2). The 30° S high pressure belt passes through Australia, causing low precipitation.
3) El Niño events (see page 9) in 2002-2003, 2004-2005 and 2006-2007 led to especially low rainfall totals in south-east Australia.
4) Scientists think that climate change may be increasing global temperatures and changing rainfall patterns. So climate change may have contributed to the Millennium Drought:
   - Temperatures in Australia were higher than normal during this period, resulting in more water evaporating than normal.
   - Weather fronts that normally bring rain to south-east Australia moved further south, away from Australia, causing annual rainfall totals to be lower.

### 2 Consequences of the Millennium Drought in Australia

1) Water levels in lakes and rivers (particularly the Murray and Darling) fell, so water supplies ran low.
2) The largest impacts were on farming:
   - Crop yields fell, and crops that rely on irrigation (watering) were particularly badly affected, e.g. rice production fell to just 2% of pre-drought totals. This increased food prices.
   - Livestock died — the number of sheep in Australia fell by around 8 million during 2002-2003.
   - Farmers' incomes fell, and over 100 000 people employed in farming lost their jobs.
3) The drought caused vegetation loss and soil erosion, and rivers and lakes suffered from outbreaks of toxic algae.
4) Dust storms caused by the drought affected inland Australia and some coastal cities.
5) The drought conditions were perfect for wildfires. Over 30 000 km² of land burned, and hundreds of houses were destroyed. 8 people were killed.

### 3 Responses to the Millennium Drought in Australia

1) Water conservation measures were introduced. E.g. the 3 million people who rely on the River Murray for their water supply had their allocation reduced.
2) Cities such as Sydney built desalination plants that can turn sea water into drinking water.
3) The Australian government provided more than 23 000 rural families and 1500 small businesses with income support to help them survive.
4) The government is also investing in improving drought forecasts so farmers can prepare better, improving irrigation schemes and developing drought-resistant crops.

## Australia's drought had a huge impact on rural and farming communities

The farming industry suffered a lot during the drought — crop yields fell and livestock died, which reduced farmers' incomes. However, the government's responses to the drought have helped these communities to recover.

# Worked Exam Questions

These exam questions are similar to the type you'll get in the exam — except they've got the answers written in for you already. Have a look to see the sorts of things you should be writing.

1 Study **Figure 1**, a map showing the areas affected by tropical storms.

a) Using **Figure 1**, describe the global distribution of tropical storms.

*All tropical storms form near the equator, then move westwards and away from the equator.*
[2]

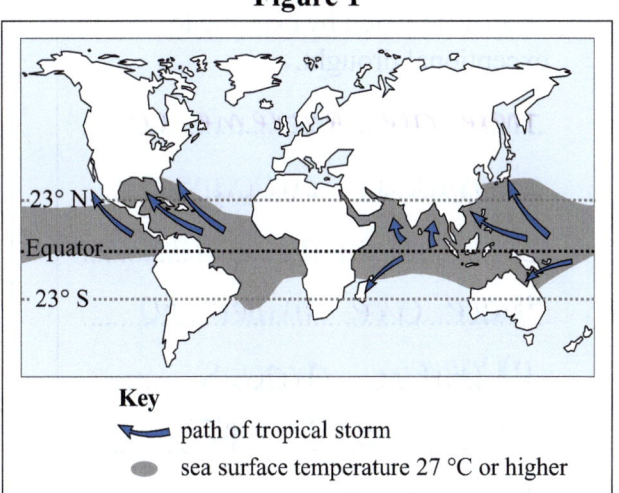

**Figure 1**

Key
← path of tropical storm
● sea surface temperature 27 °C or higher

b) Explain why tropical storms are only found in the areas shown in **Figure 1**.

*Tropical storms only form over water that's 27 °C or higher. This explains why they all form near the equator where the water is warmer.*
[2]

[Total 4 marks]

2 **Figure 2** shows normal atmospheric and oceanic circulation patterns in the South Pacific Ocean.

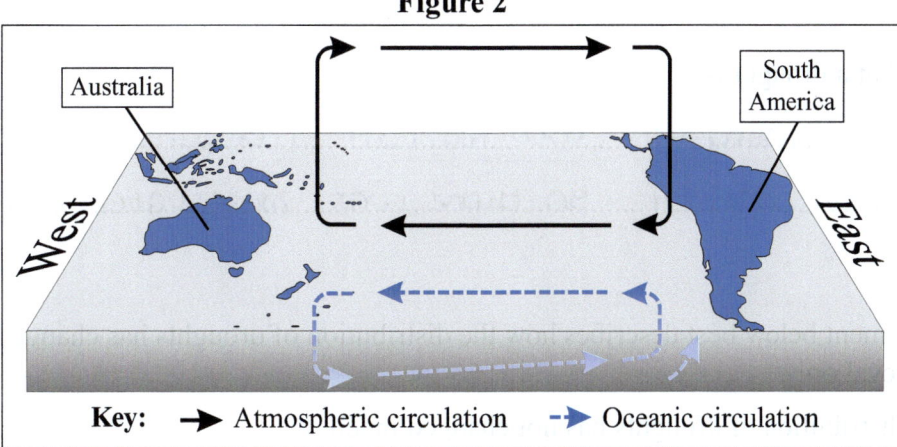

**Figure 2**

Key: → Atmospheric circulation  --▶ Oceanic circulation

a) Describe how the circulation patterns shown in **Figure 2** change during an El Niño event.

*During an El Niño event, normal atmospheric circulation is reversed, so air rises in the eastern Pacific and falls in the west. This causes wind direction to reverse. Oceanic circulation also reverses direction or becomes weaker, and cold water stops rising in the east.*
[4]

b) Explain how El Niño events can cause droughts in some areas.

*During an El Niño event, there is sinking air in the high pressure area over the western Pacific. This leads to unusually dry weather, which can cause droughts.*
[2]

[Total 6 marks]

Topic 1 — Global Hazards

16

# Exam Questions

1 Study **Figure 1**, which shows the global distribution of areas affected by drought in November 2008.

**Figure 1**

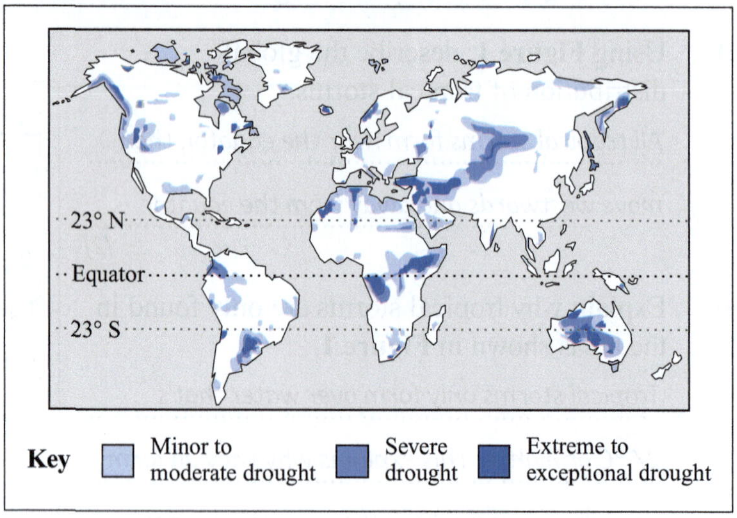

a) Describe the global distribution of areas affected by extreme to exceptional drought.

There are extreme to exeptional drought close to the equator. There are miner to moderate drouts 23°N & 23°N S of the equator.

[4]

b) Describe what a drought is.

When a country has low rainfall, temperatures are higher than normal so there was more water evaparating.

[1]

c) Which statement below best describes how the distribution of droughts has changed over time? Shade **one** oval only.

A   The distribution of droughts has not changed much.   ○
B   There have been more droughts in the Americas and Russia since 1950.   ○
C   There have been more droughts in Africa and Asia since 1950.   ●
D   There have been fewer droughts in Africa and Asia since 1950.   ○

[1]
[Total 6 marks]

2 Answer this question using a case study of **either** a drought **or** a heat wave event.

**Chosen weather hazard event:**..................................................................................

Outline the consequences of this weather hazard event and the responses to it.

[Total 8 + 3 SPaG]

Topic 1 — Global Hazards

# Tectonic Plates

*The **Earth's surface** is made of **huge floating plates** that are constantly moving...*

## The **Earth's Surface** is Separated into **Tectonic Plates**

1) At the centre of the Earth is the core — it has an inner bit and an outer bit. The inner core is a ball of solid iron and nickel. The outer core is liquid.
2) Around the core is the mantle, which is semi-molten rock that moves very slowly.
3) The outer layer of the Earth is the crust. It's about 10-70 km thick.
4) The crust is divided into slabs called tectonic plates that float on the mantle.
5) Plates are made of two types of crust — continental and oceanic:

- Continental crust is thicker and less dense.
- Oceanic crust is thinner and more dense.

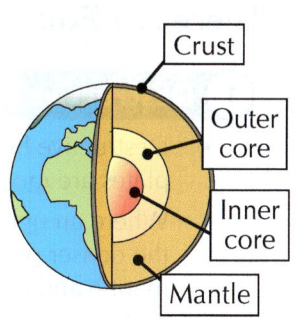

## Tectonic Plates **Move** due to **Convection Currents** in the **Mantle**

1) The lower parts of the mantle are sometimes hotter than the upper parts. When these lower parts heat up they become less dense and slowly rise.
2) As they move towards the top of the mantle they cool down, become more dense, then slowly sink.
3) These circular movements are called CONVECTION CURRENTS — they cause tectonic plates to move.

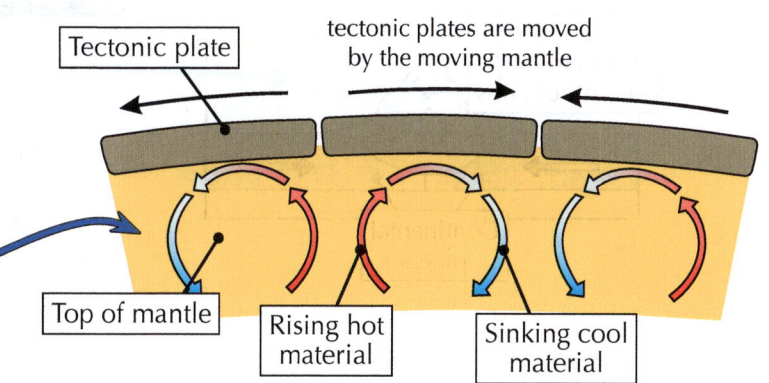

## **Plate Boundaries** are where Tectonic Plates **Meet**

The places where plates meet are called plate boundaries or plate margins:

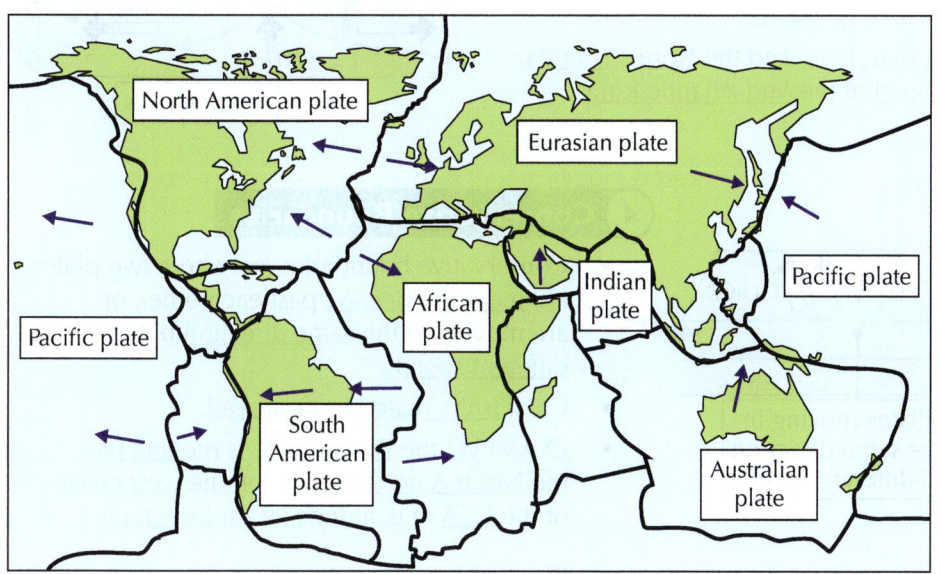

---

## Earth's structure = core, then mantle, then crust on the outside

Make sure you understand the Earth's structure and what tectonic plates are. Spend some time getting convection currents clear in your head as well. Oh, and don't forget about plate margins too. Sorted? Then move on...

Topic 1 — Global Hazards

# Plate Boundaries

*Tectonic plate boundaries* are where **plates meet**. How the plates meet is to do with the **direction** they're moving in.

## There are **Four Types** of **Plate Boundaries**

### 1) Destructive Boundaries

- Destructive boundaries are where two plates are moving towards each other.
- Where an oceanic plate meets a continental plate, the denser oceanic plate is forced down into the mantle and destroyed. This often creates volcanoes and ocean trenches (very deep sections of the ocean floor where the oceanic plate goes down).
- EXAMPLE: the Pacific plate is being forced under the Eurasian plate along the east coast of Japan.

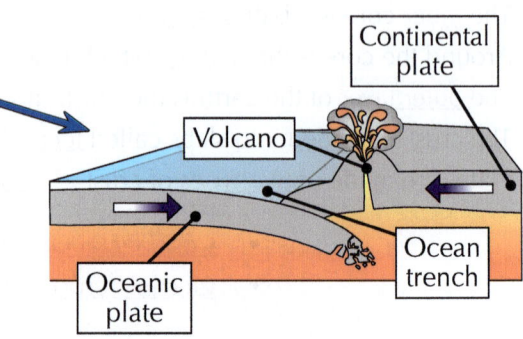

### 2) Collision Plate Boundaries

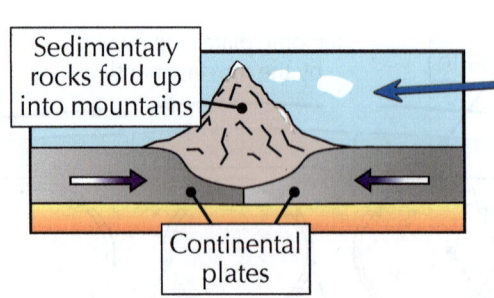

- In collision plate boundaries, both plates are made from continental crust and move towards each other.
- Neither plate is forced down into the mantle — instead both plates are folded and forced upwards, creating fold mountains.
- EXAMPLE: the Eurasian and Indian plates are colliding to form the Himalayas.

### 3) Constructive Boundaries

- Constructive boundaries are where two plates are moving away from each other.
- Magma (molten rock) rises from the mantle to fill the gap and cools, creating new crust.
- EXAMPLE: the Eurasian plate and the North American plate are moving apart at the Mid-Atlantic Ridge.

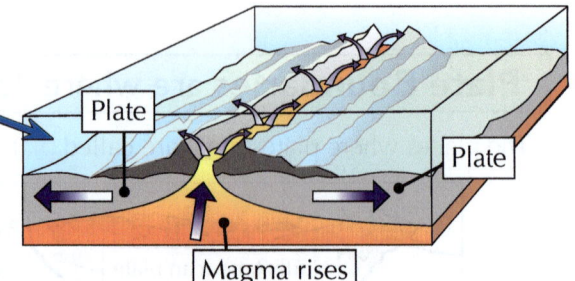

### 4) Conservative Boundaries

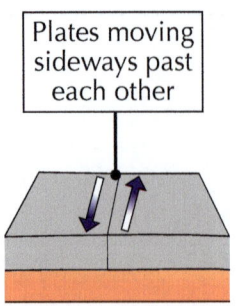
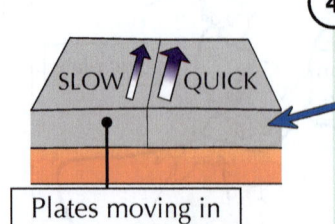

- Conservative boundaries are where two plates are moving sideways past each other, or are moving in the same direction but at different speeds.
- Crust isn't created or destroyed.
- EXAMPLE: the Pacific plate is moving past the North American plate on the west coast of the USA, e.g. at the San Andreas fault.

---

 **Make sure you understand the differences between each boundary**
Each plate boundary has different characteristics — the direction the plates move in affects what happens there. Practise sketching and labelling the diagrams on this page to learn how tectonic plates move.

Topic 1 — Global Hazards

# Earthquakes

*Earthquakes happen more often than you think. Obviously there are the **big ones** that cause loads of **damage** and make the headlines on the news, but there are also lots of **weak earthquakes** every year that hardly anyone notices.*

## Earthquakes Occur at All Four Types of Plate Boundaries

1) Earthquakes are caused by the tension that builds up at all four types of plate boundaries:

   Destructive boundaries — tension builds up when one plate gets stuck as it's moving down past the other into the mantle.

   Collision boundaries — tension builds as the plates are pushed together.

   Constructive boundaries — tension builds along cracks within the plates as they move away from each other.

   Conservative boundaries — tension builds up when plates that are grinding past each other get stuck.

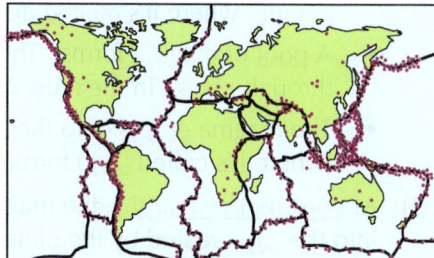

2) The plates eventually jerk past each other, sending out shock waves (vibrations). These vibrations are the earthquake.

3) The shock waves spread out from the focus — the point in the Earth where the earthquake starts. Near the focus the waves are stronger and cause more damage.
4) The epicentre is the point on the Earth's surface straight above the focus.
5) Earthquakes are measured using the moment magnitude scale (which measures the energy released by an earthquake) or the Mercalli scale (which measures the effects). You may still see some references to the Richter scale, which also measures the energy released but is no longer used.

Damage after the magnitude 7.8 earthquake in Nepal in 2015

## Earthquakes Occur at Various Depths

1) The focus of an earthquake can be at the Earth's surface, or anywhere up to 700 km below the surface.
2) Shallow-focus earthquakes are caused by tectonic plates moving at or near the surface. They have a focus between 0 km and 70 km below the Earth's surface.
3) Deep-focus earthquakes are caused by crust that has previously been subducted into the mantle moving towards the centre of the Earth, heating up or decomposing. They have a focus between 70 km and 700km below the Earth's surface.
4) In general, deeper earthquakes do less damage at the surface than shallower earthquakes. Shock waves from deeper earthquakes have to travel through more rock to reach the surface, which reduces their power (and the amount of shaking) when they reach the surface.

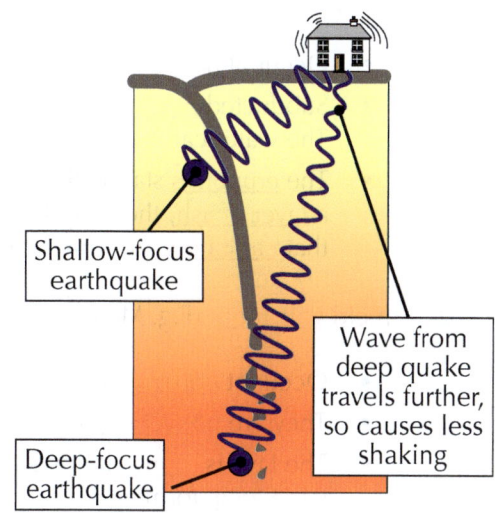

## Shallow earthquakes usually do the most damage

I'd better say this now... don't be put off by maps like the one at the top of the page — you won't ever have to draw them in your exam. But you should know where earthquakes happen and why, so have another read of this page.

Topic 1 — Global Hazards

# Volcanoes

*Volcanoes usually look like mountains... until they **explode** and throw **molten rock** everywhere.*

## Volcanoes are Found at Destructive and Constructive Plate Margins

1) At destructive plate margins the oceanic plate goes under the continental plate because it's more dense.
   - The oceanic plate moves down into the mantle, where it's melted and destroyed.
   - A pool of magma forms. The magma rises through cracks in the crust called vents.
   - The magma erupts onto the surface (where it's called lava) forming a volcano.
2) At constructive margins the magma rises up into the gap created by the plates moving apart, forming a volcano.
3) When a volcano erupts, it emits lava and gases. Some volcanoes emit lots of ash, which can cover land, block out the sun and form pyroclastic flows (super-heated currents of gas, ash and rock).

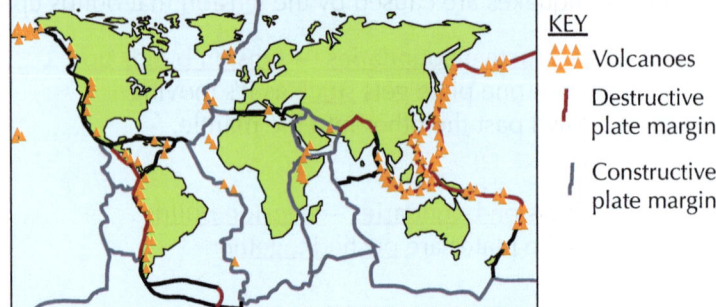

## Hotspots are Found Away From Plate Boundaries

Most volcanic activity occurs at plate boundaries, but there are some areas of intense volcanic activity that aren't at any plate boundaries. These areas are called hotspots:

1) A hotspot is a bit of the Earth's crust that is hotter than normal. They occur where a plume of hot magma from the mantle moves towards the surface, causing an unusually large flow of heat from the mantle to the crust.
2) Sometimes the magma can break through the crust and reach the surface. When this happens, there is an eruption and a volcano forms.
3) Hotspots can be found in oceanic or continental crust, and can be near or far from plate boundaries.
4) Hotspots remain stationary over time, but the crust moves above them. This can create chains of volcanic islands, e.g. Hawaii is a chain of volcanic islands in the middle of the Pacific plate.

## There are Different Types of Volcano

1) Composite volcanoes (E.g. Mount Fuji in Japan)

   - Occur at destructive plate boundaries (see p.18).
   - Subducted oceanic crust contains lots of water. The water can cause the subducted crust to erupt.
   - The eruptions start with ashy explosions that deposit a layer of ash, then erupt a layer of thick, sticky lava that can't flow far. This forms a steep-sided cone.

2) Shield volcanoes (E.g. Mauna Loa on the Hawaiian islands)

   - Occur at hotspots or constructive plate boundaries.
   - They are not very explosive and are made up of only lava.
   - The lava is runny. It flows quickly and spreads over a wide area, forming a low, gentle-sided volcano.

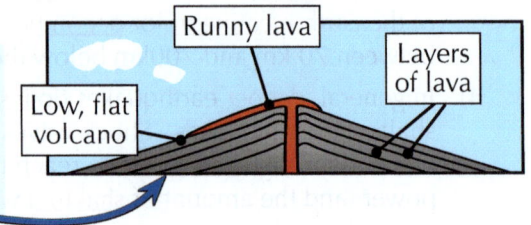

## Volcanoes only occur in some parts of the world

Make sure you can describe the global pattern of volcanic activity, and remember that not all volcanoes are on plate boundaries. Examiners love asking about hotspots, so make sure you understand how they work as well.

Topic 1 — Global Hazards

# Tectonic Hazards

*Don't think you could get away without learning a **real-world example** of a tectonic event...*

## There was a **Deadly Earthquake** in **Pakistan** in **2005**

Place: Kashmir, Pakistan
Date: 8th October, 2005
Size: 7.6 on the moment magnitude scale

Although the epicentre and most serious effects were in Pakistan, it also affected neighbouring countries including India, Afghanistan and China.

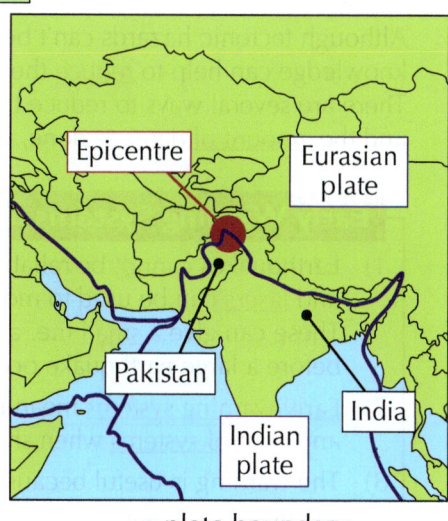

~ plate boundary

### 1  Causes of the 2005 Pakistan Earthquake

1) The Eurasian plate and the Indian plate meet at a collision plate boundary (see p.18) that runs through the middle of Pakistan.
2) The area is very prone to seismic activity as the plates meet and fold, forming the Himalayan fold mountain range.
3) On 8 October 2005, strain that had built up along the fault was suddenly released in a powerful earthquake.

### 2  Consequences of the 2005 Pakistan Earthquake

1) Around 80 000 deaths, mostly from collapsed buildings.
2) Tens of thousands of people were injured.
3) Hundreds of thousands of buildings were damaged or destroyed, including whole villages.
4) Around 3 million people were made homeless.
5) Water pipelines and electricity lines were broken, cutting off supply.
6) Landslides buried buildings and people. They also blocked access roads and cut off water supplies, electricity supplies and telephone lines.
7) Diarrhoea and other diseases spread due to little clean water.
8) Freezing winter conditions shortly after the earthquake caused more casualties and meant rescue and rebuilding operations were difficult.
9) Children's education was affected as schools were destroyed and not rebuilt quickly.

### 3  Responses to the 2005 Pakistan Earthquake

1) International aid and equipment such as helicopters and rescue dogs were brought in, as well as teams of people from other countries.
2) Despite this, help didn't reach many areas for days or weeks, and many people had to be rescued by hand without any equipment or help from emergency services.
3) Tents, blankets and medical supplies were distributed, although it took up to a month for them to reach most areas.
4) 40 000 people from one destroyed town were relocated to a new settlement.
5) Government money was given to people to rebuild their homes, but many had to use it for food. After 3 years, thousands of people were still living in temporary tents.
6) Aid was given to rebuild schools, but some schools were still not rebuilt 10 years after the earthquake, with pupils being taught outside.

## 80 000 dead, 3 million homeless — this 2005 earthquake was deadly

To put that in context, it's roughly the same as if every single person in Wales lost their home. You might have studied a different tectonic hazard event — either way, make sure you know the causes, consequences and responses.

Topic 1 — Global Hazards

# Managing the Impacts of Tectonic Hazards

*Plenty of people* live in areas affected by tectonic hazards, so they need ways to *reduce* the *impact* of them.

## Technology can Reduce the Impact of Tectonic Hazards

Although tectonic hazards can't be prevented, modern technology and knowledge can help to reduce the threat from earthquakes and volcanoes. There are several ways to reduce the number of people killed and injured, and the amount of damage done, when tectonic hazards occur:

### Early Warning Systems for Earthquakes

1) Earthquakes cannot be reliably predicted in advance, but networks of seismometers and lasers can be used to monitor earth movements in areas at risk of earthquakes. These can give a small (i.e. a few seconds or minutes) but vital amount of warning before a large earthquake occurs.
2) Early warning systems mean that warnings can be communicated quickly and automatically to people and control systems when shaking is detected, using the internet, SMS networks and sirens.
3) The warning is useful because:
   - People can get under cover (e.g. under tables) before the shaking starts.
   - People doing delicate or dangerous jobs can stop what they're doing and make the situation safe, e.g. surgeons can stop delicate procedures and cooks can turn off stoves.
   - Utilities like gas can be shut off, preventing leaks and fires.
   - Trains can start slowing down, making derailments due to damaged track less likely.

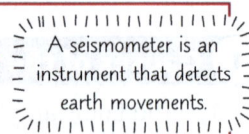
A seismometer is an instrument that detects earth movements.

### Predicting and Monitoring Volcanoes

1) Volcanic eruptions can be predicted if the volcano is well-monitored. Predicting when a volcano is going to erupt gives people time to evacuate — this reduces the number of injuries and deaths.
2) Scientists can monitor the tell-tale signs that come before a volcanic eruption. Remotely operated seismometers, lasers and other sensors can detect indications that an eruption is likely, such as tiny earthquakes, escaping gas and changes in the shape of the volcano (e.g. bulges in the land where magma has built up under it).
3) Volcanoes are also monitored during eruptions, which helps authorities respond appropriately, for example:
   - Evacuation zones can be extended if the eruption becomes more violent.
   - Ash clouds that can damage aircraft can be tracked — this means that flights can be diverted or cancelled, so passengers aren't put at risk.
   - If ash and poisonous gases spread, authorities can warn people to put on gas masks.

### Building Design

Modern building technologies can be used to design buildings that don't collapse in earthquakes or when covered in volcanic ash. This reduces deaths and injuries from falling masonry and reduces the cost of repairs and rebuilding afterwards too.
1) Buildings can be designed to withstand earthquakes, e.g. by using materials like reinforced concrete or building special foundations that absorb an earthquake's energy.
2) Existing buildings and bridges can be strengthened (e.g. by wrapping pillars in steel frames).
3) Pipelines (e.g. for gas and water) can be designed to flex and not break during earthquakes. This helps to prevent deaths and damage to property caused by flooding and fires.

## Early warning systems allow people to find a safe place to take shelter

None of the examples on this page can prevent earthquakes or volcanic eruptions from happening — they're all about reducing the impacts of tectonic hazards. Make sure you learn them all — it'll be worth it for the exam.

Topic 1 — Global Hazards

# Worked Exam Questions

Time for a few exam-style questions to test what you know. The first page has the answers already filled in to help you understand how to answer exam questions effectively. It's over to you for the second page though.

1    Study **Figure 1**, which shows the Earth's tectonic plates and the distribution of earthquakes.

**Figure 1**

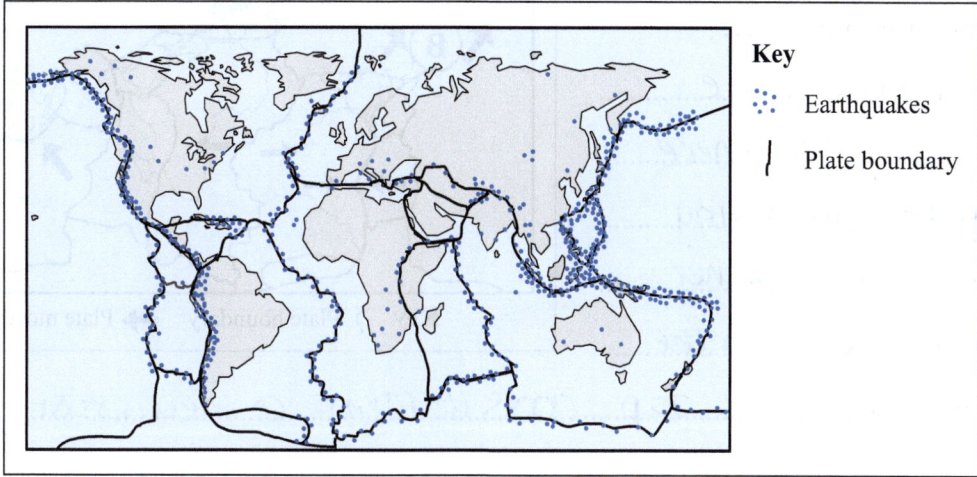

a)   Describe the distribution of earthquakes around the world.

*Almost all earthquakes are found along plate boundaries but some occur in the middle of plates.*

*[2]*

b)   Describe what a shallow-focus earthquake is.

*A shallow-focus earthquake is an earthquake that has a focus between 0 km and 70 km*

*below the Earth's surface.*

*[1]*

*[Total 3 marks]*

2    Study **Figure 2**, which shows a cross-section through a shield volcano.

a)   Explain how the volcano gets its characteristic shape.

**Figure 2**

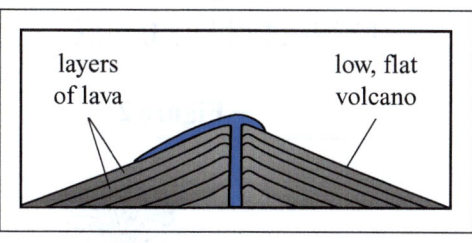

*The lava that comes out of shield volcanoes is runny.*

*This means the lava flows quickly down the sides and spreads*

*over a wide area, forming a low, flat volcano.*

*[2]*

b)   Contrast the characteristics of shield volcanoes and composite volcanoes.

*Shield volcanoes are low and flat, whereas composite volcanoes are steep sided. Composite volcanoes*

*are made of layers of lava and ash, whereas shield volcanoes are made of layers of lava only. The lava*

*that comes out of shield volcanoes is runny, whereas the lava that comes out of composite volcanoes is*

*thick. Ash is released from composite volcanoes, but not from shield volcanoes.*

*[4]*

*[Total 6 marks]*

Topic 1 — Global Hazards

# Exam Questions

**1** Study **Figure 1**, which shows the Earth's tectonic plates.

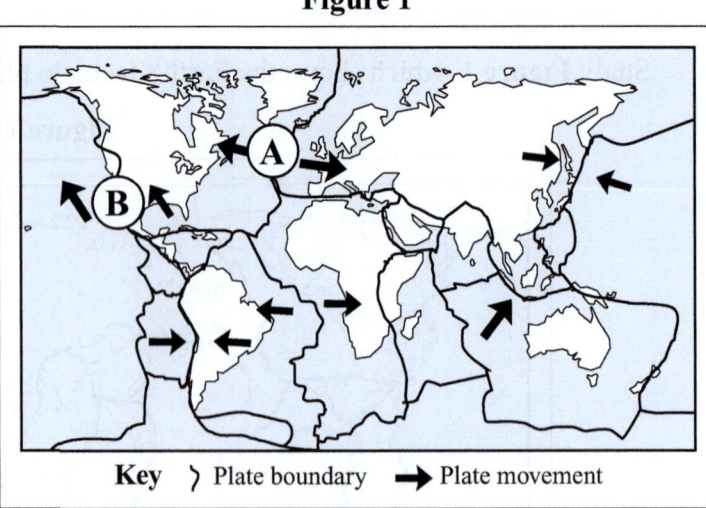
**Figure 1**

a) Name the type of plate boundary labelled A in **Figure 1** and explain why new crust forms there.

*constructive plate boundary are where two plates are moving away from eachother. magma rises from the mantle to fill the gap, cools to form a new crust*
[3]

b) Name the type of plate boundary found at the location labelled B on **Figure 1**.

*conservative plate boundry*
[1]

c) Describe **two** ways that tectonic plates could move in relation to each other at the type of plate boundary you identified in b).

*plates move in the same direction but at different speeds.*
[2]

d) Study **Figure 2**, which is a diagram of a plate boundary. Name the type of plate boundary shown.

*destructive plate boundary*
[1]

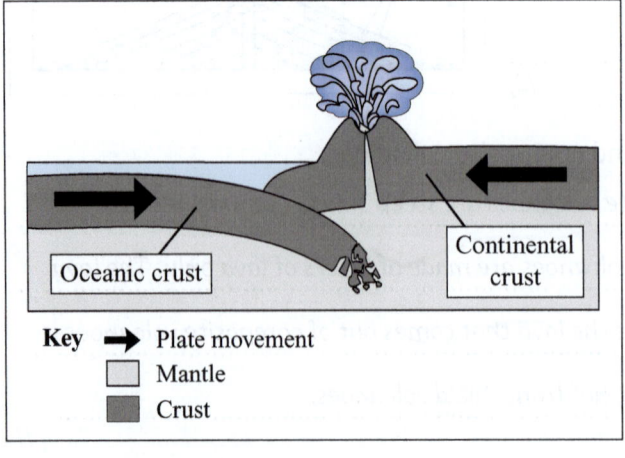
**Figure 2**

e) Describe the processes that operate at a collision plate boundary.

*two plates are moving towards eachother, where the oceanic plate meets the continental plate. the deanser the oceanic plate is forced down into the mantle and destroyed*
[2]

[Total 9 marks]

Topic 1 — Global Hazards

# Revision Summary

You've almost reached the end of Topic 1 — just one more page of questions to go.
- Try these questions and tick off each one when you get it right.
- When you've done all the questions under a heading and are completely happy with it, tick it off.

## Global Atmospheric Circulation (p.2-4) ☐
1) How does global atmospheric circulation lead to high and low pressure belts?
2) How do high and low pressure belts create climatic zones?
3) How does global atmospheric circulation cause extremes of precipitation in some parts of the world?

## Extreme Weather (p.5-14) ☐
4) What conditions are required for a tropical storm to develop?
5) What causes tropical storms to rotate?
6) What are the extreme weather conditions caused by tropical storms?
7) How has the distribution of tropical storms varied over time?
8) How has the frequency of tropical storms varied over time?
9) What is El Niño?
10) What is La Niña?
11) How has the frequency of droughts varied over time?
12) What were the consequences of a flash flood or tropical storm that you have studied?
13) What were the responses to a flash flood or tropical storm that you have studied?
14) What were the causes of a heat wave or drought that you have studied?

## Tectonic Plates (p.17-18) ☐
15) Describe the Earth's structure.
16) What is the mantle?
17) What are the places where tectonic plates meet called?
18) Why do tectonic plates move?
19) Name the type of plate boundary where two plates of continental crust are moving towards each other.
20) Name the type of plate boundary where two plates are moving sideways against each other.

## Tectonic Hazards (p.19-22) ☐
21) What causes earthquakes?
22) How do volcanoes form at destructive plate boundaries?
23) What is a hotspot?
24) What is a composite volcano?
25) For a tectonic hazard event you have studied:
    a) Describe the causes of the hazard event.
    b) Give three consequences of the hazard event.
    c) What were the responses to the hazard event?
26) How can early warning systems reduce the impact of tectonic hazards?
27) How can building design reduce the impact of tectonic hazards?

# Topic 2 — Changing Climate

## Evidence for Climate Change

*We British like to talk about the weather, so global climate change should give us plenty to go on...*

### The Earth is Getting Warmer

Climate change is any significant change in the Earth's climate over a long period. The climate constantly changes — it always has, and it always will.

1) The Quaternary period is the most recent geological time period, spanning from about 2.6 million years ago to the present day.

*The Quaternary period includes the whole of human history.*

2) In the period before the Quaternary, the Earth's climate was warmer and quite stable. Then things changed a lot.

3) During the Quaternary, global temperature has shifted between cold glacial periods that last for around 100 000 years, and warmer interglacial periods that last for around 10 000 years.

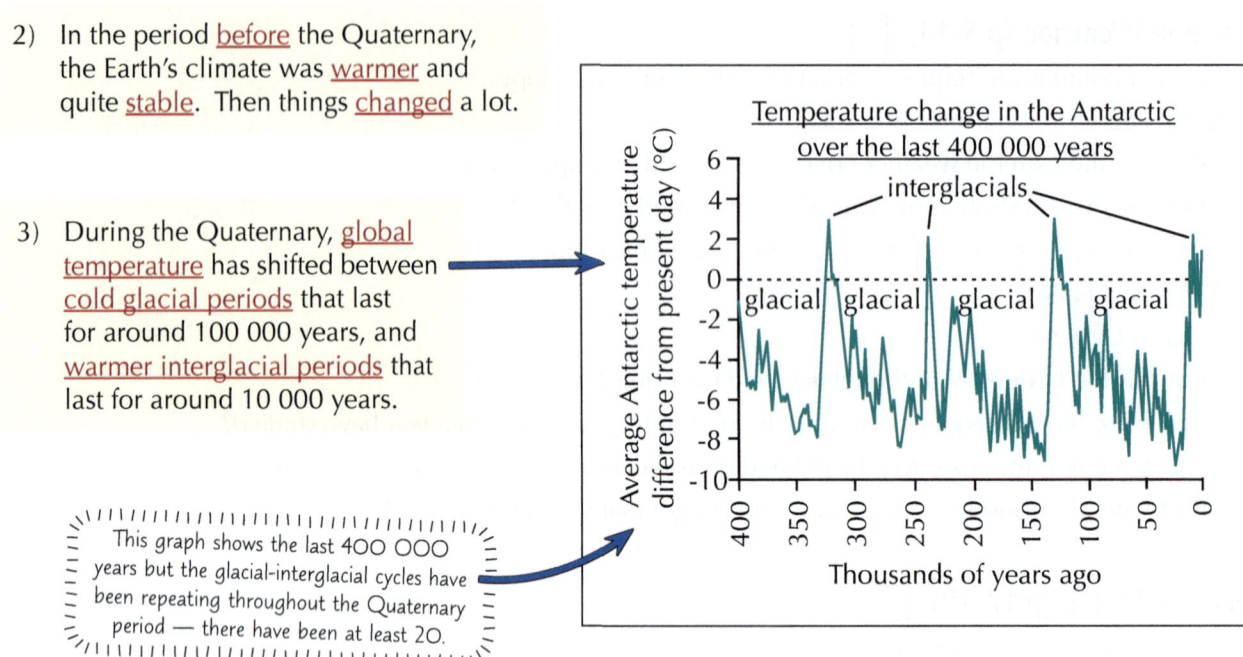

*This graph shows the last 400 000 years but the glacial-interglacial cycles have been repeating throughout the Quaternary period — there have been at least 20.*

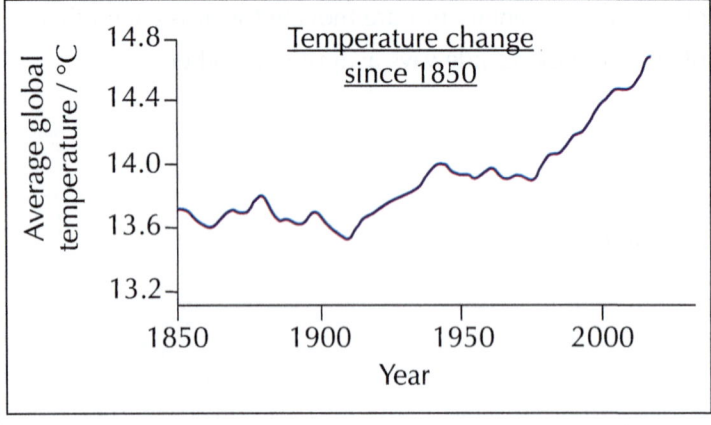

4) The last glacial period ended around 15 000 years ago. Since then the climate has been warming.

5) Global warming is the term used to describe the sharp rise in global temperatures over the last century. It's a type of climate change.

## Global warming has been occurring for the last century

There's going to be loads about climate change and global warming over the next few pages so you need to make sure you know the difference between them. Cover the page, jot down a definition of each, then see if you're right.

Topic 2 — Changing Climate

# Evidence for Climate Change

*There is a variety of evidence that **scientists and researchers** can use to demonstrate that **climate change** is occurring. Not all of the evidence is equal though — some sources are a lot more **reliable** than others.*

## Evidence for Climate Change Comes from Many Sources

Scientists can work out how the climate has changed over time using a range of methods. For example:

### Ice Cores

1) Ice sheets are made up of layers of ice — one layer is formed each year.
2) Scientists drill into ice sheets to get long cores of ice.
3) By analysing the gases trapped in the layers of ice, they can tell what the temperature was each year.
4) One ice core from Antarctica shows the temperature changes over the last 400 000 years (see graph on the previous page).
5) Data collected from ice cores is very detailed and reliable.

### Temperature Data

1) Since the 1850s, global temperatures have been measured accurately using thermometers. This gives a reliable but short-term record of temperature change.
2) However, weather stations are not evenly distributed across the world — data from some areas is patchy.

### Diaries and Paintings

1) Historical diaries can show what the climate was like in the past, e.g. by giving the number of days of rain or snow and the dates of harvests (e.g. an early harvest suggests warm weather).
2) Paintings of fairs and markets on frozen rivers show that winters in Europe were regularly much colder 500 years ago than they are now.
3) However, diaries and paintings aren't very reliable, as they just give one person's viewpoint.

### Sea Ice Positions

1) Sea ice forms around the poles in winter when ocean temperatures fall below -1.8 °C and melts during the summer when it's warmer.
2) By observing the maximum and minimum extent of sea ice each year, scientists can tell how ocean temperatures are changing.
3) The data is very reliable, but accurate records don't go very far back.

## Learn the evidence for climate change

There were no thermometers 2.6 million years ago but scientists can reconstruct climates using the clever methods shown on this page. Some of the methods produce more reliable data than others, but they can all be useful for working out what the climate used to be like in the past. Make sure you learn this stuff inside out before the exam.

Topic 2 — Changing Climate

# Causes of Climate Change

*Climate change* goes back **long before** humans roamed the Earth — this has been caused by **natural factors**.

## Some **Natural Factors** are Possible **Causes** of **Climate Change**

### 1) Milankovitch Cycles

1) Milankovitch cycles are variations in the way the Earth moves round the Sun.
   - Stretch — the path of the Earth's orbit around the Sun changes from an almost perfect circle to an ellipse (an oval) and back again about every 96 000 years.
   - Tilt — the Earth is tilted at an angle as it orbits the Sun. This tilt (or axis) changes over a cycle of about 41 000 years.
   - Wobble — the axis of the Earth wobbles like a spinning top on a cycle of about 22 000 years.
2) These cycles affect how far the Earth is from the Sun, and the angle that the Sun's rays hit the Earth. This changes the amount of solar radiation (how much of the Sun's energy) the Earth receives. If the Earth receives more energy, it gets warmer.
3) Tilt and wobble also affect how much solar radiation is received at different latitudes at different times of year.
4) Orbital changes may have caused the glacial and interglacial cycles of the Quaternary period.

### 2) Sunspots

1) Sunspots are cooler areas of the Sun's surface that are visible as dark patches. They increase the Sun's output of energy.
2) Sunspots come and go in cycles of about 11 years. There may also be longer sunspot cycles of several hundreds or thousands of years.
3) Periods when there are very few sunspots and solar output is reduced may cause the Earth's climate to become cooler in some areas.
4) Most scientists think that changes in solar output don't have a major effect on global climate change.

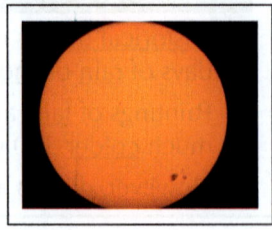

### 3) Volcanic Activity

1) Major volcanic eruptions eject large quantities of material into the atmosphere.
2) Some of these particles reflect the Sun's rays back out to space, so the Earth's surface cools.
3) Volcanic activity may cause short-term changes in climate, e.g. the cooling that followed the eruption of Mount Pinatubo in 1991.

*Volcanoes also release $CO_2$ (a greenhouse gas — see p.29), but not enough to cause warming.*

---

## Many natural factors have contributed to historical climate change

It's important to remember that climate change is not a new phenomenon — it's been happening for thousands of years. Examiners love to ask about climate change, so it's important that you understand how each natural factor can lead to climate change. Try jotting down in your own words how each factor can impact global temperatures.

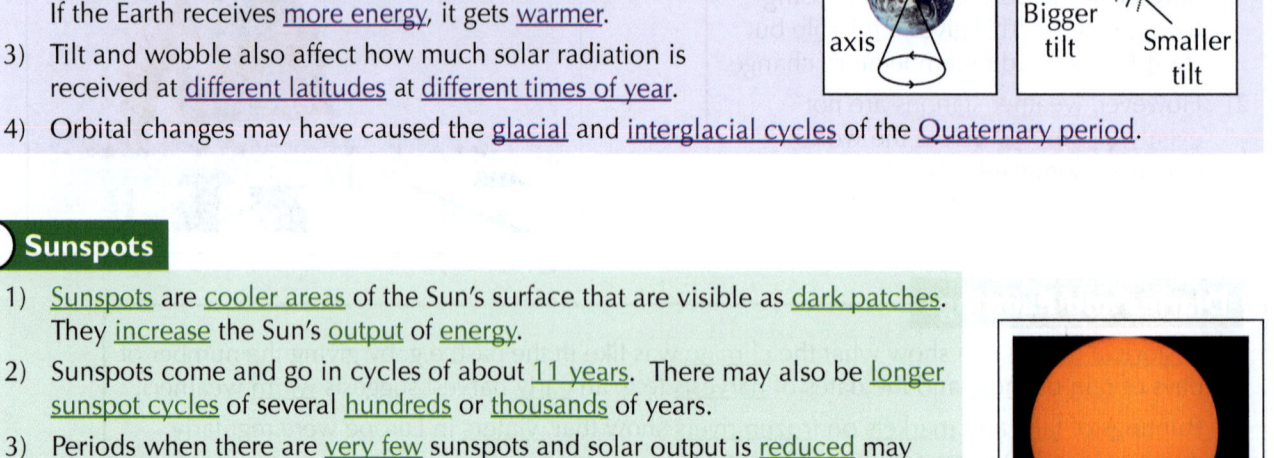

Topic 2 — Changing Climate

# Causes of Climate Change

*In the last 150 years or so **human activities** have begun to have an **impact** on the Earth's climate.*

## The Natural Greenhouse Effect is Essential for Keeping Our Planet Warm

1) The temperature of the Earth is a balance between the heat it gets from the Sun and the heat it loses to space.

2) Gases in the atmosphere naturally act like an insulating layer — they trap outgoing heat, helping to keep the Earth at the right temperature.

3) This is called the greenhouse effect ('cos it's a bit like a greenhouse trapping heat).

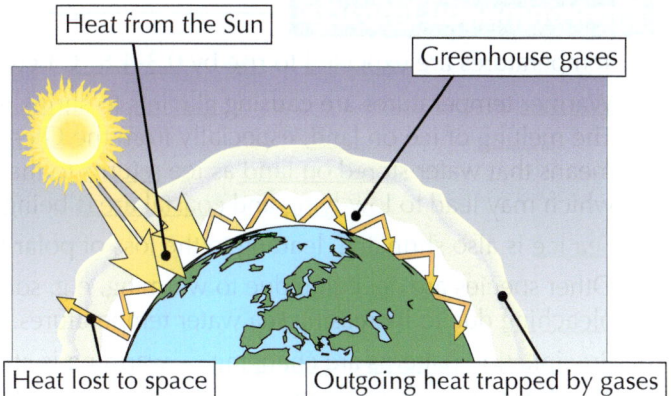

4) Gases that trap heat are called greenhouse gases — they include carbon dioxide ($CO_2$) and methane ($CH_4$).

## Human Activities are Contributing to the Greenhouse Effect

1) The rate of the recent rise in global temperature (global warming) is unheard of.
2) There's a scientific consensus (general agreement) that human activities are causing global warming by making the greenhouse effect stronger. This is called the enhanced greenhouse effect.
3) Too much greenhouse gas in the atmosphere means too much energy is trapped and the planet warms up.
4) Humans are increasing the concentration of greenhouse gases by:

### Farming
1) Farming of livestock produces a lot of methane — cows love to fart...
2) Rice paddies contribute to global warming, because flooded fields emit methane.

### Burning Fossil Fuels
$CO_2$ is released into the atmosphere when fossil fuels like coal, oil, natural gas and petrol are burnt, e.g. in thermal power stations or in cars.

### Cement Production
Cement is made from limestone, which contains carbon. When cement is produced, lots of $CO_2$ is released into the atmosphere.

### Deforestation
1) Plants remove $CO_2$ from the atmosphere and convert it into organic matter using photosynthesis.
2) When trees and plants are chopped down, they stop taking in $CO_2$.
3) $CO_2$ is also released into the atmosphere when trees are burnt as fuel or to make way for agriculture.

---

## Global warming is caused by a stronger greenhouse effect
You may have to explain the causes of climate change in your exam — try writing an explanation in your own words of how human activities can cause the greenhouse effect to become stronger.

Topic 2 — Changing Climate

# Global Effects of Climate Change

*Whether **human** or **natural** factors are to blame, scientists are **pretty sure** climate change is having an **impact**...*

## Climate Change has Environmental, Economic and Social Impacts

### Environmental Impacts

1) Temperatures are expected to rise by 0.3-4.8 °C between 2005 and 2100.
2) Warmer temperatures are causing glaciers to shrink and ice sheets like Greenland to melt. The melting of ice on land, especially from the Greenland and Antarctic ice sheets, means that water stored on land as ice returns to the oceans. This causes sea level rise, which may lead to low-lying and coastal areas being flooded more regularly.
3) Sea ice is also shrinking, leading to the loss of polar habitats.
4) Other species are declining due to warming, e.g. some coral reefs are suffering from bleaching due to increasing sea water temperatures.
5) Precipitation patterns are changing — warming is affecting how much rain areas get.
6) The distribution and quantity of some species could change and biodiversity could decrease:
   - Some species are now found in higher latitudes due to warming temperatures.
   - Some habitats are being damaged or destroyed due to climate change — species that are specially adapted to these areas may become extinct.

*"High latitude" means far from the equator, both north and south.*

### Economic Impacts

1) Climate change means the weather is getting more extreme. This means more money has to be spent on predicting extreme weather events (e.g. floods, droughts and tropical storms), reducing their impacts and rebuilding after them.
2) Rising temperatures are causing areas of permafrost (see p.68) to melt — this can lead to the collapse of buildings, pipelines etc. built on it. However, it's easier to extract natural resources from unfrozen ground.
3) Climate change is affecting farming in different ways around the world:
   - Globally, some crops have suffered from climate change (e.g. maize crops have got smaller due to warming in recent years).
   - But some farmers in high-latitude countries are finding that crops benefit from warmer conditions.
4) Water shortages might affect our ability to generate power — hydroelectric power and thermal power stations require lots of water.

### Social Impacts

1) In some places, reduced rainfall means there's an increased threat from wildfires. These can damage homes and also put people's lives at risk.
2) Some areas could become so hot and dry that they're difficult or impossible to inhabit. Low-lying coastal areas could be lost to the sea or flood so often that they also become impossible to inhabit. This could lead to migration and overcrowding in other areas.
3) Some areas are struggling to supply enough water for their residents due to problems with water availability caused by changing rainfall patterns. This can lead to political tensions, especially where rivers cross borders.
4) Lower crop yields could increase malnutrition, ill health and death from starvation, particularly in lower latitudes.

## Rising temperatures affect rainfall patterns and cause ice sheets to melt

Scientists still don't know what the exact impacts of climate change will be, but some effects are already being seen. Make sure you know how climate change could have environmental, economic and social impacts.

Topic 2 — Changing Climate

# Effects of Climate Change on the UK

*The **effects** of climate change aren't just happening in places far away — the impacts can be felt in the **UK** too.*

## Climate Change in the UK Causes Environmental Impacts...

**Climate**
1) Temperature will increase. The increase is expected to be greatest in southern England, where the average summer temperature is projected to increase by 3.9 °C by 2080.
2) Winter rainfall is expected to increase by 16% in parts of the western side of the UK.
3) Summer rainfall is expected to decrease by 23% in parts of southern England.

**Extreme Events**
1) Droughts are expected to be more frequent and intense, especially in southern England.
2) Flooding will become more common due to increased rainfall and sea level rise.

**Sea Level Rise**
1) Sea level is expected to rise by 12-76 cm by 2095.
2) This will lead to the loss of habitats, e.g. saltmarsh.

**Wildlife**
Climate change will change the UK's habitats. Some species have already left their original habitats and moved north to areas with lower temperatures (e.g. the comma butterfly). This can upset the balance of natural ecosystems (see p.57) and lead to species extinction.

## ...Economic Impacts...

**Tourism**
1) Warmer weather in the UK could boost the tourist industry if more people decide to holiday at home.
2) However, in some areas, it could also lead to a decline, e.g. skiing in the Cairngorms.

**Agriculture**
1) Temperature increase and a longer growing season may increase productivity of some crops, e.g. asparagus, onions, courgettes, peas and beans.
2) New crops adapted to warmer climates could be grown in southern England (e.g. soya and grapes), but reduced rainfall and droughts would increase the need for irrigation and water storage schemes.

**Fishing**
1) The UK fishing industry could also be affected — more extreme UK weather conditions could put fishing infrastructure (e.g. ports, boats) at risk from storm damage.
2) Fishermen's livelihoods could be affected by changing fish populations and species found in UK waters.

## ...and Social Impacts

**Floods**
Flooding from increased rainfall and sea level rise might damage homes and businesses, especially those on estuaries (e.g. in cities such as Hull, Cardiff, Portsmouth and London) and low lying areas near the coast (e.g. large areas of Norfolk).

**Water Shortages**
Drier summers will affect water availability, particularly in areas of south east England where population density is increasing.

**Health**
Deaths from cold-related illnesses may decrease, but health services may have to treat more heat-related illnesses, e.g. heat exhaustion.

**Many impacts on the UK are the same as other places**
If you concentrate on learning the specific details of the environmental, economic and social impacts of climate change in the UK, you'll find you've also learned some of the information on page 30.

Topic 2 — Changing Climate

# Worked Exam Questions

Working through exam questions is a great way of testing what you've learned and practising for the exam. These worked examples will give you an idea of the kind of answers examiners are looking for.

1 Study **Figure 1**, which shows global temperature between 1850 and 2018.

a) How much did global temperature rise by between 1850 and 2018?

*0.95 °C*
*[1]*

b) Describe the change in average global temperature shown by the graph.

*Temperature stayed around 13.7 °C from 1850 to 1910, then rose to 14 °C by 1940. It plateaued until about 1975, then rose steadily to 14.7 °C by 2018.*
*[2]*

[Total 3 marks]

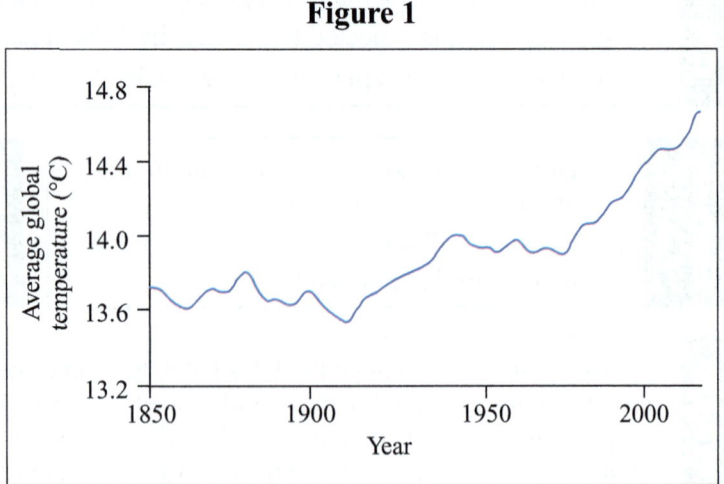

Figure 1

2 Study **Figure 2**, which shows data on sea level rise between 1900 and 2100.

a) What is the average predicted rise in sea level between 2050 and 2100?

*30 cm*
*[1]*

b) Suggest **one** way in which the rise in sea level might affect the environment.

*Low-lying and coastal areas may be flooded more regularly.*
*[1]*

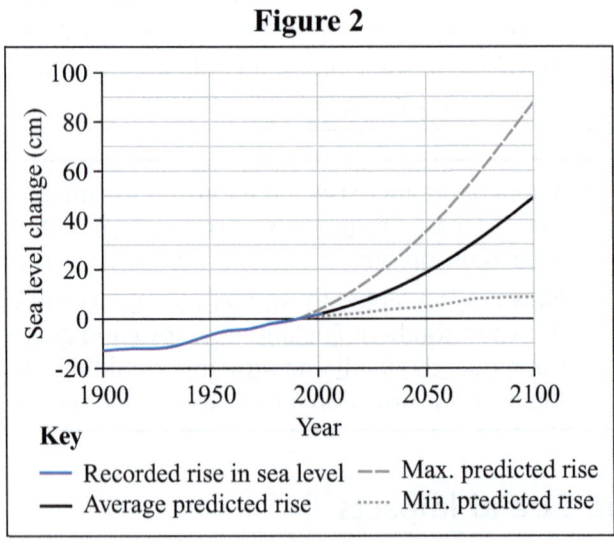

Figure 2

c) Apart from sea level rise, outline **two** possible environmental impacts of climate change.

1: *Climate change is causing precipitation patterns to change, which is affecting how much rain some areas get.*

2: *Some species that are adapted to particular climates may decline if they don't adapt to the changing climate.*
*[2]*

[Total 4 marks]

Topic 2 — Changing Climate

# Exam Questions

1 Study **Figure 1**, a newspaper article about tourism in the UK.

**Figure 1**

**Bank Holiday Weekend Tourist Boom**

Thousands of tourists flocked to the South West's beaches over the bank holiday weekend to enjoy unusually warm temperatures.

In some areas there were highs of 32 °C, which attracted thousands of beachgoers and holiday-makers.

It's thought the good weather has encouraged many UK residents to take a 'staycation' instead of travelling abroad to continental destinations.

This is good news for the South West's tourism industry. Tourists contribute an average of £4 billion every year to the local economy — an important source of income for the region.

a) Using **Figure 1** and your own knowledge, describe the positive impacts that climate change may have on the UK.

*The temperature gets as high as 32 °C which will attract thousands of tourists. The weather makes people want to stay in the UK.*

[3]

b) Outline **two** possible social impacts of climate change in the UK.

1: ................................................................................................

2: ................................................................................................

[4]

[Total 7 marks]

Topic 2 — Changing Climate

# Revision Summary

Well done for reaching the end of Topic 2. Here are some revision questions to test your knowledge.
- Try these questions and tick off each one when you get it right.
- When you've done all the questions under a heading and are completely happy with it, tick it off.

## Evidence for Climate Change (p.26-27) ☐
1) What is the Quaternary period?
2) Describe how climate has changed from the beginning of the Quaternary period to the present day.
3) Why are ice cores a useful source of information about past climate?
4) How do sea ice positions provide evidence for climate change?
5) Describe how diary entries and paintings can give evidence of climate change.
6) Why might data provided by weather stations be unreliable as a record of global climate?

## Causes of Climate Change (p.28-29) ☐
7) a) What are Milankovitch cycles?
   b) How do they affect the Earth's climate?
8) How might sunspots affect the Earth's climate?
9) Describe how volcanic activity might cause climate change.
10) What is the natural greenhouse effect?
11) Name two greenhouse gases.
12) What is the enhanced greenhouse effect?
13) Give four ways that human activities increase the concentration of greenhouse gases in the atmosphere.

## Global Effects of Climate Change (p.30) ☐
14) What effect might increasing temperatures have on polar habitats?
15) How might species distribution be affected by climate change?
16) Outline the possible global economic impacts of extreme weather.
17) Describe one possible economic impact of climate change on areas of permafrost.
18) Give one possible social impact of sea level rise.
19) Give one way that climate change might have an impact on health.

## Effects of Climate Change on the UK (p.31) ☐
20) Give two ways that extreme weather events in the UK might be affected by climate change.
21) Give one possible environmental impact of sea level rise in the UK.
22) Outline the possible economic impacts of climate change on agriculture in the UK.
23) How might the UK fishing industry be affected by climate change?

# Topic 3 — Distinctive Landscapes

## The UK Landscape

*Ah, the UK landscape. Majestic **mountains**, luscious **lowlands** and rugged **rocks**.*

### A Landscape is Characterised by Specific Geographic Features

1) Landscapes are made up of all the visible features of an area of land.
2) A landscape with more physical features, such as mountains or forest, is described as a natural landscape.
3) If a landscape has more visible human features, like a town or a city, it's described as a built landscape.

Natural landscape

Built landscape

### The UK's Upland and Lowland Areas Have Distinctive Characteristics

1) The UK's natural landscape can be split into upland, lowland and glaciated landscapes.
2) The geology, climate and land uses in these landscapes give them distinctive characteristics.

#### Upland Areas

- These are mostly found in the north and west of the UK.
- They are generally formed of harder rocks which resist erosion, e.g. slate, granite and some limestones.
- Many are glaciated landscapes, e.g. Snowdonia.
- The gradient of the land is often steep.
- The climate tends to be cooler and wetter.
- The harsh climate and thin soils allow rough vegetation to thrive, and some upland areas are used for forestry.
- Land uses include sheep farming, quarrying and tourism.

■ Upland
■ Lowland

#### Lowland Areas

- These are mostly found in the south and east.
- They are generally formed from softer rocks, e.g. chalk, clay and some sandstones.
- The landscape is flatter with gently rolling hills.
- The climate tends to be warmer and drier.
- Vegetation grows easily in the more fertile soils and includes grassy meadows and deciduous forests (see page 60).
- Land uses include quarrying and tourism, as well as dairy and arable farming (growing crops).
- Most urban areas and industries (e.g. factories) are located in lowland areas.

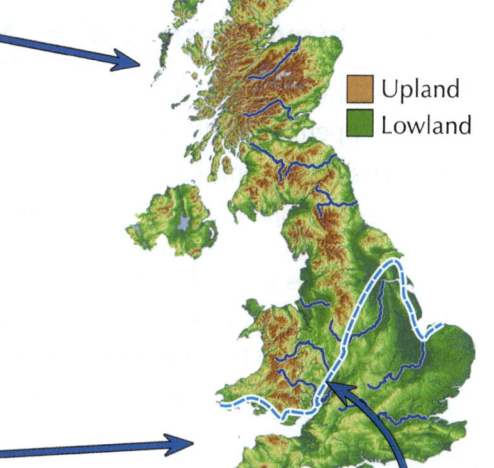

#### Glaciated Landscapes

- During the last glacial period (p.29), ice covered the UK roughly as far south as this line, so glaciated landscapes are mostly found in upland areas in the north-west of the UK.
- Ice is very powerful, so it was able to erode the landscape, carving out valleys. It also deposited lots of material as it melted.
- Landscapes formed by glacial meltwater and deposits extend south of this line.

### Most uplands are found in the north and west of the UK

This is a nice introduction to the rest of the distinctive landscapes section. Make sure you know the difference between natural and built landscapes, and the distribution of upland, lowland and glaciated landscapes in the UK.

Topic 3 — Distinctive Landscapes

# Weathering and Erosion

*Weathering* and *erosion* are examples of *geomorphic processes*. Don't let the fancy terminology scare you — "geomorphic" is just the name given to processes that **change the shape** of a landscape and **create landforms**.

## Rock is Broken Down by Mechanical and Chemical Weathering

1) Mechanical weathering is the breakdown of rock without changing its chemical composition. The main type of mechanical weathering that affects landscapes in the UK is freeze-thaw weathering:

   1) It happens when the temperature alternates above and below 0 °C (the freezing point of water).
   2) Water gets into rock that has cracks, e.g. granite. When the water freezes it expands, which puts pressure on the rock. When the water thaws it contracts, which releases the pressure on the rock.
   3) Repeated freezing and thawing widens the cracks and causes the rock to break up.

   Salt weathering is a similar process caused by the build-up of salt crystals deposited in cracks by waves.

2) Chemical weathering is the breakdown of rock by changing its chemical composition. Carbonation weathering is a type of chemical weathering that happens in warm and wet conditions:

   1) Rainwater has carbon dioxide dissolved in it, which makes it a weak carbonic acid.
   2) Carbonic acid reacts with rock that contains calcium carbonate, e.g. carboniferous limestone, so the rocks are dissolved by the rainwater.

3) Biological weathering is the breakdown of rocks by living things, e.g. plant roots break down rocks by growing into cracks on their surfaces and pushing them apart.

## Mass Movement is when Material Falls Down a Slope

1) Mass movement is the shifting of rocks and loose material down a slope, e.g. a cliff or valley side. It happens when the force of gravity acting on a slope is greater than the force supporting it.
2) Mass movements cause coasts to retreat rapidly.
3) They're more likely to happen when the material is full of water — it acts as a lubricant, and makes the material heavier.
4) Undercutting of a slope by erosion will increase the chance of mass movement.
5) You need to know about TWO types of mass movement.

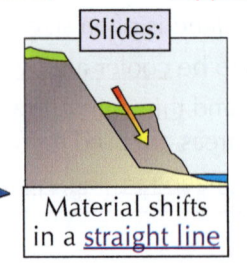

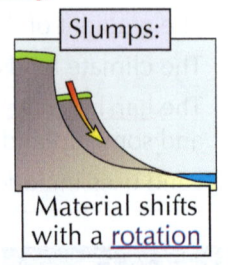

Slides: Material shifts in a straight line
Slumps: Material shifts with a rotation

## There are Four Processes of Erosion

The same four processes of erosion occur along coasts and in river channels:

1) Hydraulic action — along coasts waves crash against rock and compress the air in the cracks. This puts pressure on the rock. Repeated compression widens the cracks and makes bits of rock break off. In rivers, the force of the water breaks rock particles away from the river channel.
2) Abrasion — eroded particles in the water scrape and rub against rock in the sea bed, cliffs or river channel, removing small pieces and wearing them away. Most erosion in rivers happens by abrasion.
3) Attrition — eroded particles in the water smash into each other and break into smaller fragments. Their edges also get rounded off as they rub together. The further material travels, the more eroded it gets. E.g. attrition causes particle size to decrease between a river's source and its mouth.
4) Solution — dissolved carbon dioxide makes river and sea water slightly acidic. The acid reacts chemically with some rocks e.g. chalk and limestone, dissolving them.

---

**REVISION TIP**

### Learn the different types of weathering and erosion
This page is packed full of information, but it's just about how landscapes are worn away and rocks are broken down into smaller pieces. Make sure you can sketch the diagrams without looking at the page.

Topic 3 — Distinctive Landscapes

# Transportation and Deposition

*Material that has been **eroded** gets **pushed around** and **moved** from place to place before being **dumped** somewhere.*

## Transportation is the Movement of Eroded Material

Eroded material is moved by rivers and the sea. There are four processes of transportation:

### Traction
Large particles like boulders are pushed along the river bed or sea floor by the force of the water.

### Saltation
Pebble-sized particles are bounced along the river bed or sea floor by the force of the water.

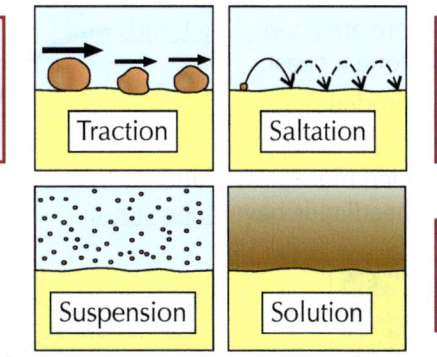

### Suspension
Small particles like silt and clay are carried along by the water.

### Solution
Soluble materials dissolve in the water and are carried along.

## Deposition is the Dropping of Material

Deposition is when material being carried by sea water or a river is dropped. It occurs when water carrying sediment loses velocity (slows down) so that it isn't moving fast enough to carry so much sediment.

### 1) Coastal Deposition

1) Waves that deposit more material than they erode are called constructive waves.
   - Constructive waves have a low frequency (6-8 waves per minute).
   - They're low and long.
   - The swash (the movement of water up the beach) is powerful and it carries material up the coast.
   - The backwash (the movement of water down the beach) is weaker and it doesn't take a lot of material back down the coast. This means there's lots of deposition and very little erosion. 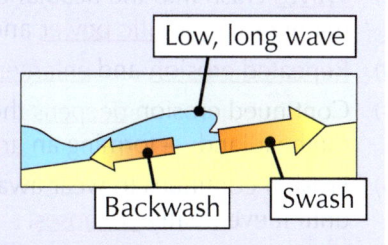
2) The amount of material that's deposited on an area of coast is increased when:
   - There's lots of erosion elsewhere on the coast, so there's lots of material available.
   - There's lots of transportation of material into the area.

### 2) River Deposition

There are a few reasons why rivers slow down and deposit material. Deposition in rivers occurs when:
- The volume of water in the river falls.
- The amount of eroded material in the water increases.
- The water is shallower, e.g. on the inside of a bend.
- The river reaches the sea or a lake at its mouth.

---

**EXAM TIP** — **The amount of erosion affects the amount of deposition elsewhere**
If you're asked to explain coastal or river processes in the exam, you might find drawing a diagram helps. It doesn't have to be a work of art — just make sure you add labels to it so it's clear what it's showing.

Topic 3 — Distinctive Landscapes

# Coastal Landforms

*Erosion* by waves forms many different **coastal landforms** over **long periods of time**, and there are quite a few that you need to know about. But don't worry, it can all be explained with a few simple **diagrams**.

## Headlands and Bays Form Where Erosion Resistance is Different

1) Some types of rocks are more resistant to erosion than others.
2) Headlands and bays form where there are alternating bands of resistant and less resistant rock along a coast.
3) The less resistant rock (e.g. clay) is eroded quickly and this forms a bay — bays have a gentle slope.
4) The resistant rock (e.g. chalk) is eroded more slowly and it's left jutting out, forming a headland — headlands have steep sides.

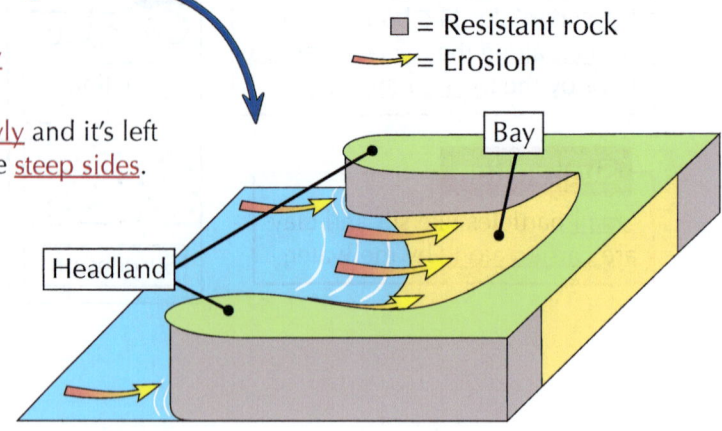

☐ = Less resistant rock
☐ = Resistant rock
→ = Erosion

Cardigan Bay, Wales

## Headlands are Eroded to form Caves, Arches and Stacks

1) Headlands are usually made of resistant rocks that have weaknesses like cracks.
2) Waves crash into the headlands and enlarge the cracks — mainly by hydraulic power and abrasion.
3) Repeated erosion and enlargement of the cracks causes a cave to form.
4) Continued erosion deepens the cave until it breaks through the headland — forming an arch, e.g. Durdle Door in Dorset.
5) Erosion continues to wear away the rock supporting the arch, until it eventually collapses.
6) This forms a stack — an isolated rock that's separate from the headland, e.g. Old Harry in Dorset.

Durdle Door, Dorset

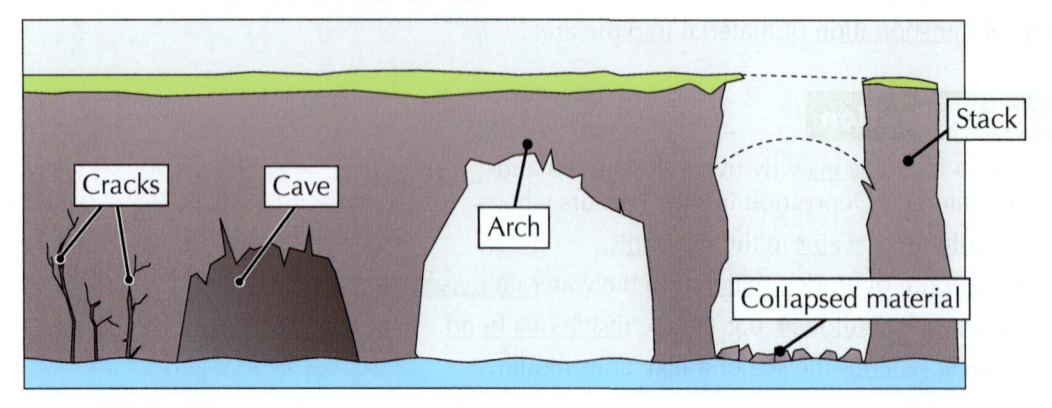

Cracks | Cave | Arch | Stack | Collapsed material

## Caves are eroded to arches, which are eroded to stacks

This page might seem quite complicated to begin with, so take your time to learn how each landform is created. You could be asked about any landform in the exam, so make sure you learn this page off by heart.

Topic 3 — Distinctive Landscapes

# Coastal Landforms

*Here are some more exciting **landforms** for you to learn about. The ones on this page are formed by **deposition**.*

## Beaches are formed by Deposition

1) Beaches are found on coasts between the high water mark (the highest point on the land the sea level gets to) and the low water mark (the lowest point on the land the sea level gets to).
2) They're formed by constructive waves (see p.37) depositing material like sand and shingle.
3) Sand and shingle beaches have different characteristics:

- Sand beaches are flat and wide — sand particles are small and the weak backwash can move them back down the beach, creating a long, gentle slope.
- Shingle beaches are steep and narrow — shingle particles are large and the weak backwash can't move them back down the beach. The shingle particles build up and create a steep slope.

## Longshore Drift can form Spits at Bends in the Coastline

1) Spits are just beaches that stick out into the sea — they're joined to the coast at one end. Spits form at sharp bends in the coastline, e.g. at a river mouth.
2) Spits are formed by longshore drift — a process that moves material along coasts:

   1) Waves follow the direction of the prevailing (most common) wind.
   2) They usually hit the coast at an oblique angle (any angle that isn't a right angle).
   3) The swash carries material up the beach, in the same direction as the waves.
   4) The backwash then carries material down the beach at right angles, back towards the sea.
   5) Over time, material zigzags along the coast.

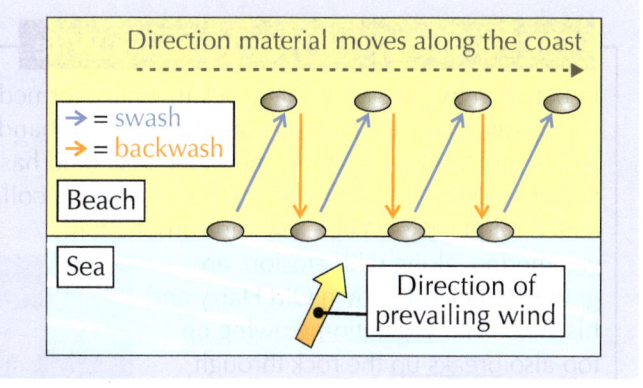

3) Longshore drift transports sand and shingle past the bend and deposits it in the sea.
4) Strong winds and waves can curve the end of the spit (forming a recurved end).

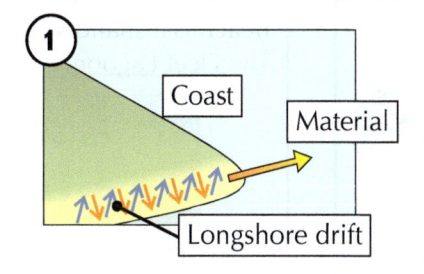

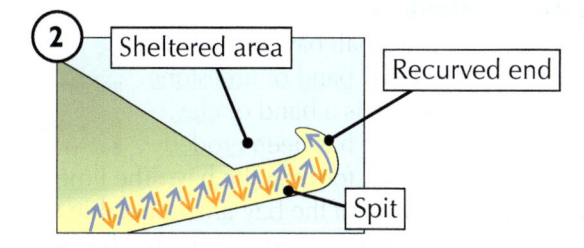

5) The sheltered area behind the spit is protected from waves — lots of material accumulates in this area, which means plants can grow there.
6) Over time, the sheltered area can become a mud flat or a salt marsh.

## Longshore drift moves material along the coast

Remember, longshore drift is caused by the waves hitting the coast at an oblique angle. The swash carries material diagonally up the beach, and the backwash then carries it back down to the sea at a right angle. This process constantly repeats, gradually moving material along the coast in the direction of the prevailing wind.

Topic 3 — Distinctive Landscapes

# UK Coastal Landscape

**CASE STUDY**

*The **Dorset coast** has lots of landforms — **headlands**, **bays**, **arches**, **stacks**, **coves**, **lagoons**...*

## The Dorset Coast is a Popular Tourist Destination in Southern England

1) The Dorset coast is located on the south coast of England.
2) It is called the Jurassic Coast because it has lots of fossils dating from the Jurassic period. Lots of people come to the area to hunt for fossils, and it's an important location for scientists studying geology.
3) It also has a variety of coastal landforms, including sandy beaches, making it a popular tourist destination.

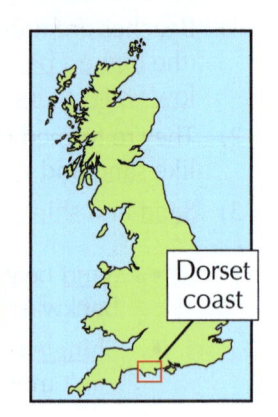

## Geomorphic Processes have Created a Variety of Landforms

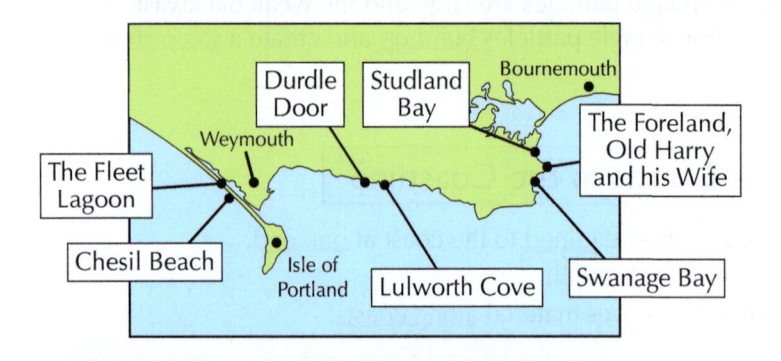

*Map showing the Dorset coast with: Weymouth, Durdle Door, Studland Bay, Bournemouth, The Foreland, Old Harry and his Wife, The Fleet Lagoon, Chesil Beach, Isle of Portland, Lulworth Cove, Swanage Bay.*

### The Foreland, Old Harry and his Wife

In between two areas of softer rock that have formed bays, there is a headland called The Foreland made from a band of harder rock (chalk). An arch at the end of the headland has collapsed to form a stack called Old Harry and a stump (a collapsed stack) called Old Harry's Wife. Salt and carbonation weathering, along with erosion, are gradually wearing down Old Harry and his Wife. The vegetation growing on top also breaks up the rock through biological weathering.

### Durdle Door

Durdle Door is a great example of an arch (see page 38). It formed on a hard limestone headland. Erosion by waves opened up a crack in the headland, which became a cave and then developed into an arch. The arch is being gradually broken down by mechanical, chemical and biological weathering.

### Lulworth Cove

Lulworth Cove is a small bay formed after a gap was eroded in a band of limestone. Behind the limestone is a band of clay. The clay is softer, so it has been eroded and transported away, forming the bay. The limestone cliffs forming the back wall of the bay are vulnerable to mass movement, and sometimes experience small slides and slumps.

### Chesil Beach

Chesil Beach is a tombolo (a type of spit that extends out to an island). It joins the Isle of Portland to the mainland. It has been formed by longshore drift. Behind Chesil Beach is a shallow lagoon called The Fleet Lagoon.

### Swanage Bay

The cliffs backing Swanage Bay are made of clay, which is a soft rock. Towards the northern end of the bay, the cliffs are covered in vegetation, stabilising them and protecting them from weathering. Elsewhere, the cliffs are not stabilised by vegetation, so wet weather weakens them and can cause slumps. Longshore drift carries material (mainly gravel) from the south to the north of the beach in the bay. Overall, erosion is the dominant process in the bay — the beach has been losing material for decades.

Topic 3 — Distinctive Landscapes

# UK Coastal Landscape

*There are several **climate** and **weather** factors that affect how **weathering** and **erosion** shape the Dorset coast. Head to page 36 if you'd like a **reminder** about how some of the different weathering and erosion processes **work**.*

## Geomorphic Processes on the Dorset Coast are Influenced by...

### ...Temperature...

1) The Dorset coast has warm, dry summers (around 21 °C in July) and mild and wet winters (average minimum temperature in January is about 3 °C).

2) Salt weathering is the dominant form of mechanical weathering, particularly in summer. The warm temperatures cause sea water to evaporate from rocks quickly, leaving a build-up of salt crystals in tiny cracks in the rock.

3) The mild winters mean that freeze-thaw weathering is less common because it's usually not cold enough for ice to form.

### ...Wind...

1) The Dorset coast's location means that it's exposed to prevailing winds from the south-west.

2) These prevailing winds can bring storms to the UK from the Atlantic Ocean. Storms bring high energy, destructive waves which increase erosion of the cliffs.

3) Hydraulic action and abrasion both increase during a storm and erode the base of the cliffs. This makes the cliffs unstable, making mass movement more likely to happen.

### ...and Rainfall

1) The Dorset coast receives relatively low amounts of rainfall annually, but can experience very wet winters, with rainfall heaviest during storm periods.

2) Soils and rocks become heavier when they're saturated, which can make them more prone to mass movement.

3) In January 2016, intense rainfall combined with high-energy waves during Storm Frank to cause the collapse of cliffs between Burton Bradstock and West Bay.

---

**REVISION TIP**

## Make sure you know the effect of weather and climate on the coast

This page has got loads of important information about the climate of the Dorset coast. Grab a piece of paper and see if you can draw some flow diagrams showing how certain climate conditions influence geomorphic processes on the rocks of the Dorset coast, or the coast you've studied in class.

Topic 3 — Distinctive Landscapes

# UK Coastal Landscape

*It's not just the climate and weather that affect the **geomorphic processes** on the Dorset coast — **geology** influences them too. **Industry** and **tourism** are also having an impact on the landscape. Read on to find out more...*

## The Geology of the Dorset Coastline Affects Geomorphic Processes

1) The coastline is made from bands of hard rock and soft rock.

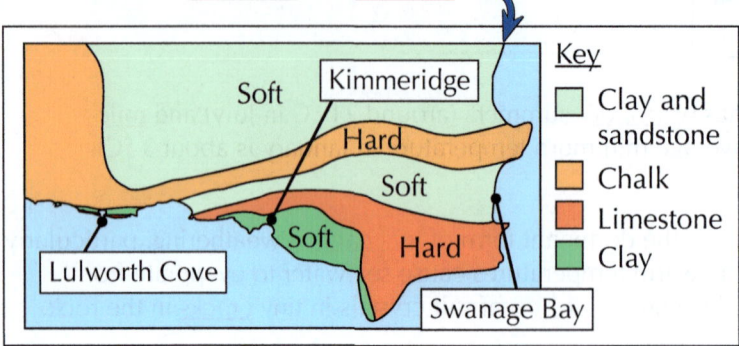

   Key:
   - Clay and sandstone
   - Chalk
   - Limestone
   - Clay
   
   (Map shows Lulworth Cove, Kimmeridge, Swanage Bay with alternating soft and hard bands.)

2) The rocks have been eroded at different rates, creating the area's coastal landforms, e.g. Lulworth Cove.
3) Soft rock like sandstone and clay are easily eroded by hydraulic action and abrasion.
4) The harder chalk and limestone cliffs are weathered and eroded more slowly, meaning that they stick out into the sea as exposed headlands. Chalk and limestone are vulnerable to erosion by solution, where the sea water chemically reacts with the rock, causing it to dissolve.
5) Weathering tends to happen gradually and cause small changes. Erosion can happen more suddenly on a much larger scale. A single storm can cause large amounts of erosion along a big stretch of the coast.

## Geology, Climate and Weather can also Interact

1) It's often a combination of climatic and geological factors that affect how erosion and weathering shape the landscape.
2) Lots of rain makes chalk and limestone vulnerable to carbonation weathering because the rain water is slightly acidic.
3) Prolonged heavy rain causes clay to become heavier, softer and more slippery, making mass movement more likely. During the winter, when there is more rainfall, there are often slides and slumps on the clay cliffs.

*Mudslides and rock falls near Kimmeridge*

## Industry and Tourism are also Shaping the Landscape

1) A lot of quarrying has taken place along the coast because limestone is a valuable building stone. There are a number of quarries on the Isle of Portland and to the west of Chesil Beach. Quarries expose large areas of rock, making them vulnerable to chemical weathering and erosion.
2) Up until the 1960s, gravel was removed from Chesil Beach for use in the construction industry. Material was removed from the beach much more quickly than the sea could replenish it, so this began to damage the landform.
3) The Dorset coast attracts large numbers of tourists every year. Coastal footpaths run along the cliff tops, and are gradually worn down as people repeatedly walk on them. Vegetation along the cliff top may be trampled and worn away by repeated use of the footpaths. This can expose the underlying soil and rock to weathering and erosion by wind and rain.

## A variety of processes work to shape the landscape of the Dorset coast

That just about rounds up the environmental and human factors that affect the coastal landscape and landforms in Dorset. There's just one human factor left to look at — the management of the coastline. Move on if you're ready.

Topic 3 — Distinctive Landscapes

# UK Coastal Landscape

*The Dorset coastline is being **managed** in order to reduce the effects of erosion. This is **impacting** the **landscape**.*

## Coastal Management Strategies are Protecting the Coastline

1) Areas of the Dorset coast are being eroded, putting properties and infrastructure at risk. There is also danger to people from landslides and rockfalls.
2) Coastal management strategies have been used to protect the coastline for roughly the last 150 years.
3) These management strategies have helped prevent erosion in some areas, but they have impacted the landscape and caused changes to the natural environment.

### Groynes

1) Groynes are wooden or stone fences that are built at right angles to the coast.
2) They trap material transported by longshore drift. This creates wider beaches which slow the waves, giving greater protection from erosion.
3) New timber groynes were put in place along Swanage beach in 2005-6. They've helped to stop the loss of beach material.
4) However, by stopping beach material from moving along the coast, they've starved areas further down the coast of sediment, making them narrower. Narrow beaches don't protect the coast as well, so there may be more erosion.

### Sea Walls

1) There are concrete sea walls in place along most of Swanage beach.
2) Sea walls reflect waves back out to sea, preventing the erosion of the coast.
3) But they can create a strong backwash, which removes sediment from the beach and can erode under the wall.
4) They also prevent the cliffs from being eroded, so there's no new material to replenish the beach. This will gradually lower the level of the beach.

### Beach Replenishment

1) In winter 2005/2006, sand and shingle dredged from the sea bed at Poole Harbour was added to the upper parts of Swanage beach.
2) This has created wider beaches, which slow the waves and help protect cliffs and coastal properties from erosion.
3) However, it cost £5 million to replenish the beach and it will need to be repeated roughly every 20 years.

## There are pros and cons to each management strategy

Coastal management strategies, together with the impacts of industry and tourism (see previous page), are all examples of ways that human activity can affect coastal landscapes. Don't worry if you didn't learn about the Dorset coast in class — it's fine if you've studied a different example. But before you go on, make sure you know the ins and outs of the landforms, physical processes and human impacts in your chosen area.

Topic 3 — Distinctive Landscapes

# Worked Exam Questions

Time to put your knowledge to the test... I've made life easier for you by giving you the answers to the first page of practice exam questions. Read over them to get an idea of what your exam answers should be like.

1   Study **Figure 1**, which shows how the coastline of an area has changed over time.

**Figure 1**

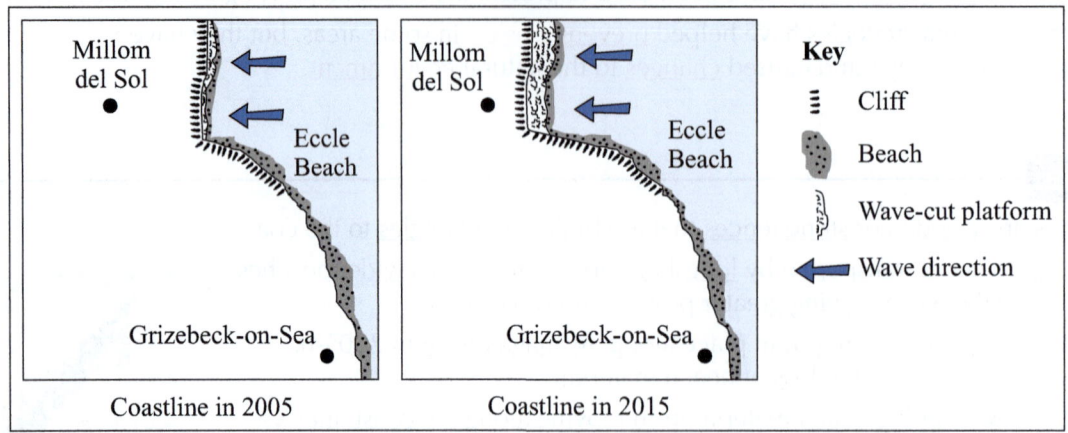

Coastline in 2005     Coastline in 2015

Key: Cliff, Beach, Wave-cut platform, Wave direction

a) Name and describe **two** processes of erosion that could have caused the coastal change shown in **Figure 1**.

1: *Hydraulic power is when waves crash against rock and compress the air in the cracks. This puts pressure on the rock. Repeated compression widens the cracks and makes bits of rock break off.*

2: *Solution is when sea water is made slightly acidic due to dissolved carbon dioxide, and reacts chemically with rocks, dissolving them.*

[4]

b) Explain how freeze-thaw weathering could cause the cliffs shown in **Figure 1** to break up.

*Freeze-thaw weathering can happen when water gets into rock that has cracks. If the water freezes it expands, which puts pressure on the rock. When the water thaws it contracts, which releases the pressure on the rock. Repeated freezing and thawing widens the cracks and causes the rock to break up.*

[4]

c) Describe **two** processes of weathering, other than freeze-thaw, that can affect landscapes.

1: *Carbonation weathering happens when carbonic acid in rainwater dissolves rock such as limestone.*

2: *Salt weathering occurs when salt builds up in cracks in the rock and forms crystals that break up the rock.*

[4]

[Total 12 marks]

Topic 3 — Distinctive Landscapes

# Exam Questions

1 Study **Figure 1**, which shows how the velocity of the River Dance varies along its course.

a) Small gravel particles are transported by velocities above 0.1 m per second.
At what distance along the River Dance does the transportation of gravel start?

.................................................................
[1]

**Figure 1**

b) At 80 km along the River Dance, pebbles are being transported.
Give the velocity of the river at this point.

.................................................................
[1]

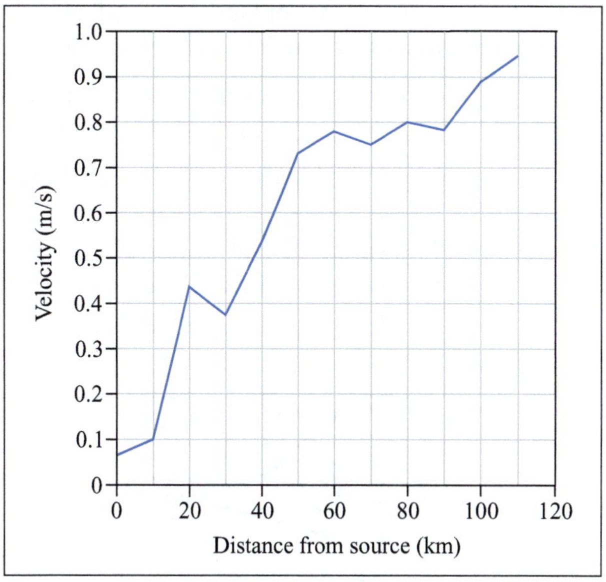

c) Using **Figure 1**, suggest why deposition is the dominant process between 20 and 30 km.

....................................................................................................................................................................

....................................................................................................................................................................

....................................................................................................................................................................

....................................................................................................................................................................
[2]

d) In the tables below, match each process of transportation with its correct description.
One has been done for you.

| Process of transportation |
|---|
| Saltation |
| Solution |
| Traction |
| Suspension |

| Description |
|---|
| Large particles like boulders are pushed along the river bed or sea floor by the force of the water. |
| Soluble materials dissolve in the water and are carried along. |
| Small particles like silt and clay are carried along by the water. |
| Pebble-sized particles are bounced along the river bed or sea floor by the force of the water. |

[2]
[Total 6 marks]

2 Answer this question using a case study of a coastal landscape in the UK.

Assess how far the impacts of human activity on one coastal landscape have been negative.

[8 + 3 SPaG]
[Total 11 marks]

# River Landforms

*Weathering, erosion, transport* and *deposition* combine to produce the **characteristic landforms** of rivers. But before you dive in to learning about river landforms, you'll need some basic river **terminology**...

## A River Basin is an Area of Land Drained by a River

1) A river basin is the area of land surrounding a river, where any rain falling on the land eventually makes its way into that river. This area is also called the river's catchment.

2) River basins are separated by a boundary called a watershed. They're ridges of high land — water falling either side of these ridges will go into different river basins.

3) Here are a few of the key features of a river basin:

   - A tributary is a smaller river (e.g. a stream) that joins a main river.
   - The source is where a river starts, usually in an upland area (e.g. mountains).
   - The mouth is where a river flows into the sea or a lake.

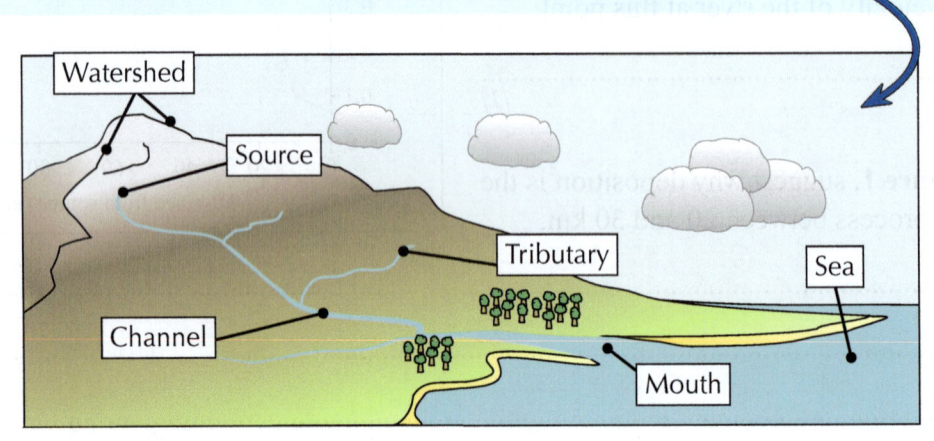

4) The path of a river as it flows downhill is called its course.

5) Rivers have an upper course (closest to the source of the river), a middle course and a lower course (closest to the mouth of the river).

6) Rivers form channels and valleys as they flow downhill.

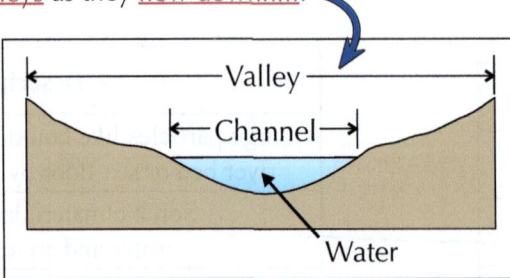

7) They erode the landscape — wear it down, then transport the material to somewhere else where it's deposited.

8) The shape of the valley and channel changes along the river depending on whether erosion or deposition is the dominant process.

## All river basins follow the same basic pattern

That was a quick introduction to the world of rivers. Some of it may seem like basic stuff, but there's a whole lot more on river landforms coming up, so a good understanding of how river basins work will really help with the rest of this topic. To help get this stuff into your brain, try drawing a labelled diagram of the key features of a river basin. Once you're done, have another look at the diagram above to see how much of it you remembered.

Topic 3 — Distinctive Landscapes

# River Landforms

*The processes of **erosion** on page 36 can **change the river landscape** and create **distinctive landforms**. Now's your chance to find out all about them, starting with **v-shaped valleys** and **waterfalls**...*

## V-Shaped Valleys are Formed by Vertical Erosion in the Upper Course

1) In the upper course of a river, fast-flowing water following heavy rain and high turbulence causes loose rough particles and boulders to be transported by the river and scraped along the river bed.

2) This causes downwards erosion of the river channel by the process of abrasion.

3) The valley sides are exposed to weathering (e.g. by freeze-thaw). The weathered material that falls down the valley sides into the river channel causes further erosion by abrasion.

4) The river doesn't have enough energy to erode sideways (laterally), so vertical erosion of the river bed is dominant, which deepens the river valley, creating a steep-sided V-shape.

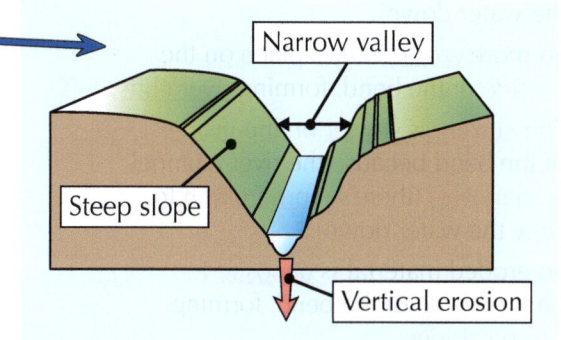

## Waterfalls and Gorges are Found in the Upper Course of a River

1) Waterfalls form where a river flows over an area of hard rock followed by an area of softer rock.

2) The softer rock is eroded (by hydraulic action and abrasion) more than the hard rock, creating a 'step' in the river.

3) As water goes over the step it erodes more and more of the softer rock.

4) A steep drop is eventually created, which is called a waterfall.

5) The hard rock is eventually undercut by erosion. It becomes unsupported and collapses.

6) The collapsed rocks are swirled around at the foot of the waterfall where they erode the softer rock by abrasion (see p.36). This creates a deep plunge pool.

7) Over time, more undercutting causes more collapses. The waterfall will retreat (move back up the channel), leaving behind a steep-sided gorge.

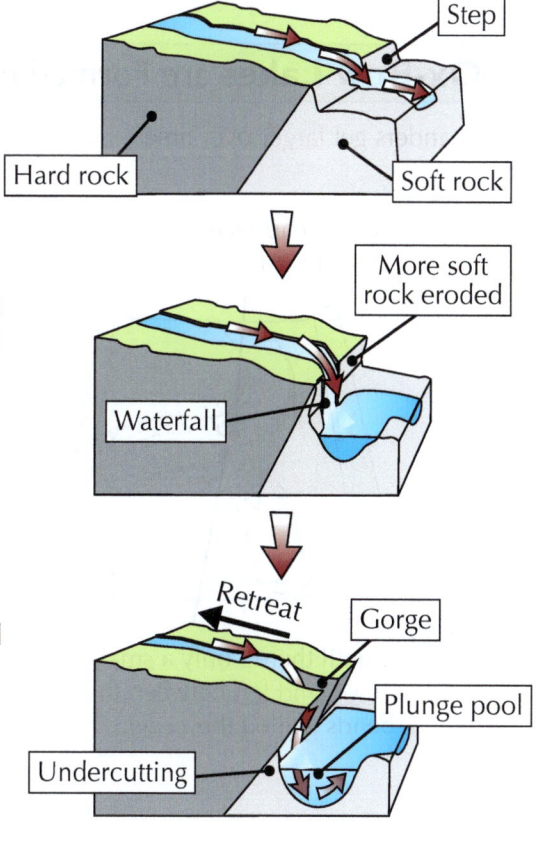

## V-shaped valleys, waterfalls and gorges are formed by erosion

Step over the hard rock and plunge into the pool — that's how I remember how waterfalls are formed. Geography examiners love river landforms (they're a bit weird like that) so make sure you learn how they form.

Topic 3 — Distinctive Landscapes

# River Landforms

*When a river's **eroding** and **depositing** material, **meanders** and **ox-bow lakes** can form.*

## Meanders are Formed by Erosion and Deposition

Rivers develop large bends called meanders in their middle and lower courses, in areas where there are both shallow and deep sections in the channel:

1) The current (the flow of the water) is faster on the outside of the bend because the river channel is deeper (there's less friction to slow the water down).

2) So more erosion takes place on the outside of the bend, forming river cliffs.

3) The current is slower on the inside of the bend because the river channel is shallower (there's more friction to slow the water down).

4) So eroded material is deposited on the inside of the bend, forming slip-off slopes.

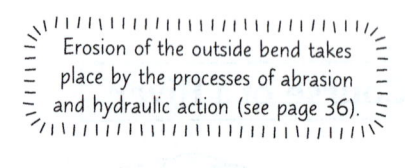

*Erosion of the outside bend takes place by the processes of abrasion and hydraulic action (see page 36).*

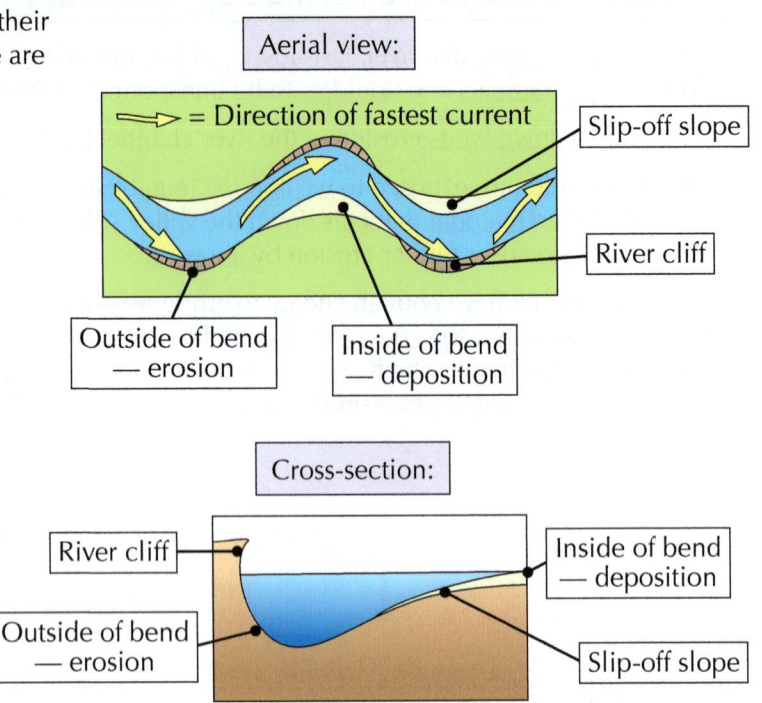

Aerial view:
= Direction of fastest current
Slip-off slope
River cliff
Outside of bend — erosion
Inside of bend — deposition

Cross-section:
River cliff
Outside of bend — erosion
Inside of bend — deposition
Slip-off slope

## Ox-Bow Lakes are Formed from Meanders

Meanders get larger over time — they can eventually turn into an ox-bow lake:

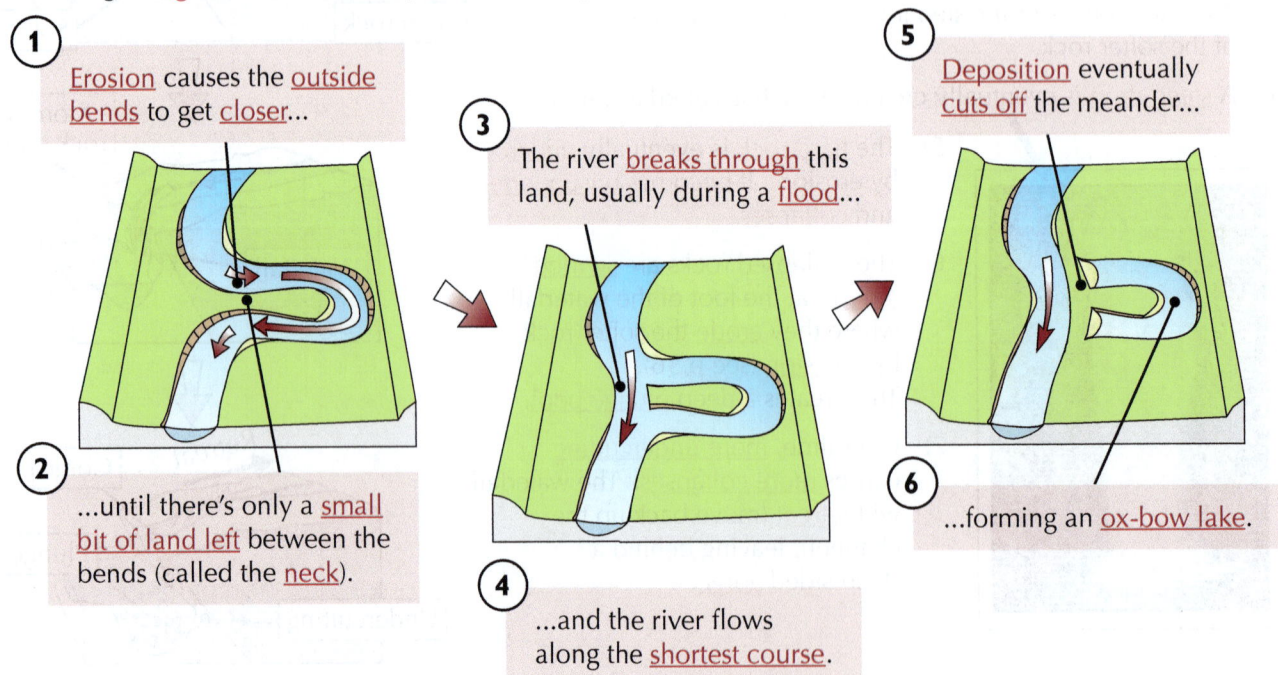

1) Erosion causes the outside bends to get closer...

2) ...until there's only a small bit of land left between the bends (called the neck).

3) The river breaks through this land, usually during a flood...

4) ...and the river flows along the shortest course.

5) Deposition eventually cuts off the meander...

6) ...forming an ox-bow lake.

---

**EXAM TIP** — **The features of meanders are formed by erosion and deposition**
In the exam, don't be afraid to draw diagrams of river landforms — examiners love a good diagram and they can help make your answer clear. Don't spend forever making them look pretty though...

# River Landforms

*Rivers are generally **fast-flowing** in their **upper** course, but tend to **slow down** as they get nearer the sea. When they **flow fast**, they **erode** the landscape. As they **slow down**, they make **landforms** through **deposition**.*

## Floodplains are Flat Areas of Land that Flood

1) The floodplain is the wide valley floor on either side of a river which occasionally gets flooded.

2) When a river floods onto the floodplain, the water slows down and deposits the eroded material that it's transporting. This builds up the floodplain (makes it higher).

3) Meanders migrate (move) across the floodplain, making it wider.

4) Meanders also migrate downstream, flattening out the valley floor.

5) The deposition that happens on the slip-off slopes of meanders also builds up the floodplain.

*Floodplains are found in the lower course of a river.*

## Levees are Natural Embankments

1) Levees are natural embankments (raised bits) along the edges of a river channel.

2) During a flood, eroded material is deposited over the whole floodplain.

3) The heaviest material is deposited closest to the river channel, because it gets dropped first when the river slows down.

4) Over time, the deposited material builds up, creating levees along the edges of the channel, e.g. along the Yellow River (Huang He River) in China.

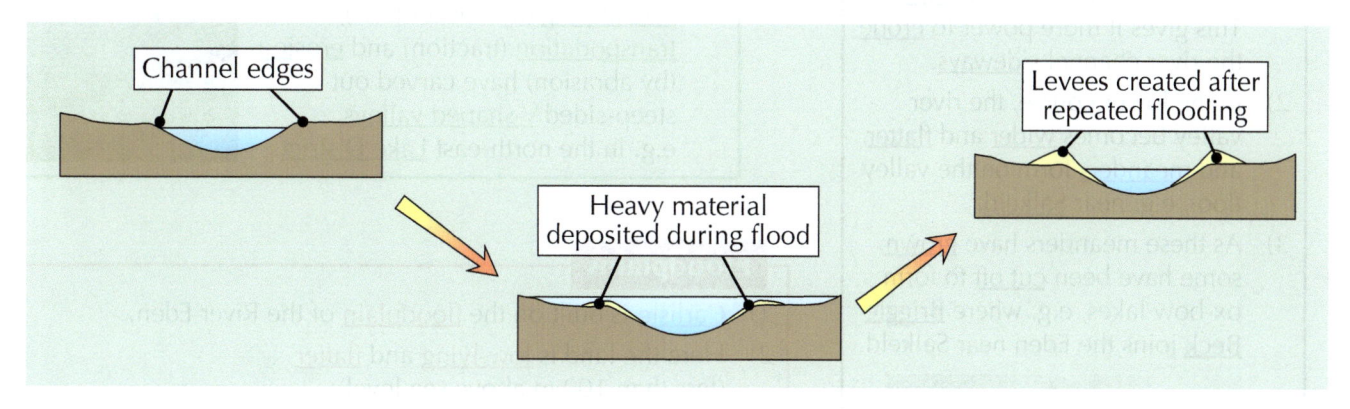

*Like floodplains, levees are also found in a river's lower course.*

Channel edges

Heavy material deposited during flood

Levees created after repeated flooding

## Deposition is common in the lower course of a river

As the river slows down in its lower course, material is dropped. This leads to the formation of different landforms. Make sure you know the characteristics of these landforms and you can describe the processes of their formation.

Topic 3 — Distinctive Landscapes

# UK River Basin

*You can see many of the **landforms** of **erosion** and **deposition** from pages 47-49 in the **Eden basin**.*

## The Eden Basin is in North-West England

1) The Eden basin is in north-west England, between the mountains of the Lake District and the Pennines.
2) The River Eden's source is in the Pennine hills in south Cumbria. It flows north-west through Appleby-in-Westmorland and Carlisle. Its mouth is in the Solway Firth at the Scottish border.
3) The river basin is a largely rural area, with many scenic landscapes that are popular with tourists. There are a variety of river landforms.

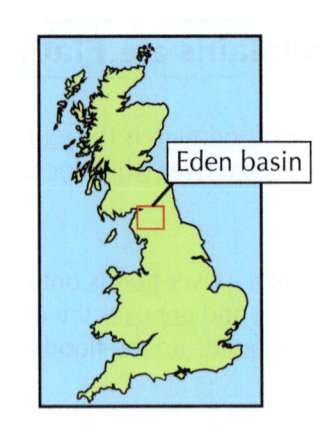

## Geomorphic Processes Created a Variety of Landforms in the Eden Basin

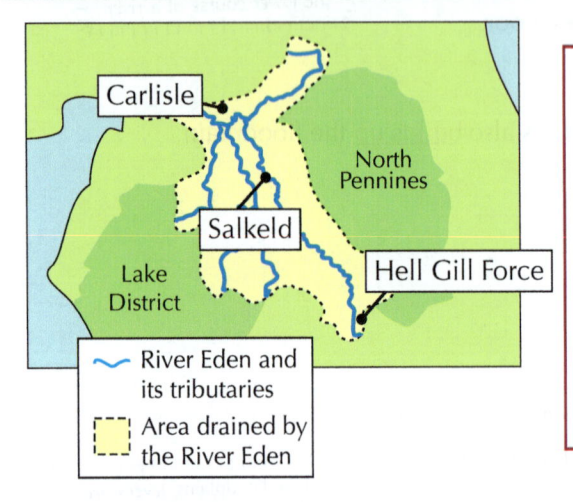

### Waterfalls

1) Hell Gill Force is a waterfall near the source of the River Eden.
2) It has formed where there is a change in the rock type from hard limestone to softer sandstone.
3) The water has eroded the soft rock, forming a step in the river channel.
4) Below the waterfall there is a steep-sided gorge, left behind as the waterfall has retreated up the valley.

### Meanders

1) As more tributaries join the River Eden, the river gets bigger. This gives it more power to erode the river channel sideways.
2) In the lower course, the river valley becomes wider and flatter, and meanders form on the valley floor, e.g. near Salkeld.
3) As these meanders have grown, some have been cut off to form ox-bow lakes, e.g. where Briggle Beck joins the Eden near Salkeld.

### V-shaped Valleys

1) Many streams flow down the steep slopes of the hillsides at the edge of the basin from about 600 m above sea level.
2) Weathering (by freeze-thaw), transportation (traction) and erosion (by abrasion) have carved out steep-sided V-shaped valleys, e.g. in the north-east Lake District.

### Floodplains

1) Carlisle is built on the floodplain of the River Eden.
2) Here the land is low-lying and flatter (less than 100 m above sea level).
3) As meanders have migrated across the valley floor, the floodplain has become wider.
4) Sediment has also been deposited when the river has flooded, building up the floodplain.

Topic 3 — Distinctive Landscapes

# UK River Basin

*Climate* and *weather* influence the *geomorphic processes* in the Eden basin. Remember — geomorphic processes are those that change the *shape* of the *landscape* and create *landforms* (see pages 36-37 for more).

## Cumbria has a Mild, Wet Climate

1) Cumbria is on the west coast of the UK, facing the prevailing south-westerly winds. As a result, Cumbria's climate is mild and wet. The area generally has cool summers and mild winters.

2) Cumbria is one of the wettest parts of the UK, often experiencing periods of intense rainfall. Many of the UK's highest rainfall records were recorded in Cumbria.

## Geomorphic Processes in the Eden Basin are Influenced by Temperature...

1) Despite the generally mild winters, temperatures can be much colder on higher ground, such as the land around the source of the River Eden. In winter, this higher ground can regularly freeze.

2) During these cold periods, freeze-thaw weathering can slowly break up the exposed rock of the valley sides in the upper course of the river. If the valley sides are weakened, sudden mass movement, such as landslides, becomes more likely.

3) Material from landslides is added to the river's load (the rocks, stones and sediment transported by the river), increasing the erosive power of the river through abrasion.

## ...and Rainfall

1) During periods of intense rainfall, the ground becomes saturated. This makes it heavier and less stable. This can cause the river banks to slide or slump into the river channel.

2) Heavy rain can flow quickly over the surface and into the river Eden and its tributaries. This can cause the volume of water in the river to rapidly increase.

A landslide near Appleby

3) The high volume of water can increase transportation of material by the river, which can cause more erosion by abrasion — particularly in the upper course of the river.

## Weather and climate affect geomorphic processes in the Eden basin

Remember, Cumbria is one of the wettest places in the country, so rainfall has a big influence on the geomorphic processes in the Eden basin. Make sure you're happy with how the temperature affects these processes, too.

Topic 3 — Distinctive Landscapes

**CASE STUDY**

# UK River Basin

*You saw on the previous page how Cumbria's weather and climate affect the **geomorphic processes** that are at work in the **Eden basin**. This page takes a look at how these processes are affected by **geology** and **human activity**.*

## Geomorphic Processes are Influenced by the Geology of the Area

1) The harder rocks around the edge of the Eden basin have remained as high ground as they are more resistant to erosion. However, exposed limestone is vulnerable to slow carbonation weathering (p.36).

2) Igneous rocks, such as those found in the west of the Eden basin, tend to be impermeable (i.e. water won't soak into the rock). Because water can't soak into the ground, high rainfall causes lots of surface streams to form, which have a lot of power to erode vertically, creating steep-sided V-shaped valleys.

3) Through the middle and lower courses of the Eden, the river valley is made up of sandstone (a softer rock). The river's increasing volume and energy in its lower course mean that there's lots of lateral (sideways) erosion of the sandstone. This widens the river channel and forms meanders and steep river cliffs.

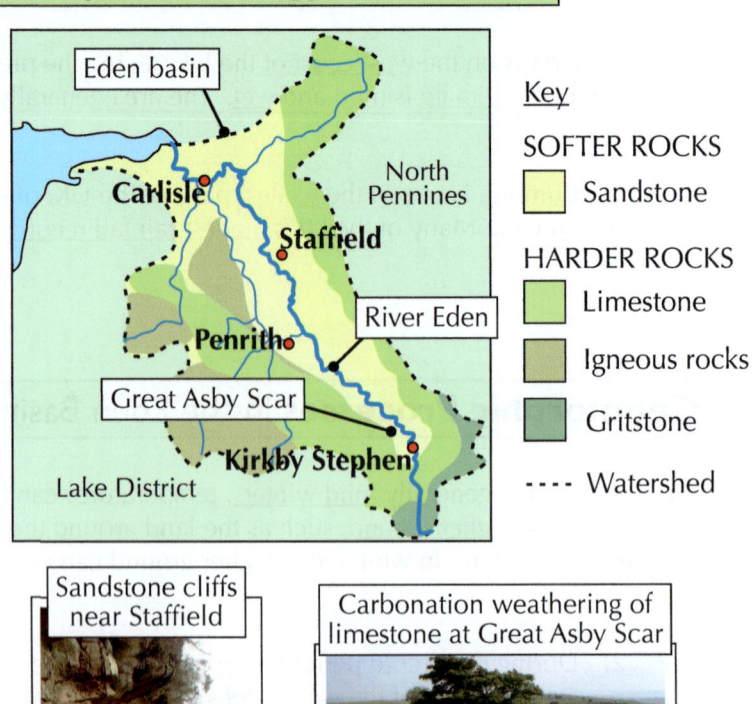

**Key**
SOFTER ROCKS
- Sandstone

HARDER ROCKS
- Limestone
- Igneous rocks
- Gritstone
- - - - Watershed

Sandstone cliffs near Staffield

Carbonation weathering of limestone at Great Asby Scar

## Human Activity on the Land also affects Geomorphic Processes

### Deforestation
Natural woodland and heathland have been cleared from many upland areas in the Eden basin. This increases surface runoff when it rains, and means that more water ends up in river channels more quickly. This increase in volume gives rivers more energy for erosion, and can cause sliding and slumping of the river banks.

### Farming
Some upland areas have been drained of moisture to make them more suitable for farming. This reduces the stability of the soil, meaning that more soil is washed into the river channel by rain. The increased load of the river increases deposition downstream, changing the floodplain landscape from its natural state.

**EXAM TIP** — **The strength of the underlying rock affects erosion in a river**
Don't panic if you're faced with a 6-mark extended answer question in the exam. Take a bit of time to plan your answer. This way, you'll be less likely to miss out an important bit of information.

Topic 3 — Distinctive Landscapes

# UK River Basin

*Nearly at the end of this case study — just one more page to go. This one's all about how the **people** that live in the Eden basin are **managing** the rivers, and the **effects** that this is having on the **landscape**.*

## The River Landscape has been Altered by Management Schemes

The rivers in the Eden basin have been managed to meet the needs of people in the area. Management strategies have affected the geomorphic processes in the river basin.

### Flood Walls & Embankments

1) 10 km of raised flood defences (flood walls and embankments) have been built along the Rivers Eden and Caldew in Carlisle.
2) These are designed to contain the water within the river channel, so that the floodplain can be built on.
3) They interrupt the natural processes of the river and can prevent the natural formation of meanders and the deposition of sediment on the floodplain.

### Reservoirs

1) Castle Carrock beck (to the south-east of Carlisle) has been dammed to create a reservoir.
2) Reservoirs limit the natural flow of water downstream. Material carried by the river is deposited in the reservoir and not along the river's natural course. This can increase erosion downstream, and reduce the natural buildup of the floodplain in the lower course of the river.

### Planting Trees

1) Near Dalston (south of Carlisle), the landscape has been changed by the planting of 1000 trees to reduce flooding and also to reduce erosion by stabilising the soil.
2) Trees intercept rainfall and reduce surface runoff. This prevents rapid increases in the volume of water in the river because it takes longer for water to reach the river channel.
3) As a result, the river will have less energy, reducing lateral and vertical erosion, meaning that meanders may take longer to form.

### Channel Management

1) In the past, the river landscape in the Eden basin was changed by channel straightening. Many sections of river were diverted into artificial channels to try to reduce flooding.
2) Channel straightening makes the water flow more quickly than it naturally would, which can increase erosion and decrease deposition. In the artificial channel, conditions aren't right for meanders to form as they normally would — so the natural river landscape is changed.
3) More recently, some areas of the Eden basin have been restored to their original state by having artificial meanders put in, e.g. on the River Lyvennet to the south-west of Appleby.
4) The meanders slow the river's flow, increasing deposition. This encourages the river to begin to meander more naturally, and allows the natural build-up of the floodplain.

## The management of rivers can have a big impact on the landscape

Whether you choose this river basin or a different one you've studied, make sure you know the landforms in the basin, and understand how geology, climate and human activity influence the processes that impact the landscape.

Topic 3 — Distinctive Landscapes

# Worked Exam Questions

Practice questions are useful for finding any areas that you need to look at again. Work through the questions on the next two pages — the first one has been done for you to help show what the examiners are after.

1   Study **Figure 1**, which is a labelled photograph of a meander.

**Figure 1**

a)  Suggest a feature likely to be found at the part of the river labelled A in **Figure 1** and explain its formation.

*A river cliff is likely to be found at A.*

*The current is faster on the outside bend of*

*the meander because the channel is deeper.*

*This means there's more erosion on the*

*outside bend, so a river cliff is formed.*

[3]

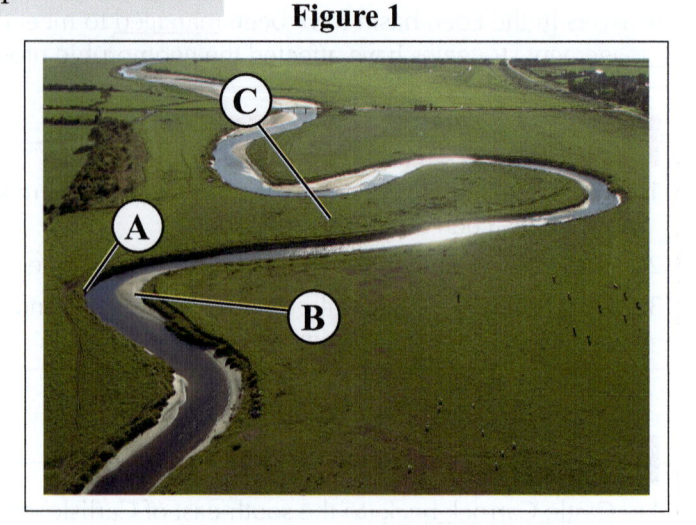

b)  Suggest a feature likely to be found at the part of the river labelled B in **Figure 1** and explain its formation.

*A slip-off slope is likely to be found at B. The current is slower on the inside bend of the meander*

*because the river channel is shallower. This means material is deposited on the inside of the*

*bend, so a slip-off slope is formed.*

[3]

c)  Name the feature labelled C in **Figure 1**.

*The neck of the meander.*

[1]

d)  Explain how an ox-bow lake could form on the river shown in **Figure 1**.

*The current is fastest at the outside bend of a meander because the channel is deeper. The fast*

*current at the outside bend means that more erosion takes place here, by the processes of abrasion*

*and hydraulic action. Erosion causes the outside bends of a meander to get closer. The outside bends*

*continue getting closer until there's only a small bit of land left between the bends (called the neck).*

*The river breaks through the neck, usually during a flood, and flows along the shortest course.*

*Material is deposited across the inlets to the old meander. This eventually cuts off the meander,*

*forming an ox-bow lake.*

[6]

[Total 13 marks]

Topic 3 — Distinctive Landscapes

# Exam Questions

1  Study **Figure 1**, which is an Ordnance Survey® map showing part of Snowdonia, Wales.

**Figure 1**

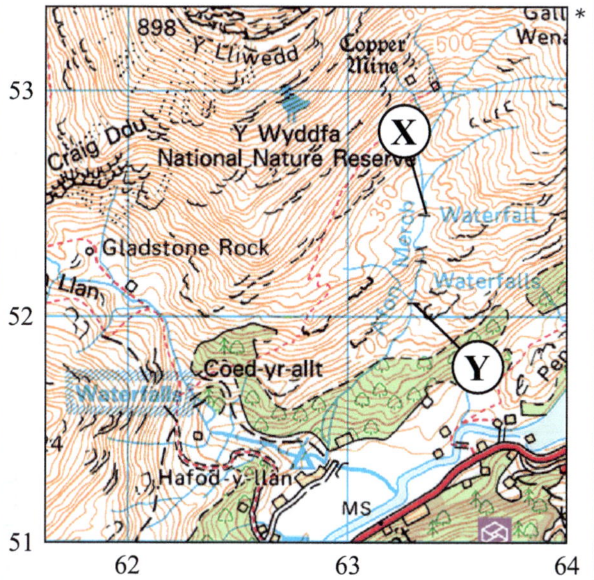

a) What is the six-figure grid reference for the waterfall, marked X on **Figure 1**? Shade one oval only.

A  525634  ◯
B  647535  ◯
C  633524  ◯
D  635535  ◯
[1]

b) There is another waterfall at point Y. State the distance between the two waterfalls.

........................................................................
[1]

c) Which waterfall, X or Y, is located on a steeper section of the river's course?

........................................................................
[1]

d) Suggest why waterfalls have formed along this stretch of the Afon Merch.

........................................................................
........................................................................
[2]

e) Explain how a gorge may form in the upper course of the Afon Merch.

........................................................................
........................................................................
........................................................................
........................................................................
........................................................................
[3]

f) Geographical Information Systems (GIS) are able to show a range of types of geographical data on separate layers. Suggest one layer that could be added to **Figure 1** to help understand the formation of river landforms.

........................................................................
........................................................................
[1]

[Total 9 marks]

*© Crown copyright 2023 OS 100034841

Topic 3 — Distinctive Landscapes

# Revision Summary

That's it for Topic 3. Now it's time to see how much information your brain has soaked up.
- Try these questions and tick off each one when you get it right.
- When you've done all the questions under a header and are completely happy with it, tick it off.

## The UK Landscape (p.35) ☑
1) a) What is a natural landscape?
   b) What is a built landscape?
2) Give three characteristics of upland areas in the UK.
3) Give three characteristics of lowland areas in the UK.
4) Describe the distribution of glaciated landscapes in the UK.

## Geomorphic Processes (p.36-37) ☑
5) Describe the process of chemical weathering.
6) What is biological weathering?
7) What are the two types of mass movement?
8) What's the difference between abrasion and attrition?
9) Name two processes of transportation.
10) When does deposition occur in rivers?

## Coastal Landforms (p.38-43) ☑
11) Are headlands made of more or less resistant rock?
12) Describe how erosion can turn a crack in a cliff into a cave.
13) What is a stack?
14) a) Which type of wave allows deposition to occur?
    b) What can increase the amount of material that is deposited?
15) What are the characteristics of shingle beaches?
16) How does longshore drift transport sediment along a coast?
17) Where do spits form?
18) a) For a named coastline, describe the climate of the region.
    b) Explain how geology and climate have affected one of the landforms found there.

## River Landforms (p.46-53) ☑
19) Describe how V-shaped valleys are formed.
20) a) Where is the current fastest on a meander?
    b) What feature of a meander is formed where the flow is fastest?
21) Name the landform created when a meander is cut off by deposition.
22) Describe the formation of a floodplain.
23) What is a levee?
24) a) For a named river basin, describe how the geology has influenced the landscape.
    b) Describe two landforms that can be found there.
    c) Explain two ways in which human activity has changed the landscape.

# Topic 4 — Sustaining Ecosystems

# Ecosystems

*Welcome to a lovely new topic — get ready to learn all about **ecosystems**.*

## An **Ecosystem** Includes all the **Living** and **Non-Living Parts** in an **Area**

1) An ecosystem is a unit that includes all the biotic (living) parts (e.g. plants and animals) and the abiotic (non-living) parts (e.g. soil and climate) in an area.

2) The organisms in ecosystems can be classed as producers, consumers or decomposers.

3) A producer is an organism that uses sunlight energy to produce food.

4) A consumer is an organism that gets its energy by eating other organisms — it eats producers or other consumers.

5) A food chain shows what eats what. A food web shows lots of food chains and how they overlap.

6) A decomposer is an organism that gets its energy by breaking down dead material, e.g. dead producers, dead consumers or fallen leaves. Bacteria and fungi are decomposers. This returns nutrients to the soil, where they can be used by plants.

**Example of a small scale ecosystem**

- A hedgerow ecosystem includes the plants that make up the hedgerow, the organisms that live in it and feed on it, the soil in the area and the rainfall and sunshine it receives.
- The producers include hawthorn bushes and blackberry bushes.
- The consumers include thrushes, ladybirds, spiders, greenfly, sparrows and sparrowhawks.

Ladybird → Sparrow → Sparrowhawk

(food web showing Sparrow, Sparrowhawk, Thrush, Ladybird, Greenfly, Spider, Bushes with berries)

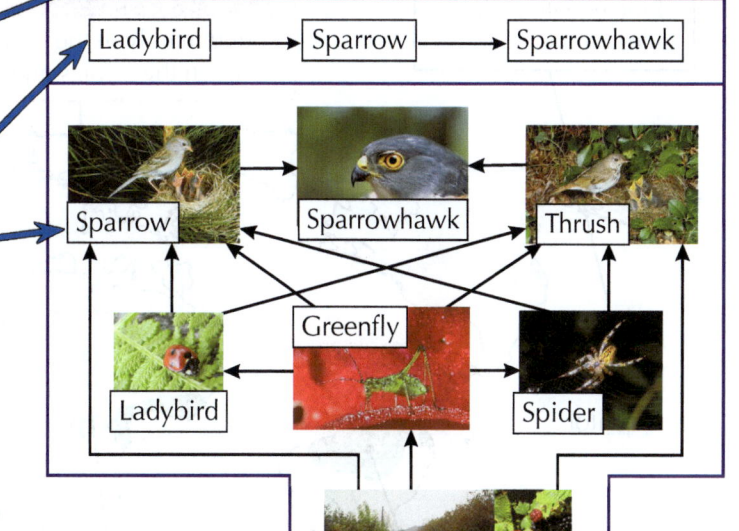

## The **Different Parts** of Ecosystems are **Interdependent**

Some parts of an ecosystem depend on the others, e.g. consumers depend on producers for a source of food and some depend on them for a habitat (a place to live). So, if one part changes it affects all the other parts that depend on it. Here are two hedgerow examples:

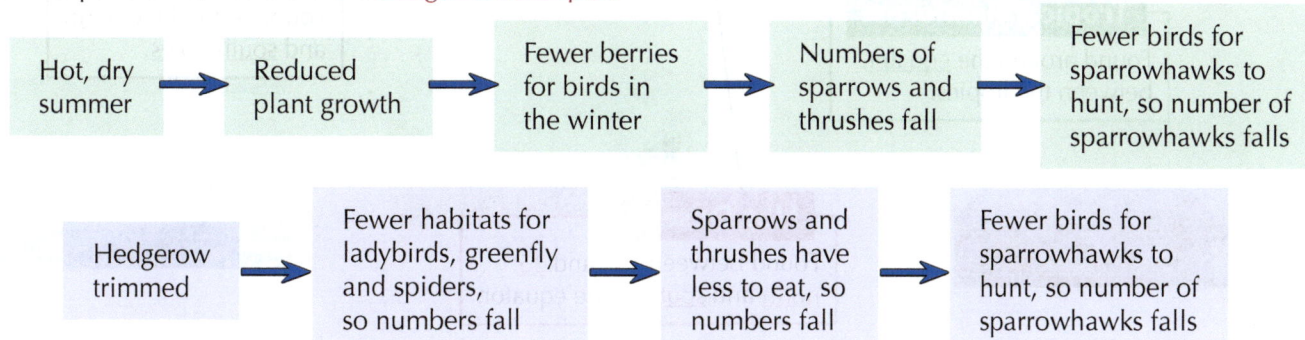

Hot, dry summer → Reduced plant growth → Fewer berries for birds in the winter → Numbers of sparrows and thrushes fall → Fewer birds for sparrowhawks to hunt, so number of sparrowhawks falls

Hedgerow trimmed → Fewer habitats for ladybirds, greenfly and spiders, so numbers fall → Sparrows and thrushes have less to eat, so numbers fall → Fewer birds for sparrowhawks to hunt, so number of sparrowhawks falls

### EXAM TIP — Food webs show multiple interlinked food chains
You may be asked how a change in an ecosystem affects the other parts. It's helpful to draw a food web for the ecosystem so you can easily see what will have more food, less food, no habitat and so on.

# Global Ecosystems

*There are loads of different **ecosystems** in the world. Time for a whistle-stop tour...*

## You Need to Know the **Global Distribution** of **Six Ecosystems**

1) The climate in an area determines what type of ecosystem forms. So different parts of the world have different ecosystems because they have different climates.
2) The map shows the global distribution of six types of ecosystem — there are a lot more, but these are some of the major ones.

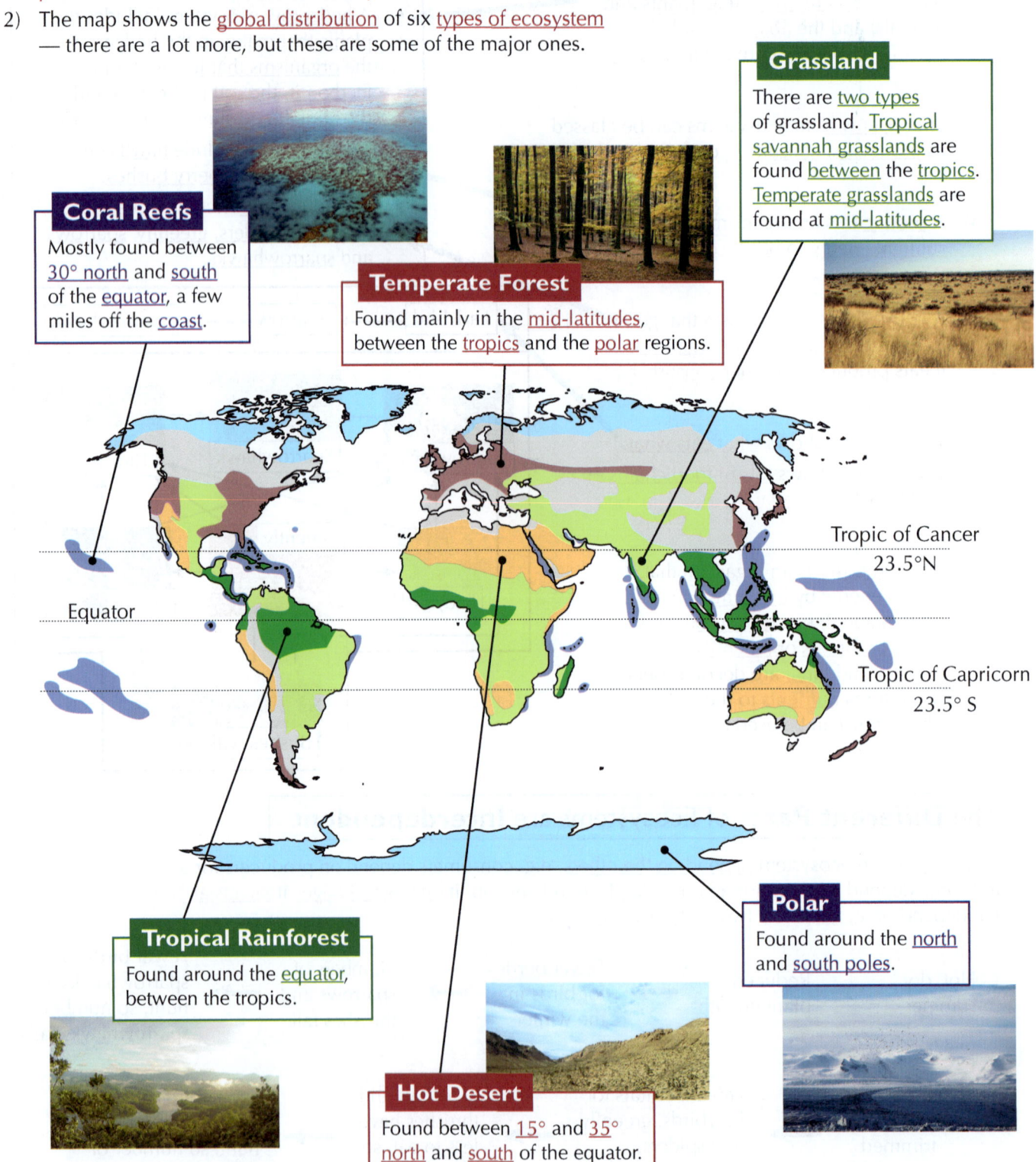

### Grassland
There are two types of grassland. Tropical savannah grasslands are found between the tropics. Temperate grasslands are found at mid-latitudes.

### Coral Reefs
Mostly found between 30° north and south of the equator, a few miles off the coast.

### Temperate Forest
Found mainly in the mid-latitudes, between the tropics and the polar regions.

Tropic of Cancer 23.5°N

Equator

Tropic of Capricorn 23.5° S

### Polar
Found around the north and south poles.

### Tropical Rainforest
Found around the equator, between the tropics.

### Hot Desert
Found between 15° and 35° north and south of the equator.

## Different ecosystems are seen as you move further from the equator
You don't need to memorise the whole map, but make sure you can describe the general distribution of these six ecosystems. You'll learn about each ecosystem's climate, animals and plants over the next few pages.

Topic 4 — Sustaining Ecosystems

# Global Ecosystems

*These are among the most **extreme** ecosystems on Earth — swelteringly **hot deserts** and freezing cold **polar regions**.*

## Hot Deserts Have Low Rainfall

**Climate**
1) There's very little rainfall — less than 250 mm per year. When it rains varies a lot — it might only rain once every two or three years.
2) Temperatures are extreme — they range from very hot in the day (e.g. 45 °C) to cold at night (below 0 °C).

**Plants**
1) Plant growth is sparse due to the lack of rainfall. Plants that do grow include cacti and thornbushes.
2) Plant roots are often very long to reach deep water supplies, or spread out wide near the surface to catch as much water as possible when it rains. Some plants (e.g. cacti) have fleshy stems and thick, waxy skin to cope with the dry climate.

**Animals**
1) Hot deserts are home to lizards, snakes, insects and scorpions. Mammals tend to be small, e.g. kangaroo rats. Many birds leave during the hottest weather.
2) Animals are adapted to cope with the harsh climate. Many animals are nocturnal, so they can stay in burrows or in the shade during the day. Some bigger animals have evolved to lose very little water and to tolerate dehydration, e.g. camels.

## Polar Ecosystems are Cold and Dry

*Plants are sometimes called flora and animals are sometimes called fauna. (I remember it because flora is like floral, meaning flowery.)*

**Climate**
1) Polar areas are very cold. Temperatures are usually less than 10 °C. Winters are normally below −40 °C and can reach almost −90 °C.
2) Rainfall (and snowfall) is low — no more than 500 mm a year (mainly in the summer).
3) There are clearly defined seasons — cold summers and even colder winters.

**Animals**
1) There are relatively few different species of animals compared with other ecosystems.
2) Polar bears, penguins and marine mammals like whales, seals, and walruses are examples of animals found in polar regions.

**Plants**
1) There are very few plants — some lichens and mosses are found on rocks, and there are a few grasses and flowering plants on the coast where it's warmer.
2) Plants grow slowly and don't grow very tall — grasses are the most common plants. Closer to the poles, only mosses and lichens can survive.
3) Some small, short trees and shrubs grow in warmer, sheltered areas.

## Hot deserts and polar ecosystems have very harsh climates

Both these ecosystems have extreme temperatures and low rainfall, making it very difficult for animals and plants to survive. But these ecosystems are not lifeless — species with adaptations can cope with these extreme climates.

Topic 4 — Sustaining Ecosystems

# Global Ecosystems

*There are two major types of forest ecosystem — **temperate forests** and **tropical rainforests**.*

## Temperate Forests Have a Mild, Wet Climate

**Climate**
1) Temperate forests have <u>four</u> distinct <u>seasons</u> — spring, summer, autumn and winter. The <u>summers</u> are <u>warm</u> and the <u>winters</u> are <u>cool</u>.
2) <u>Rainfall</u> is very <u>high</u> (up to 1500 mm per year) and there's <u>rain all year</u> round.
3) The forests that receive the <u>highest amount of rainfall</u> are sometimes called <u>temperate rainforests</u>.

**Animals**
1) Temperate forests support lots of different species of <u>mammals</u> (e.g. foxes, squirrels), <u>birds</u> (e.g. woodpeckers, cuckoos) and <u>insects</u> (e.g. beetles, moths).
2) <u>Streams</u> and <u>ponds</u> are <u>habitats</u> for insects (e.g. <u>mosquitoes</u>) to breed. Insects provide food for <u>fish</u>, including trout and salmon.

**Plants**
Temperate forests have lots of <u>trees</u>. The type of vegetation depends on the <u>type of forest</u>:
1) <u>Deciduous forests</u> have <u>broad-leaved trees</u> that <u>drop their leaves</u> in autumn (e.g. oak), <u>shrubs</u> (e.g. brambles) and <u>undergrowth</u> (e.g. ferns). <u>Forest-floor plants</u> (e.g. bluebells) often flower in <u>spring</u> before the trees grow leaves and <u>block out</u> the light.
2) <u>Coniferous forests</u> have <u>evergreen trees</u> (e.g. pine, fir) and an <u>understory</u> of grasses and low-growing plants. Trees are evergreen so they can make use of available <u>sunlight all year</u> round.

## Tropical Rainforests Have a Hot, Wet Climate

*See pages 64-67 for more on rainforests.*

**Climate**
1) The climate is <u>the same all year</u> round — there are <u>no definite seasons</u>.
2) It's <u>hot</u> (the temperature is generally between <u>20-28 °C</u> and only varies by a few degrees over the year). This is because near the <u>equator</u>, the <u>Sun</u> is <u>overhead</u> all year round.
3) <u>Rainfall</u> is very <u>high</u>, around 2000 mm per year. It <u>rains every day</u>, usually in the <u>afternoon</u>.

**Animals**
1) Rainforests are believed to contain <u>more animal species</u> than any other ecosystem. Gorillas, jaguars, anacondas, tree frogs and sloths are all <u>examples</u> of rainforest animals. There are also loads of species of <u>insects</u> and <u>birds</u>.
2) Many animals are <u>camouflaged</u>, e.g. leaf-tailed geckos look like leaves so they can <u>hide</u> from <u>predators</u>. Other animals are <u>nocturnal</u> (active at <u>night</u>), e.g. sloths. They <u>sleep</u> through the day and <u>feed</u> at night when it's <u>cooler</u> — this helps them to <u>save energy</u>.

**Plants**
1) Most trees are <u>evergreen</u> (they don't <u>drop</u> their <u>leaves</u> in a particular <u>season</u>) to take advantage of the <u>continual growing season</u>.
2) Vegetation cover is <u>dense</u>, so very <u>little light</u> reaches the forest floor. There are lots of <u>epiphytes</u> (plants that grow on other living plants and take <u>nutrients</u> and <u>moisture</u> from the air), e.g. orchids and ferns.
3) The rainforest has <u>four distinct layers</u> of plants with different adaptations. For example, trees in the highest layer (<u>emergents</u>) are <u>very tall</u>, have big roots (called <u>buttress roots</u>) to support their trunks and <u>only</u> have branches at their <u>crown</u> (where <u>most light</u> reaches them). Plants lower down in the <u>undercanopy</u> have <u>large leaves</u> to absorb as <u>much light</u> as possible.

## The climate in an area determines the type of ecosystem found there

Both these ecosystems need high rainfall, but tropical rainforests are only found in hot regions where the climate doesn't change much over the year. Temperate forests are seen in cooler areas that experience different seasons.

Topic 4 — Sustaining Ecosystems

# Global Ecosystems

*Here are the last two ecosystems you need to know about — **grasslands** and **coral reefs**.*

## There are **Two Types** of **Grassland**

**Climate**
1) Savannah grasslands have quite low rainfall (800-900 mm per year) and distinct wet and dry seasons. Temperatures are highest (around 35 °C) just before the wet season and lowest (about 15 °C) just after it.
2) Temperate grasslands have hot summers (up to 40 °C) and cold winters (down to −40 °C). They receive 250-500 mm precipitation each year, mostly in the late spring and early summer.

**Plants**
1) Savannah grasslands consist mostly of grass, scrub and small plants, with a few scattered trees, e.g. acacia tree. Plants are adapted to cope with low levels of rainfall — many have long roots to reach deep water or small, waxy leaves to reduce water loss.
2) Temperate grasslands are also dominated by grasses and small plants. They have very few trees. Grasses often have roots that spread out wide to absorb as much water as possible.

**Animals**
1) Savannah grasslands are home to lots of insects, including many species of grasshoppers, beetles and termites. Larger animals include lions, elephants, giraffes, zebras and antelope.
2) Temperate grasslands are home to fewer animal species than savannah grasslands. Mammals include bison and wild horses, and rodents such as mole rats.
3) In both types of grassland, grazing animals (e.g. antelope) travel long distances in search of food and water, while other animals (e.g. mole rats) dig burrows to escape the harsh climate.

## **Coral Reefs** Support a Large Number of **Animals**

**Climate**
1) Coral reefs are most common in warm areas that receive lots of sunlight.
2) They grow best in shallow, clear, salty water.

**Plants**
1) Coral reefs form underwater, so few plants grow there.
2) Tiny algae (plant-like organisms) live inside the tissue of corals. The algae and the coral depend on each other for nutrients.

**Animals**
1) Coral itself is an animal — it's a bit like a sea anemone, but some species create a hard outer coating for protection.
2) Around 25% of all marine species live in coral reefs, including fish, molluscs, sea snakes, turtles and shrimps. Many fish have flat bodies so they can easily swim through and hide in small gaps in the coral.

---

### REVISION TIP: Think about how each ecosystem is different
Look back over the last few pages and jot down the similarities and differences you notice among the six ecosystems. Compare their climates and the types of plants and animals found there.

Topic 4 — Sustaining Ecosystems

# Worked Exam Questions

Make sure you pay attention to this page — it will show you how to answer exam questions to get the highest marks. When you've read it through, have a go at the questions on the next page on your own.

**1** Study **Figure 1**, which shows part of a food web for a coastal ecosystem.

a) Using **Figure 1**, describe how the sea snail and the periwinkle are connected to each other.

*The periwinkle is a food source for the sea snail.*
[1]

b) Give **one** non-living component that could be part of this ecosystem.

*Sunlight*
[1]

**Figure 1**

c) Using **Figure 1**, explain how the populations of octopuses and seaweed in this ecosystem might be affected if a disease reduced the crab population.

**Octopuses:** *The population will decrease because there will be fewer crabs for them to eat.*

**Seaweed:** *The population of seaweed will increase because less of it will be being eaten by the crabs.*
[2]
[Total 4 marks]

**2** Study **Figure 2**, which shows climate data for a hot desert.

a) What is the average maximum temperature for December?

*40* °C
[1]

**Figure 2**

b) With reference to **Figure 2**, describe **two** characteristics of the hot desert climate.

**Characteristic 1:** *Temperature shows a high daily variation, being very hot in the day and much colder at night. Figure 2 shows that the difference between maximum and minimum temperature in January is about 20 °C.*

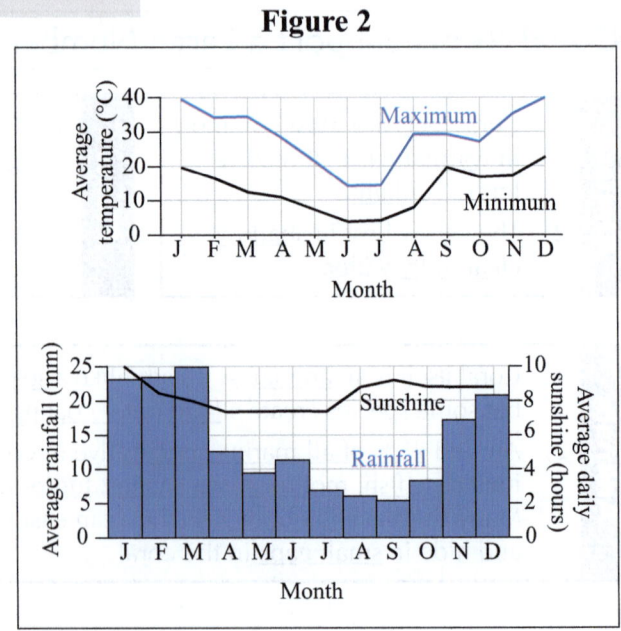

**Characteristic 2:** *There is very little rainfall. Figure 2 shows that the average rainfall peaks at about 25 mm a month but can be as low as about 5 mm a month.*
[4]
[Total 5 marks]

Topic 4 — Sustaining Ecosystems

# Exam Questions

1   Study **Figure 1**, a photograph of savannah grassland.

a)   Where are grasslands found?

...................................................................................

................................................................................... *[1]*

**Figure 1**

b)   Which of the following is **not** a characteristic of the climate of grasslands? Shade **one** oval only.

   A   Cold winters (down to –40 °C)   ◯
   B   Distinct wet and dry seasons    ◯
   C   High rainfall (over 1500 mm/yr) ◯
   D   Hot summers (up to 40 °C)       ◯   *[1]*

c)   Using **Figure 1** and your own knowledge, describe the flora of grassland ecosystems.

..........................................................................................................................................

..........................................................................................................................................

..........................................................................................................................................
*[2]*

d)   Describe **one** way that soil and plants are dependent on one another in land-based ecosystems.

..........................................................................................................................................

..........................................................................................................................................

..........................................................................................................................................
*[2]*

*[Total 6 marks]*

**Figure 2**

**Diet:** Plants
**Length:** 5-15 cm
**Behaviour:** Nocturnal. Live in burrows.

2   Study **Figure 2**, a mini fact file about the desert jerboa.

Using **Figure 2** and your own knowledge, explain **two** ways in which jerboas are characteristic of the animals found in the hot deserts.

1:..........................................................................................

..........................................................................................

2:..........................................................................................

..........................................................................................
*[Total 4 marks]*

Topic 4 — Sustaining Ecosystems

# Tropical Rainforests

*Time to venture **deep** into the heart of the **rainforest** and find out just how they **function**. First up is the **water cycle**.*

## The Water Cycle Shows How Water Moves in Tropical Rainforests

1) The water cycle has different parts — bodies of water (e.g. rivers and lakes), the land and the atmosphere.

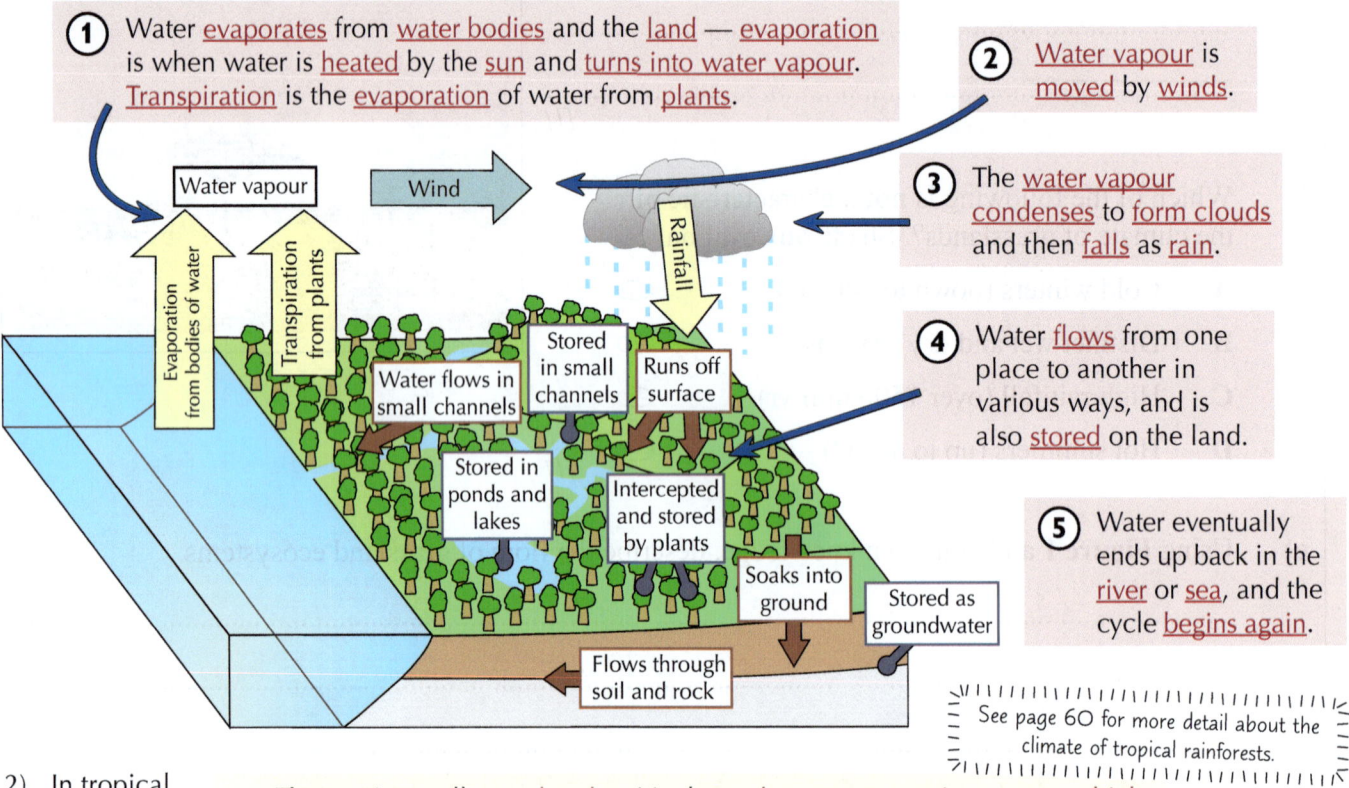

① Water evaporates from water bodies and the land — evaporation is when water is heated by the sun and turns into water vapour. Transpiration is the evaporation of water from plants.

② Water vapour is moved by winds.

③ The water vapour condenses to form clouds and then falls as rain.

④ Water flows from one place to another in various ways, and is also stored on the land.

⑤ Water eventually ends up back in the river or sea, and the cycle begins again.

*See page 60 for more detail about the climate of tropical rainforests.*

2) In tropical rainforests:
- The sun is usually overhead so it's always hot — evaporation rates are high.
- High evaporation rates mean there's lots of water vapour, so rainfall is high.
- Vegetation is dense, so lots of water is intercepted and stored by plants.

## Nutrients are Cycled Quickly in Tropical Rainforests

1) The nutrient cycle is the way that nutrients move through an ecosystem.
2) In tropical rainforests:

- Trees are evergreen, so dead leaves and other material fall all year round.
- The warm, moist climate means that fungi and bacteria decompose the dead organic matter quickly, releasing nutrients into the soil.
- Rainwater soaks into the soil and the nutrients are dissolved in the water.
- Dense vegetation and rapid plant growth mean that the nutrient-rich water is rapidly taken up by plants' roots.

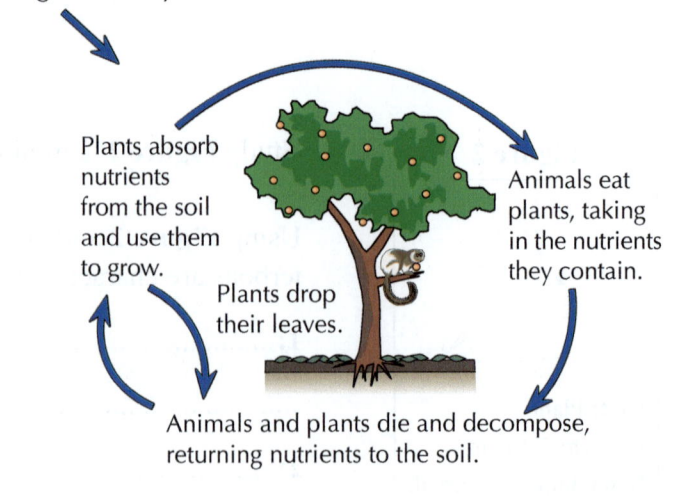

Plants absorb nutrients from the soil and use them to grow.

Animals eat plants, taking in the nutrients they contain.

Plants drop their leaves.

Animals and plants die and decompose, returning nutrients to the soil.

---

**REVISION TIP**

### Water and nutrients are cycled through tropical rainforests
You need to know the characteristics of water and nutrient cycles in tropical rainforests. Use this page to draw and label your own water and nutrient cycles — keep doing this until you've got it all memorised.

Topic 4 — Sustaining Ecosystems

# Tropical Rainforests

*The **warm**, **moist** conditions combined with the **nutrient** cycle give rainforest **soils** distinct characteristics.*

## Rainforest Soils are Low in Nutrients

Soils in tropical rainforests are often very deep but they only have a very thin fertile layer and are generally nutrient poor. This is a result of the combination of high temperatures and high rainfall:

1) The hot, wet climate means that chemical weathering is rapid. This means there is usually a deep layer of soil — the bedrock can be up to 30 m below the surface.
2) The trees drop their leaves all year round, so there is a constant supply of dead leaves and twigs falling onto the soil surface, forming a thick leaf layer.
3) This is quickly broken down (see previous page) to form humus, which then gets mixed with the soil.
4) The layer of humus is thin because the high density, fast-growing plants quickly absorb the nutrients.
5) Nutrients are also leached (washed downwards) through the soil by the heavy rainfall, making the soil nutrient poor.
6) Trees and other vegetation have roots close to the surface, where the nutrients are — there are lots of roots in the humus layer.

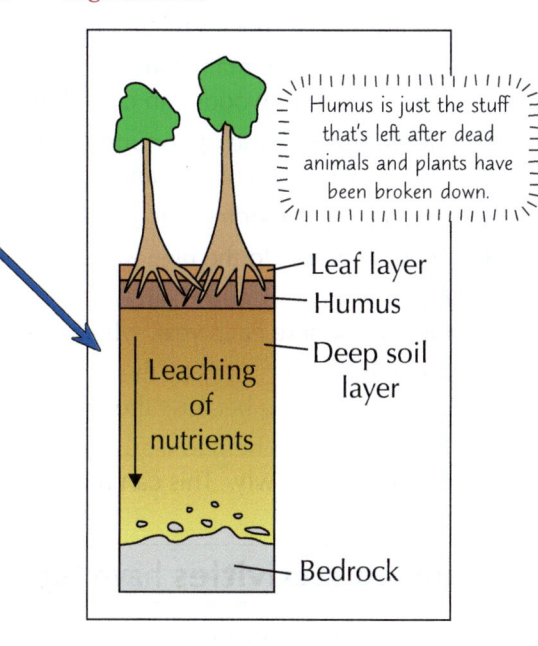

*Humus is just the stuff that's left after dead animals and plants have been broken down.*

- Leaf layer
- Humus
- Deep soil layer
- Leaching of nutrients
- Bedrock

## Rainforests are Interdependent Ecosystems

All the parts of the rainforest (climate, soils, water, plants, animals and people) are dependent on one another — if any one of them changes, everything else is affected. For example:

1) The warm and wet climate means that plants grow quickly — the dense leaf cover protects the forest floor from wind and heavy rainfall, while root systems hold the soil together — this stops it being eroded.
2) The lack of wind near the forest floor means that many plants there have to rely on bees, butterflies, or other animals for pollination. Symbiotic relationships between plants and animals (where they each depend on the other for survival) are very common in tropical rainforests. For example:

> Agouti (a rodent) are one of the only animals who can crack open the hard seed pod of the Brazil nut to eat the nut inside. Sometimes, the agouti bury the nuts — these can sprout into new seedlings. If the agouti became extinct, the Brazil nut trees would decline and so could all the other animals who live in or feed on the Brazil nut trees. People who sell Brazil nuts to make a living may also be affected.

3) There are lots of epiphytes (plants that grow on other plants) in rainforests. They get access to light by growing high up on other plants, but they don't have access to the nutrients in the soil — they are dependent on rainfall to provide water and nutrients.
4) Changes to the rainforest ecosystem can have knock-on effects on the whole ecosystem. For example, deforestation reduces the amount of $CO_2$ being absorbed from the atmosphere, which adds to the greenhouse effect and changes the climate (see p.29).

## Interdependence means everything affects everything else

Make sure you know the characteristics of rainforest soils and how the plants, animals and so on are all interdependent. Cover the page and note down what you know to check you've got it all before you move on.

Topic 4 — Sustaining Ecosystems

# Tropical Rainforests — Human Impacts

*Tropical rainforests are really **important**, but **human activities** are having huge **impacts** on them.*

## Tropical Rainforests Provide Lots of Goods and Services

High biodiversity (the range of plants and animals found there) means rainforests are a rich source of goods:

- Many products, including rubber, coffee, chocolate and medicines, are sourced from the rainforest. Undiscovered species might give us new medicines and other new products.
- Hardwoods, e.g. mahogany, are widely used for furniture and building. Logging of hardwoods can contribute a huge amount to a country's economy.
- Rainforests provide opportunities for farming and mining if the vegetation is cleared. This provides lots of jobs and income in many rainforest areas.

Rainforests also provide services through their impact on the global climate and local environment:

- They are home to the highest diversity of animal and plant species on the planet.
- Rainforest plants absorb around 0.7 billion tonnes of carbon dioxide ($CO_2$) from the atmosphere each year, which helps to reduce climate change (see p.29).
- Rainfall is intercepted by the high density of vegetation — this reduces the risk of local flooding because the movement of water to rivers is slowed down.
- Rainforests also help to regulate the global water cycle by storing water and releasing it into the atmosphere slowly. This can reduce the risk of drought and flooding in areas a long way away.

*Rainforests also directly provide services for people, e.g. tourists visit to see the plants and animals.*

## Human Activities have Big Impacts on the Rainforest

Although human activities can bring jobs and wealth, they also have lots of negative impacts:

**Logging**
- With no trees to hold the soil together, heavy rain washes away the soil (soil erosion). Eroded soil can enter rivers, silting up habitats that fish use for breeding.
- The removal of trees interrupts the water cycle — this can lead to some areas becoming very dry with an increased risk of wildfires, while other areas become more likely to flood.
- Logging requires the building of new roads, which opens up the rainforest to further development.

**Agriculture**
- Land is often cleared using slash-and-burn techniques. Burning vegetation produces $CO_2$, which adds to the greenhouse effect.
- Without trees to intercept rainfall, more water reaches the soil. Nutrients are washed away, so soil fertility is reduced — rainforest soils usually lose their fertility in 3-5 years.
- Artificial fertilisers added to improve soil fertility are washed into streams, threatening wildlife.

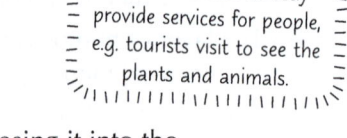

*Clearing trees can also make an area less appealing to tourists, so income from tourism decreases.*

**Mineral Extraction**
- Mining of precious metals, e.g. gold, often requires heavy machinery and the removal of trees.
- Toxic chemicals used to extract and purify the metals are washed into streams and rivers, killing wildlife and polluting people's drinking water.
- There can also be conflict with local people over rights to the land.

**Tourism**
- Tourists may scare wildlife, e.g. causing nesting birds to abandon their young.
- They may also damage vegetation and leave behind lots of litter.
- If tourism is unregulated, a lack of infrastructure, e.g. sewers, can lead to pollution of waterways. In order to build infrastructure (e.g. roads and airports), vegetation must be cleared.

## Human threats to rainforests may lead to goods and services being lost

The damage done to rainforests by human activity doesn't just threaten the species that inhabit them — we might lose access to important rainforest products and suffer more severely from climate change, flooding and drought.

Topic 4 — Sustaining Ecosystems

# Tropical Rainforests — Sustainable Management

CASE STUDY

*Rainforests* face a lot of **threats**, but it's not all **doom and gloom** for them. This page is all about ways people are trying to **manage** the biggest rainforest of them all — the mighty **Amazon**.

## People are Trying to Use and Manage the Amazon Sustainably

1) The Amazon rainforest is in the north of South America and covers an area of around 8 million km², including parts of Brazil, Peru, Colombia, Venezuela, Ecuador, Bolivia, Guyana, Suriname and French Guiana.
2) Some management strategies aim to use the Amazon rainforest in a way that's sustainable — that is, allowing people today to get the things that they need, without stopping people in the future getting what they need. Here are some of the ways they're doing it:

### Sustainable Forestry

1) Sustainable forestry balances the removal of trees to sell with the conservation of the forest as a whole. It can involve selective logging, where only some trees are felled so that the forest is able to regenerate, or planting new trees to replace the ones that were cut down.
2) International agreements try to reduce illegal logging, and promote wood from sustainably managed forests. For example, the Forest Stewardship Council® (FSC) is an organisation that marks sustainably sourced timber products with its logo so that consumers can choose sustainable products.
3) Precious Woods Amazon is a logging company operating in Brazil. They place limits on the number of trees that can be cut down, to make sure the forest can regenerate. They also use a variety of species, so that no species is over-exploited. They are FSC®-certified.

### Community Programmes

1) Natütama is an organisation in Puerto Nariño in Colombia that is working with the local community to protect river species, e.g. the Amazon river dolphin.
2) It employs local people to teach other people in the community how they can protect endangered river animals and their habitats.
3) Local fishermen collect information about the number and distribution of species, and report any illegal hunting or fishing that is taking place.
4) The team also organise clean-up days to remove litter from the local rivers.

### Ecotourism

Ecotourism is tourism that minimises damage to the environment and benefits the local people.

1) Yachana Lodge is an ecotourism project in Ecuador, in a remote area of the Amazon rainforest where local people rely on subsistence farming to provide a living.
2) It employs local people, giving them a more reliable income and a better quality of life.
3) It also encourages the conservation of the rainforest so that visitors continue to want to visit.
4) Tourists visit in small groups so that harm to the environment is minimised, and take part in activities to raise awareness of conservation issues.
5) Tourists have to pay entrance fees — this brings in more money for rainforest conservation. Profits are invested in education projects to promote conservation in the local community.

### Biosphere Reserves

A biosphere reserve is an internationally recognised protected area that aims to combine conservation and sustainable use.

1) The Central Amazon Conservation Complex (CACC) in Brazil is the largest protected area in the rainforest, covering around 60 000 km². It's home to loads of different species of plants and animals, e.g. black caimans and river dolphins.
2) Access to the CACC is restricted, and there are strict limits on hunting, logging and fishing.
3) Scientific research projects and environmental education activities are encouraged to make people more aware of conservation issues.

## There are several strategies for increasing sustainability in the Amazon

You need to learn a case study involving attempts to sustainably manage a tropical rainforest. This doesn't have to be the Amazon — if you've studied a different rainforest in class, you can use that one instead.

Topic 4 — Sustaining Ecosystems

# Polar Environments

*It's time for a foray into the ice-cold world of polar environments...*

## Antarctica and the Arctic have Distinctive Characteristics

Antarctica and the Arctic are both polar ecosystems but they are slightly different. The Arctic is usually defined as the region north of the Arctic Circle (about 66° N).

*Some people define the Arctic as anywhere north of the tree line or where average summer temperatures are less than 10 °C.*

|  | The Arctic | Antarctica |
|---|---|---|
| Climate | Average summer temperatures are less than 10 °C and winter temperatures are about -20 °C to -40 °C. Annual precipitation is usually less than 500 mm. | Antarctica is colder than the Arctic. Summer temperatures are usually -20 °C to -5 °C and winter temperatures can reach almost -90 °C. Annual precipitation is also lower (only 50 mm inland and 200 mm at the coast). |
| Features of the land and sea | The majority of the Arctic is made up of ocean, which has lots of drifting pack ice and icebergs. The sea ice extends further in winter. On land there are mountainous regions, areas that are permanently covered with snow and ice, and areas of treeless tundra (where only a surface layer of the soil thaws each summer). | Antarctica is a land mass which is 99% covered with an ice sheet. A few mountains poke up out of the ice, e.g. the Transantarctic Mountains, which run across the continent. The sea freezes in the winter, nearly doubling the size of the continent. |
| Flora (plants) | Low-growing shrubs, lichen, moss, some flowering plants, e.g. Arctic poppies. | Much less vegetation — mainly moss and lichen. The sea contains lots of phytoplankton. |
| Fauna (animals) | E.g. whales, seals, fish, wolves, polar bears, reindeer, caribou and lots of birds. Most animals are adapted to the specific conditions of the Arctic. *Caribou* | E.g. whales, seals, penguins, sea-birds. All the animals in Antarctica rely on the sea, e.g. for food or to provide a habitat for breeding. *Penguins* |

## Cold Environments are Fragile, Interdependent Ecosystems

The biotic (living) components of cold environments (plants, animals and people) and the abiotic (non-living) components (climate, soils, water) are closely related — if one of them changes, the others are affected.

1) The cold, dry climate means that biodiversity is low in the Arctic and Antarctica.
2) Ocean currents and winds open up gaps in the sea ice. This increases light levels in the water, meaning algae and other producers can produce more food. This causes populations of fish, e.g. cod, to increase, supporting consumers such as seals, penguins and polar bears.
3) If temperatures increase (e.g. due to climate change caused by human activities) more sea ice melts in the summer — animals such as seals and polar bears rely on sea ice for breeding and hunting, so if sea ice cover decreases, these animals are threatened.
4) In the Arctic tundra, the cold climate causes plants to grow slowly and decompose slowly. This means that the soil is low in nutrients, further reducing growth rates. In summer, the surface layer of soil thaws and plant cover increases. Plants absorb heat from the Sun, and prevent the permanently frozen ground below (permafrost) from thawing. Slow melting of the upper layer of permafrost provides water for plants.
5) In the Antarctic there are very few plants — phytoplankton in the sea are the most important producers. These form the basis of all the food chains, e.g. they are eaten by krill, which are eaten by fish, which are eaten by penguins or sea-birds. Phytoplankton depend on nutrient-rich currents of seawater rising to the surface from deep underwater — if these were reduced, the whole ecosystem would be threatened.

### EXAM TIP — The Arctic and Antarctica have similarities and differences

You need to know the characteristics of both the Arctic and Antarctic for the exam, but you only need to learn about interdependence in one polar ecosystem — you can choose either the Arctic or Antarctic.

Topic 4 — Sustaining Ecosystems

# Polar Environments — Human Impacts

*No surprises here — you've learnt about the **characteristics** of polar environments, so now it's time to hear about all the **negative things** people are doing to them (and a few of the positive things too).*

## Human Activities Impact Polar Ecosystems

### Tourism
1) Tourism occurs in both the Arctic and Antarctica.
2) It increases shipping and air travel, leading to water and air pollution. There is also a risk of boats grounding, which can cause oil spills.
3) Tourists can disturb breeding colonies of birds and seals. Trampling damages fragile vegetation and erodes the landscape, leaving paths.
4) Litter and waste disposal damages habitats and can harm wildlife, especially because decomposition rates in the cold environments are so slow.
5) In Antarctica, there is concern over the introduction of non-native species, which could alter food webs, changing the ecosystem irreversibly.

### Fishing
1) Commercial fishing takes place in both the Arctic and Antarctic oceans.
2) Over-fishing threatens many species, e.g. in Antarctica the Patagonian Toothfish has been fished to near extinction.
3) Reduced fish populations have knock-on effects on other species in the food chain, e.g. the larger fish and birds that eat them.
4) Other species can also be affected, e.g. albatrosses and petrels get caught in the fishing lines and drown.

### Indigenous People
1) There are no permanent inhabitants in Antarctica and the Arctic only has a population of about 4 million, including the Inuit of Greenland and Canada.
2) Traditional indigenous people rely on reindeer herding, or fishing and hunting to support themselves — but they only take what they need and don't upset the balance of the ecosystem.
3) Many indigenous people now live in modern towns and cities, e.g. Anchorage in Alaska — this impacts the environment through waste disposal, air and noise pollution from vehicles, and heat from buildings, which can melt permafrost.

### Scientific Research
1) Scientists use polar environments for important research, e.g. on global climate change. This has a positive impact on global environmental management, and on management of polar ecosystems.
2) In the past, some scientists working in Antarctica dumped rubbish in the sea and abandoned broken equipment. This polluted the land and sea, damaging habitats and posing a risk to wildlife.
3) Research stations and ships produce chemical and sewage pollution. However, research organisations try to limit this.

### Mineral Extraction
1) The Arctic has large gas and oil reserves, e.g. at Prudhoe Bay in Alaska, as well as other mineral deposits, e.g. uranium and phosphate are mined in Arctic Russia.
2) Drilling for gas and oil is risky — oil spills are difficult to clean up and can harm habitats and kill wildlife.
3) Pipelines also have to be built to transport the oil and gas — these can melt the permafrost below and interrupt the migration routes of caribou herds.
4) The extraction of metals from mined rocks produces lots of pollution, damaging ecosystems in the surrounding area.

*There are mineral reserves in Antarctica too but they're not allowed to be extracted (see next page).*

### Whaling
1) Whaling was a big industry in both the Arctic and Antarctic during the last two centuries.
2) Many species of whale were hunted to near extinction, e.g. Blue, Fin and Minke whales.
3) Whales are very slow breeders, so it takes a long time for their populations to recover.
4) Whaling in polar areas has mostly stopped, and numbers of some whale species are slowly recovering.

---

### REVISION TIP — Exploiting resources has negative impacts on polar environments
Cover the page and write down all six activities that are affecting polar ecosystems. Then see how many details about the impacts of each activity you can add. Bonus points for any examples you remember.

Topic 4 — Sustaining Ecosystems

# Managing Polar Environments

*Polar environments are **fragile** areas — **sustainable management** can be used to **protect** them from damage.*

## Tourism is Being Managed Sustainably on Svalbard

1) Svalbard is a group of islands in the Arctic Circle, north of Norway, that is promoting sustainable tourism.
2) Over 60% of Svalbard is protected. For example, there are strict limits on the use of off-road motorised vehicles, and tour operators and visitors have to get permission to visit the nature reserves.
3) Different zones have different levels of protection — nature reserves allow very little access, while tourism areas have fewer regulations.
4) Here's an example of how tourism is being managed sustainably in one part of Svalbard:

> **Ny-Ålesund**
> 
> Ny-Ålesund is the most northerly settlement in the world and is run by a company called Kings Bay AS. The population is mostly made up of scientific researchers. The company and researchers have taken actions to limit the impact of tourism on the area. For example:
> - Cruise ships are required to tell passengers about the rules visitors have to follow, e.g. not disturbing nesting birds or leaving litter.
> - Visitors have to stick to the 1.5 km path around the settlement and there are lots of boards with environmental information, to make tourists aware of the issues.
> - The ships are only allowed to remain anchored for a few hours — this reduces the amount of pollution from e.g. diesel fumes entering the local environment.

5) More recently there has been a ban on the most polluting fuels used by cruise ships — this means that the bigger cruise ships are now unable to visit Ny-Ålesund, as well as some other areas around Svalbard.

## The Antarctic Treaty is an Example of Global Sustainable Management

1) The Antarctic Treaty is an agreement made by twelve countries in 1959 about how to sustainably manage Antarctica's ecosystems.
2) The environmental protocol (which came into force in 1998) sets out 6 basic principles for human activity:
   - no mineral exploitation is allowed
   - plants and animals must be conserved
   - areas of the environment must be protected
   - there are rules for waste disposal and waste must be minimised
   - there are regulations for the discharge of sewage from vessels
   - activities must have an Environmental Impact Assessment before they are able to go ahead
3) There are strict rules about the introduction of non-native species so that ecosystems aren't disturbed, e.g. visitors have to wear disinfected overboots when they land and there are restrictions on eating, drinking and weeing whilst ashore.
4) There are also globally agreed rules amongst tour operators — only 100 visitors are allowed to land at any one time and cruise ships of over 500 passengers are prevented from stopping.
5) There have been no major problems with the treaty and some people think it should be extended to cover the ocean surrounding Antarctica so that there is more protection for marine life, e.g. whales and fish.

---

### Tourism is managed in many cold environments to protect ecosystems

Sustainable management occurs on different scales. You need to know two case studies in polar environments — one that's on a small scale (e.g. sustainable tourism on Svalbard) and one on a global scale (e.g. the Antarctic treaty).

Topic 4 — Sustaining Ecosystems

# Worked Exam Questions

It's not enough just to learn some facts for the exam — you'll also need to know how to put them into a good exam answer. So here are some worked examples to help you on the way.

**1** Study **Figure 1**, a diagram showing part of the nutrient cycle in a tropical rainforest ecosystem.

**Figure 1**

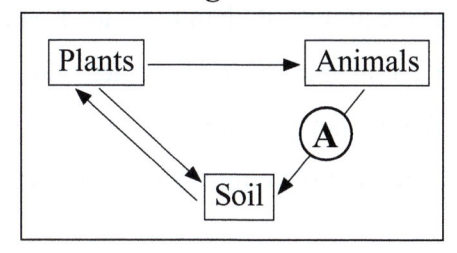

a) State how nutrients are transferred along the arrow labelled A in **Figure 1**.

*The decomposition of dead animals returns nutrients to the soil.*

*[1]*

b) Describe how nutrients are recycled in the rest of the tropical rainforest ecosystem in **Figure 1**.

*In tropical rainforests, dead leaves and other plant material containing nutrients fall all year round. The dead organic matter is decomposed by fungi and bacteria. The nutrients released are then dissolved by rainwater soaking in to the soil. The nutrients are rapidly taken up by plants' roots due to the dense vegetation and rapid plant growth.*

*[4]*
*[Total 5 marks]*

**2** Study **Figure 2**, a diagram of an epiphyte in a tropical rainforest. Epiphytes are plants that grow on other plants, but which do not obtain nutrients from their hosts.

a) State **one** possible reason why epiphytes grow high up in the canopy.

*So that they can get more light.*

*[1]*

**Figure 2**

b) Using **Figure 2** and your own knowledge, suggest how epiphytes are dependent on other parts of the ecosystem.

*Epiphytes are dependent on the climate, as they need frequent rainfall to provide them with a source of water. They are dependent on their host plant to allow them to grow high enough to get the light they need. Epiphytes may also be dependent on animals for pollination.*

*[3]*
*[Total 4 marks]*

Topic 4 — Sustaining Ecosystems

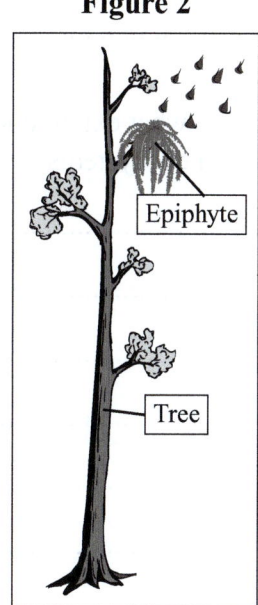

# Exam Questions

**1** Human activities have a variety of impacts on polar environments.

a) Which **two** of the following statements best describe how fishing can have a negative impact on polar ecosystems? Shade **one** oval only.

    **1** Indigenous people often take more fish than they need, causing fish populations to decline.
    **2** Commercial overfishing is threatening some species with extinction.
    **3** Birds can get caught in fishing nets and drown.
    **4** Fishermen kill whales to stop them eating the fish they want to catch.

    **A** 1 and 2 ○
    **B** 2 and 3 ● 
    **C** 1 and 4 ○
    **D** 3 and 4 ○

[1]

b) Outline **one** possible impact that mineral extraction may have on the environment in polar regions.

*Oil spills can occur and it is very hard to clean up so this will release toxic chemicals into the enviroment.*

[2]

c) Describe **two** impacts of tourism on the Arctic ecosystem.

.....................................................................................................................................
.....................................................................................................................................
.....................................................................................................................................
.....................................................................................................................................
.....................................................................................................................................

[4]

d) To what extent does scientific research in polar environments have a positive effect on ecosystems?

.....................................................................................................................................
.....................................................................................................................................
.....................................................................................................................................
.....................................................................................................................................
.....................................................................................................................................
.....................................................................................................................................

[6]

[Total 13 marks]

Topic 4 — Sustaining Ecosystems

# Revision Summary

That's Topic 4 sorted. Time for some quick revision questions — you'll find the answers in the section.
- Try these questions and tick off each one when you get it right.
- When you've done all the questions under a heading and are completely happy with it, tick it off.

## Global Ecosystems (p.57-61)
1) What is an ecosystem?
2) Give two abiotic features of ecosystems.
3) What is a producer?
4) Describe the role of decomposers in ecosystems.
5) Where are temperate forests found?
6) What type of ecosystem is mostly found between the Tropics of Cancer and Capricorn?
7) What kinds of plants grow in hot deserts?
8) Describe the vegetation in temperate forest ecosystems.
9) Describe the climate of tropical rainforests.
10) What sorts of animals are found in coral reef ecosystems?

## Tropical Rainforests (p.64-67)
11) Outline the main features of the water cycle in tropical rainforests.
12) Why is there rapid nutrient cycling in tropical rainforests?
13) Why is the humus layer thin in rainforest soils?
14) Why are tree roots usually close to the soil surface in tropical rainforests?
15) Give an example of interdependence in the tropical rainforest ecosystem.
16) Why is it important to protect tropical rainforests?
17) What are two environmental services that tropical rainforests perform for the planet?
18) What effects can agriculture have on tropical rainforests?
19) What are the effects of mineral extraction on tropical rainforests?
20) Give one example of how ecotourism is being used to manage rainforests sustainably.
21) What is a biosphere reserve?

## Polar Environments (p.68-70)
22) How does the climate differ between the Arctic and Antarctica?
23) What are the main features of the land and sea in the Arctic?
24) Describe the animals found in Antarctica.
25) Give one example of interdependence in either the Arctic or Antarctic ecosystem.
26) What are the impacts of whaling on polar ecosystems?
27) Describe a small-scale example of sustainable management in either the Arctic or Antarctica.
28) How is either the Arctic or Antarctica being managed sustainably on a global scale?

# Topic 5 — Urban Futures

## Urban Growth

*Urban areas (towns and cities) are growing at different rates in different parts of the world.*

### Urbanisation is Happening Fastest in Poorer Countries

1) Urbanisation is the growth in the proportion of a country's population living in urban areas.
2) It's happening in countries all over the world — more than 50% of the world's population currently live in urban areas (3.9 billion people) and this is increasing every day.
3) The rate of urbanisation differs between countries that are richer and those that are poorer.
4) Advanced countries (ACs) are more economically developed, e.g. UK, Japan and Germany. Urbanisation happened earlier in ACs than in less developed countries, e.g. during the Industrial Revolution, and most of the population now already live in urban areas.
5) ACs have very slow rates of urban growth, and many people desiring a better quality of life are moving away from overcrowded cities to rural areas. Good transport and communication networks mean that people in ACs can live in rural areas and commute to cities, or work from home.
6) Low-income developing countries (LIDCs) are less economically developed, e.g. Ethiopia, Nepal and Afghanistan. Not many of the population in LIDCs currently live in urban areas. In general, the fastest rates of urbanisation in the world are in LIDCs.
7) Emerging and developing countries (EDCs) are those where economic development is increasing, sometimes rapidly, e.g. Brazil, China, Russia, India. The percentage of the population living in urban areas varies. Some EDCs, such as Thailand, Mexico and China, are experiencing rapid urban growth.

*See p.92 for more on ACs, LIDCs and EDCs.*

### The World's Biggest Cities are Now Found in Poorer Countries

1) There are two types of city that you need to know about:

   - Megacity — an urban area with over 10 million people living there. A megacity can be a single city, or a conurbation — where neighbouring towns and cities have spread and merged together.
   - World city — a city that has an influence over the whole world. World cities are centres for trade and business. Lots of people and goods from international destinations pass through them. They also tend to be hubs of culture and science, with international media centres.

2) In 1950 most of the biggest and most influential cities were in advanced countries. There were only 2 megacities — Tokyo and New York.
3) By 2014 there were 28 megacities and this number is still growing — it's predicted to rise to 41 by 2030. More than two-thirds of current megacities are in poorer countries (EDCs and LIDCs), mostly in Asia, e.g. Jakarta in Indonesia and Mumbai in India.
4) In 1950, the only world cities were London, Paris, Tokyo and New York.
5) The number of world cities has also increased, but it's difficult to put an exact number on how many there are. Most are still in ACs but some, e.g. Dubai, Moscow and Rio de Janeiro, are in EDCs.

Key
- ACs
- LIDCs
- EDCs
- □ Megacity

---

### Urbanisation happened earlier in richer countries than in poorer countries

Most countries are urbanising, but rates of urbanisation are usually fastest in developing and emerging countries. As a result, most megacities are found in poorer countries. They can be found in developed countries too though.

Topic 5 — Urban Futures

# Urbanisation in LIDCs

*You saw on the previous page that **urbanisation** is happening **fastest** in **less developed** countries.*
*You're about to find out the main **reasons** why people want to move from **rural** to **urban** areas in the first place.*

## Urbanisation is Caused by Rural-Urban Migration...

1) Rural-urban migration is the movement of people from the countryside to the cities. The rate of rural-urban migration in LIDCs is affected by push factors (things that encourage people to leave an area) and pull factors (things that encourage people to move to an area).

2) Rapid urbanisation in LIDCs is being caused by a combination of push and pull factors:

### Push factors

1) Natural disasters, e.g. floods and earthquakes, can damage property and farmland, which people can't afford to repair.
2) Mechanisation of agricultural equipment — farms require fewer workers so there are fewer jobs.
3) Drought (see p.10) can make land unproductive, so people can no longer support themselves.
4) Conflict or war can cause people to flee their homes.

### Pull factors

1) There are more jobs in urban areas that are often better paid.
2) Access to better health care and education.
3) To join other family members who have already moved.
4) People think they will have a better quality of life.

## ...and Internal Growth

1) Urbanisation is also caused by internal growth (when the birth rate is higher than the death rate).

2) The birth rate tends to be higher in cities because it's normally young people that move to urban areas (to find work). These people then have children in the cities — increasing the urban population.

3) In LIDCs, better healthcare can be found in cities than in rural areas. This means people living in urban areas live longer, reducing death rates and increasing the proportion of people in urban areas.

## People usually move to cities to look for better jobs and services

There's nothing too tricky here — rural-urban migration and internal growth work together to cause urbanisation in developing countries. Try scribbling down all the push and pull factors that cause people to move into urban areas.

Topic 5 — Urban Futures

# Urbanisation in LIDCs

*The previous page covered the **reasons** why the number of **people** living in **urban areas** in LIDCs is **increasing**. Now it's time to take a look at some of the **consequences** of this rapid urban **growth**.*

## Rapid Urbanisation can cause Lots of Problems in LIDCs

1) Cities offer lots of opportunities for the people migrating there — e.g. better access to education, healthcare and employment.

2) The growing population can also help increase the wealth and economic development of the city, as well as the country it's in.

3) However, very rapid growth puts pressure on cities, causing problems:

### Economic Consequences

1) There may not be enough jobs for everyone, leading to high levels of unemployment.

2) Lots of people work in the informal sector, where the jobs aren't taxed or regulated by the government. People often work long hours in dangerous conditions for little pay.

3) People may not have access to education so they are unable to develop the skills needed to get better jobs.

### Social Consequences

1) There aren't enough houses for everyone — many people end up in squatter settlements that are badly built and overcrowded.

2) Infrastructure can't be built fast enough — people often don't have access to basic services, e.g. clean water, proper sewers or electricity. This can cause poor health.

3) There can be high levels of crime.

### Environmental Consequences

If cities grow rapidly, waste disposal services, sewage systems and environmental regulations for factories can't keep pace with the growth.

1) Rubbish often isn't collected or it may end up in big rubbish heaps. This can damage the environment, especially if it's toxic.

2) Sewage and toxic chemicals can get into rivers, harming wildlife.

3) The road system may not be able to cope with all the vehicles. Congestion causes increased greenhouse gas emissions and air pollution.

## Learn the problems caused by urbanisation in LIDCs

The consequences of rapid urban growth can be applied to most fast-growing cities in developing countries. If you learn everything on this page it'll help you with the LIDC case study later on in this topic (see pages 85-87).

Topic 5 — Urban Futures

# Suburbanisation

*Trends in **urbanisation** are a bit **different** in **richer** countries than in LIDCs. There are **three** main types of urban movement that you need to know about. First up is **suburbanisation** — basically people moving to the **suburbs**.*

## Suburbanisation is Taking Place in Advanced Countries

Suburbanisation is the movement of people from city centres to the outskirts.
It's caused by a combination of push and pull factors:

### Push Factors

1) Urban areas can be overcrowded, polluted, have high crime rates and may have little green, 'natural' space. Some people believe that their quality of life is lower in the inner city than it would be in the suburbs.
2) As countries develop, governments often clear low quality city centre housing and provide new houses outside the city for residents. E.g. slum clearances in England between 1950 and 1970 moved people to council estates on the outskirts of urban areas.
3) Deindustrialisation in city centres (when manufacturing moves out of an area) leads to people having to leave cities in search of employment in new industrial areas.
4) As unemployment increases in the city, people have less money to spend there, so local shops and services may be forced to close. This means there are fewer local services for people living in the city centre.

### Pull Factors

1) Suburban areas can offer a lower population density, more open green spaces and a perception of being safer and more family-friendly.
2) Planning laws may be more relaxed outside city centres, so it's easier to build houses. In the UK, developers build new housing estates on the edges of urban areas, offering large, modern houses with gardens.
3) Improvements in public transport and increasing car ownership mean that people can live in the suburbs and commute in to the city to work.
4) Rents are often cheaper on the outskirts of cities, which attracts businesses. Jobs and services then become available in the suburbs — encouraging people to move there.

## Suburbanisation has Social, Economic and Environmental Consequences

### Economic

1) There are fewer people living in inner city areas and parts of cities that are mainly offices can be deserted after work hours. Shops, restaurants and other amenities may struggle for customers and close.
2) As businesses leave, unemployment increases, which leads to lower living standards and poverty.

### Social

1) As people and businesses move out to the suburbs, buildings in the city centre are abandoned and may become derelict. This can lead to the city centre becoming run down.
2) Wealthier middle-class people may move to the suburbs where there is a better quality of life. The people left behind are poorer and are often foreign immigrants. This can lead to economic and ethnic segregation.

### Environmental

1) New housing estates are often built on open countryside, which affects wildlife habitats.
2) As urban areas spread, more ground is concreted over. This can increase surface run-off (when water flows quickly overland) and the risk of flooding.
3) Most people who live in the suburbs own cars and may commute into the city to work. This means that the number of cars on the roads increases, causing congestion and air pollution.

## Suburbanisation can cause the city centre to become run down

Suburbanisation can have knock-on effects. E.g. if lots of people leave the inner city for the suburbs, businesses might start moving out of the inner city too, which can lead to buildings in the city centre becoming derelict.

Topic 5 — Urban Futures

# Counter-Urbanisation

*This page covers another type of **urban-rural movement** that you need to know about — **counter-urbanisation**.*

## Counter-Urbanisation is Taking Place Around Some Cities in ACs

Counter-urbanisation is the movement of people away from large urban areas to smaller settlements and rural areas. As well as the push factors from the previous page, it's also caused by these push and pull factors:

### Push Factors
1) Suburbs and city centres often have problems with traffic congestion and parking.
2) Housing in central urban areas and the suburbs is often very expensive. People feel they are not getting value for money and move further from the city, where prices are often lower.

### Pull Factors
1) Houses in smaller settlements and rural areas are often bigger and have more outside space than those in city centres and the suburbs.
2) Improved communication services (e.g. high-speed internet connections) make it easier for people to live in rural areas and work from home.
3) Improvements to communication services also mean that some companies no longer need to be in a city centre and can move to rural areas where land is cheaper. This creates jobs in rural areas.
4) Increased car ownership and improved public transport mean that people can live further from the city and commute to work.

## There are Consequences to Counter-Urbanisation

Lots of the impacts of counter-urbanisation on cities are similar to those caused by suburbanisation (see previous page). There are also impacts on rural areas:

### Social
1) In some villages, the existing houses are improved, e.g. farm buildings are renovated. But some developments (e.g. unattractive new housing) can affect the character of rural settlements.
2) It can lead to the creation of commuter settlements — where people live in rural areas but continue to work in the city. This may force shops and services in rural areas to close because of reduced demand — people spend most of their time away from the area at work.
3) There is more demand for houses, so house prices increase. Younger people may not be able to afford to buy a house, which can mean the population is dominated by older people.
4) Schools in rural areas may close if the new residents are older people rather than families with children.
5) Rural roads and infrastructure may struggle to cope with the additional traffic.

### Economic
1) Some services in rural areas see an increase in business (e.g. pubs that have restaurants). This is because the newer residents are often professionals or retired people who have higher disposable incomes.
2) But some rural shops and services (e.g. bus services) may close — wealthier residents who own cars are more likely to travel to use shops and services in urban areas.
3) Farmers are able to make money by selling unwanted land or buildings for housing.

### Environmental
1) Most people in rural areas own a car, and the additional traffic can cause an increase in air pollution and congestion.
2) New housing estates are often built on open countryside, which affects wildlife habitats.

## Counter-urbanisation can cause a strain on rural infrastructure

Suburbanisation and counter-urbanisation may seem very similar, but there is one key difference between them. Remember — suburbanisation is the movement of people from the inner city to the city's outskirts, and counter-urbanisation is when people move out of the city completely (often to a smaller town or a rural area).

Topic 5 — Urban Futures

# Re-Urbanisation

*Re-urbanisation does exactly what it says on the tin. It's when people **move back** into **urban areas**.*

## Some Cities in ACs are Experiencing Re-Urbanisation

Re-urbanisation is the movement of people back into urban areas. And you guessed it, it's caused by these push and pull factors:

*Greenfield sites are sites that have never been built on. Brownfield sites have been developed before but left derelict.*

### Push Factors

1) There may be a lack of jobs in some rural or suburban areas.
2) Rural areas provide fewer leisure or entertainment facilities (e.g. nightlife).
3) Counter-urbanisation may cause high house prices in rural areas (see p.78).

### Pull Factors

1) The movement of industry and businesses out of cities as a result of deindustrialisation (see p.77) may leave land derelict. Government policies often favour redevelopment of brownfield sites in city centres over development of greenfield sites. People are attracted back to the city by new developments (e.g. high quality apartments).
2) Most universities are based in urban areas, so young people move there for education, and many stay.
3) Young, single people often want to live close to their work in areas with good entertainment services (e.g. bars and nightclubs). For example, Notting Hill in London attracts young, affluent workers because it is a lively area that is well connected to the city centre.
4) Once re-urbanisation has started it tends to continue — as soon as a few businesses invest and people start to return, it encourages other businesses to invest.

## Re-Urbanisation has Social, Economic and Environmental Consequences

### Economic

1) As people move back into the city centre, new shops and services open, which boosts the economy in the city.
2) But jobs created in new businesses may not be accessible to the original residents, many of whom are unskilled or semi-skilled.
3) Tourism in the city may increase if the city centre is improved. Increased tourism brings money into the city which can be spent on improving the area even more, e.g. building new attractions or improving public transport.

### Environmental

1) Re-developing derelict brownfield sites in cities instead of greenfield sites in the open countryside protects countryside wildlife habitats.
2) But some brownfield sites have been derelict for a long time, so redeveloping them can destroy urban wildlife habitats.

### Social

1) As shops and businesses return, jobs are created. This means there is less unemployment, which can help to reduce certain types of crime, e.g. theft.
2) Local state schools can benefit from the increased number of students. However, wealthier people moving into an area may choose to send their children to private schools or better-performing schools away from the city centre.
3) Original residents in the area being re-urbanised are often on low incomes and may not be able to afford housing as prices increase. They may have to move to cheaper areas of the city.
4) There may be tension between the original residents and the new residents, which could lead to crime or violence.
5) Shops and services catering to the newer, more wealthy residents (e.g. cafés and designer clothes shops) may replace shops and services targeted at original residents (e.g. grocery stores and launderettes).

### Learn the factors that draw people to urban areas

**REVISION TIP** — Learning all of the push and pull factors that affect the processes of suburbanisation, counter-urbanisation and re-urbanisation can seem daunting. To help get them sorted in your head, draw three tables and fill them with the push and pull factors for each different process. You can even use some colour, if you like.

Topic 5 — Urban Futures

# Worked Exam Questions

Here are some worked exam questions — for an extra bit of practice, try covering the answers and thinking about how you would answer each question before you read the suggested answer.

1  There is a range of push and pull factors that lead to suburbanisation in advanced countries (ACs).

a) What is suburbanisation?
*The movement of people from city centres to the outskirts of cities.*
[1]

b) Which one of the following is **not** a pull factor leading to suburbanisation? Shade **one** oval only.
- A  Planning laws outside the city centre are relaxed, so it's easier to build houses. ○
- B  Suburban areas have more green spaces, so quality of life is higher. ○
- C  Public transport is often good in suburban areas, so commuting is easy. ○
- D  Suburban areas have many nightclubs and bars, so entertainment is easily accessible. ●

[1]

c) Outline the push factors that contribute to suburbanisation in advanced countries (ACs).
*Urban areas can be overcrowded and polluted, so some people believe that their quality of life is lower in the inner cities than it would be in the suburbs. Industries such as manufacturing have moved out of many AC city centres, so there are fewer jobs in these industries. This has caused people to leave the city centres to look for employment in new industrial areas.*
[4]

[Total 6 marks]

2  Study **Figure 1**, which shows the rural and urban populations of the Republic of the Congo in 1990 and 2014.

**Figure 1**

|      | Rural | Urban |
|------|-------|-------|
| 1990 | 1100  | 1300  |
| 2014 | 1600  | 3000  |

Population in thousands

a) Calculate the ratio of the rural to urban population in the Republic of the Congo in 2014. Give your answer in its simplest form.
*8:15*
[1]

b) Suggest **two** pull factors that encourage people in LIDCs to move to cities from rural areas.
1: *There are more jobs in urban areas, and they are often better paid.*
2: *To get access to better health care and education.*
[2]

[Total 3 marks]

Topic 5 — Urban Futures

# Exam Questions

**1** Study **Figure 1**, a graph showing the change in the urban population of richer countries (ACs) and poorer countries (EDCs and LIDCs) between 1960 and 2010.

a) Complete the graph to show that the urban population of EDCs and LIDCs in 2010 was 2.72 billion. *[1]*

b) In 1960 the urban population of EDCs and LIDCs was 0.56 billion. Calculate the percentage change in the urban population between 1960 and 2010.

...................................................................
...................................................................
...................................................................
................................................................... *[1]*

**Figure 1**

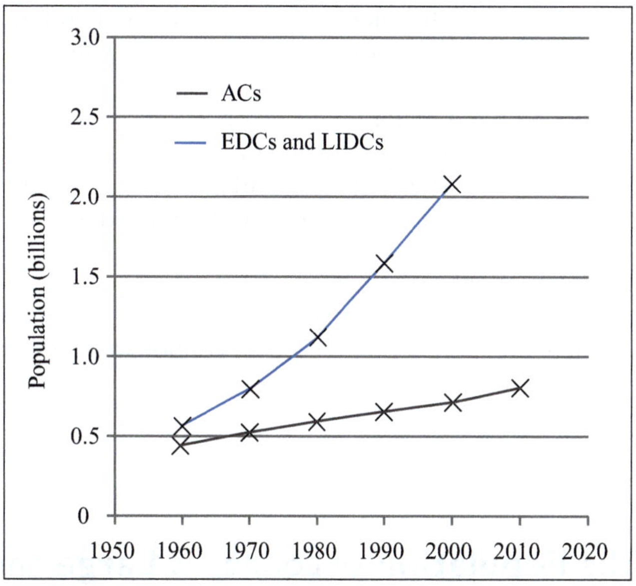

c) Suggest reasons for the difference in the rate of urbanisation in richer and poorer countries shown in **Figure 1**.

...........................................................................................................................................
...........................................................................................................................................
...........................................................................................................................................
...........................................................................................................................................
...........................................................................................................................................
...........................................................................................................................................
...........................................................................................................................................
........................................................................................................................................... *[6]*

d) Describe the environmental consequences of rapid urban growth in LIDCs.

...........................................................................................................................................
...........................................................................................................................................
...........................................................................................................................................
...........................................................................................................................................
........................................................................................................................................... *[4]*

*[Total 12 marks]*

Topic 5 — Urban Futures

# London

*Right, now that you know the basics of **urban growth**, it's time to get into the specifics with a couple of case studies. First up, **London** — a classic example of how growth of a city provides both **opportunities** and **challenges**.*

## London is a World City in South East England

1) London is the UK's capital city and is an essential part of the UK's economy. Over 20% of the UK's income comes from London. It is also the centre of the UK's transport system — with road, rail, air and shipping links.

2) London has a major influence on its surrounding area. Companies are attracted to the region by the proximity to London, which increases jobs and wealth. The South East and East of England are the two biggest regional economies in the UK outside London.

3) It's important globally too — it's a world city and, along with New York, one of the two most important financial centres in the world. There are more foreign banks in London than anywhere else.

## The Population of London is Large and Growing

1) The population of London is now over 8.5 million people and it's growing because:

- International migration — around 100 thousand more people arrived in London than left in 2014.

- National migration — within the UK, young adults move to the city for work or to study but there is also counter-urbanisation (see page 78) as older people and families move out of the city.

- Internal population growth — the young population means there are more births than deaths in the city.

*If you include the whole urban area of London, the population is about 14 million — London is a megacity.*

*National migration is the movement of people within a country. International migration is the movement of people from one country to another.*

2) There are several top-class universities, e.g. UCL, LSE and Imperial College, so the city has a large student population. Students come from all over the world — nearly 20% of the students are from overseas.

3) Population growth has meant that average population density is very high — over 5000 people per km².

4) Migration has been a major part of life in London for centuries. As a result it is now the most ethnically diverse city in the UK — less than half of the city's population is White British and more than half of new babies each year are born to international immigrants.

5) London's character has been strongly influenced by migration — people with the same ethnicity tend to settle in the same place, creating distinctive areas, e.g. Brick Lane is famous for its curry houses due to the Bangladeshi community, and Southall has a large Indian market.

### London's population is increasing due to migration and internal growth

**EXAM TIP:** You might be asked to write about how migration is affecting the population growth and character of a named city in an AC — London is a really good example, but if you've learnt about a different one in class then go ahead and use that instead. Don't forget to talk about international and national migration in your answer — both types of migration will have some sort of effect on the city you've studied.

Topic 5 — Urban Futures

# London

*London is a diverse city with many **unique areas** and **cultures** from across the world. There are also plenty of special **events** which take place in London. These factors all play a role in what **life** is actually like in the city.*

## There are Distinctive Ways of Life in London

1) London's West End is home to many theatres where the world's top musicals and plays are regularly performed. Some of the UK's most popular museums and art galleries are in London, e.g. the British Museum and the National Gallery. The city is also a centre for fashion — London Fashion Week is one of the four biggest fashion events in the world.

2) London has very high ethnic diversity, and some areas, e.g. Chinatown, have a high proportion of people from one ethnic background. Lots of food, music and goods from that culture can be found in the area and many people are attracted to these areas to shop and eat.

3) There are also many big festivals celebrating different cultures and ethnic backgrounds, for example, the annual Afro-Caribbean Notting Hill Carnival, Chinese New Year parade, Proms and Eid in the Square.

*Chinatown*

4) Housing in richer areas (mainly west London and the suburbs, e.g. Sutton) tends to be modern apartments or large houses with gardens. In poorer areas (mainly the inner city and east London, e.g. Newham) the housing density is higher and many buildings have been split to house multiple families.

5) Many leisure facilities are available for people in London — cinemas, concert venues, clubs and pubs are all popular and the city is also home to some of the best restaurants and shopping areas in the UK. There are many large parks in the centre of the city, e.g. Hyde Park, and there are many popular visitor attractions, such as the Tower of London and the London Eye.

*The Tower of London*

6) London has many world-class sports facilities and hosted the Olympic Games in 2012. Each year there are lots of popular mass participation sporting events around London, e.g. the London Marathon.

7) London's wealth means that it consumes a huge amount of resources — food, water and energy etc. E.g. Londoners consume nearly 7 million tonnes of food every year, most of which is imported.

---

**REVISION TIP**

### Many world-famous events and festivals take place in London
Try writing a summary of everything on this page in just a couple of paragraphs. Not only will this help get it in your head, it'll give you some practice at writing in the style of a long-answer exam question.

Topic 5 — Urban Futures

# London

**CASE STUDY**

## Modern London faces lots of Challenges

### 1) Housing Availability

1) London's population has been growing rapidly, but homes have not been built at the same pace.
2) As a result, the supply of homes is not enough to meet the demand of those who want to live in London so house prices and rents are rising.
3) Average rents in London are about double the UK average and house prices are some of the least affordable in the world.
4) As a result, workers on lower incomes often can't afford to live near to where they work, many people can't afford to buy homes, and adults house-sharing is becoming more common.

### 2) Transport Provision

London has a very good transport system but the rising population and increasing number of commuters is stressing the transport network.

1) Roads are frequently congested. Average traffic speed between 7am and 7pm in central London is only 8 miles per hour.
2) About 1 million passengers arrive by train each day — many trains are overcrowded.
3) The London Underground is increasingly filled beyond its capacity — delays due to overcrowding more than doubled between 2013 and 2015.

### 3) Access to Services

London provides some of the best healthcare and education in the UK. However, its large population means that access to these services can be difficult, especially for poorer people.

1) Healthcare — healthcare is free on the NHS but services are often overwhelmed. Waiting times for appointments have increased and ambulances have to cope with increasing traffic.
2) Education — the best state schools are very over-subscribed and difficult to get into. Wealthy parents are able to send their children to fee-paying schools, but many children from poorer families end up in under-performing schools.

### 4) Inequality

1) London is home to the richest and the poorest people in the UK and the gap is widening. Average income in Kensington and Chelsea is more than £130 000 but less than £35 000 in Newham. More than 25% of the population are living in poverty, due to unemployment and low wages. This makes it harder for them to afford things like rent, food and fuel.
2) Unhealthy lifestyles, e.g. drinking, smoking and poor diets, are more common in deprived areas — life expectancy is about 5 years lower in poorer areas of the city than in wealthier areas.

## There are Sustainable Solutions to London's Transport Problem

A sustainable solution means improving things for people today without negatively affecting future generations. The Mayor's Transport Strategy is an initiative that aims to improve London's transport network and make it more sustainable by easing congestion and reducing air pollution. For example:

1) A new railway, the Elizabeth line, has been built by Crossrail east to west across the city to increase rail capacity in central London by 10%. The Bakerloo Line is to be extended to Lewisham.
2) Rail and Underground capacity is being increased by running more trains every hour, increasing the number of carriages on trains and making parts of the Underground service 24 hour. These improvements should help to reduce overcrowding on rail services.
3) More dedicated bus lanes are to be created and roads have been made more suitable for cyclists by constructing two-way cycleways throughout the city, e.g. between the Oval and Pimlico. Cycling is encouraged in London — bikes are already available to hire easily using self-service machines.
4) Congestion charges have been introduced to discourage drivers from entering the city centre, in order to decrease the amount of congestion and air pollution caused by vehicles.

## Revise the details of London or another city in an advanced country

Make sure you're clear on the location, importance and ways of life in the city, and how urban growth has created opportunities and challenges in London — or another place you've studied. You should also know about sustainable solutions to one of the challenges that the city faces. Keep going over the details 'til you know them inside out.

Topic 5 — Urban Futures

# Lagos

*Lagos is another great example of the growth in cities due to migration and the **benefits** and **problems** this causes.*

## Lagos is the Biggest City in Africa

1) Lagos is a city on the coast of Nigeria built around the western shore of a large lagoon.

2) Nigeria is a low-income developing country (LIDC) despite having the biggest economy in Africa (because most people are really poor but there are a few who are mega rich). The city's population is around 21 million, and is one of the fastest-growing urban areas in the world. The population of Lagos is growing by over 500 000 people a year.

3) The city was under British rule during colonial times and was a centre of trade. It was the national capital until 1991, and it remains the main financial centre for the whole of West Africa.

4) Lagos has an international port and airport, making it an important centre for regional and global trade. The city contains 80% of Nigeria's industry and lots of global companies are located there.

## Migration is Causing the City to Grow Rapidly

1) The population of Lagos is growing rapidly, largely due to rural-urban migration. Large numbers of migrants arrive in the city every year, creating an outwards urban sprawl of the city into the surrounding countryside and engulfing nearby towns.

2) The majority of people come from within Nigeria, and they come seeking better jobs — incomes are about 4 times higher than those in rural areas.

3) International migration from neighbouring countries, e.g. Niger and Chad, also contributes to the growth of Lagos. There is also some migration from countries further afield, including the USA, the UK and China — this is mainly people who are employed by foreign businesses operating in Lagos.

4) Migration has impacted the city's character. From its origins as a small fishing settlement inhabited by the Yoruba people (one of Nigeria's ethnic groups), it now has a very diverse population with people from each ethnic group within Nigeria, as well as many people with different nationalities.

5) The city has become overcrowded, congested and polluted. Lagos's location on the coast means there isn't much space to expand so population densities are very high.

## Lagos has grown incredibly quickly

Plenty to learn on this page about the importance of Lagos, its growth and how this has affected the character of the city. Make sure you've got it sorted — there's more to come on the city. The next couple of pages cover the different ways of life in Lagos, the challenges that Lagos faces, and the potential solutions to some of the city's problems.

Topic 5 — Urban Futures

# Lagos

*As the level of **development** in Nigeria increases, **traditional** ways of life in **Lagos** are starting to be mixed with an increasing '**western**' influence. Have a read of this page and you'll see what I mean.*

## There are Distinctive Ways of Life in Lagos

1) Lagos has a big film industry, which produces popular 'Nollywood' films. There is also a thriving music scene, which has introduced music styles such as Afrobeat and Afro hip-hop.

2) Western-style fashion is becoming common among the richer inhabitants, but many people still retain their traditional dress and ways of life, e.g. fishing in the lagoon, or making crafts to sell.

3) There are around 250 different ethnic groups living in Lagos and there can be ethnic tension, particularly between those with different religions, e.g. Christians and Muslims.

4) About two-thirds of the population live in slums. For those who can afford proper housing, it's a mix of old and new — some of the old colonial buildings remain, alongside new high-rise flats and skyscrapers in the central business district. The very rich live in gated communities, e.g. on Banana Island.

5) Street parties, pool parties and nightclubbing are all popular leisure activities in Lagos, and there are many festivals held throughout the year (e.g. Lagos International Jazz Festival, Badagry Festival, Eyo Festival) celebrating music, food and local culture.

6) Shopping is also popular in Lagos — there are loads of street vendors, lots of markets specialising in different products and rows and rows of small shops. The central business district on Lagos Island has been modernised and has more western-style shops and supermarkets, selling international foods.

7) Consumption of all resources is rising in Lagos — as people get wealthier, they can afford to buy more consumer goods and use more resources. Consumption of energy is rapidly increasing in Nigeria, and Lagos is responsible for more than half of this increase.

## Retail in Lagos ranges from street vendors to shopping centres

The majority of the residents of Lagos still live in slums, but the city is gradually growing richer. This is leading to an increase in the amount of resources that people are consuming, and the amount of goods that they purchase.

Topic 5 — Urban Futures

# Lagos

## Lagos faces Challenges in Housing, Health, Waste and Jobs

### 1) Squatter Settlements

Over 60% of the city's population live in slums, e.g. Makoko.

1) Houses in Makoko are flimsy, wooden huts built on stilts in the lagoon. These are illegally built — people face eviction if slums are demolished to clean up the city.
2) There is only one primary school in Makoko and many families can't afford to send their children to school.
3) Communal toilets are shared by 15 households and most of the waste goes straight into the lagoon below — it's always full of rubbish and raw sewage.
4) Water can be bought in Makoko from a communal water point but that is up to 3 km from some homes. The only electricity comes from illegal connections that often cut out.
5) There are high levels of crime in Makoko — the slum is patrolled by gangs called 'area boys' who both commit crimes and act as informal 'police' in the slum.

### 2) Health

1) Most of the city doesn't have access to proper sewers or clean water. This causes health problems, e.g. cholera.
2) Malaria is also a problem — the stagnant water provides a breeding ground for mosquitoes.
3) There aren't enough healthcare facilities and many people can't afford to pay for treatment.
4) Many rural migrants distrust western medicine and prefer to seek help from traditional healers.

### 3) Informal Sector Jobs

1) There aren't enough formal jobs for all the migrants — people have to make money any way they can, e.g. by scavenging in the Olusosun rubbish dump for items to sell.
2) About 60% of the population work in informal jobs, e.g. street sellers, barbers, carpenters.
3) There's no protection for informal workers — they often work long hours for little pay. Lots of people live on less than $1.25 per day.
4) Street-sellers' stalls are bulldozed to make way for new developments and road widening.

### 4) Waste Disposal

1) The huge population produces lots of waste — approximately 9000 tonnes per day.
2) Only about 40% of rubbish is officially collected and there are large rubbish dumps, e.g. Olusosun, which contain toxic waste.
3) Waste disposal and emissions from factories are not controlled, leading to air and water pollution.

## Sustainable Solutions can Help with the Waste Management Problem

The Lagos State Integrated Waste Management Project is an initiative that is trying to improve sustainability by reducing the amount of waste that goes to landfill sites and reducing the air pollution landfill causes. Strategies include:

1) The World Bank is financing a project to collect waste from food markets to turn into compost. This stops the waste from going to landfill sites, where it releases methane (a greenhouse gas) as it decomposes. Instead, a useful product is created that can be used to fertilise farming land, increasing food supplies.
2) Where waste still ends up in rubbish dumps, the government aims to generate electricity from it by burning the methane released. This is already happening at Ikosi Fruit Market, where electricity generated from rotting fruit is used to provide lighting for the market. A larger-scale project is also underway at the landfill site at Olusosun — pipes are being placed into the rubbish to collect the methane so that it can be taken to generators. The electricity generated will be used to power the dump, which is open 24 hours a day.

---

**EXAM TIP: Include lots of facts and figures when you write about a case study**

It's fine if you've got a different example of urban growth in an LIDC that you'd rather write about in the exam — just make sure you have enough info to cover the key points on these last three pages.

Topic 5 — Urban Futures

# Worked Exam Questions

Another set of worked exam questions to have a look at here. Remember, these answers are just suggestions — there are other correct answers — but they should give you an idea of the kinds of things to write.

1   Study **Figure 1**, a graph showing the migration of males into and out of London in 2013 across a range of age groups.

**Figure 1**

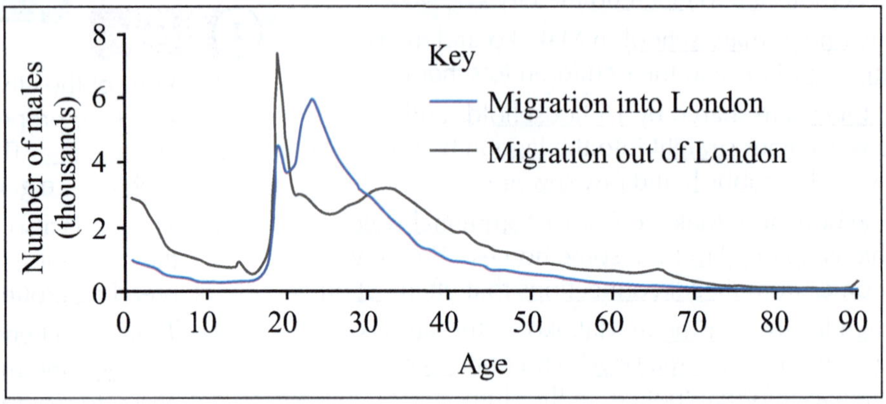

a) Using **Figure 1**, which age group experienced a net increase in population due to migration? Shade **one** oval only.

   A   0-10 years    ◯
   B   11-20 years   ◯
   C   21-30 years   ●
   D   31-40 years   ◯
   [1]

b) What is meant by national migration?
   *The movement of people within a country.*
   [1]

c) Describe how international migration is changing the growth and character of a named AC city.
   *In London, international migration has led to an increase in population, e.g. about 100 000 more people arrived in London than left in 2014. International migration has also led to London becoming a very ethnically diverse city, which has influenced its character, creating distinctive ethnic areas, e.g. the Brick Lane Bangladeshi curry houses.*
   [4]

d) Describe how migration has affected the growth of a city in an EDC or an LIDC.
   *Large numbers of migrants move to Lagos every year, and the population is increasing very rapidly. The urban area is growing outwards into the surrounding countryside. The housing supply has not been able to keep up, with over 60% of the population of Lagos living in slums.*
   [3]
   [Total 9 marks]

Topic 5 — Urban Futures

# Exam Questions

1 Study **Figure 1**, a graph showing population change in London from 2004 to 2014 and **Figure 2**, a graph showing house prices and the number of new houses built in London from 2004 to 2016.

**Figure 1**

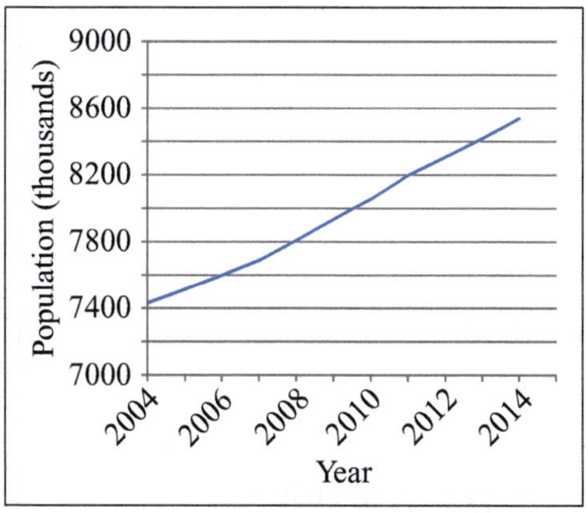

**Figure 2**

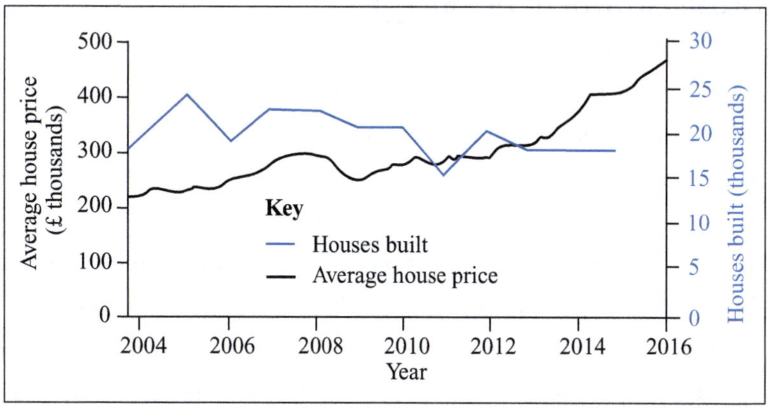

a) Describe the trend in the population of London shown in **Figure 1**.

...................................................................................................................................................................
...................................................................................................................................................................
[1]

b) Using **Figure 1** and **Figure 2**, suggest why London is facing a housing crisis.

...................................................................................................................................................................
...................................................................................................................................................................
...................................................................................................................................................................
...................................................................................................................................................................
[3]

c) Describe the challenges created by inequality in an AC city you have studied, and outline how these challenges have affected life in the city.

...................................................................................................................................................................
...................................................................................................................................................................
...................................................................................................................................................................
...................................................................................................................................................................
...................................................................................................................................................................
[4]

d) For a named AC city, describe **one** initiative that is being used to make it more sustainable.

...................................................................................................................................................................
...................................................................................................................................................................
...................................................................................................................................................................
...................................................................................................................................................................
...................................................................................................................................................................
[4]

[Total 12 marks]

Topic 5 — Urban Futures

# Revision Summary

You're nearly at the end of Topic 5. Just one page of questions standing between you and a chocolate biscuit.
- Try these questions and tick off each one when you get it right.
- When you've done all the questions under a heading and are completely happy with it, tick it off.

## Urban Growth (p.74-76) ☐
1) What is urbanisation?
2) Where is urbanisation taking place most rapidly?
3) Describe the trend in urbanisation in ACs.
4) What is a megacity?
5) Give two characteristics of a world city.
6) Describe the change in the global distribution of megacities since 1950.
7) Give three push factors that lead to rural-urban migration.
8) Give one factor, other than migration, that causes urbanisation.
9) Describe the social challenges that have been caused by rapid urban growth in LIDCs.

## Urban Trends in Advanced Countries (p.77-79) ☐
10) Give two pull factors that lead to suburbanisation.
11) Describe the environmental consequences of suburbanisation.
12) Define counter-urbanisation.
13) Give two push factors that lead to counter-urbanisation.
14) Describe the social consequences of counter-urbanisation.
15) What is re-urbanisation?
16) Give two pull factors that lead to re-urbanisation.
17) Describe the economic consequences of re-urbanisation.

## Challenges and Opportunities in Cities — Case Studies (p.82-87) ☐
18) For a city in an advanced country (AC) that you have studied:
    a) Describe the city's importance within its region.
    b) Describe the pattern of national migration.
    c) Describe the ways of life in the city.
    d) Outline the problems with the availability of housing in the city.
    e) Describe the challenges of access to services in the city.
19) For a city in a low-income developing country (LIDC) or an emerging and developing country (EDC) that you have studied:
    a) Describe the city's importance within its region.
    b) Describe the patterns of national and international migration.
    c) Give two distinctive characteristics of the ways of life in the city.
    d) Describe the challenges of squatter settlements in the city.
    e) Outline the challenges caused by waste disposal in the city.
    f) Outline one initiative that is making the city more sustainable.

# Topic 6 — Dynamic Development

## Measuring Development

*This topic is a little **tricky** — but this **page** will set you up well, so make sure you take a **good look** at it.*

### Development is when a Country is Improving

1) When a country develops it basically gets better for the people living there. There are different aspects to development:
   - Economic development — progress in economic growth, e.g. how wealthy a country is, its level of industrialisation and use of technology.
   - Social development — improvement in people's standard of living, e.g. better health care and access to clean water.
   - Environmental development — advances in the management and protection of the environment, e.g. reducing pollution and increasing recycling.

*An increase in economic development often leads to social and environmental improvements.*

2) The level of development is different in different countries, e.g. France is more developed than Ethiopia.

### There Are Loads of Measures of Development

Development is pretty hard to measure because it includes so many things. But you can compare the development of different countries using 'measures of development'.

| Name | What it is | A measure of... | As a country develops, it gets... |
|---|---|---|---|
| Gross Domestic Product (GDP) | The total value of goods and services a country produces in a year. It's often given in US$. | Wealth | Higher |
| GDP per capita | The GDP divided by the population of a country. It's often given in US$ and is sometimes called GDP per head. | Wealth | Higher |
| Gross National Income (GNI) | The total value of goods and services produced by a country in a year, including income from overseas. It's often given in US$. | Wealth | Higher |
| GNI per capita | The GNI divided by the population of a country. It's also often given in US$ and is sometimes called GNI per head. | Wealth | Higher |
| Birth rate | The number of live babies born per thousand of the population per year. | Women's rights | Lower |
| Death rate | The number of deaths per thousand of the population per year. | Health | Lower |
| Life expectancy | The average age a person can expect to live to. | Health | Higher |
| Infant mortality rate | The number of babies who die under 1 year old, per thousand babies born. | Health | Lower |
| Literacy rate | The percentage of adults who can read and write. | Education | Higher |
| Human Development Index (HDI) | This is a number that's calculated using life expectancy, education level (e.g. average number of years of schooling) and income per head. Every country has an HDI value between 0 (least developed) and 1 (most developed). | Lots of things | Higher |
| Happy Index | This is calculated by dividing a country's life expectancy, well-being and level of inequality by its environmental impact. Countries are graded green (good), amber (medium) or red (bad). | Lots of things | No overall pattern |

### There are lots of ways of measuring development

These measures of development could well come up in the exam, so make sure you know what each of them means and whether it gets higher or lower as a country develops. In fact, shut the book and test yourself now.

# Uneven Development

*Now you know what **development** is all **about**, it's time to find out how it **varies** across the world.*

## Uneven Development has Consequences

Level of development is different in different countries. Comparing development measures for different countries shows the consequences of uneven development — differences in wealth, health and education. For example:

Wealth — People in more developed countries have a higher income than those in less developed countries. E.g. GNI per capita shows that income in the UK is around 20 times higher than in Chad.

Health — Better health care means that people in more developed countries live longer than those in less developed countries. E.g. people in the UK live almost 30 years longer than people in Chad.

Education — People in more developed countries tend to be better educated than those in less developed countries. E.g. people in the UK spend more than twice as long in education as people in Chad.

|  | Chad | UK |
|---|---|---|
| GNI per head (US $) | 880 | 43 440 |
| life expectancy (years) | 51.6 | 80.7 |
| education level (average years of school) | 7.4 | 16.2 |

## Levels of Development Vary across the World

The most developed countries are in North America, Europe and Australasia, and the least developed are in central Africa and parts of Asia. The International Monetary Fund (IMF) classifies countries by their level of development:

### Low-Income Developing Countries (LIDCs)

LIDCs are the poorest countries in the world — GNI per capita is very low and most citizens have a low standard of living. Their economy is often based on primary industry (e.g. agriculture), and they don't export many goods. LIDCs don't have much money to spend on development (e.g. new schools, hospitals or roads), so their level of development stays low. Examples: Afghanistan, Somalia, Mali and Nepal.

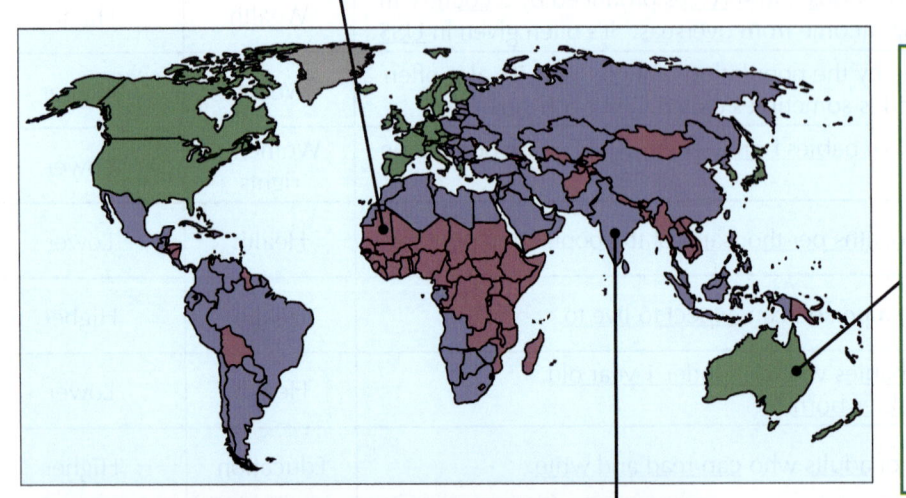

### Advanced Countries (ACs)

ACs are the wealthiest countries in the world — GNI per capita is high and most citizens have a high standard of living. Their economy is based on tertiary and quaternary industry (e.g. services). ACs have lots of money to spend on improving education, transport and health care, so people tend to be well-educated and have a high life expectancy. Examples: UK, USA, France, Canada, Australia.

### Emerging and Developing Countries (EDCs)

EDCs are generally getting richer as their economy is moving from being based on primary industry (e.g. mining) to secondary industry (manufacturing), and exports of manufactured goods are generally high. Exports and increasing wages mean that there's money to spend on development, so health care, education and transport are generally improving. This means that standard of living for many citizens is also improving. Examples: China, Brazil, Russia, India.

> **REVISION TIP** — **Uneven development creates differences in wealth, health and education**
> You don't need to learn how every country is classified but you should have a good understanding of the characteristics and global distribution of ACs, LIDCs and EDCs. Try learning a few examples of each too.

Topic 6 — Dynamic Development

# Factors Affecting Development

*You need to know the **reasons why** there are **global inequalities** — i.e. why **countries differ** in how **developed** they are. These same reasons can make it difficult for countries to **break out** of **poverty**.*

## Physical Factors can Affect How Developed a Country is

A country is more likely to be less developed if it has...

### 1) A Poor Climate

1) If a country has a poor climate (really hot or really cold or really dry) not much will grow. This reduces the amount of food produced. In some countries this can lead to malnutrition, e.g. in Chad and Ethiopia. People who are malnourished have a low quality of life.
2) People also have fewer crops to sell, so less money to spend on goods and services. This also reduces their quality of life.
3) The government gets less money from taxes (as less is sold and bought). This means there's less to spend on developing the country, e.g. to spend on improving healthcare and education.

### 2) Few Natural Resources

1) Countries without many raw materials like coal, oil or metal ores tend to make less money because they've got fewer products to sell.
2) This means they have less money to spend on development.
3) Some countries do have a lot of raw materials but still aren't very developed because they don't have the money to develop the infrastructure to exploit them (e.g. roads and ports).

### 3) A Poor Location

1) In countries that are landlocked (don't have any coastline) it can be harder and more expensive to transport goods into and out of the country.
2) This means it's harder to make money by exporting goods, so there's less to spend on development.
3) It's also harder to import goods that might help the country to develop, e.g. medicine and farm machinery.

### 4) Lots of Natural Hazards

1) A natural hazard is a natural process which could cause death, injury or disruption to humans or destroy property and possessions (e.g. an earthquake, flood or volcanic eruption). A natural disaster is a natural hazard that has actually happened.
2) Countries that have a lot of natural disasters (e.g. Bangladesh, which floods regularly) have to spend a lot of money rebuilding after disasters occur.

## Learn these physical causes of uneven development

Basically, if a country's climate is rubbish for farming or it's a hotspot for natural disasters then it's going to struggle to develop. There are a few exceptions though, e.g. Japan gets battered by natural hazards but is developed.

Topic 6 — Dynamic Development

# Factors Affecting Development

*You saw on the previous page how **development** can be affected by physical factors.
Now it's time to take a look at some of the **human factors** that determine how **developed** a country is.*

## There are Human Factors that Influence Development

Human factors can also affect a country's level of development and stop it from breaking out of poverty...

### Conflict

1) War, especially civil wars, can slow or reduce levels of development.
   E.g. health care becomes much worse and things like infant mortality increase a lot.

2) Money is spent on arms and fighting instead of development,
   people are killed and damage is done to infrastructure and property.

3) Countries have to spend money repairing this damage when the fighting ends.

### Debt

1) LIDCs often borrow money from other countries and international organisations,
   e.g. to help them cope with the aftermath of a natural disaster.

2) This money has to be paid back (usually with interest),
   so any money the country makes can't be used to develop.

### Disease and Healthcare

1) In some LIDCs, lack of clean water and poor health care mean that a
   large number of people suffer from diseases such as malaria and cholera.

2) People who are ill can't work, so they're not contributing to the
   economy. They may also need expensive medicine or health care.

3) Lack of economic contribution and increased spending on health care
   means that there's less money available to spend on development.

### Politics

1) Corrupt governments can hinder development, e.g. by taking money that's intended for
   building new infrastructure or improving facilities for people. They might also prevent a
   fair election from happening, so there is no chance for a democratically elected government
   (chosen by the people) to gain power.

2) If a government is unstable (i.e. likely to lose power at any time), companies and other
   countries are unlikely to invest or want to trade, meaning that level of development stays low.

3) Governments need to invest in the right things to help a country develop, e.g. transport
   and schools. If they invest in the wrong areas, the country won't develop as quickly.

Topic 6 — Dynamic Development

# Factors Affecting Development

## Education

1) Educating people produces a more skilled workforce, meaning that the country can produce more goods and offer more services (e.g. ICT). This can bring money into the country, through trade or investment.

2) Educated people also earn more, so they pay more taxes. This provides money that the country can spend on development.

## Trade

1) Trade is the exchange of goods and services. Countries can import goods and services (buy them in from another country) or can export them (sell them to another country).

2) Countries that export goods and services of greater value than they import have a trade surplus, while countries that import goods and services of greater value than they export have a trade deficit. A trade deficit means a country has less money coming in than going out, so it tends to be poorer.

3) World trade patterns (who trades with whom) seriously influence a country's economy and so affect their level of development. If a country has poor trade links (it trades a small amount with only a few countries) it won't make a lot of money, so there'll be less to spend on development.

4) What a country trades also affects its level of development — exporting primary products (e.g. wood, stone) is less profitable than exporting manufactured goods (e.g. cars, phones). Countries that export mostly primary products tend to be less developed.

## Tourism

Tourism can provide increased income as there will be more money entering the country. This money can be used to increase the level of development.

## Aid

1) Aid is help given by one country to another. Some countries receive more than others, so they can develop faster.

*There's more about aid on p.99.*

2) Aid can be spent on development projects (e.g. building schools or improving water supplies), helping to increase development.

3) However, if countries come to rely on aid it might stop them from developing trade links that could be a better way of developing.

---

**EXAM TIP**

### Money from taxes can increase development in a country

If you get a long-answer question about the factors that affect development, scribble down a quick plan with the key points before starting your answer — examiners are looking for a logical structure.

Topic 6 — Dynamic Development

# Worked Exam Questions

Here are some handy worked exam questions to get you in the exam mood. Use them wisely.

**1** Study **Figure 1**, which shows measures of development for Canada, Malaysia and Angola.

a) Which of the following is a measure of economic development? Shade **one** oval only.

- A  GNI per capita  ●
- B  Birth rate  ○
- C  Life expectancy  ○
- D  Literacy rate  ○

[1]

**Figure 1**

|  | Canada | Malaysia | Angola |
|---|---|---|---|
| GNI per capita | $51 770 | $11 120 | $4800 |
| Birth rate | 10.28 | 19.71 | 38.78 |
| Death rate | 8.42 | 5.03 | 11.49 |
| Infant mortality rate | 4.65 | 13.27 | 78.26 |
| Life expectancy | 81.76 | 74.75 | 55.63 |
| Literacy rate | 97.1% | 94.6% | 71.1% |
| HDI value | 0.913 | 0.779 | 0.532 |

b) What is meant by the Gross National Income (GNI) per capita of a country?

*The total value of goods and services produced by a country in a year (including income from overseas) divided by the population of the country.*

[2]

c) Explain why the Human Development Index (HDI) values given in **Figure 1** may be a better measure of development than any of the other measures.

*Individual indicators can be misleading if they are used on their own because as a country develops, some aspects develop before others. HDI is calculated using several different indicators, so it is likely to give a much more accurate idea of how developed a country is.*

[2]

d) Using **Figure 1**, suggest how uneven development might have consequences for the health of people in LIDCs.

*Uneven development means that many LIDCs have a very low income, e.g. in Angola, GNI per capita is only $4800, so they don't have much money to spend on health care. This means that people can die from treatable diseases, so death rates and infant mortality rates are high, e.g. infant mortality rate in Angola is more than sixteen times higher than in Canada.*

[4]

e) Explain which of the countries shown in **Figure 1** is the most developed.

*Canada is the most developed country. It has a higher GNI per capita than Malaysia or Angola, suggesting that its citizens are wealthy. Canada has relatively low birth and infant mortality rates and a high life expectancy, suggesting that health care there is good. It also has a higher literacy rate than the other countries, suggesting that it has a successful education system.*

[4]

[Total 13 marks]

Topic 6 — Dynamic Development

# Exam Questions

1   Study **Figure 1**, an article about Libya written in 2016.

**Figure 1**

Libya is the fourth largest country in Africa. It's located on the northern edge of the Sahara desert. More than 90% of the country is a desert or semi-desert environment.

There has been ongoing conflict in Libya since 2011, leading to economic decline and worsening living standards. GDP per capita has decreased by about 30% since 2013.

Oil is an important industry in Libya. It accounts for 97% of the country's exports and 80% of Libya's GDP. However, oil companies started to leave the country after the outbreak of violence.

a)   Using **Figure 1**, explain how climate may have affected the level of development of Libya.

   ....................................................................................................................................................

   ....................................................................................................................................................

   ....................................................................................................................................................

   ....................................................................................................................................................

   ....................................................................................................................................................
   [4]

b)   Outline **two** other physical factors that can affect how developed a country is.

   **1:**..............................................................................................................................................

   ....................................................................................................................................................

   **2:**..............................................................................................................................................

   ....................................................................................................................................................
   [4]

c)   Using **Figure 1**, suggest how conflict may have affected Libya's level of development.

   ....................................................................................................................................................

   ....................................................................................................................................................

   ....................................................................................................................................................

   ....................................................................................................................................................

   ....................................................................................................................................................

   ....................................................................................................................................................
   [4]

   [Total 12 marks]

Topic 6 — Dynamic Development

# Increasing Development — Stages and Goals

*The next few pages are jam-packed with useful info for your **development case study**, so learn them well...*

## Rostow's Model shows Five Stages of Economic Development

1) Rostow's model predicts how a country's level of economic development changes over time — it describes how a country's economy changes from relying mostly on primary industry (e.g. agriculture), through secondary industry (e.g. manufacturing goods) to tertiary and quaternary industry (e.g. services and research).
2) At the same time, people's standard of living improves.
3) Stage 1 is the lowest level of development and Stage 5 is the highest.

**1 Traditional society**
Subsistence based. Farming, fishing and forestry. Little trade.

**2 Preconditions for take-off**
Manufacturing starts to develop. Infrastructure is built, e.g. roads, power networks. International trading begins.

**3 Take-off**
Rapid, intensive growth. Large-scale industrialisation. Increasing wealth.

**4 Drive to maturity**
Economy grows so people get wealthier. Standards of living rise. Widespread use of technology.

**5 Mass consumption**
Lots of trade. Goods are mass produced. People are wealthy, so there are high levels of consumption.

## The Millennium Development Goals Aimed to Help LIDCs Develop

1) The Millennium Development Goals (MDGs) aimed to improve life in LIDCs. They were targets set by the United Nations (UN) in 2000 — all UN member states agreed to try to achieve the goals by 2015.
2) There were eight MDGs, which aimed to:

   1) Halve the number of people living in extreme poverty or suffering from hunger.
   2) Make sure that all children had a primary education.
   3) Increase the number of girls and women in education and in paid employment.
   4) Reduce death rates in children under five years old by two-thirds.
   5) Reduce death rates amongst women caused by pregnancy or childbirth by three-quarters.
   6) Stop the spread of major diseases, including HIV/AIDS and malaria.
   7) Protect the environment and make sure development was sustainable, while improving quality of life.
   8) Make sure that countries around the world worked together to help LIDCs develop.

3) By 2015, the UN had gone some way to achieving these goals, but success was variable in different parts of the world. The UN has set a new series of Sustainable Development Goals (SDGs) to achieve by 2030.

## You'll meet Rostow's model and the MDGs again in a few pages' time

All this stuff might seem a bit dry and theoretical now, but you need to understand the theory to make sense of your LIDC case study (p.101-105). It's dead important, so make sure you've got your head around it before moving on.

Topic 6 — Dynamic Development

# Increasing Development — Aid

*There are lots of different things that can **help** a country to develop, but none of them are **trouble-free**...*

## Aid can Help Countries to Develop

1) Aid is given by one country to another, either as money or as resources (e.g. food, doctors).
2) Money can be spent on development projects, e.g. building schools to improve literacy rates, making dams to provide clean water or providing farming education and equipment to improve agriculture.
3) There are different types of aid, all with advantages and disadvantages for development:

| Type of Aid | What it is | Advantages | Disadvantages |
|---|---|---|---|
| 'Top-down' | When an organisation or government receives the aid and decides how it should be spent. | • Often used for large projects, e.g. dams for hydroelectric power (HEP) or irrigation schemes.<br>• These can solve large scale problems and improve the lives of lots of people.<br>• Projects can improve the country's economy, helping with long-term development. | • The country may have to pay back the money (if it's a loan).<br>• Large projects are often expensive.<br>• They may not benefit everyone — e.g. HEP may not supply power to remote areas.<br>• If governments are corrupt, they may use the money for their own purposes, so it doesn't help development. |
| 'Bottom-up' | Money is given directly to local people, e.g. to build or maintain a well. | • Local people have a say in how the money will be used, so they get what they need.<br>• Projects often employ local people, so they earn money and learn new skills. | • Projects may be small-scale, so they don't benefit everyone.<br>• Different organisations (e.g. charities) may not work together, so projects may be inefficient. |
| Short-term | Aid sent to help countries cope with emergencies, e.g. natural disasters. | • Gives immediate relief, so the country recovers faster.<br>• Money allocated for development doesn't have to be used to cope with the emergency instead. | • Often doesn't help with longer-term recovery, e.g. rebuilding infrastructure. This may restrict further development.<br>• Food aid may limit the price farmers can charge for their crops, so their income is reduced. |
| Long-term | Aid given over a long period to help countries develop. | • Most projects aim to be sustainable, e.g. by helping people meet their own needs.<br>• Projects can improve life for lots of people in the long-term.<br>• May help to build trade links between the donor and recipient countries. | • May make the recipient country dependent on aid.<br>• Aid is sometimes 'tied' — money has to be spent on goods and services from the donor country, which may be more expensive than from other sources. |
| Debt relief | A country doesn't have to pay back part or all of the money it has borrowed. | • Frees up money that can be spent on development.<br>• Donor countries can specify how the cancelled debt should be spent, e.g. on health care or education. | • Donor countries may be reluctant to cancel debts for countries with corrupt governments.<br>• Imposing conditions can mean that the money isn't used where it's most needed. |

## There are pros and cons to each type of aid

The type of aid that a country receives will depend on its individual circumstances, but development is a complicated matter with no easy solutions. There's more on the advantages and disadvantages of different ways to increase development on the next page but, for now, concentrate on learning everything in the table above.

Topic 6 — Dynamic Development

# Increasing Development — Trade and TNCs

*Here are **two more ways** of increasing development, each with their own **pros** and **cons**.*

## Trade has Advantages and Disadvantages...

*For more on trade, see p.95.*

1) Trade between an LIDC and other countries can help the LIDC to develop by:

   - Creating jobs and bringing money into the country. This improves people's standard of living.
   - Increasing the amount of money a country has to spend on things like health care and education, and on development projects, such as improving transport infrastructure.

2) However, there are problems with countries relying on trade to help them develop:

   - Some LIDCs can't afford the technology to produce goods quickly and cheaply (e.g. agricultural machinery). This means they might not be able to match the prices of other countries.
   - Conflict can make the supply of goods unreliable, so countries may not have goods to trade.
   - In countries where diseases such as HIV/AIDS are a major problem, money has to be spent on treating people, so there's less money to invest in developing trade.
   - Trade can have a negative effect on people. E.g. to keep prices low, wages and working conditions may be very poor. So increased trade won't necessarily improve quality of life for everyone.
   - LIDCs often export primary products such as grain or wood. These products don't create much profit, so they don't provide much money for development. They can also be unreliable, e.g. if crops fail because of drought.
   - Countries are often dependent on trading one product, e.g. coffee or cotton. If the demand for that product falls, the country's income can decrease sharply.

## ...and so do Trans-National Companies

1) TNCs (trans-national companies) are companies that are located in or produce and sell products in more than one country. E.g. Sony® is a TNC — it makes electronic products in China and Japan.
2) TNC factories are usually located in poorer countries because labour is cheaper, and there are fewer environmental and labour regulations, which means they make more profit.
3) They can improve the development of countries they work in by transferring jobs, skills and money to less developed countries, reducing the development gap.
4) TNC offices and headquarters are usually located in richer countries because there are more people with administrative skills (because education is better).

TNCs have advantages and disadvantages:

| Advantages | Disadvantages |
|---|---|
| • TNCs create jobs in all the countries they're located in.<br>• Employees in poorer countries get a more reliable income compared to jobs like farming.<br>• TNCs spend money to improve the local infrastructure, e.g. airports and roads.<br>• New technology (e.g. computers) and skills are brought to poorer countries. | • Employees in poorer countries may be paid lower wages than employees in richer countries.<br>• Employees in poorer countries may have to work long hours in poor conditions.<br>• Most TNCs come from richer countries so the profits go back there — they aren't reinvested in the poorer countries the TNC operates in.<br>• The jobs created in poorer countries aren't secure — the TNC could relocate the jobs to another country at any time. |

### REVISION TIP
**TNCs are companies that do business in more than one country**
International trade and TNCs can help poorer countries to develop industry, infrastructure, health care and education. However, there are often downsides too. Close the book and see if you can draw up a table of the advantages and disadvantages of increasing development through trade and TNCs.

Topic 6 — Dynamic Development

# LIDC Development

*Now you've covered a bit of the **theory** behind development, it's time to get to grips with what it looks like out there in the **real world** — this case study is about development in the **Democratic Republic of the Congo**.*

## The Democratic Republic of the Congo is one of the Poorest Countries

1) The Democratic Republic of the Congo (DRC) is a huge country in central Africa. It is nearly landlocked — it just has a tiny stretch of coastline.
2) It has a population of around 96 million. A high birth rate is causing the population to grow quite rapidly, so there are increasing numbers of people who need food, clean water, education etc.
3) The DRC has very rich natural resources, including copper, gold, oil and diamonds. Its fertile soil and climate make it ideal for growing crops such as coffee, sugar and cotton.
4) The DRC also has rich deposits of minerals ores such as coltan and wolframite, which are used in laptops, mobile phones and cameras.
5) Despite this, it is a very poor country with a low level of development.

| | |
|---|---|
| GNI per capita | US $550 |
| Life expectancy | 60 years |
| Literacy rate | 77% |
| HDI | 0.48 |

## Political and Social Factors Have Hindered Development

1) The DRC was a Belgian colony from 1885 to 1960. By 1960, the country was quite developed in some ways — industry was booming, and education and health care were improving.
2) However, most of the massive wealth created from mines and farms was passed back to other countries. Native people were not allowed to vote, and were allowed only a very basic education.
3) The DRC gained independence from Belgium in 1960, and there was conflict over who would lead the country. In 1965, Mobutu Sese Seko seized power. His rule prevented the DRC from developing:

- Corruption was very widespread — President Mobutu allowed armed forces to loot the country, taking goods and money. This led to huge inequality in wealth — a small number of very rich people, and a huge number of very poor people.
- Large companies paid bribes to gain access to mineral resources. Much of the resulting wealth left the country, so it didn't benefit the local people.
- Mobutu forced many foreign-owned businesses to leave the country, leading to loss of jobs and wealth. He refused to pay back debts to Belgium, who cancelled development projects in the DRC.
- There was conflict over leadership for much of his rule. This caused damage to crops, property and infrastructure, forced people to flee their homes and made it hard for them to access medical care.

4) Mobutu was overthrown in 1997. This led to civil war, which lasted until 2003. *Peace is fragile and fighting still continues in some areas.*
5) Joseph Kabila, who became president in 2001, promised to focus on improving infrastructure, health, education, housing, jobs and access to resources such as water and power.
6) There have been signs of economic growth since 2012, but development remains relatively slow.

## The Democratic Republic of the Congo has struggled to develop

**EXAM TIP** You may not have studied the DRC in class, but you do need to learn a case study from an LIDC. This case study covers lots of different aspects of the DRC's development over the next few pages. Make sure you learn lots of details for the exam — it's good to be able to back up an answer with facts and figures.

Topic 6 — Dynamic Development

# LIDC Development

*This page gives **two more factors** that have **hindered development** in the DRC, then takes a look at whether **Rostow's model** can be used to **predict** how the country might develop in the **future**.*

## 'Conflict Minerals' Have Held Back Development

1) Growing global demand for electronic products has increased demand for minerals ores such as coltan and wolframite. In parts of the DRC, armed groups force people to work in dangerous conditions to mine the mineral ores.
2) Fighting over ownership of the mines has caused the deaths of millions of people, causing these resources to become known as 'conflict minerals'.
3) Many companies are now buying minerals from other countries, where forced labour and war aren't an issue. This makes it difficult for the DRC to sell the resources it has, which is hindering economic development.

## The Environment Creates Challenges for Development

1) Although the DRC is rich in resources (see p.101), its geography makes it hard for them to be exploited:

   - The country is so large that goods have to be transported thousands of miles.
   - The small amount of coastline limits ocean transport. Building roads and railways is difficult and expensive because much of the country is covered in forest and there are lots of rivers.
   - The Congo River, which runs east to west across the country, has the potential to provide hydroelectric power for large parts of Africa. However, the difficult terrain means that setting up infrastructure to transmit this electricity is very difficult.

2) Food production in some areas is difficult, causing malnutrition and poverty — the centre and south of the country have a long dry season, and droughts can occur between April and November.
3) The DRC experiences frequent floods — this can ruin crops, as well as destroying settlements and infrastructure that require money to rebuild. This hinders further development.

## Rostow's Model May Help to Show How the DRC will Develop

*See p.98 for more on Rostow's model*

1) The DRC has an economy that's based on both primary goods (e.g. metal and mineral extraction, agriculture) and secondary goods (e.g. shoes and cement).
2) The DRC appears to be at Stage 2 of Rostow's model of development — 'Preconditions for take-off'.

   *In Stage 2, a country starts to manufacture goods and has surplus produce to trade. It develops infrastructure, e.g. transport networks.*

3) Rostow's model suggests that Stage 3 ('Take-off') is the next step for the DRC, with rapid industrialisation and increasing wealth. This should trigger increased trade and investment, leading to further development.
4) However, the DRC doesn't fit neatly into Stage 2 and may not develop as Rostow's model suggests:

   - Transport infrastructure is very poor, with few paved roads and limited railways. This limits the country's potential for exports and trade, which will slow its development.
   - Only around 10% of people have access to electricity, and this value is much lower in rural areas. Power cuts are common. This makes it hard for industry to operate, which hinders development.

## Rostow's model isn't totally applicable to the DRC

Development models can be really useful when trying to predict how an LIDC like the DRC might develop in the future, but it's important to realise that models have their limitations, too. If a country doesn't exactly match the set of conditions laid out in the model, it may not actually develop in the way that the model predicts.

Topic 6 — Dynamic Development

# LIDC Development

*Before you read this page, it might help to have a quick look back the **Millennium Development Goals** on page 98.*

## The **Millennium Development Goals** have been **Partially Met** in the DRC

The DRC has made some progress towards meeting the MDGs (see p.98) — most measures of development show some improvement since 2000, but the DRC is still one of the least developed countries in the world.

### 1) Reduce Poverty and Hunger
1) The percentage of people living in poverty decreased from 71% in 2005 to 63% in 2012.
2) However, the number of people suffering from undernutrition increased from 19 million in 2005 to 35.6 million in 2020.

### 2) Provide Education For All
The percentage of children who completed a primary school education increased from 35% in 1999 to around 70% in 2015.

### 3) Promote Gender Equality
1) The percentage of girls finishing primary school doubled from 32% in 1999 to 65% in 2013. However, the percentage of boys finishing primary school grew more over the same period, so inequality has increased.
2) There are fewer women than men in paid work, and on average they earn less than men doing the same job.

### 4) Reduce Child Death Rates
1) The death rate of children under five decreased from about 159 per thousand births in 2000 to about 81 per thousand births in 2020.
2) Despite efforts to vaccinate children against measles, only 35% of under 5s were fully vaccinated as of 2019.

### 5) Reduce Maternal Death Rates
1) The number of women dying in childbirth decreased from around 760 per 100 000 births in 2000 to around 473 per 100 000 births in 2017.
2) The availability of health care for mothers before and during childbirth has increased since 1990.

### 6) Stop the Spread of Diseases
1) The percentage of people with HIV/AIDS has decreased from about 5% to about 1% since 2000. This is partly due to better education and increased access to contraception.
2) The proportion of people with malaria halved between 2000 and 2015, due partly to a huge increase in the availability of mosquito nets.

### 7) Make Development Sustainable
1) About 52% of the population have access to clean water — a small increase from 2000.
2) There are efforts to preserve the rainforests, e.g. the government has created protected areas and put bans on new logging operations.

### 8) Promote International Links
1) In 2008, China gave the DRC US $6 billion to spend on infrastructure, in return for access to some of its mineral resources.
2) Other countries have invested in trade (see p.104) and offered aid (see p.105).

## The DRC has been working towards some of the MDGs since 2000

International schemes like the MDGs can help development, but things may not quite turn out as planned. A fair amount of progress has been made in the DRC, e.g. the death rate for children has decreased in the past 20 years. But it's not been perfect — e.g. there are more people suffering from malnutrition now than in the year 2000.

Topic 6 — Dynamic Development

**CASE STUDY**

# LIDC Development

*The DRC's **links** to **other countries** have been **increasing**, which has led to an increase in **trade**.*

## The DRC is **Increasing** its **Trade Links**

1) Until recently, the DRC had a trade deficit (it imported more than it exported). More money was being sent to other countries than was being received from them, which weakened the DRC's economy.
2) The DRC now exports roughly as much as it imports (about US $22.2 billion of goods each year).
3) The DRC exports mostly primary products, including crude oil, minerals, wood and coffee. Minerals and metals, such as diamonds, gold and copper, account for about 90% of exports.
4) The DRC's main imports are manufactured goods, such as machinery, vehicles and electrical equipment.
5) Until recently, many countries were reluctant to trade with DRC because of human rights violations, corruption and conflict. Since 1997, trade links have increased and the DRC now trades with a number of countries — its main trading partners are Belgium, China, Italy, France and Australia. The DRC is also a member of several trade communities, designed to increase free trade in Africa.

## Trade Brings **Benefits** and **Problems** to the DRC

1) The increase in trade in the DRC has had significant advantages for the country:

   - The economy of the DRC grew by 7% from 2010 to 2012, and this growth rate is expected to increase. Increased wealth improves standard of living and gives opportunities for investment in e.g. education and healthcare.

   - Establishing links with other countries makes them more likely to invest in the DRC (e.g. by locating branches of TNCs there) or to offer aid, which can be used for development.

2) However, it has also caused some problems:

   - The DRC's reliance on trading primary goods, e.g. minerals, makes it vulnerable to falling prices — in 2008 and 2009, global economic problems caused a sharp fall in the value of these products, which hindered economic growth in DRC.

   - The DRC's reliance on importing manufactured goods makes it vulnerable to increased prices. These goods are generally more valuable than primary products, so the DRC has to pay a lot for them — this has also limited its economic development.

   - Demand from richer countries for mineral ores such as coltan and wolframite (see p.101) led to uncontrolled exploitation of these resources. Their extraction often involved human rights abuses such as slavery, and helped to fund armed rebels in the DRC. There are now international efforts to make extraction and trade of these mineral ores safe, legal and profitable for the DRC.

---

**REVISION TIP**

### The DRC can grow its economy by increasing its trade links

A good way of testing whether you really know something is to try and teach it to someone else. Without looking at the page, try and explain all the positive and negative impacts that increasing trade has had on the DRC to e.g. a friend or parent. You'll soon find out whether you need to revise a bit more.

Topic 6 — Dynamic Development

# LIDC Development

**CASE STUDY**

## Few TNCs are Located in the DRC

1) Relatively few TNCs currently operate in the DRC, but their number is increasing — particularly mining companies such as AngloGold Ashanti (based in South Africa) and Barrick (based in Canada).
2) TNCs have helped economic development in the DRC, but they have also caused problems:

### Advantages
1) TNCs provide employment — the Kibali mine, majority-owned by AngloGold Ashanti and Barrick, employs around 2500 people in the DRC.
2) TNCs can contribute to environmental conservation, e.g. Barrick supports projects in the DRC's Garamba National Park.
3) TNCs bring money into the DRC through taxes and spending — in 2021, the DRC government received US $78 million from the Kibali mine.
4) TNCs invest money in infrastructure — the companies that own the Kibali mine have built roads and hydroelectric plants in the DRC.

### Disadvantages
1) TNCs can pull out of the country, taking jobs and wealth with them — in 2009, mining company De Beers announced that it would stop looking for new diamond reserves in the DRC.
2) Some profits from TNCs leave the DRC, e.g. some of Barrick's profits return to Canada.
3) Some large mining companies have been accused of forcing small mines to close and people to leave their homes to make way for large mines.
4) TNCs can cause environmental problems, e.g. construction of roads to give access to mines causes deforestation.

## The DRC Receives a Lot of Aid

1) The DRC receives billions of dollars of aid every year — some of the highest amounts of any country. The main donors include the USA, UK, Belgium and the World Bank. Aid has pros and cons for the DRC:

### Advantages
1) Aid funds projects to improve living conditions, health, education and infrastructure, e.g. the UK has funded the construction of 1700 km of new roads.
2) Emergency aid programmes have provided food and shelter for people who are affected by ongoing conflicts over land and resources.

### Disadvantages
1) Some early aid was in the form of weapons to arm government forces. This promoted fighting and didn't directly benefit civilians.
2) Some aid has conditions, e.g. in 2008 China gave the DRC US $9 billion, but insisted that it be used to develop mining and infrastructure — this may not benefit the poorest people.

2) Both top-down and bottom-up aid projects have been used in the DRC:

|  | Project | Advantages | Disadvantages |
| --- | --- | --- | --- |
| 'Top-down' | Proposed construction of Grand Inga Dam on the Congo River. Cost: US $80 billion Donors: African Development Bank and others | • Could provide cheap, clean and reliable energy for all of the DRC, plus extra to sell. • Will promote industry in the DRC, providing jobs and boosting the economy. | • Risk that money may be lost to corrupt officials/companies. • Little provision for transmitting energy to poor, rural communities. • Flooding of the Bundi Valley and relocation of 30 000 people. |
| 'Bottom-up' | Involving teachers, students and parents in improving rural schools and increasing the number of children in education. Cost: £390 000 Donor: Comic Relief | • Local people have a say in how their schools should be improved. • Better-educated people earn more, so contribute more to economic development. | • Not enough funding to improve all schools, so not everyone benefits. • Some families need children to earn a living, so they can't afford to send them to school. • Doesn't tackle large-scale issues. |

## Bottom-up aid strategies can be really beneficial for rural communities

It's totally fine if you studied a different LIDC in class — but for whichever country you studied, make sure you're fully clued-up about all the different factors in its development that have been covered on the last few pages.

Topic 6 — Dynamic Development

# Worked Exam Questions

With the answers written in, it's very easy to skim these worked examples and think you've understood. But that's not going to help you, so take the time to make sure you've really understood everything here.

1  Study **Figure 1**, which shows the global distribution of sites of a Trans-National Company (TNC).

**Figure 1**

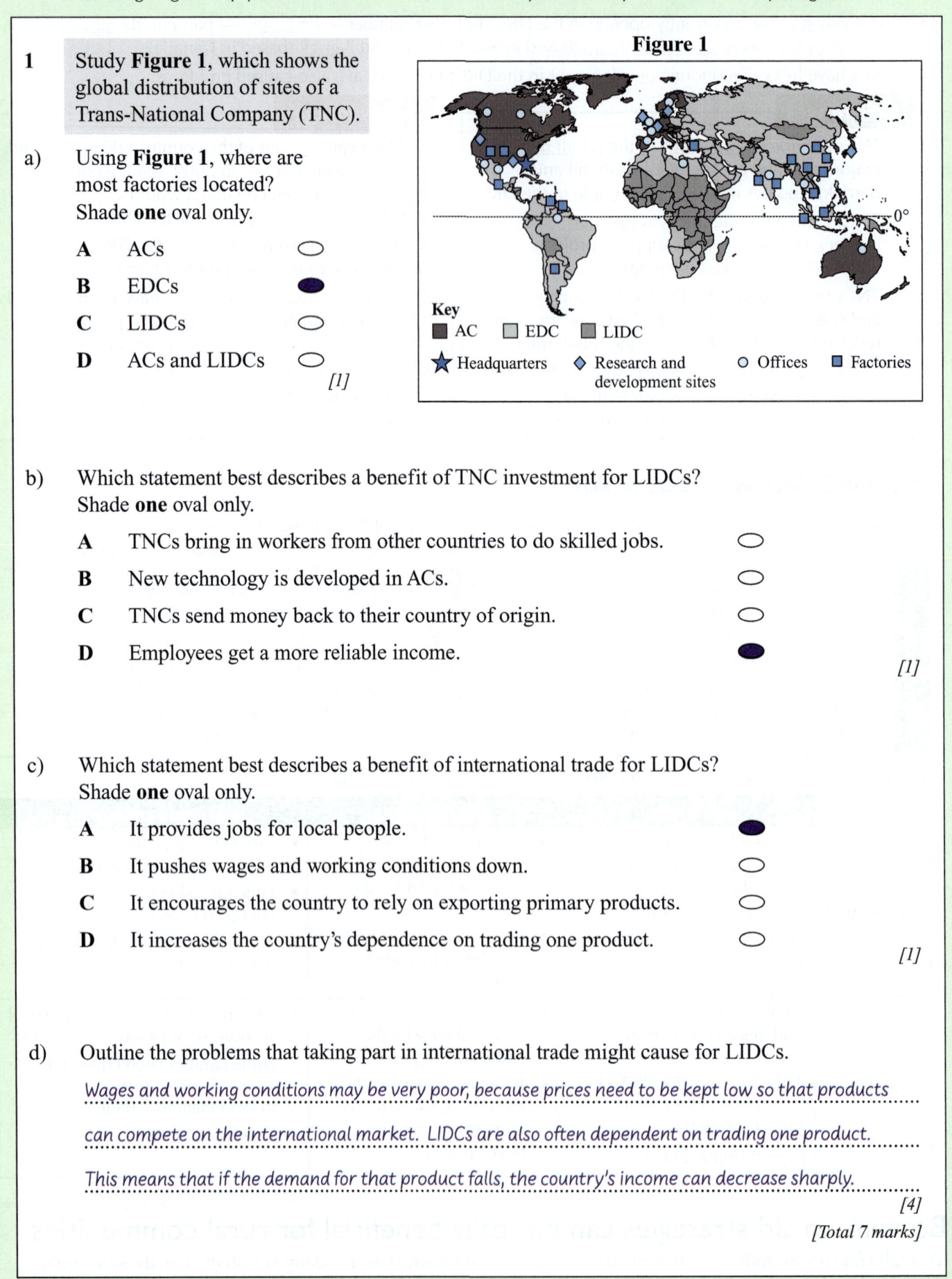

Key
- AC
- EDC
- LIDC
- ★ Headquarters
- ◇ Research and development sites
- ○ Offices
- ■ Factories

a) Using **Figure 1**, where are most factories located? Shade **one** oval only.

- A   ACs           ○
- B   EDCs          ●
- C   LIDCs         ○
- D   ACs and LIDCs ○

[1]

b) Which statement best describes a benefit of TNC investment for LIDCs? Shade **one** oval only.

- A   TNCs bring in workers from other countries to do skilled jobs.   ○
- B   New technology is developed in ACs.                              ○
- C   TNCs send money back to their country of origin.                 ○
- D   Employees get a more reliable income.                            ●

[1]

c) Which statement best describes a benefit of international trade for LIDCs? Shade **one** oval only.

- A   It provides jobs for local people.                              ●
- B   It pushes wages and working conditions down.                    ○
- C   It encourages the country to rely on exporting primary products. ○
- D   It increases the country's dependence on trading one product.   ○

[1]

d) Outline the problems that taking part in international trade might cause for LIDCs.

*Wages and working conditions may be very poor, because prices need to be kept low so that products can compete on the international market. LIDCs are also often dependent on trading one product. This means that if the demand for that product falls, the country's income can decrease sharply.*

[4]

[Total 7 marks]

Topic 6 — Dynamic Development

# Exam Questions

1 Study **Figure 1**, an article about an aid project in Ghana.

**Figure 1**

> **UK Government Support for Ghana**
>
> The UK is the second largest aid donor to Ghana. The UK Government's Department for International Development (DFID) gave over £205 million between 2005 and 2007 towards Ghana's poverty reduction plans. This level of aid continues, with donations of around £85 million per year. The aid is used in several ways, including to improve healthcare, education and sanitation.
>
> About 15% of the UK's funding in 2008 was used to support the healthcare system in Ghana —
>
> £42.5 million was pledged to support the Ghanaian Government's 2008-2012 health plan. On top of that, in 2008 the UK gave nearly £7 million to buy emergency equipment to reduce maternal deaths.
>
> Thanks to a £105 million grant from the UK in 2006, Ghana has been able to set up a ten year education strategic plan. It was the first African country to do this. The UK pledged additional money to help 12 000 children in North Ghana to get a formal basic education.

a) Which of the statements below best describes the aid projects described in **Figure 1**? Shade **one** oval only.

    A    Short-term, 'top-down' aid    ○

    B    Short-term, 'bottom-up' aid    ○

    C    Long-term, 'top-down' aid    ○

    D    Long-term, 'bottom-up' aid    ○

[1]

b) Outline **one** potential advantage and **one** potential disadvantage for the recipient country of long-term aid projects.

    **Advantage:**......................................................................................................................

    ............................................................................................................................................

    **Disadvantage:**..................................................................................................................

    ............................................................................................................................................

[2]

c) Outline **one** potential advantage and **one** potential disadvantage for the recipient country of short-term aid projects.

    **Advantage:**......................................................................................................................

    ............................................................................................................................................

    **Disadvantage:**..................................................................................................................

    ............................................................................................................................................

[2]

d) For an LIDC you have studied, evaluate the success of **one** top-down and **one** bottom-up development strategy.

[8 + 3 SPaG]

[Total 16 marks]

Topic 6 — Dynamic Development

# Revision Summary

That's it for Topic 6. Now it's time to see how much information you've remembered.
- Try these questions and tick off each one when you get it right.
- When you've done all the questions under a heading and are completely happy with it, tick it off.

## Development (p.91-92) ☐
1) What is economic development?
2) What is social development?
3) List five measures of development.
4) What is meant by 'uneven development'?
5) What do LIDC, AC and EDC stand for?
6) Where are most ACs found?

## Factors Affecting Development (p.93-95) ☐
7) Give four physical factors that can affect how developed a country is.
8) For one physical factor, describe how it can affect development.
9) Give four human factors that can affect how developed a country is.
10) For one human factor, describe how it can affect development.

## Increasing Development (p.98-100) ☐
11) Briefly describe the five stages of Rostow's model of economic development.
12) Describe two of the Millennium Development Goals.
13) Explain the difference between 'top-down' and 'bottom-up aid.'
14) What is the difference between short-term and long-term aid?
15) Explain how debt relief can help a country to develop.
16) What is a TNC?
17) How can TNCs help the development of a country?
18) Give one disadvantage of TNCs for developing countries.

## Development in the Democratic Republic of the Congo (p.101-105) ☐
19) True or false: the DRC is landlocked.
20) Explain how being a colony might have hindered development in the DRC.
21) Explain how political factors have affected development in the DRC.
22) What are 'conflict minerals'?
23) Describe two physical factors that have hindered development in the DRC.
24) For two Millennium Development Goals, describe how far they've been met in the DRC.
25) What stage of Rostow's development model does the DRC fall into? Explain your answer.
26) a) What are the DRC's main exports? What are its main imports?
    b) What effect might this have on its economy?
27) Give one advantage and one disadvantage to the DRC of increasing trade.
28) a) Name a TNC that operates in the DRC.
    b) Describe the advantages and disadvantages of TNCs to the DRC.
29) a) Describe one aid project taking place in the DRC.
    b) Describe the advantages and disadvantages of this aid project to the DRC.

*If you've learned about a different country, try answering these questions for the country you've studied instead.*

# Topic 7 — UK in the 21st Century

## Characteristics of the UK

*Time to learn stuff about the UK. First up, some information on the UK's population density, rainfall and land use...*

### The Characteristics of the UK Change Across the Country

**UK population density**

Population density (the number of people per unit area, e.g. per km²) varies:

- Population density is highest in cities, e.g. London, Glasgow, Birmingham — in London it's about 5500 people per km².
- It's also high in areas around major cities, or where there are clusters of cities, e.g. the south-east, Midlands and central Scotland.
- Mountainous regions such as northern Scotland and central Wales have low population densities.
- Other areas of low population density are north England and west Wales. Eden in Cumbria has a population density of about 24 people per km².

High population density can cause problems:

- There may be a shortage of available housing — e.g. in London, up to 60 000 new homes are needed every year to keep up with population growth. A shortage can drive up the price of houses, so some people can't afford to live there.
- There may be pressure on services such as health care and schools — there can be long waiting lists to see doctors, and children may have to attend a school a long way from home.

### UK average annual rainfall

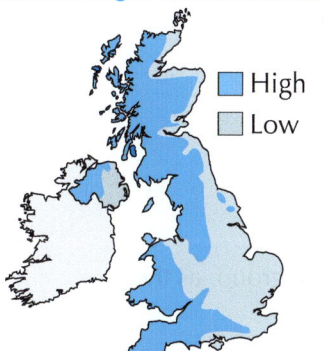

The UK gets quite a lot of rain, but the amount varies hugely around the country:

- The north and west of the UK generally have high rainfall. E.g. Aultbea in northwest Scotland has an average annual rainfall of 1470 mm.
- The south and east of the UK generally have lower rainfall. E.g. London has an annual average rainfall of 560 mm.
- Rainfall tends to be higher in coastal areas than inland.
- Rainfall is also higher in areas of higher elevation — mountainous areas get more rainfall than low-lying areas.

*The UK's relief (see p.35) helps to determine patterns of population density, rainfall and land use.*

Areas with high population density use a lot of resources, e.g. water. If the area also has low rainfall, this can cause water stress — there isn't enough water to meet people's needs. London experiences severe water stress.

Land use is how land is used, e.g. housing or farming. It varies across the UK:

**UK land use**: Built-up areas, Natural land, Agricultural land, Wetlands

- Most of the UK (about 70%) is agricultural land. Arable farming (growing crops) is more common in the south and east of the country, and grazing animals is more common in the north and west.
- Less than 10% of the UK is built on — buildings are concentrated in large urban areas, especially in south-east England, the Midlands and central Scotland. These urban areas are expanding.
- Forest covers about 13% of the land — some of this is natural and some has been planted and is managed by people.
- Some areas are not used as much by humans and have been left in a fairly natural state, e.g. mountainous or boggy areas in north Scotland.

## Population density, weather and land use vary across the UK

Don't worry too much about learning specific details on this page — the main thing to learn is the rough patterns of population density, rainfall, land use and relief (see p.35), and some of the issues these patterns can cause.

# The Changing Population of the UK

*Since 2001, the **population** of the UK has **changed** a lot — there are **more** of us, and the **average age** is **increasing**.*

## The UK's Population is Increasing

1) In 2001, the population of the UK was about 59 million. By 2015, it was about 65 million.

2) Population has increased every year since 2001, but growth rate has slowed down since 2011.

## UK Population Structure Can be Shown with Population Pyramids

1) The changing population structure of the UK (the number of men and women in different age groups) is shown using population pyramids:

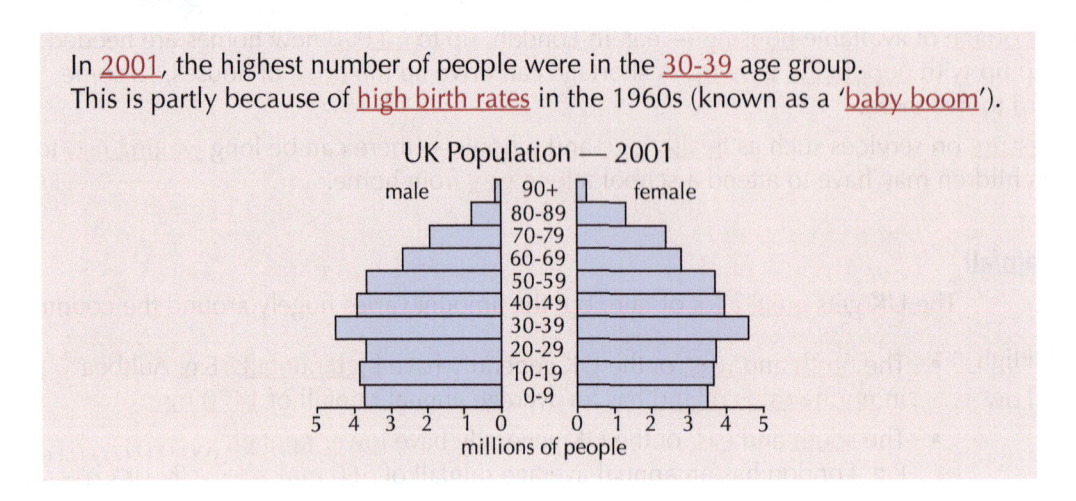

In 2001, the highest number of people were in the 30-39 age group. This is partly because of high birth rates in the 1960s (known as a 'baby boom').

*UK Population — 2001*

By 2015, the highest number of people were in the 40-49 age group, as the 1960s 'baby boom' generation got older.

*UK Population — 2015\**

2) Between 2001 and 2015, the number of people aged 20-29 increased — this was partly due to increasing numbers of young migrants (see page 112).

3) The number of people aged 0 to 39 increased by about 3%, and the number of people aged over 39 increased by about 18% — this shows that the UK's population is getting older (see p.113).

---

### Population pyramids can show changes in the UK's population structure

In the exam you might be given a population pyramid on the UK and asked to interpret it. Have a good look at the examples above and make sure you know what a population pyramid shows about population structure.

*\*Constructed using data from Population Division, World Population Prospects, the 2015 revision, by Department of Economic and Social Affairs. © United Nations 2023. Accessed 23.06.2016. Reprinted with the permission of the United Nations.*

# The Changing Population of the UK

*As a country **develops**, there are predictable changes in **birth rate**, **death rate** and **population size**.*

## The UK is at Stage 4 of the Demographic Transition Model

1) The Demographic Transition Model (DTM) shows how a country's population is likely to change as it develops, based on changing birth and death rates.

2) At stage 1, birth and death rates are high, and population is low. As a country develops, healthcare improves, so death rate falls and population grows. Over time, better education and increased access to contraception means that birth rate falls, so population growth begins to slow down.

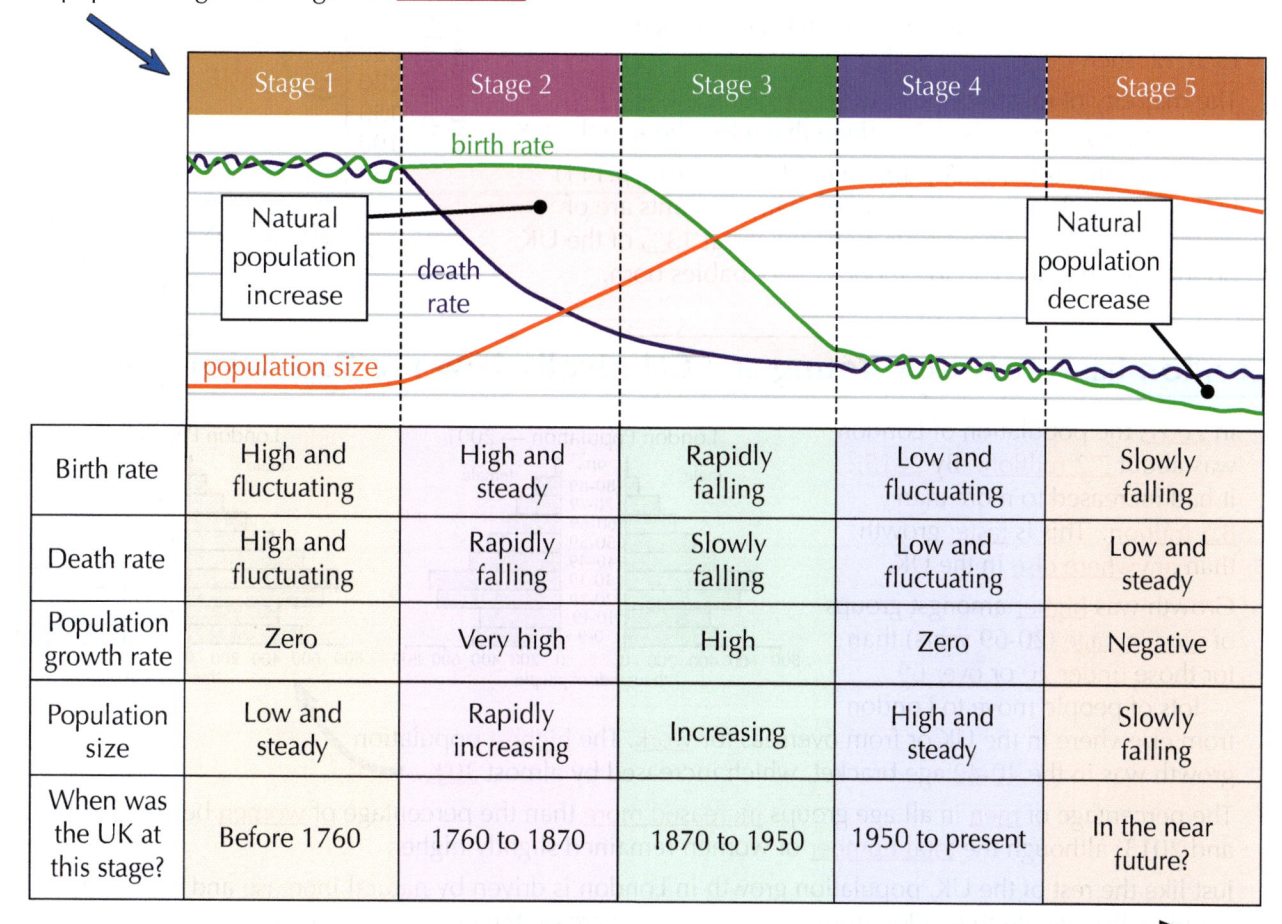

|  | Stage 1 | Stage 2 | Stage 3 | Stage 4 | Stage 5 |
|---|---|---|---|---|---|
| Birth rate | High and fluctuating | High and steady | Rapidly falling | Low and fluctuating | Slowly falling |
| Death rate | High and fluctuating | Rapidly falling | Slowly falling | Low and fluctuating | Low and steady |
| Population growth rate | Zero | Very high | High | Zero | Negative |
| Population size | Low and steady | Rapidly increasing | Increasing | High and steady | Slowly falling |
| When was the UK at this stage? | Before 1760 | 1760 to 1870 | 1870 to 1950 | 1950 to present | In the near future? |

DEVELOPMENT →

3) In the UK:

- Birth rate and death rate have fallen over the past 300 years — it has been through stages 1-3 of the DTM.

- Birth rate is now 12 births per thousand people and death rate is 9 deaths per thousand people. These are both quite low, but population is still growing slowly — this shows that the UK is at stage 4 of the DTM.

*The DTM doesn't account for migration — see next page.*

4) The UK hasn't yet reached stage 5 — when death rate is higher than birth rate, and population size starts to decrease.

## Population often increases rapidly as countries start to develop

Lots of information here, but don't panic — you don't have to memorise all the information on the diagram. Just make sure you know that the UK is at stage 4 of the Demographic Transition Model, and that you understand why.

Topic 7 — UK in the 21st Century

# The Changing Population of the UK

*Migration* into the UK is increasing its **population size** and **ethnic diversity** — especially in big cities like **London**.

## There's Lots of Migration to the UK

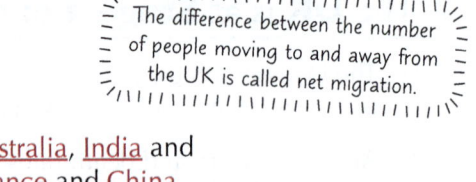

1) Roughly half the UK's population growth (see page 110) is driven by natural increase (more births than deaths), and about half by migration.
2) In 2015, over 600 000 people moved to the UK, mostly from China, Australia, India and Poland. About 300 000 people moved overseas, mostly to Australia, France and China.
3) The number of people moving to the UK has been greater than the number leaving in every year since 2001.
4) Net migration to the UK increased from 2001 to 2004, stayed fairly constant from 2004 to 2010, decreased to 2012, then increased sharply. 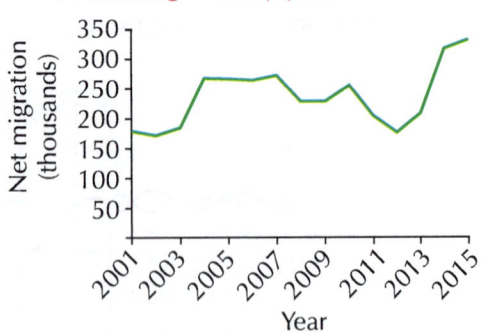
5) The majority of migrants move to London and the south-east — population growth is higher there than elsewhere in the UK.
6) Migration affects the UK's position on the DTM (see p.111) by increasing the birth rate, because many migrants are of child-bearing age. Immigrants make up about 13% of the UK population, but account for about 27% of babies born.

*The difference between the number of people moving to and away from the UK is called net migration.*

## London has a Relatively Young and Ethnically Diverse Population

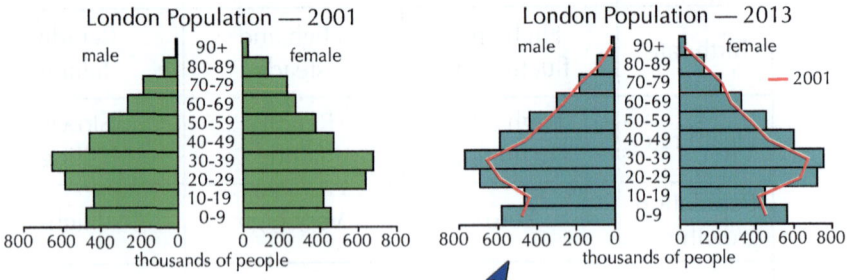

1) In 2001, the population of London was about 7.2 million. By 2015, it had increased to more than 8.5 million. This is faster growth than anywhere else in the UK.
2) Growth was higher amongst groups of working age (20-69 years) than for those under 20 or over 69 — lots of people move to London from elsewhere in the UK or from overseas for work. The highest population growth was in the 40-49 age bracket, which increased by almost 30%.
3) The percentage of men in all age groups increased more than the percentage of women between 2001 and 2013, although the total number of women remained slightly higher.
4) Just like the rest of the UK, population growth in London is driven by natural increase and migration. People who migrate to London from other countries increase the city's ethnic diversity.

### Ethnic Diversity

1) Across the UK as a whole, about 13% of the population were born in another country. In London, this value is about 37%.
2) Ethnic diversity in London has increased between 2001 and the present — in 2001, 60% of the population were white British, but by 2011 this had fallen to 45%.
3) The change was driven by an increase in the percentage of white non-British people (particularly from Poland and Romania), as well as Black African and Asian people.

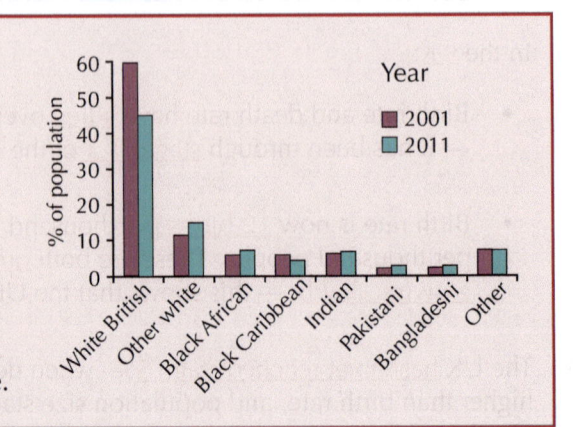

## Migration is partly responsible for UK population growth

The population of London is growing even faster and is younger and more diverse than the UK as a whole. A higher rate of migration into London than into other parts of the UK is a major reason for these differences.

Topic 7 — UK in the 21st Century

# The UK's Ageing Population

*An **ageing population** is one that has an increasingly **high proportion** of **older people**. Ageing populations can face some **economic** and **social** problems — the government has several ways to tackle these issues.*

## The UK has an Ageing Population

In the UK, around 18% of the population are over 65. The proportion of older people is increasing because:

1) Birth rates are low because couples are having fewer children — in the UK, the average number of children per family decreased from 2.9 in 1964 (the peak of the 1960s 'baby boom') to 1.8 in 2014. Also, more women are choosing not to have children than in the past.

2) People are living longer due to better medical care and a healthier lifestyle (e.g. not smoking). Life expectancy in the UK increased from 72 years in 1964 to 81 years in 2015.

## The Number of Older People Varies Around the UK

**Proportion of people over 65**

Key: Low, Medium, High, Very high

1) The proportion of older people isn't the same everywhere in the UK.
2) It's lower in Northern Ireland and Scotland than in England and Wales.
3) It's generally lower in big cities, such as London, Bristol and Manchester — people often live in cities to be closer to their jobs, so a higher proportion of the population is of working age.
4) The percentage of older people is high in coastal areas, especially in east and south-west England, because lots of people move there when they retire.

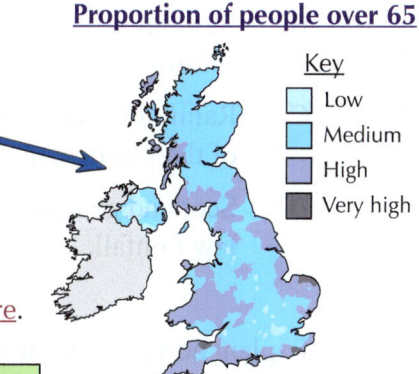

## The Ageing Population has Social and Economic Effects

### Social

1) Healthcare services are under pressure because demand for medical care has increased.
2) Some people act as unpaid carers for older family members in their free time, so they have less leisure time and are more stressed.
3) People may not be able to afford to have lots of children when they have dependent older relatives. This may lead to a further drop in birth rate.
4) Many retired people do voluntary work, e.g. in hospitals. This benefits the community.

### Economic

1) Taxes for working people rise to pay for healthcare and services such as pensions and retirement homes.
2) Older people who aren't working pay less tax, so their economic contribution decreases.
3) However, some older people look after their grandchildren, so their children can work.
4) Many older people have disposable income, which they spend on goods and services that boost the economy.

## There are Different Responses to the UK's Ageing Population

1) As the number of older people increases, the government may need to increase taxes or cut spending in other areas (e.g. education or defence) to fund more support and medical care.
2) The government is raising the age at which people can claim a pension — people stay in work longer, so they contribute to taxes and pensions for longer.
3) The government is encouraging people to save more money to help pay for their retirement. For example, in 2015 the government launched savings accounts for over-65s, known as 'pensioner bonds' — these offered a higher rate of interest than many savings accounts, so older people could save more.
4) The UK government currently offers a winter fuel allowance to all older people. In future, this may only be given to older people who can't afford to heat their homes, meaning less money is spent overall.

---

**REVISION TIP**

### An ageing population impacts the UK's society and economy
You need to know the causes, distribution, effects and responses to the UK's ageing population. Check that you have a good grasp of them by covering the page and jotting down a few points for each.

Topic 7 — UK in the 21st Century

# Worked Exam Questions

These worked exam questions are here to give you an idea about how to approach questions about the characteristics and population of the UK. Have a go at tackling some yourself on the next page.

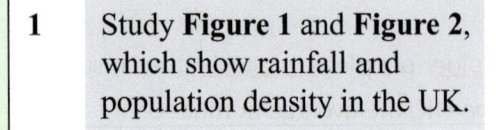

1. Study **Figure 1** and **Figure 2**, which show rainfall and population density in the UK.

   a) Which of these statements is correct? Shade **one** oval only.
   - A The south of the UK receives little rain.
   - B Rainfall is higher in Cardiff than in London. ●
   - C Rainfall is higher in the east of the UK than in the west.
   - D Scotland generally has low rainfall.

   [1]

   **Figure 1** — UK average annual rainfall (Key: High, Low)
   **Figure 2** — UK regional population density (Key: Very high, High, Medium, Low)

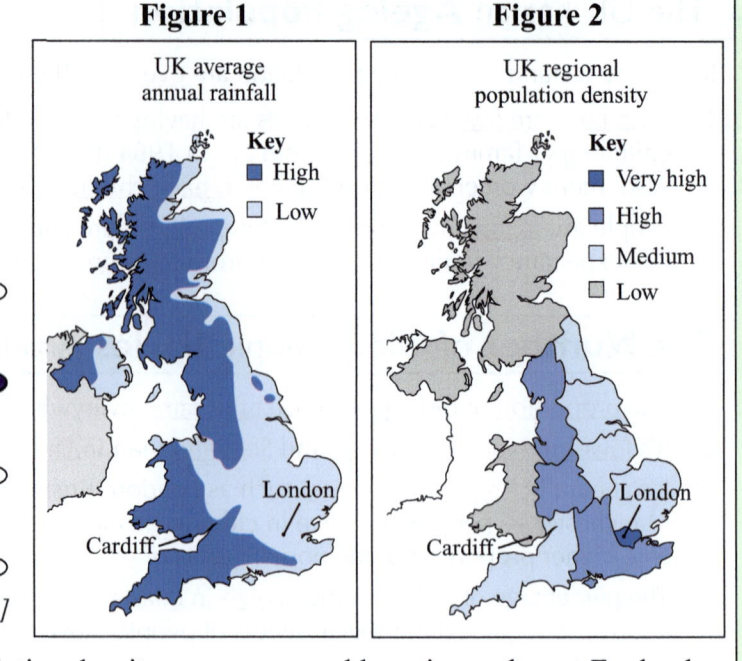

   b) Explain how patterns of rainfall and population density may cause problems in south-east England.

   *In south-east England, population density is high but rainfall is low. Areas with high population densities use lots of water, so there may be water shortages in the area.*

   [3]
   [Total 4 marks]

2. Study **Figure 3**, which shows the demographic transition model, together with UK birth and death rates for 2015.

   **Figure 3**

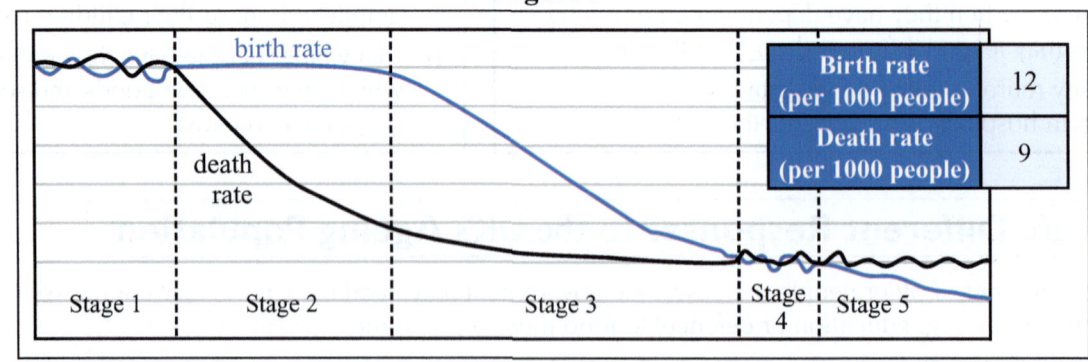

   | Birth rate (per 1000 people) | 12 |
   | Death rate (per 1000 people) | 9 |

   Suggest what stage of the demographic transition model the UK is at.
   Use **Figure 3** to justify your answer.

   *The UK is at stage 4 of the demographic transition model. Birth rate and death rate are relatively low, which suggests the UK is at a late stage of the DTM, but birth rate is slightly higher than death rate, suggesting that the UK has not yet reached stage 5.*

   [Total 3 marks]

Topic 7 — UK in the 21st Century

# Exam Questions

1   Study **Figure 1**, population pyramids for the UK for 2001 and 2015.

a) Complete **Figure 1** to show that there were 3 500 000 girls aged 0-9 years old in 2001.
[1]

b) How many people aged 40-49 were there in the UK in 2001?

7.5 million
[1]

c) What is the modal class of the UK population in 2001?

..............................................................
[1]

d) Using **Figure 1**, describe how the age structure of the UK population changed from 2001 to 2015.

there has been an increase in elderly people (90+) due to improving health care.

[3]
[Total 6 marks]

2   For a named location in the UK, describe how its population structure and ethnic diversity have changed since 2001.

In the city of London, the population size has increased by 16.6%, from around 7,400 in 2011 to 8,600 in 2021. This is higher than the overall increase for england (6.6%), where the population grew by nearly 3.5 million to 56,489,800.

[Total 6 marks]

# The Changing Economy of the UK

*The **UK's economy** is **changing** all the time — a lot of it has to do with **politics**. You need to understand how politics **influences** the economy, and how **employment sectors** and **working hours** have changed since 2001.*

## Changes to the Economy Have Been Driven by Politics

1) Between <u>1997</u> and <u>2007</u>, the UK economy <u>grew strongly</u> and unemployment <u>decreased</u>. This was partly because of the <u>government's priorities</u>:

   - Encouraging <u>investment</u> in new <u>technologies</u>, e.g. computing industries.
   - Investing in <u>university education</u>, leading to a more <u>skilled workforce</u>.

   *Investment in technology and education boosted growth of quaternary industries (see below).*

2) However, in <u>early 2008</u> the UK entered a <u>recession</u>. Businesses <u>failed</u>, <u>GDP decreased</u> and <u>unemployment increased</u>. The government had to <u>change</u> their priorities to <u>end</u> the recession:

   - <u>Supporting businesses</u> so they didn't <u>collapse</u> — their collapse would increase <u>unemployment</u>.
   - <u>Decreasing taxes</u> on goods to <u>encourage spending</u> and international <u>trade</u>.
   - <u>Borrowing money</u> from e.g. private companies and overseas investors.

   *Getting people into work means there are fewer people claiming benefits and more paying taxes.*

3) The recession ended in <u>late 2009</u>. The government had to focus on <u>paying off</u> money <u>borrowed</u> during the recession and helping people to find <u>jobs</u>:

   - Cutting spending on <u>public services</u> such as pensions, education and defence to <u>raise money</u>.
   - Providing <u>training</u> for <u>job-seekers</u> and support for <u>new businesses</u> to decrease <u>unemployment</u>.

## The UK's Employment Sectors Have Changed

1) Since 2001, jobs in <u>quaternary</u> industries (e.g. education and research, ICT) have <u>increased</u> most, while jobs in <u>secondary industries</u> (e.g. manufacturing) have <u>decreased</u>.

2) Over the same period, the number of people employed in <u>primary production</u> (e.g. farming and mining) and <u>tertiary</u> industries (e.g. retail) stayed <u>fairly steady</u>.

3) The biggest increases have been in <u>professional</u> and <u>technical</u> jobs (e.g. law, computing, research and development).

4) Employment in manufacturing decreased most, partly due to <u>cheaper materials</u> and <u>labour</u> being available <u>overseas</u>.

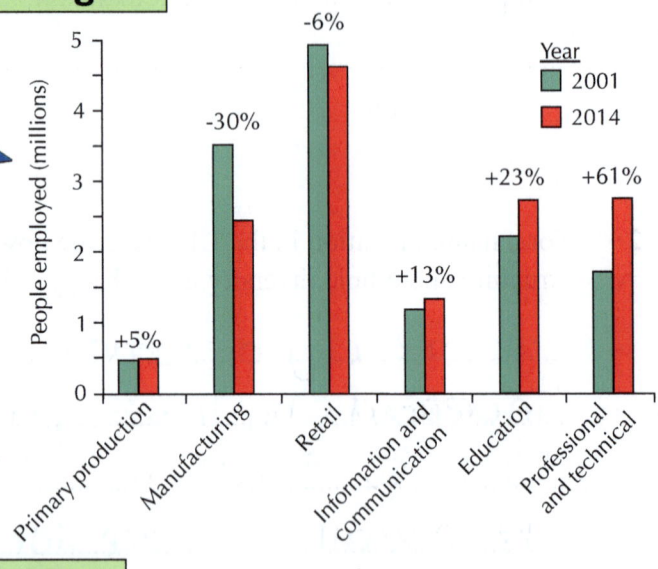

Bar chart — People employed (millions), Year 2001 vs 2014:
- Primary production: +5%
- Manufacturing: -30%
- Retail: -6%
- Information and communication: +13%
- Education: +23%
- Professional and technical: +61%

## Working Hours Have Decreased Since 2001

1) Overall, working hours are decreasing — the average number of hours worked in a week was <u>34.7</u> in <u>2001</u> and <u>33.1</u> in <u>2014</u>. The number of hours worked <u>decreased</u> slightly more for <u>men</u> than for <u>women</u> over this time.

2) There has been an increase in people doing <u>part-time jobs</u> and <u>zero-hours contracts</u> (where the employee <u>isn't</u> guaranteed <u>any</u> hours of work).

3) However, the number of families with <u>both</u> parents in <u>full-time work</u> has <u>increased</u> since 2003, when the government <u>increased financial support</u> for low-income working parents.

*Since 1998, the maximum working time per week is 48 hours, and workers are entitled to at least 5.6 weeks of holiday each year.*

---

**REVISION TIP: There have been major economic changes in the UK in recent years**
There's some complex information here. Learn this page and then test yourself — see if you can write a detailed description of the changes in political priorities, employment sectors and working hours.

Topic 7 — UK in the 21st Century

# UK Economic Hubs

*Industries are not evenly spread across the UK — they're clustered around a number of **economic centres**.*

## An Economic Hub is an Economically Important Place

1) Economic hubs are places where economic activity is concentrated — e.g. they often have lots of businesses. They have economic influence beyond the hub itself, for example companies located in the hub may trade with companies in other countries.

2) Economic hubs occur at a range of scales — e.g. they can be an entire region, a town or city, or a single street within a city. For example:

- Region — South Wales is home to lots of new digital and media companies, which are rapidly increasing their takings and staff numbers. This is helping to boost the economy of Wales and the UK as a whole.
- City — London is an economic hub for the UK, and has a global economic influence, e.g. through trade and financial markets. The headquarters of many banks and other businesses (both UK-based and global) are located there, and the city creates 22% of the UK's GDP.
- Part of city — Electric Works, a large office building in central Sheffield, is home to many digital, creative and media companies.

## The UK's Core Economic Hubs are Often in Cities

1) Many of the main economic hubs in the UK have a high concentration of tertiary and quaternary industries (see p.116). These are often based in cities, or in science or business parks on the outskirts of cities where there are good transport links and links with universities.

2) Economic hubs are concentrated in the south-east of England — cities like London, Brighton and Cambridge are experiencing more rapid growth in new businesses and jobs than cities elsewhere in the UK. However, the UK government is encouraging investment outside the south-east, and many companies are setting up sites in other areas. Some examples of current economic hubs and some of the industries located in them are:

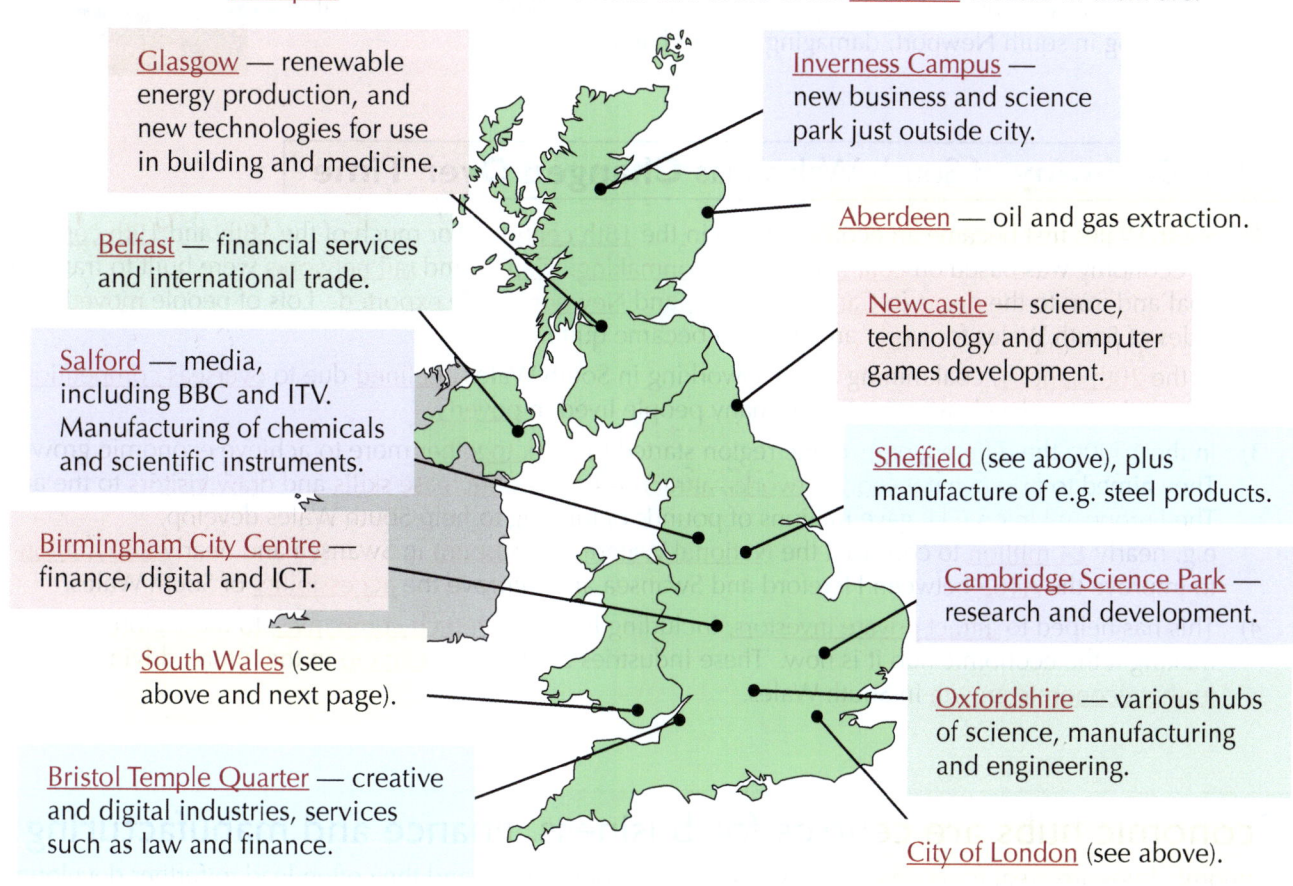

Glasgow — renewable energy production, and new technologies for use in building and medicine.

Belfast — financial services and international trade.

Salford — media, including BBC and ITV. Manufacturing of chemicals and scientific instruments.

Birmingham City Centre — finance, digital and ICT.

South Wales (see above and next page).

Bristol Temple Quarter — creative and digital industries, services such as law and finance.

Inverness Campus — new business and science park just outside city.

Aberdeen — oil and gas extraction.

Newcastle — science, technology and computer games development.

Sheffield (see above), plus manufacture of e.g. steel products.

Cambridge Science Park — research and development.

Oxfordshire — various hubs of science, manufacturing and engineering.

City of London (see above).

*Topic 7 — UK in the 21st Century*

# UK Economic Hubs

## South Wales is an Economic Hub

1) Wales is less wealthy than the UK as a whole. However, South Wales is much richer than other parts of Wales — e.g. GDP per capita in Cardiff is £22 000 compared to £15 500 in Wales as a whole.

2) The difference in wealth between South Wales and the rest of Wales is caused by the large number of companies that have located in the south, and the high number of visitors the area attracts:

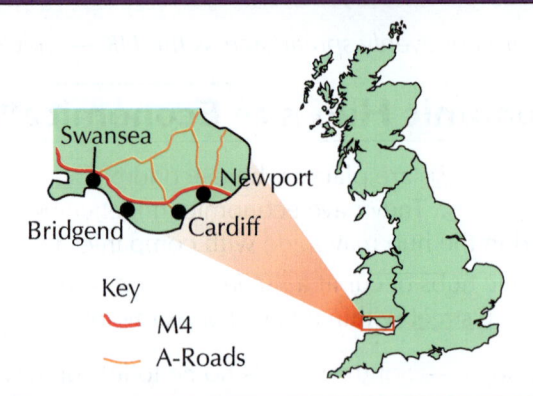

- Manufacturing — e.g. GE Aviation Wales has a plant in Nantgarw that employs around 1000 people.
- Services — e.g. insurance providers Admiral have their headquarters in Cardiff, as well as offices in Newport and Swansea, and employ over 5000 people in South Wales.
- Digital — digital companies in South Wales grew by 87% between 2010 and 2013 — much faster than in the UK as a whole. TechHub in Swansea was set up in 2016 to provide office space, networking opportunities and advice for new digital companies.
- Media — over 50 000 people are employed in media and creative industries in Wales as a whole, with the highest concentration in South Wales. The head office of BBC Cymru Wales is in Cardiff, and programmes made there, such as Doctor Who and Casualty, are exported worldwide (see p.120).
- Tourism — 600 000 people visit Cardiff each year, contributing £130 million to the local economy.

3) Most companies are based in the cities, creating inequalities in wealth between the cities and surrounding areas. However, growth has a positive effect on the whole region by creating jobs, attracting visitors and prompting further development, e.g. out-of-town shopping centres.

4) Through business investment, employment and exports, South Wales contributes significantly to the economy of Wales and the UK as a whole.

5) Economic growth in South Wales has had environmental impacts on the region. For example, various manufacturing industries have been built on wetlands at Wentloog in south Newport, damaging natural habitats.

## The Economy of South Wales Has Changed Over Time

1) South Wales first became an economic hub in the 18th century. For much of the 18th and 19th centuries, its economy was based on coal mining and ironmaking. Canals and rail networks were built to transport coal and iron to the docks in Cardiff, Swansea and Newport, to be exported. Lots of people moved to the cities of South Wales for work, and the area became quite wealthy.

2) In the 20th century, coal mining and ironworking in South Wales declined due to overseas competition. Unemployment levels were high, and many people lived in poverty.

3) In the 1990s, the different parts of the region started to work together more to achieve economic growth. They aimed to improve transport networks, attract businesses, increase skills and draw visitors to the area. The European Union (EU) gave millions of pounds of funding to help South Wales develop, e.g. nearly £4 million to construct the National Waterfront Museum in Swansea and nearly £80 million to improve the A465 between Hereford and Swansea and improve the accessibility of South Wales.

4) This has helped to attract private investors, including lots of high-tech companies, to the region, making it the economic hub it is now. These industries are likely to expand in the future, driving further economic growth in South Wales.

## Economic hubs are centres for business, finance and manufacturing

Economic hubs are great for economic growth and job opportunities, and they often lead to further development. Make sure you know how one particular economic hub affects its regional economy, as well as the UK economy.

# The UK's Role in the World

*The UK may be a relatively **small** state, mostly surrounded by **water**, but that hasn't stopped us getting **involved** in things all around the world — we work closely with other countries to promote **peace** and **reduce conflict**.*

## The UK is a Member of Several International Organisations

1) Lots of international organisations have been set up to try to avoid conflict, and to ensure that member countries work together to help resolve conflict elsewhere.
2) The UK is a member of several international groups, such as:

- The North Atlantic Treaty Organisation (NATO) is a group of 30 countries, including the USA and many European countries, who work together to ensure their own security. They aim to prevent conflict by promoting cooperation and to resolve conflicts by political means (e.g. overseeing negotiations) and military means (as a last resort).
- The United Nations (UN) is made up of 193 member states. It was founded in 1945, at the end of WWII, to maintain peace. The UN tries to solve issues that can't be dealt with by individual countries, e.g. helping countries develop sustainably and delivering aid during crises.
- The Group of Seven (G7) has seven members — the US, Canada, France, the UK, Japan, Germany and Italy. Members meet once a year to discuss relevant issues, including economic policies, conflict, energy supply and security, and come to agreements about how best to approach them.

*The UK used to be a member of the European Union (EU), which was set up after WWII to prevent further conflict in Europe. In 2020, the UK left the EU.*

## The UK has been Involved in Trying to Resolve Conflict in Ukraine

**EXAMPLE**

1) Ukraine is a country in eastern Europe — it is bordered by Russia to the north and east. Ukraine was governed by Russia until 1991.
2) In 2013, backed by Russia, the Ukraine government decided not to form closer trade links with the EU, but to strengthen their ties with Russia instead. This was unpopular with many Ukrainians, who wanted to build a closer relationship with western Europe, and there were protests and violence. The president was removed from office and a pro-EU president was elected.
3) In 2014, the Russian President, Vladimir Putin, took control of Crimea (part of Ukraine) and moved large numbers of Russian troops to the Russia-Ukraine border. Years of fighting between the Ukrainian army and pro-Russian Ukrainians followed.
4) International organisations in which the UK plays a part have reacted in various ways:

*In 2022, the conflict worsened when Russia invaded Ukraine.*

**NATO** supports negotiations between the two sides to try to settle the conflict. In 2015, they created a rapid-response force of around 5000 soldiers stationed in surrounding countries to try to deter future attempts by Russia to gain territory. The rapid-response force is being led by different countries in rotation — the UK led it in 2017, as well as supplying troops and RAF jets.

**UN** The UN supports peace talks between Russian and Ukrainian leaders and provides aid (e.g. food, medicine and blankets) to people forced to leave their home because of fighting. In 2015, the UK gave £15 million in aid to Ukraine, as well as military support and training for the Ukrainian army.

**G7** used to be G8 — the other countries forced Russia out in 2014, after its seizure of Crimea. The UK, along with the other G7 countries, has imposed sanctions on Russia — e.g. restricting the money that Russian banks can borrow and limiting trade with Russia. By threatening the Russian economy, they hope to convince Russia to agree to a ceasefire and the withdrawal of troops.

---

**EXAM TIP** | **The UK is involved in many different global peacekeeping efforts**
If you've studied a different example of the UK's role in an international conflict, feel free to discuss it in the exam. Just make sure you have enough information about the UK's part in that conflict.

Topic 7 — UK in the 21st Century

# UK Media Exports

*The UK's **media** and **culture** is one of its most **important exports** — British **books** and **films** can be found all over the world and have helped **shape** what people in different parts of the world **imagine Britain to be like**.*

## The UK Exports Lots of Media Products

1) Media products are things like films, TV and radio shows, music and books.
2) The UK produces lots of media and exports it all over the world. This makes a big contribution to the UK's economy — in 2012, media industries employed nearly 1.7 million people and exported over £17 billion of products worldwide.
3) Some examples of media products that have been exported from the UK are:

- TV drama series — e.g. 'Downton Abbey' is watched by around 120 million people in more than 100 countries, including the USA and China.
- TV reality shows — e.g. 'The X Factor UK' is watched by more than 360 million people in 147 territories, and 51 countries have produced their own national version.
- Films — UK films are distributed all over the world, but are most popular in New Zealand, Australia and Europe. For example, 'The King's Speech' took over US $400 million at the box office, of which two-thirds was outside the UK.
- Music — UK artists account for nearly 14% of global album sales each year. Adele, Ed Sheeran and One Direction were three of the biggest-selling artists in the world in 2015.
- Books — e.g. the 'Harry Potter' series by J. K. Rowling has been translated into 68 languages and has sold more than 400 million copies in more than 200 territories.

## The UK's Media Exports Have a Global Influence

Media produced in the UK and reflecting life here are distributed all over the world, and some successful British artists have become internationally famous. This means that media exports have a big influence:

- Most exported UK media are in English, so people in other countries develop a better understanding of the English language. However, the accents and phrases they learn may not be representative of the UK as a whole.
- The different lifestyles, values and beliefs of UK residents become more widely known and understood. However, this can be misleading — e.g. most people in the UK don't have servants or live in a house like Downton Abbey.
- Media exports affect the way the UK is perceived in other countries — e.g. in some films and TV shows it is portrayed as an ugly, industrial country, while in others it is shown as scenic and rural.
- Seeing the UK portrayed positively in different media makes people want to come here — either to work, to study or just to visit. For example, tourism in the UK increased after the 2012 Olympic Games in London, which was broadcast on TV around the world.
- Exports of similar media products may increase, strengthening the UK's economic influence.
- UK media exports can inspire people or companies in other countries to create or develop new media products — e.g. the quiz show 'The Weakest Link' started in the UK but the format was bought by more than 40 other countries, including the USA, Australia and France.
- Some people copy the clothes or hairstyles of celebrities they admire, so British celebrities have an impact on fashion around the world, and can boost sales of products that they use or endorse.

## Media exports are an important part of the UK's economy

TV shows, films, music and books exported from the UK bring a lot of money into the country, but their influence goes beyond the economic effects — they can change people's opinion of the UK in a positive or negative way.

# Multicultural UK

*It's not just the UK that **influences** the rest of the world — the **rest of the world** influences what life's like **here**.*

## Ethnic Groups Influence Life and Culture in the UK

1) The UK is a multicultural country — for centuries, people have moved here from all over the world. High proportions of ethnic minorities come from India, Pakistan and Africa.
2) People moving to the UK bring their own culture, which they share — e.g. by setting up businesses such as shops and restaurants or building religious centres.
3) People from the same ethnic background often settle in the same area of a city, creating a distinctive character in that area (because of e.g. the architecture and types of businesses that people create there).
4) Ethnic groups have influenced food, media and fashion in the UK:

China Town in Liverpool

### Food

1) Food that originates in other countries has become a staple for many Brits, e.g. curry and pizza.
2) Restaurants producing authentic ethnic food are popular with people of that ethnic background, and of many other ethnic backgrounds, including white British people.
3) Different national dishes need different ingredients, so shops specialising in those ingredients often open in areas with a high number of people from a particular ethnic background — e.g. London Road in Sheffield has a large Asian community, and lots of shops selling Indian and Chinese produce.
4) In recent years, mainstream supermarkets have increased the amount of ethnic food that they sell — many large supermarkets have a 'world food' aisle, and even small supermarkets offer ready-made curry paste, noodles and other ingredients for ethnic dishes.

### Media

People from ethnic minorities have made the media scene in the UK more diverse. This has helped different groups to understand and empathise with each other. For example:
1) People from ethnic minorities have written, acted in and produced a number of successful TV shows, such as 'The Kumars' and 'Youngers'.
2) Music styles including soul, reggae and dubstep all have roots in Black African and Caribbean music. They have been extremely influential in shaping music in the UK.
3) Authors from other cultures write books exploring their heritage or experiences in the UK, e.g. 'Yoruba Girl Dancing' by Nigerian writer Simi Bedford.
4) There have been numerous crossovers between traditional British culture and ethnic culture — e.g. several Shakespeare plays, including 'Hamlet', have been performed as Bollywood musicals.

### Fashion

1) As with food, in areas with a high population of people from an ethnic minority background, shops selling traditional clothes for those countries are likely to open. E.g. Stratford Road in Birmingham has a lot of shops selling saris and other traditional Indian clothes.
2) As these clothes become more common, people from other cultures start to wear them. Asian and middle-eastern fashion has become popular in the UK, e.g. harem trousers and kaftans.
3) Fashion houses and high-street shops start to sell their own versions of these clothes, often combining traditional and UK styles — e.g. Indonesian-style batik prints on strapless tops.

## Incoming migrants bring their culture and customs to the UK

UK culture has been shaped by historical and modern migration — food, media and fashion have all been affected by immigration. Cover the page and see if you can explain some ways migration has influenced life in the UK.

Topic 7 — UK in the 21st Century

# Worked Exam Questions

Another set of worked exam questions to look at here. It's tempting to skip over them without thinking, but it's worth taking time to look carefully — similar questions might just come up in your own exams...

1    Study **Figure 1**, a graph showing change in the percentage of people employed in different sectors in the UK between 2001 and 2014.

a)   Use **Figure 1** to complete the following sentences.

    i) The sector with the greatest percentage decrease in employment was .....*manufacturing*..... [1]

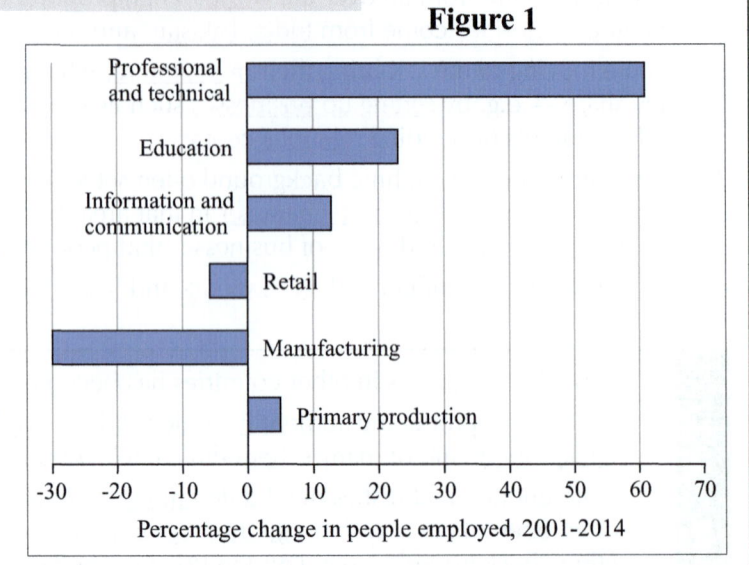

    ii) The percentage of people employed in education increased by ...*23%*... [1]

**Figure 1**

*[Bar chart showing percentage change in people employed, 2001-2014, for sectors: Professional and technical (~60), Education (~23), Information and communication (~12), Retail (~-5), Manufacturing (~-30), Primary production (~5)]*

b)   Suggest how changing political priorities might have affected the UK economy since 2001.

*From 1997 to 2007, the government invested heavily in new technologies, such as the computing industry, which helped to drive economic growth. During the economic recession in 2008-2009, the government had to borrow money to support struggling businesses. Since the recession ended, the government has focused on paying off money it borrowed, meaning that the economy has gradually become stronger.*

[4]
[Total 6 marks]

2    Describe how ethnic groups have contributed to UK culture by influencing **one** of food, media or fashion.

*Lots of food that originates in other countries, such as pizza and curry, has become a staple part of many people's diet in the UK. Restaurants producing authentic ethnic food are popular with people of that ethnic background, and of many other ethnic backgrounds, including white British people. Different national dishes need different ingredients, so shops specialising in those ingredients often open in areas with a high number of people from a particular ethnic background. As food from ethnic minorities has become more popular, mainstream supermarkets have started selling more of it, increasing its influence.*

[Total 4 marks]

Topic 7 — UK in the 21st Century

# Exam Questions

1  Study **Figure 1**, which shows the top ten countries by box office takings for the 2012 UK film 'Skyfall'.

**Figure 1**

|  | Box office takings (million US $) |
|---|---|
| USA | 304.4 |
| UK | 158.3 |
| Germany | 85.2 |
| France | 59.1 |
| China | 59.0 |
| Australia | 50.8 |
| Japan | 30.6 |
| Netherlands | 23.0 |
| Russia | 22.8 |
| Switzerland | 20.2 |

a) Calculate how much more money was taken in the USA than in the UK.

...................................................................................................
[1]

b) In total, 'Skyfall' made US $1110 million at the box office. Calculate the percentage of total box office takings that came from the UK.

...................................................................................................

...................................................................................................
[1]

c) **Figure 2** shows tourists in the UK photographing a set from a 'Harry Potter' film. Using **Figure 2**, explain how media exports might encourage people to visit the UK.

**Figure 2**

...................................................................................................

...................................................................................................

...................................................................................................

...................................................................................................
[1]

d) Using **Figure 1**, **Figure 2** and your own knowledge, explain how UK films have a global influence.

...................................................................................................

...................................................................................................

...................................................................................................

...................................................................................................

...................................................................................................

...................................................................................................

...................................................................................................

...................................................................................................

...................................................................................................
[6]

[Total 9 marks]

Topic 7 — UK in the 21st Century

# Revision Summary

Well done for making it to the end of Topic 7. Time for some revision questions to check what you know.
- Try these questions and tick off each one when you get it right.
- When you've done all the questions under a heading and are completely happy with it, tick it off.

## UK Characteristics (p.109)
1) Which areas of the UK have a high population density?
2) Give two problems that high population density might cause.
3) Briefly describe the pattern of rainfall across the UK.
4) What is meant by 'water stress'?
5) What is most land in the UK used for?
6) Roughly what percentage of the UK is built on?

## Changing UK Population (p.110-113)
7) Briefly describe what has happened to the number of people in the UK since 2001.
8) True or false: There are more older people in the UK now than there were in 2001.
9) What changes in the UK population would show that it's reached stage 5 of the DTM?
10) 'The UK has positive net migration.' What does this mean?
11) How might migration affect the UK's position on the DTM?
12) True or false: Population growth in London is slower than in the UK as a whole.
13) Name two areas of the UK where the proportion of older people is high.
14) a) Give two social effects of an ageing population on the UK.
    b) Give two economic effects of an ageing population on the UK.
15) Give one way that the UK government has tried to overcome the negative effects of an ageing population.

## Changing UK Economy (p.116-118)
16) Briefly describe how the economy of the UK has changed between 2001 and now.
17) Give one example each of an industry in the primary, secondary, tertiary and quaternary sectors.
18) a) What has happened to the number of people employed in secondary industries since 2001?
    b) What has happened to the number of people employed in quaternary industries since 2001?
19) Describe how average working hours have changed since 2001.
20) What is an economic hub?
21) Give three examples of economic hubs in the UK.
22) Give two examples of major industries in South Wales.
23) How is industry in South Wales different now compared to the 19th century?

*If you've studied an economic hub other than South Wales, you can answer about that instead.*

## UK's Global Significance (p.119-121)
24) Give two examples of international organisations that the UK is a member of.
25) a) Give an example of an international conflict that the UK has been involved in trying to resolve.
    b) Describe one way in which an international organisation involving the UK has reacted to this conflict.
26) Name two media products that the UK exports.
27) Give two ways in which media exports may have influenced people in other countries.
28) a) Give one example each of ethnic media and fashion.
    b) For each example, give one way in which it has influenced UK life or culture.

# Topic 8 — Resource Reliance

## Resource Supply and Demand

*Resources* are just all the things that we *use* — and in this case we're talking about *food*, *water* and *energy*.

### Everyone Needs Food, Energy and Water

Resources, such as food, energy and water, are needed for basic human development:
1) Food — without enough nutritious food, people can become malnourished. This makes them more likely to get ill, and may stop them from working or doing well at school.
2) Energy — a good supply of energy is needed for a basic standard of living, e.g. to provide lighting and heat for cooking. It's also essential for industry and transport.
3) Water — people need a constant supply of clean, safe water for drinking, cooking and washing. Water is also needed to produce food, clothes and lots of other products.

### Demand for Resources is Increasing

Consumption of food, water and energy around the world is increasing. There are two main reasons for this:

#### 1 Rising Population

1) The global population is increasing — in 2011 it was just over 7 billion and it's expected to reach 9 billion by 2040. More people require more resources.
2) Increased demand for one resource can increase demand for another — e.g. more people means that more food needs to be grown, which increases demand for water.

#### 2 Economic Development

1) Economic development means that people are getting wealthier, especially in emerging and developing countries (EDCs — see p.92).
2) Wealthier people have more disposable income, which affects their resource consumption:
   - They have more money to spend on food and they often buy more than they need.
   - They can afford cars, fridges, televisions etc., all of which use energy. Manufacturing these goods and producing energy to run them also uses a lot of water.
   - More people can afford flushing toilets, showers, dishwashers etc. This increases water use.

### Supply of Resources isn't Increasing Fast Enough

Many countries are trying to increase supplies of food, water and energy. However, there are also lots of factors that limit these supplies, meaning that supply can't meet demand. For example:

1) Climate — some countries have very low rainfall, so water supplies are limited. This also limits how much food they can grow. Climate change may change rainfall patterns, affecting water availability and crop growth (see p.30).
2) Geology — some countries don't have reserves of fossil fuels such as coal and oil, and may not have a suitable landscape for generating renewable energy from e.g. wind or hydropower. Geology can also limit water supply — when rain falls on permeable rock, e.g. sandstone, it flows into the rock and can form underground water stores that are hard to get to.
3) Conflict — war can disrupt transport of resources, e.g. by damaging roads, water pipes or power lines.
4) Poverty — some countries can't afford the technology (e.g. agricultural machinery, nuclear power plants) to exploit the natural resources that are available.
5) Natural hazards — events such as tropical storms, earthquakes and volcanic eruptions can damage agricultural land and destroy infrastructure such as water pipes and power lines.

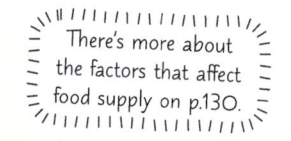

*There's more about the factors that affect food supply on p.130.*

### People in richer countries consume more food, water and energy

That was a quick dash through some pretty big ideas. There's more coming up on the effects of resource supply and demand — if you can get your head round this page, it'll really help with the rest of the topic, so read it again.

# Human Use of the Environment

*We humans change the **environment** to get more food, energy and water, but it's **not trouble-free**...*

## Farming is Becoming More Mechanised

1) Since the 1960s, there has been a growth in large-scale, industrial farming where processes are increasingly done by machines, e.g. tractors and combine harvesters, rather than people.
2) Industrial farming can increase the amount of food that can be produced, because processes such as milking, ploughing and harvesting can be done more quickly.
3) However, changes to farms have had impacts on ecosystems and the environment:

- Field sizes have increased so that food can be produced more cheaply. Removal of hedgerows has led to a decline in biodiversity.
- The amount of chemicals used in food production has been increasing — large quantities of artificial fertilisers and pesticides are applied to crops, and animals are given special feed to encourage growth. If they enter water courses (e.g. rivers), these chemicals can harm or kill organisms.
- Increased use of heavy machinery, e.g. in planting and harvesting, can cause soil erosion.

## Commercial Fishing Methods Increase Fish Catches

1) Global demand for fish is increasing. Most fish and seafood is provided by commercial fishing methods — these include trawling (towing huge nets behind boats) and dredging (dragging a metal frame along the seabed to harvest shellfish such as oysters and scallops).
2) Since the 1950s, fishing has become increasingly mechanised — this means that boats can now carry bigger nets and haul in bigger catches than used to be possible, helping to meet demand for fish.
3) Fish farms (aquaculture) are also being used to breed fish and shellfish in contained spaces.
4) Commercial fishing is having a number of impacts on ecosystems and the environment:

- Over-fishing of some fish (e.g. cod) means that some species are now endangered. Decreasing the number of one species in an ecosystem can have knock-on impacts on other species (see p.57).

- Dredging can damage seafloor habitats and disturb organisms such as sea urchins and starfish.

- Fish farms are often overcrowded, and the large number of fish produce a lot of waste. If this waste is released into the natural environment, it can cause large blooms of algae. The algae absorb a lot of oxygen from the water, causing other plants and animals to die.

## New farming and fishing methods are having an environmental impact

Many new farming and fishing methods are very damaging for wildlife, but remember that they're beneficial too — they've allowed us to produce more food and keep up with the increasing demand (see p.130).

Topic 8 — Resource Reliance

# Human Use of the Environment

*It's not just our **demand for food** that's causing **damage** to the **environment** — our **need for energy** is too.*

## Demand for Energy is Increasing Deforestation

1) Deforestation is the removal of trees from forests. Increasing energy demand increases deforestation — trees are burnt as fuel or cleared to make way for power stations.

2) In some countries where a large river runs through an area of forest (e.g. the Amazon River in the Amazon rainforest in Brazil), forest is being destroyed to make way for hydroelectric power (HEP) stations. HEP provides renewable energy that will help us meet our increasing energy needs. However, the initial construction of HEP stations involves building a dam, which floods large areas of forest.

3) Deforestation has many environmental impacts:

- Trees remove $CO_2$ from the atmosphere, and burning vegetation to clear forest releases $CO_2$. So deforestation means more $CO_2$ in the atmosphere, which adds to global warming (see p.29).
- Forests provide an important habitat — around 70% of all land-based plant and animal species live in forests. If the forests are cut down, these habitats are lost and species may die out.
- Removing trees exposes the soil and makes it easier to erode — eroded soil can enter rivers and streams, damaging the habitats of fish and other freshwater organisms.
- Trees intercept rainfall, so removing them makes flooding more likely — this can damage habitats.

## Mining has Environmental Impacts

1) Fossil fuels, e.g. coal, gas and oil, are a major source of energy. They are removed from the ground by mining.

2) Surface mining is where large areas of vegetation, soil and rock are stripped away so that miners can reach the materials they want. Sub-surface mining involves digging deep shafts below the ground surface.

3) Recently, a technique called fracking has been developed to extract shale gas — natural gas that is trapped underground in shale rock. Liquid is pumped into the rock at high pressure. This causes the rock to crack (fracture), releasing the gas, which is then collected as it comes out of the production well.

4) Mining has lots of impacts on the environment and ecosystems:

- Waste from mines can pollute soil, groundwater, drinking water and air. Pollutants include mercury and lead, which are very toxic to plants, animals and people.
- Habitats are destroyed to make way for mines, leading to loss of biodiversity.
- Mining uses a huge amount of water (a limited resource).
- Coal, oil and gas are not sustainable energy sources. They're non-renewable, and release $CO_2$ when they're burned — this contributes to global warming (see p.29).

### Energy production can affect the environment and ecosystems

**REVISION TIP:** Make a table to help you remember these environmental impacts — have one column for deforestation and one for mining. Describe each impact simply, e.g. habitat loss, to help you to remember them all.

Topic 8 — Resource Reliance

# Human Use of the Environment

*Reservoirs* and methods of *water transfer* are often needed to *improve the water supply* in an area.

## Reservoirs Can Provide a Reliable Water Supply

1) Seasonal variations in rainfall or unpredictable rainfall can cause a water shortage at certain times of year. One way of coping with this problem is by increasing storage.
2) Building a dam across a river traps a large amount of water behind the dam, creating a reservoir — this provides a reliable source of water all year. However, dams and reservoirs have environmental impacts:

- Reservoirs flood large amounts of land, destroying habitats and agricultural land.
- Reservoirs impact local ecosystems. Water is often released through the dam at regular intervals making the river flow much more uniform — this often reduces species diversity. Dams also act as a barrier to species' movements, e.g. salmon that migrate upstream to lay their eggs.
- The natural flow of sediment downstream is disrupted, reducing the fertility of areas downstream.
- Reservoirs create new aquatic environments, which can become home to non-native species.

## Water Transfer Moves Water to Places Where It's Needed

1) Water is often not where it is most needed. E.g. the south and east of the UK is much drier than the north and west, and has a higher population density, so there isn't always enough water to go round.
2) Water transfers use canals and pipes to move water from a river that has surplus water to a river that has a water shortage. This can cause problems for ecosystems and the environment:

1) Large-scale engineering works are needed to create new channels. These can damage ecosystems.

2) There may be water shortages in areas where the water is coming from, particularly in dry years. This can put pressure on local ecosystems.

3) Lots of energy is needed to pump the water over long distances if there isn't a natural downhill route. This can release greenhouse gases, adding to climate change.

4) Water transfer schemes often involve building dams and reservoirs (see above).

## Strategies for increasing water supply have environmental costs
These solutions both require large-scale construction projects — they can be very effective in drastically improving water supply, but such large modifications of landscapes and habitats can cause major disruption to ecosystems.

Topic 8 — Resource Reliance

# Food Security

*Food security is a pretty **complex** issue — there are loads of factors that affect **how much food** is available.*

## Food Security is When People Have Enough to Eat

### Food Security
1) Food security is when people have access to enough nutritious food to stay healthy and active.
2) Countries that produce a lot of food or are rich enough to import the food they need have food security.

### Food Insecurity
1) Food insecurity is when people aren't able to get enough food to stay healthy or lead an active life.
2) Countries that don't grow enough to feed their population and can't afford to import the food they need have food insecurity.

## Food Security is Affected by Physical and Human Factors

Food security is affected by how much food is being produced and whether people can access food supplies. Food production and accessibility are affected by both physical and human factors:

**Physical Factors**

1) Climate — countries with climates that are too cold or have too little rainfall can't grow much food. Extreme weather events (e.g. floods and droughts) also affect food supply.
2) Water stress — crops and livestock need water to survive. Areas that have low rainfall or where water for irrigation is scarce struggle to grow enough food.
3) Pests and diseases — pests reduce yields by consuming crops, e.g. rats cause big problems by eating stored grain, and huge locust swarms eat all the vegetation in their path. Diseases affect most crops and livestock and can cause a lot of damage if they spread through crops and herds, e.g. 37% of the world's wheat crops are under threat from a disease called wheat rust.

**Human Factors**

1) Poverty — people living in poverty often can't afford to buy food and often don't have their own land where they can grow food. Poverty also affects people's ability to farm the land effectively, e.g. they may not be able to buy the fertilisers or pesticides they need. At a global scale, poverty means that countries which can't grow enough can't afford to import food from countries with a surplus.
2) Technology — the mechanisation of farm equipment (see p.126) increases the amount of food that can be grown by making the process more efficient. New technologies (e.g. genetic engineering — see p.133) can protect plants from disease and increase their yields.
3) Conflict — fighting may damage agricultural land or make it unsafe, making it difficult to grow enough food. Access to food becomes difficult for people who are forced to flee their homes. Conflicts also make it difficult to import food because trade routes are disrupted and political relationships with supply countries may break down.
4) Over-farming — grazing too much livestock can decrease vegetation cover and cause soil erosion. Intensive arable farming can use up soil nutrients and make the land infertile. In both cases, the land can no longer be used to produce food, unless it's given enough time to recover.
5) Food prices — the prices of certain foods change depending on supply and demand. If the price of basics such as corn and rice increases too much, poorer people can't afford them and go hungry.

---

**EXAM TIP**

## Food insecurity can be caused by many different factors
If you're asked about the causes of food insecurity, think about how one factor could affect others — e.g. an outbreak of disease might cause a shortage of a certain food, which would increase its price.

Topic 8 — Resource Reliance

# Access to Food

*This page is all about which countries **have food**, which **don't**, and what might happen when there's **not enough**...*

## Access to Food Varies Around the World

1) A country's access to food depends on how much it can grow and how much it can afford to import. Generally, richer countries have better access to food — if they can't grow it themselves, they can buy it.

2) There are several ways of showing how access to food varies globally. For example:

The daily calorie intake of people in different countries shows the amount that people eat.

Daily calorie (kcal) intake per person (2011-2013)
- Over 3539
- 3358 to 3539
- 3266 to 3358
- 3095 to 3266
- 2546 to 3095
- Less than 2546
- No data available

The Global Hunger Index shows how many people are suffering from hunger or illness caused by lack of food. The index gives a value for each country from 0 (no hunger) to 100 (extreme hunger). Countries are divided into categories depending on the severity of the problem.

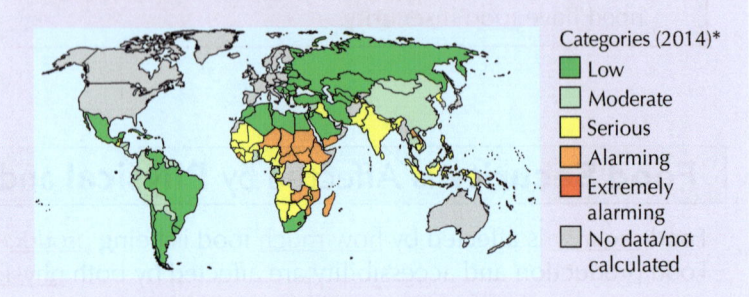

Categories (2014)*
- Low
- Moderate
- Serious
- Alarming
- Extremely alarming
- No data/not calculated

3) Both measures show a similar pattern:
- More developed areas like Europe and North America eat a lot.
- Less developed areas like Africa, Central America and parts of Asia consume less food per person, and more people suffer from hunger and hunger-related illnesses.
- EDCs (see p.92) are eating more and hunger is decreasing as wealth increases, e.g. China.

*The Global Hunger Index doesn't calculate values for advanced countries (see p.92).*

4) However, neither method shows up variations within countries — even in a country with a high calorie intake and a low score on the Global Hunger Index, some people may have limited access to food.

## Malthus and Boserup Had Different Theories About Food Supply

Malthus and Boserup both came up with theories about how population growth and food availability are related:

### Malthus's Theory
- Thomas Malthus was an 18th-century economist. He thought that population would increase faster than food supply. This would mean that eventually there would be too many people for the food available.
- He believed that, when this happened, people would be killed by catastrophes such as famine, illness and war, and the population would return to a level that could be supported by the food available.

### Boserup's Theory
- Ester Boserup was a 20th-century economist. Her theory was that however big the world's population grew, people would always produce sufficient food to meet their needs.
- She thought that, if food supplies became limited, people would come up with new ways to increase production (e.g. by making technological advances) in order to avoid hunger.

Neither theory has been proved completely right or completely wrong. There have been famines in some areas, but on a global scale, food production has so far kept up with population growth.

## Malthusian and Boserupian theories are different

Don't be put off by all the theory — basically, Malthus thought that the size of the population was controlled by food availability, whereas Boserup thought that food availability was controlled by the size of the population.

Topic 8 — Resource Reliance

# Worked Exam Questions

You know the routine by now — work carefully through these examples and make sure you understand them. Then it's on to the real test of doing some exam questions yourself.

1   Study **Figure 1**, a graph showing real and projected changes in global population from 1950 to 2050.

a)  Using **Figure 1** and your own knowledge, describe how changes in global population are affecting demand for resources.

*The global population increased from about 2.6 billion in 1950 to about 7.3 billion in 2015, and is predicted to continue to rise. The increase in population means more resources, e.g. food, water and energy, are required. Increasing demand for one resource can also increase the demand for other resources, e.g. more people means more food needs to be grown, which increases the demand for water.*

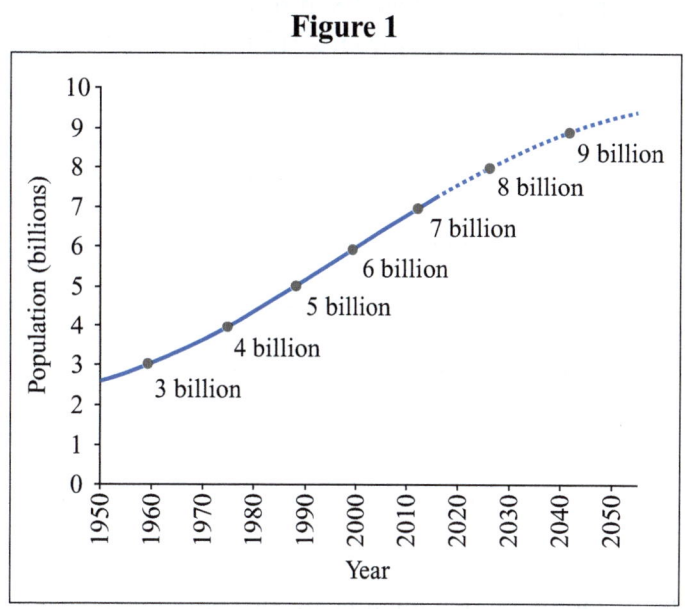

[3]

b)  Outline **one** other factor that is affecting global demand for resources.

*Global economic development is increasing the demand for resources because as people get wealthier they have more money to spend on resources, so consumption increases.*

[2]

[Total 5 marks]

**Figure 1**
(graph showing population in billions from 1950 to 2050: 3 billion, 4 billion, 5 billion, 6 billion, 7 billion, 8 billion, 9 billion)

2   Study **Figure 2**, a table showing forest cover in Terra Spoglio between 1970 and 2010.

a)  Using **Figure 2**, calculate the percentage change in forest cover between 1970 and 2010.

$\frac{4.04 - 5.42}{5.42} \times 100 = -25\%$

[1]

b)  The total area of Terra Spoglio is 19 million hectares. What percentage of Terra Spoglio was covered by forest in 1990?

$\frac{4.89}{19} \times 100 = 26\%$

[1]

**Figure 2**

| Year | Area of forest cover remaining (million ha) |
|---|---|
| 1970 | 5.42 |
| 1980 | 5.40 |
| 1990 | 4.89 |
| 2000 | 4.61 |
| 2010 | 4.04 |

c)  Describe how deforestation can increase energy supply.

*Trees that are cut down can be used as fuel. Deforestation can also make land available for power stations, e.g. HEP stations.*

[2]

[Total 4 marks]

Topic 8 — Resource Reliance

# Exam Questions

**1** Study **Figure 1**, which shows the production of cereals by country from 2012 to 2014.

a) Using **Figure 1**, describe the distribution of countries that produced less than 2.8 million tonnes of cereals from 2012 to 2014.

...........................................................................................................................................

...........................................................................................................................................
[2]

**Figure 1**

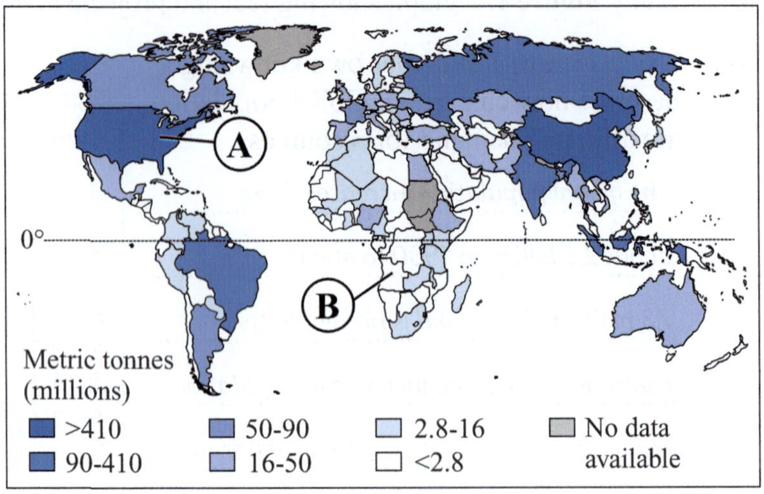

Metric tonnes (millions)
- >410
- 90-410
- 50-90
- 16-50
- 2.8-16
- <2.8
- No data available

b) Outline **one** human factor that could be causing the difference in the quantity of cereals produced by the USA (an advanced country (AC), labelled A in **Figure 1**) and Angola (a low-income developing country (LIDC), labelled B in **Figure 1**).

...........................................................................................................................................

...........................................................................................................................................
[2]

c) Describe what food security means.

...........................................................................................................................................
[1]

d) Explain the physical factors that can contribute to food insecurity.

...........................................................................................................................................

...........................................................................................................................................

...........................................................................................................................................
[4]

[Total 9 marks]

Topic 8 — Resource Reliance

# Increasing Food Production

*If you've read about **food insecurity** on p.129, you'll know that we need to **produce more** food — this page is about ways people are trying to increase food supply in a sustainable way.*

## Attempts to Increase Food Security Can be Sustainable

1) There are lots of ways that food production can be increased to help achieve food security.
2) They can be environmentally, economically and socially sustainable:
   - Environmental sustainability means keeping the environment in a healthy state in the long-term.
   - Economic sustainability means making sure the wealth of individuals and countries continues to grow.
   - Social sustainability means maintaining a high quality of life for everyone indefinitely.

### Organic Farming

1) Organic farming uses natural processes to return nutrients to the soil, so that soil stays fertile and food can continue to be produced. E.g. natural products are used instead of artificial chemicals (e.g. cow manure is used instead of artificial fertilisers), and animals aren't given vaccinations.
2) Limiting artificial chemical use helps to protect natural ecosystems and preserve biodiversity — this makes organic farming more environmentally sustainable than conventional farming.
3) However, organic food is more expensive than non-organic food, so not everyone can afford it — this limits its social sustainability.

### Intensive Farming

*Mechanisation (see p.126) is also an example of intensification of farming.*

1) Intensive farming aims to produce as much food in as small a space as possible. Farmers often use large quantities of fertilisers and pesticides to maximise crop yields. They may also keep animals inside in small spaces and give them food with added antibiotics and growth hormones to prevent disease and encourage growth.
2) Artificial chemicals (e.g. fertilisers, pesticides and antibiotics) can make their way into natural ecosystems and disrupt their balance — i.e. harming some species and favouring others. This reduces the environmental sustainability of intensive farming.
3) These chemicals are also expensive and have to be applied year after year to maintain crop yields — this increases the cost of food production, so it becomes less economically sustainable.

### Genetic Modification

1) Genetically modified (GM) crops allow more food to be grown in smaller areas with fewer resources. For example, GM crops can be designed to have higher yields, resistance to drought, disease or pests (increasing yields and reducing the need for pesticides) or higher nutritional values.
2) Increasing yields and growing more nutritious food increases food security, which makes GM crops more socially sustainable. Decreased use of artificial chemicals means that the cost of food production decreases, so GM crops may be economically sustainable for poorer farmers.
3) However, there are environmental concerns about GM crops, which reduce their sustainability:
   - They may reduce biodiversity because fewer varieties of crops are planted.
   - GM plants may interbreed with wild plants and pass on their genes or disrupt ecosystems.

### Hydroponics

1) Hydroponics is a method of growing plants without soil — plants are grown in a nutrient solution, and are monitored to make sure they get the right amount of nutrients. This maximises crop yield.
2) Less water is required than for plants grown in soil, and reduced risk of disease and pests means less need for pesticides. This increases their environmental sustainability.
3) However, hydroponics is very expensive, so it is currently only used for high-value crops. Not everyone can afford to buy these crops, which makes them less socially sustainable.

---

**EXAM TIP** — **Learn the pros and cons of these food production strategies**
If you're asked how sustainable a method of food production is, think about whether it'll help produce more food in the long-term without costing too much, harming people or damaging the environment.

Topic 8 — Resource Reliance

# Ethical Consumerism

*It's not just food **production** that can be made more sustainable — **consumption** is just as important.*

## Ethical Consumerism Can Help to Increase Food Security

1) Ethical consumerism means choosing to buy goods that have been produced with minimal harm to people and the environment. It's also about how we use goods — e.g. whether we throw lots of food away.
2) Ethical consumerism can help to increase food security and sustainability by:
   - reducing damage to agricultural land caused by food production, so land remains fertile.
   - making food production profitable, so farmers can afford to carry on producing it.
   - paying more money to poorer countries for goods, so poverty decreases.
   - reducing the amount of greenhouse gases emitted by transport and waste disposal. This may help to limit climate change and therefore prevent decreases in food production (see p.30).

## There are Lots of Ways of Making Food Consumption More Ethical

### Buy Fair Trade Products

1) Companies who want to sell products labelled as 'fair trade' have to pay farmers a fair price. This helps farmers in poorer countries make enough to improve their quality of life.
2) Food produced under fair trade schemes is ethical and sustainable because:
   - Buyers pay extra on top of the fair price to help develop the area where the goods come from, e.g. to build schools or health centres. This makes buying fair trade products more socially sustainable.
   - Only producers that treat their employees well can take part in the scheme, e.g. all employees must have a safe working environment. This improves the workers' quality of life.
   - There are rules about how fair trade food is grown — farmers must use environmentally friendly methods that e.g. protect biodiversity, limit greenhouse gas emissions and preserve soil health.

### Reduce Waste

1) Globally, one third of food that is produced is wasted — reducing this will make more food available, so less needs to be grown to feed people. This will increase environmental and social sustainability.
2) Schemes such as 'Think.Eat.Save' and 'Love Food Hate Waste' encourage individuals, businesses and governments to be less wasteful with food. E.g. by helping people plan their meals better and sharing recipe ideas for using up leftovers. They also encourage people to compost waste rather than putting it in the bin (food in landfill sites produces methane, which is a greenhouse gas).
3) Consumers can also choose food that has less packaging — this reduces the amount of resources that are used, and means that less plastic etc. goes into landfill, increasing environmental sustainability.

### Buy Local and Seasonal Food

*Buying organic food is also an example of ethical consumerism (see p.133).*

1) In many wealthy countries, people expect to buy the foods they like all year round. This means that foods have to be imported for all or part of the year.
2) Consumers can choose to eat more food that has been produced locally (e.g. choosing potatoes that have been grown on a nearby farm). They can also eat seasonally — this means eating foods that grow locally at that time of year (e.g. only eating strawberries in summer, when they are grown in the UK).
3) Local and seasonal consumption reduces the amount of food that is imported, which reduces greenhouse gas emissions from transport. This makes it more environmentally sustainable.

## Consumers' food choices can affect how sustainable food supplies are

It's not just farmers and agricultural companies that affect how sustainable food supplies are — what people choose to buy and eat is important too. Learn a few examples of each way of making food consumption more ethical.

Topic 8 — Resource Reliance

# Small-Scale Food Production

*Increasing food security isn't just about giant farms and international schemes. Sometimes, **less is more**.*

## Individuals and Communities Can Increase Food Production

1) Small-scale food production (e.g. growing fruit and vegetables in the garden) is an alternative to large-scale agriculture. It relies on individuals and communities, rather than governments or large organisations — because of this, it's known as a 'bottom-up' approach.
2) It can help to increase food security:
   - Food is grown in gardens, on balconies etc., so overall food production increases.
   - People can grow exactly what they want and pick it fresh each day, which reduces waste.
   - Methods are often organic and non-intensive — this helps keep the land fertile.
   - People are less reliant on expensive imported food, helping poorer people to eat healthily.
3) Small-scale approaches are usually less damaging to the environment than large-scale farming methods.

## Small-Scale Approaches Make Food Supplies More Sustainable

**Permaculture**

1) Permaculture is all about sustainable food production and consumption. People are encouraged to grow their own food and change their eating habits — eating fewer animal products and more fruit and vegetables, and buying local, organic or fair trade food wherever possible.
2) Food is grown in a way that recreates natural ecosystems — this protects the soil and wildlife, so it's environmentally sustainable. It also means that the growing site is low maintenance, so food can be grown with less time and effort — this increases its social sustainability.
3) Food production is designed to keep soils healthy so that crops can continue to grow. For example, mixed cropping is used, which involves having plants of different heights and different types in one area. This means the available space and light are used better, there are fewer pests and diseases and less watering is required. Using few resources increases environmental sustainability.

**Urban Gardens**

1) Urban gardens use spaces such as empty land, roof tops and balconies in towns and cities to grow food. Many urban gardens are community projects, where people work together to grow food and improve their environment.
2) Urban gardens make food locally available, reducing the need to transport food long distances. This means it is often fresher and more nutritious and can also be cheaper — improving the food security of poorer residents.
3) They add greenery to cities, making them healthier and more attractive places to live, so they're socially sustainable. It also makes urban areas less dependent on buying food produced by large-scale agriculture — this can help make it economically and environmentally sustainable.

**Allotments**

1) Allotments are areas of land in villages, towns or cities that are divided into plots and rented to individuals or small groups of people to grow plants, including fruit and vegetables.
2) Many people in towns and cities have little or no garden, so an allotment lets them grow food.
3) Like urban gardens, allotments are environmentally and socially sustainable because they allow people to grow cheap, healthy food close to home.

---

**REVISION TIP**

### Permaculture, urban gardens and allotments work on a small scale
You need to know how these methods improve the environmental, economic and social sustainability of food production. Pick a method and talk about it out loud (just to yourself) to see how much you know.

Topic 8 — Resource Reliance

# UK Food Security

*The way we **grow** food, and the **amount** and **variety** we **consume**, has **changed** dramatically in the **UK** since 1940.*

## Food Consumption Has Decreased Since 1940...

1) Average daily calorie intake in the UK increased from about 2350 in 1940 to about 2600 in 1960, then decreased to about 1750 by 2000.

2) However, this data doesn't include calories from drinks, sweets or meals out. If you include these food types, calorie intake in 2000 was around 2150 — this is still lower than in 1940.

3) There are several reasons for this decrease in consumption:

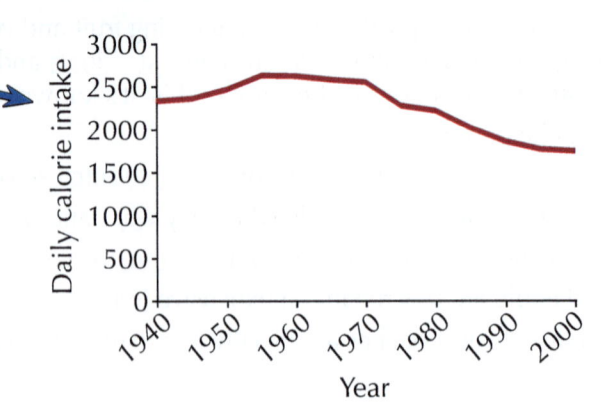

- People were more active in the past, so they needed more calories — fewer people have physical jobs now, and more people own cars and use them instead of e.g. walking or cycling.
- There's more awareness of and concern about obesity and good nutrition now — e.g. the government regularly publishes recommendations that people eat less high-calorie food such as fat and sugar.
- There have been spikes in the cost of food — e.g. the price of wheat and rice peaked in 2008. This can make it difficult for the poorest people to afford food, so their consumption decreases.

## ... but Food Availability Has Increased

1) In the UK, food availability is high — most people have enough to eat. The UK produces about 60% of the food it needs and imports the rest. Food security is affected by where food comes from — e.g. home-grown food availability can decrease if crops fail, and imports can decrease if prices go up.

2) Food availability has changed over time:

- There was less food available during World War II — there were global food shortages, and imports to the UK were disrupted by German attacks on ships carrying food. The UK government introduced rationing of foods such as meat, cheese, eggs and sugar to make sure that everyone had enough.

- The Common Agricultural Policy (CAP) was introduced in the 1950s — it increased production of crops such as wheat by intensifying agriculture (see p.133). Since the 1990s, food production has been more sustainable, and yields have been fairly stable.

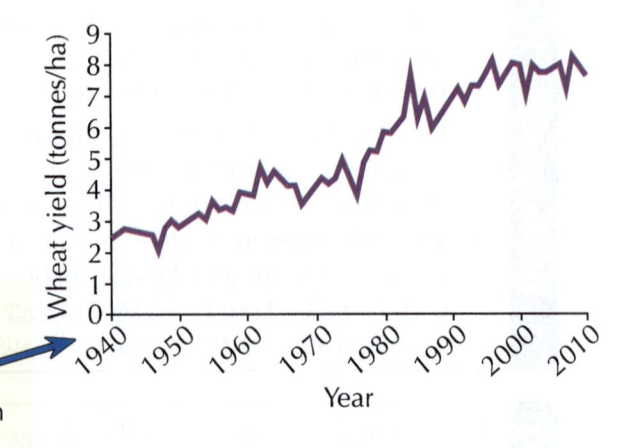

- Since the 1960s, there has been a growing demand for seasonal products (e.g. strawberries) all year round and high-value foods, such as exotic fruits, coffee and spices. Imports of these foods into the UK have increased, so they are constantly available — we produce only 22% of the fruit and vegetables we consume.

## Learn the general trends in UK food consumption and availability

In the UK, there's been a decrease in food consumption and an increase in food availability since the 1940s. Make sure you learn a few of the reasons behind each change so you can explain the trends in the exam.

Topic 8 — Resource Reliance

# UK Food Security

*Food banks increase food security **locally**, while the **intensification of farming** has increased it on a **national scale**.*

## Food Banks Have Helped Increase Food Security in Newcastle

1) Although food availability in the UK is high, there are about 5 million people who don't have enough to eat.
2) One way of tackling this is with food banks — people and companies donate food, which is handed out to those in need. Recipients get a package containing enough nutritious food to last them for three days.
3) One city where food banks are needed is Newcastle — around 8% of people in the city have used one of the food banks there. West End food bank is the busiest in the country, giving food to around 1000 people each week. Food banks in Newcastle have helped increase food security:

   - They help reduce hunger and improve people's diets — this also improves their health.
   - Some shops and bakeries donate unsold fresh food at the end of the day, reducing waste.
   - Some food banks give lessons in cooking and budgeting, to help people with limited money eat healthily and to increase food security in the longer term.

4) However, food banks don't solve underlying problems, such as low wages and benefit cuts.
5) It's difficult for food banks to store fresh food, so a lot of the food that is given out is processed (e.g. biscuits, tinned soup) — this can have lots of added salt and sugar, which can cause health problems in the long-term.

## Intensification Increased Food Supplies in the UK

Intensification of farming from the 1940s to the 1980s was an attempt to increase food security by increasing production. The methods used included:

- Higher yielding crops and animals (developed by breeding individuals that gave higher yields initially).
- Monoculture — growing just one crop over a large area.
- Irrigation technologies, e.g. groundwater pumping, electric sprinklers.
- Chemicals, e.g. fertilisers, pesticides and herbicides.
- Mechanisation, e.g. use of machines for sowing, harvesting, weeding and spraying.

This was effective in increasing food security in the UK — in 1940, the UK imported 70% of its cereal crops, but by 1980 this had decreased to 20%. However, intensification also had negative impacts, such as:

1) Monoculture crops could be wiped out by a single pest, drought or disease, e.g. cereal crop yields decreased by about 500 000 tonnes because of drought in 1976.
2) Intensive methods caused environmental damage, for example:
   - Monoculture reduced biodiversity, especially of flowering plants and insects.
   - The chemicals used caused pollution of land and water, disrupting ecosystems.
   - Over-exploiting the land led to reduced soil fertility and increased soil erosion in some areas.

## There's lots of food in the UK, but not everyone has enough to eat

Intensification of farming has increased the amount of food available and improved food security in the UK as a whole. However, many people cannot afford enough food to eat and rely on food banks for their food security.

Topic 8 — Resource Reliance

# UK Food Security

*As you've seen on the previous page, **intensification** of farming in the UK has **increased food security** in the past. You also need to know about an attempt to improve food security in the **present** — **hydroponics** is a great example.*

## Hydroponics Can Increase Food Security

1) Recently, the UK government has promoted 'sustainable intensification', which aims to increase food security without damaging the environment. One method of sustainable intensification is using new technology, such as hydroponics (see p.133), to increase food production.

2) Hydroponics is used on a large scale in abandoned WWII tunnels under London, and at Thanet Earth in Kent, which produces over 10% of the UK's peppers, cucumbers and tomatoes in huge greenhouses.

3) Hydroponics schemes can help to increase food security in the UK, and they have other benefits:

- Salad vegetables can be grown in the UK all year round, reducing reliance on imports. This means that the UK is less likely to be affected by e.g. shortages or price increases of food.

- Food can be grown in spaces that would otherwise not be used (e.g. underground tunnels), so food production increases overall.

- Many schemes aim to be environmentally sustainable — e.g. they recycle water and use natural predators to kill pests — this reduces the need for artificial pesticides.

- They also create jobs, e.g. Thanet Earth employs 500 people.

4) However, they also have some disadvantages:

- Schemes can be expensive to set up and run, which increases the cost of the food produced — this may mean that some people can't afford it.

- Some schemes, e.g. Thanet Earth, have been built in rural areas, so natural habitats have been lost.

- Schemes like Thanet Earth require a large amount of energy to power the greenhouses, as well as to package and deliver the produce to the shops.

## There are pros and cons to hydroponic schemes in the UK

You need to know about food security in one country — it doesn't have to be the UK. Just make sure you know about one attempt to improve food security at a local scale (e.g. food banks), and one past and one present attempt to achieve food security at a national scale too (e.g. intensification of farming and hydroponics) for that country.

Topic 8 — Resource Reliance

# Worked Exam Questions

Exams can be pretty scary, but the best preparation you can do is practise answering exam questions.
Read this page to get an idea of how to answer them, then turn over and have a go at the next lot yourself.

1   Study **Figure 1**, which shows the annual income of a farmer in Mali between 2006 and 2014. He joined a fair trade cooperative in 2008.

**Figure 1**

a)  In 2014, the farmer earned £490.
    Complete the graph using this information.
    *[1]*

b)  What was the farmer's income in 2011?
    *£380*
    *[1]*

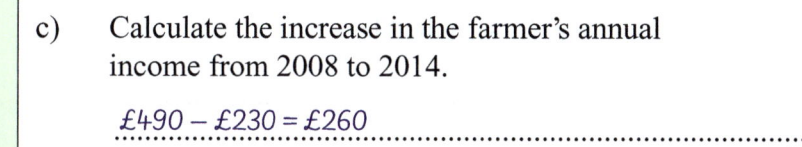

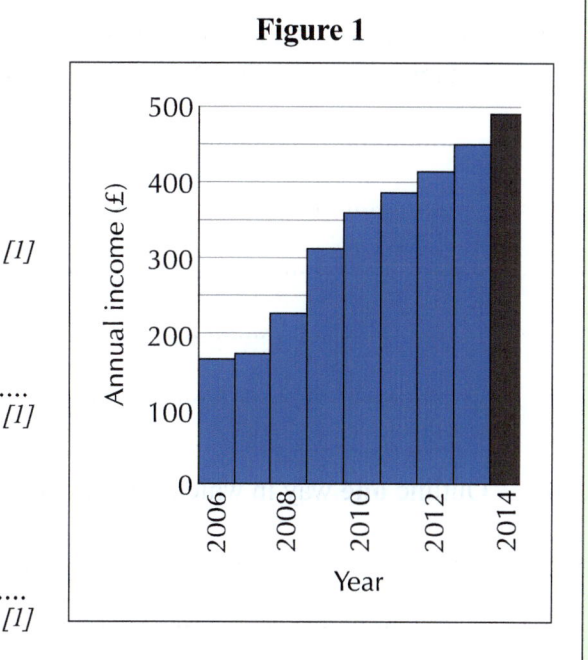

c)  Calculate the increase in the farmer's annual income from 2008 to 2014.
    *£490 − £230 = £260*
    *[1]*

d)  Other than buying fairly traded goods, outline **one** way of making food consumption more ethical.
    *Reducing food waste by e.g. using leftovers, means that less food needs to be produced,*
    *which helps to protect the environment.*
    *[2]*
    *[Total 5 marks]*

2   For a country you have studied, evaluate the success of a local-scale attempt to increase food security.

*Food banks in Newcastle hand out donated food to people in the local area who don't have enough to eat. Many people have been helped by food banks, with around 8% of people in Newcastle having used one. The food banks help people by reducing their hunger and improving their diets, so they have increased food security there. Shops donate fresh food that would not otherwise be sold, so waste is reduced, and many food banks offer advice on cooking and budgeting, to increase food security in the longer-term. However, the food banks don't solve underlying problems, such as low wages and benefit cuts, and some of the food given out isn't very healthy, which may cause health problems for people. In conclusion, food banks in Newcastle have successfully increased food security in the short term but can't solve all the problems in the longer term.*

*[Total 6 marks]*

Topic 8 — Resource Reliance

# Exam Questions

1 Study **Figure 1**, a graph showing the area of land used to grow organic crops in Finland from 1999 to 2015.

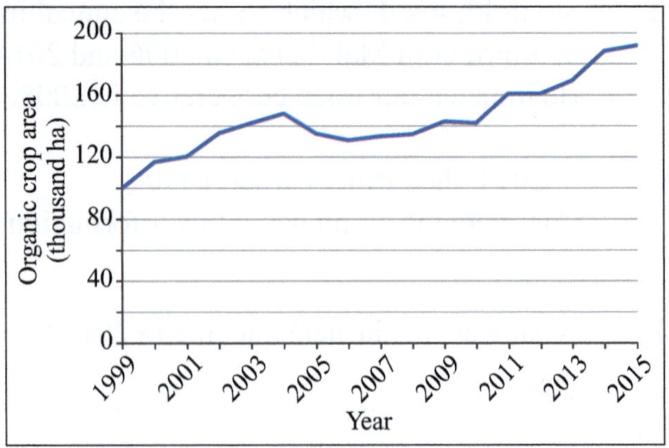

a) Describe how the area of land used to grow organic crops changed from 1999 to 2015.

...................................................................
...................................................................
...................................................................
...................................................................
...................................................................
[2]

**Figure 1**

b) Outline **one** way in which organic farming is environmentally sustainable.

...................................................................................................................................
...................................................................................................................................
...................................................................................................................................
[2]

c) Which of the following is a way of intensifying farming? Shade **one** oval only.

    A    Reducing the amount of resources used. ◯

    B    Increasing the size of the area in which food is produced. ◯

    C    Increasing the amount of chemicals used on crops. ◯

    D    Ensuring animals have access to outside space. ◯

[1]

d) Assess how far technological developments that increase food production are sustainable.

...................................................................................................................................
...................................................................................................................................
...................................................................................................................................
...................................................................................................................................
...................................................................................................................................
...................................................................................................................................
...................................................................................................................................
...................................................................................................................................
...................................................................................................................................
[6]

[Total 11 marks]

Topic 8 — Resource Reliance

# Revision Summary

Make sure you've remembered all the information on Topic 8 by having a go at these questions.
- Try these questions and tick off each one when you get it right.
- When you've done all the questions under a heading and are completely happy with it, tick it off.

## Resource Use and Production (p.125-128) ☑
1) Give two ways that food is important to people's well-being.
2) Give two ways that energy is important to people's well-being.
3) How can climate limit food supply?
4) What impact might geology have on a country's energy supply?
5) Describe one way in which farming has changed since the 1960s.
6) Give two environmental impacts of commercial fishing.
7) Give three environmental impacts of mining.
8) a) What is water transfer?
   b) Give one way in which it might damage ecosystems.

## Food Supplies (p.129-130) ☑
9) Give a definition of food insecurity.
10) Explain how conflict can affect food security.
11) Briefly describe how food consumption varies around the world.
12) a) What did Malthus believe would happen to food supply as population increased?
    b) What did Boserup believe would happen to food supply as population increased?

## Increasing Food Production (p.133-135) ☑
13) What is meant by environmental sustainability?
14) a) Give two ways that intensive farming can increase food supply.
    b) Give two ways in which intensive farming is unsustainable.
15) Apart from intensive farming, give two ways in which food supply can be increased.
16) What is ethical consumerism?
17) Describe how permaculture can sustainably increase food supply.

## UK Food Security (p.136-138) ☑
18) True or false: daily calorie consumption in the UK is higher now than in 1940.
19) How has food availability in the UK changed since 1940?
20) How did the Common Agricultural Policy affect food availability?
21) a) Give one example of a national attempt to increase food security.
    b) Give one advantage of this attempt.
    c) Give one disadvantage of this attempt.

# Geographical Exploration

*Knowing the **facts** isn't quite enough to get you through your exams — you'll also have to use a **Resource Booklet** to answer questions, including one where you'll be asked to come to a **decision** about a geographical dilemma.*

## Geographical Exploration is about Analysing and Interpreting Information

Paper 3 (the Geographical Exploration) tests you on a range of topics from the course.

1) In the exam, you'll be given a Resource Booklet with loads of information about a country.
2) You need to study all the information carefully and work out what it all means.
3) You'll have to answer questions, using the information you're given and your knowledge of Geography from the rest of the course:
   - The questions might be about physical (Our Natural World) or human (People and Society) geography topics, or a mix of the two.
   - They could cover any of the content you've studied during the course.
   - Some questions will only use one source, but for others you'll have to use several sources.
4) There'll also be a longer answer question, where you'll need to make a decision about something related to the information you've been given, and justify that decision (see below).

## There'll be Lots of Different Information Sources in the Resource Booklet

1) The booklet could include several different types of information, such as maps, graphs, photographs, diagrams, statistics, newspaper articles and quotes from people involved.
2) All the information will be related in some way — e.g. you might be given a newspaper article on a non-governmental organisation, photos of a city in an LIDC and a data table about measures of development in that LIDC.
3) The information you're given is there to help you answer the questions in the exam paper. Each question will be linked to certain parts of the Resource Booklet.
4) Some questions will probably ask you to demonstrate geographical skills, including reading graphs and charts (see pages 157-161) and calculating statistics (see pages 162-163).
5) Questions with extended written answers will ask you to refer to information in the Resource Booklet.

## The Final Question is a Decision-Making Exercise

1) You'll be asked to make a decision about something using the information, e.g. suggesting a strategy for how an area could best be managed to meet the needs of everyone involved. There's no single right or wrong answer — but you need to be able to justify your decision, so make sure you can use the information to support it.

2) Whatever your decision is, you need to write a balanced answer. Try to think of the potential economic, political, social and environmental impacts of your decision, and how any negative impacts could be reduced.

3) The question is likely to be about a complex issue with lots of different parties involved. So think about possible conflicts that your decision might cause between different groups of people, or between people and the environment, and how they could be resolved.

## You'll need to justify your decision by giving reasons why you chose it

Paper 3 may seem daunting, but don't panic — make sure you're comfortable writing about what you've learnt in the rest of the course, and use the information you're given. Do that and you're well on the way to exam success.

# Fieldwork

*For your Geography GCSE you need to complete **two** bits of **fieldwork** — you'll be asked about them in the exam.*

## You have to Write About **Two Geographical Enquiries** in the Exam

1) Fieldwork is assessed in the second part (Section B) of Papers 1 and 2. There's no assessed coursework, but you need to be able to write about fieldwork that you have done in the exam.
2) You need to have done at least one human and one physical geographical enquiry. You will be asked about the physical one in Paper 1 and the human one in Paper 2.
3) The fieldwork part of the exam has two types of questions:
   - In some questions you'll be asked about fieldwork techniques in unfamiliar situations. You might have to answer questions about techniques for collecting data, how to present data you've been given or how useful the different techniques are.
   - In some questions you have to answer questions about your investigation — you might be asked about your question or hypothesis, methods, what data you collected and why, how you presented and analysed it, how you could extend your research and so on.

*'Geographical enquiry' is just fancy exam-speak for fieldwork.*

## For **Each** of your **Enquiries**, You'll **Need to Know**...

### 1) Why You Chose Your Question

You'll need to explain why the question or hypothesis you chose is suitable for a geographical enquiry.

You'll also need to know the geographical theory behind your question.

Make sure you know what the risks associated with collecting your data were, how they were reduced, and why the location you chose was suitable.

### 2) How and Why You Collected Data

You need to describe and justify what data you collected. This includes whether it was primary data (data that you collected yourself) or secondary data (data that someone else collected and you used), why you collected or used it, how you measured it and how you recorded it.

### 3) How You Processed and Presented Your Data

The way you presented your data, and why you chose that option, could come up.

You'll need to describe what you did (e.g. what maps, graphs and diagrams you used), explain why it was appropriate, and how you adapted your presentation method for your data. You might also be asked for a different way you could have presented your data.

*There's more on analysing, concluding and evaluating on pages 144-145.*

### 4) What Your Data Showed

You'll need to know:
- A description of your data.
- How you analysed your data.
- An explanation of your data.

This might include links between your data sets, the statistical techniques you used, and any anomalies (odd results) in the data that you spotted.

You might have to link your data to geographical theory and case studies.

*There's more on graphs and statistical techniques on pages 157-163.*

### 5) The Conclusions You Reached

You'll need to summarise your data and explain how it provides evidence to answer the question or support the hypothesis you set at the beginning.

### 6) What Went Well, What Could Have Gone Better

You might be asked to evaluate your fieldwork:
- Were there problems in your data collection methods?
- Were there limitations in your data?
- What other data would it have been useful to have?
- How reliable are your conclusions?
- How did it improve your geographical understanding?

## Plan your fieldwork before you start...

... but don't worry if it doesn't quite go to plan. It's more important that you can write about it and say why things went wrong. It does help if you at least attempt to make it work though — so have another read through the page.

# Analysing and Concluding

*Analysing* your data and drawing *conclusions* from it can be pretty tricky — here's a summary of what you need to do, and there's some more help with *analysing data* on pages 157-163.

## You need to Describe and Explain what the Data Shows

When you analyse and interpret data, you need to:

### Describe

1) Describe what the data shows — you need to describe any patterns and correlations (see pages 157-161) and look for any anomalies.
2) Make sure you use specific points from the data and reference what graph, table etc. you're talking about.
3) You might also need to make comparisons between different sets of data.
4) Statistical techniques (see pages 162-163) help make the data more manageable, so it's easier to spot patterns and make comparisons.

*You might be asked to do some calculations based on results you have been given in the exam.*

### Explain

1) Explain what the data shows — you need to explain why there are patterns and why different data sets are linked together.
2) Use your geographical knowledge to help you explain the results and remember to use geographical terms.

Here's an example:

> 38% of people who visited Cliffthorpe Valley in 2016 visited the tarn — 40 000 people (see Diagram 1). The tarn area may attract visitors due to its beauty and services such as a free car park, café and tourist information centre (see Leaflet 1). However, the largest amount of litter was found at the valley head (see Graph 1), which was the fourth most popular attraction (9.5% of visitors). There are fewer bins at the valley head, and more people tend to picnic there (see Table 1), which could be why there's more litter.

## Conclusions are a Summary of the Results

A conclusion is a summary of what you found out in relation to the original question. It should include:

*Be careful when drawing conclusions. Some results show a link or correlation, but that doesn't mean that one thing causes the other.*

1) A summary of what your results show.
2) An answer for the question you are investigating, and an explanation for why that is the answer.
3) An explanation of how your conclusion fits into the wider geographical world — think about how your conclusion and results could be used by other people or in further investigations.

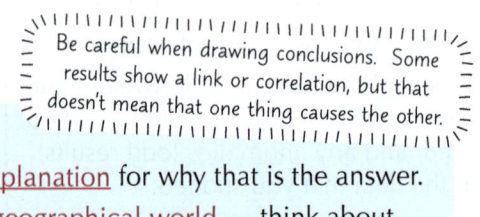

---

**EXAM TIP** — **You'll have to analyse your own data and data you're given**
In the exam, you'll need be able to write about how you analysed your data and your conclusion, so make sure you have some points ready before you hit the exam. You might also be asked to analyse some data that you're given and draw conclusions from it — the more practice you get now, the easier that'll be.

Fieldwork

# Evaluating

*Evaluating* data is all about working out how **accurate** it is, and whether it lets you **answer** your research question. You also need to think about how your investigation could be **improved** if you were to do it again.

## Evaluations Identify Problems in the Investigation

Evaluation is all about self assessment — looking back at how good or bad your study (or the data you are given in the exam) was. You need to be able to:

1) Identify any problems with the methods used and suggest how they could be improved. Think about things like the size of the data sets, if any bias (unfairness) slipped in and if other methods would have been more appropriate or more effective.

2) Describe how accurate the results are and link this to the methods used — say whether any errors in the methods affected the results.

3) Comment on the validity of your conclusion. You need to talk about how problems with the methods and the accuracy of the results affect the validity of the conclusion. Problems with methods lead to less reliable and accurate results, which affects the validity of the conclusion.

| Accurate | Reliable | Valid |
|---|---|---|
| Accurate results are as near as possible to the true answer — they have few errors. | Reliable means that data can be reproduced. | Valid means that the data answers the original question and is reliable. |

For example:

> I concluded that the river flowed faster further downstream. However, one problem with my data collection method was that it was difficult to put the float in at exactly the same point each time. This reduced the accuracy of my measurements. To make my investigation more accurate, I could have placed a tape measure across the river to mark the exact point of entry. Another problem was that I only took two readings at each site and I only used one upstream site and one downstream site. To make my data more reliable I could have taken more readings at each site, and used a larger number of sites both upstream and downstream. These improvements would have produced a more valid conclusion.

## Be critical of your results — if you think some are unreliable, say so

You can do some preparation for this bit as you're going along. While you're collecting your data, think about whether your results would be different if you'd chosen a different day or time, or if you were in a different location. Explain how they'd be different, and why. And don't forget to discuss the validity of your conclusions.

Fieldwork

# Worked Exam Questions

Remember, in the exam you'll be asked to write about someone else's fieldwork as well as about your own. Here are a couple of worked examples, and then you can practise both types of question on the next page.

1   A student wanted to investigate how people's food shopping habits have changed over time. As part of his fieldwork enquiry, he collected data on the amount of organic food that people buy. The data was collected through a door-to-door survey in a village with an organic farm shop. The results are shown in **Figure 1**.

a) Complete the graph to show that nine households in the survey buy 20-29% of their weekly shop from organic sources. *[1]*

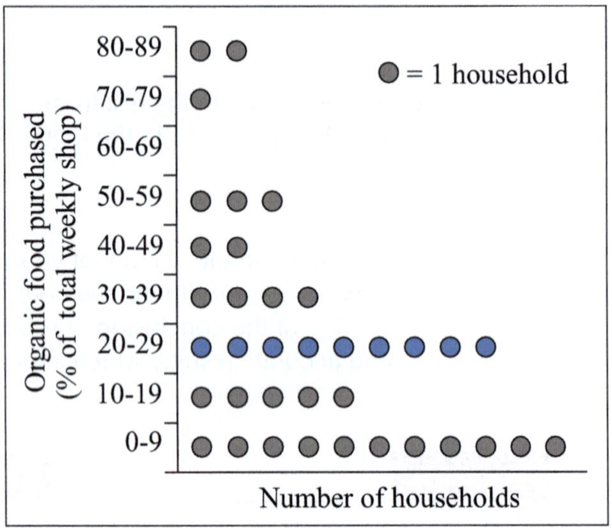

b) What is the modal class of the data shown in **Figure 1**?

   *0-9%* *[1]*

c) Outline **one** limitation of the data collection technique used in this enquiry.

   *People may not know what proportion of their weekly shop is organic so their answer may be inaccurate.* *[2]*

   *[Total 4 marks]*

**Figure 1**

(dot plot: Organic food purchased (% of total weekly shop) vs Number of households; ● = 1 household)

2   This question is about your **physical geography** fieldwork.

a) Justify **one** of the primary data collection techniques that you used.

   *I analysed pebble size at different points along the river to find out how it changed due to attrition.*
   *I took a random sample of 10 pebbles at every site to make sure that the data collected was reliable.*
   *The data showed that pebble size decreased as the distance from the source of the river increased,*
   *so I was able to answer my original question.* *[3]*

b) Outline **two** strengths of **one** of the data presentation techniques that you used.

   **Data presentation technique:** *Pie charts*

   **Strength 1:** *Pie charts clearly show the proportion of each class of data investigated, so using a pie chart for each place makes it easy to see the patterns between different places.*

   **Strength 2:** *Pie charts allow a large amount of data to be summarised, so pie charts make the data easier to understand.* *[4]*

   *[Total 7 marks]*

Fieldwork

# Exam Questions

**1** This question is about your **human geography** fieldwork.

*You might not have completed your fieldwork yet — don't do this question until your enquiry is finished.*

a) Justify the data presentation technique(s) you used.

...................................................................................................................................................
...................................................................................................................................................
...................................................................................................................................................
...................................................................................................................................................
...................................................................................................................................................
[4]

b) Outline **one** way in which your data collection methods could have been improved.

...................................................................................................................................................
...................................................................................................................................................
...................................................................................................................................................
[2]
[Total 6 marks]

**2** A student wanted to investigate how wave characteristics affect the cross-profile of a beach. **Figure 1** shows the method she used to find the cross-profile of the beach. She measured the profile at three points along the beach.

a) Describe **two** possible sources of inaccuracy in the method used.

**Figure 1**

Angle between ranging poles, measured with a clinometer
Ranging poles placed at 5m intervals
5m
Beach
Sea
Measurements started at low tide mark and repeated to top of beach

**Source 1:** ....................................................
...................................................................
...................................................................

**Source 2:** ....................................................
...................................................................
...................................................................
[2]

b) Suggest **one** way in which the reliability of the data could be improved.

...................................................................................................................................................
...................................................................................................................................................
...................................................................................................................................................
[2]
[Total 4 marks]

# Geographical Skills

## Answering Questions

*This section is filled with **techniques** and **skills** that you need for your **exams**. It's no good learning the **content** of this book if you don't learn the skills you need to pass your exam too. First up, answering questions properly...*

### Make Sure you Read the Question Properly

It's dead easy to misread the question and spend five minutes writing about the wrong thing. Four simple tips can help you avoid this:

1) Figure out if it's a case study question — they helpfully say CASE STUDY in friendly capitals at the start of the question. If you see this, you need to include a case study you've learnt about in your answer.

2) Underline the command words in the question (the ones that tell you what to do):

| Command word | Means write about... |
|---|---|
| Describe | what it's like |
| Explain | why it's like that (i.e. give reasons) |
| Compare | the similarities AND differences |
| Discuss | give both sides of an argument |
| Suggest why | give reasons for |
| Outline | give main points |

Answers to questions with 'explain' in them often include the word 'because' (or 'due to').

When writing about differences, 'whereas' is a good word to use in your answers, e.g. 'HICs have a high level of development whereas LICs have a lower level'.

If a question asks you to describe a pattern (e.g. from a map or graph), make sure you identify the general pattern, then refer to any anomalies (things that don't fit the general pattern). E.g. to answer 'describe the global distribution of volcanoes', first say that they're mostly on plate margins, then mention that a few aren't (e.g. in Hawaii).

3) Underline the key words (the ones that tell you what it's about), e.g. volcanoes, tourism, migration, counter-urbanisation, debt relief.

4) If the question says 'using Fig. 2', make sure you've talked about what Figure 2 shows. Don't just write out all of your geographical knowledge and forget all about the photo you're supposed to be talking about. Re-read the question and your answer when you've finished, just to check.

### Some Questions are Level Marked

Questions worth 6 marks or more with longer written answers are level marked, which means you need to do these things to get the top level and a high mark:

1) Read the question properly and figure out a structure for your answer before you start. Your answer needs to be well organised and structured, and written in a logical way.

2) If it's a case study question, include plenty of relevant details:

- This includes things like place names, dates, statistics, names of organisations or companies.
- Don't forget that they need to be relevant though — it's no good including the exact number of people killed in a flood when the question is about the causes of a flood.

3) One of the questions in each paper has 3 extra marks available for spelling, punctuation, grammar and specialist terminology (SPaG). To get top marks you need to:

- Make sure your spelling, punctuation and grammar are consistently correct.
- Write in a way that makes it clear what you mean.
- Use a wide range of geographical terms (e.g. sustainable development) correctly.

*SPaG questions are marked with a pencil symbol (✎).*

---

### Answers to level marked questions should be well structured

This stuff may all seem a bit simple to you, but it's really important to understand what you're being asked to do. It can be tricky — sometimes the differences between the meanings of the command words are quite subtle.

# Labelling and Comparing

*These next few pages give you some advice on what to do for **specific types** of questions. First up, here's how you should answer questions that ask you to **label** or **compare** things.*

## You Might Have to Label Photos, Diagrams or Maps

If you're asked to label something:

1) Figure out from the question what the labels should do, e.g. describe the effects of an earthquake, label the features of a landform, identify human influences on the landscape, etc.
2) Add at least as many labels as there are marks.
3) When describing the features talk about things like the size, shape and relief. Make sure you use the correct geographical names of any features, e.g. arête, wave cut platform, meander.

**Q: Label the characteristics of this coastline**

A:
- Arch caused by wave erosion (abrasion and hydraulic power).
- Cave
- Cracks and weaknesses in the rock making it susceptible to erosion.
- Stack formed from a collapsed arch.
- Some vegetation on top of the cliffs.
- Sandstone cliffs, easily eroded.

## Look at Shapes When You Compare Plans and Photos

You might be given two items, like a plan and an aerial photograph, and be asked to use them together to answer some questions. Plans and aerial photos are a bit like maps — they show places from above. Here are some tips for questions that use plans and photos:

1) The plan and photo might not be the same way up.
2) Work out how the photo matches the plan — look for the main features on the plan like a lake, a big road or something with an interesting shape, and find them on the photo.
3) Look at what's different between the plan and the photo and think about why it might be different.

Q: Look at the development plan for Crystal Bay (2000) and the photo taken after development in 2009.
  a) Name the area labelled A in the photo.
  b) Give two differences you can see between the photo and the plan.

A: a) Madeleine Park
   b) The roads have been built in slightly different areas. There's a small harbour area in front of the apartments.

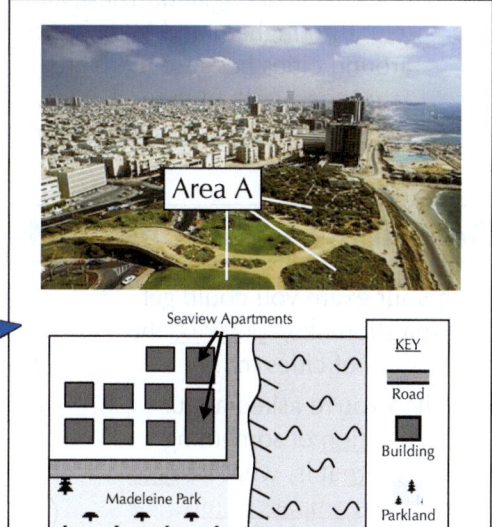

### Read the question carefully

**EXAM TIP:** Check what the question is asking you to label — you might just have to write a name, or you might have to add a bit more detail. If you're just asked for a name, you won't get extra marks for writing more.

Geographical Skills

# Maps

*Maps* are a **staple** of most Geography exams, so make sure you know how to **read** them.

## Latitude and Longitude are Used for Global Coordinates

1) The position of anywhere on Earth can be given using coordinates if you use latitude and longitude.
2) Lines of latitude run horizontally around the Earth. They measure how far north or south from the equator something is.
3) Lines of longitude run vertically around the Earth. They measure how far east or west from the Prime Meridian (a line of longitude running through Greenwich in London) something is.
4) Latitude and longitude are measured in degrees.
5) For example, the coordinates of London are 51° N, 0° W. New York is at 40° N, 74° W.

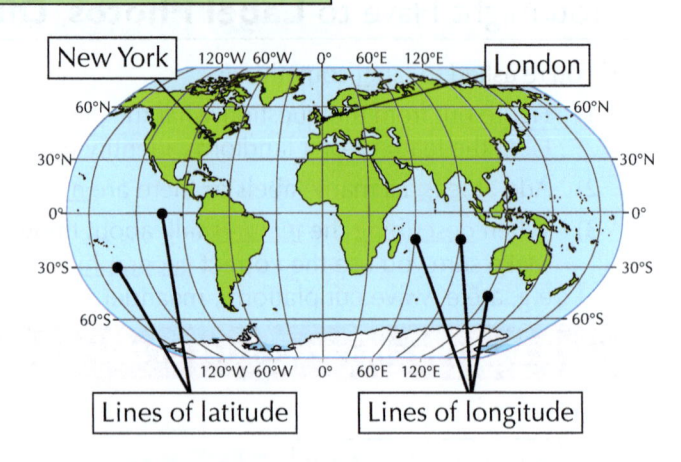

## Describing Distributions on Maps — Describe the Pattern

1) In your exam you could get questions like, 'use the map to describe the distribution of volcanoes' and 'explain the distribution of deforestation'.
2) Describe the general pattern and any anomalies (things that don't fit the general pattern).
3) Make at least as many points as there are marks and use names of places and figures if they're given.
4) If you're asked to give a reason or explain, you need to describe the distribution first.

Figure 1 — Population density of Britain

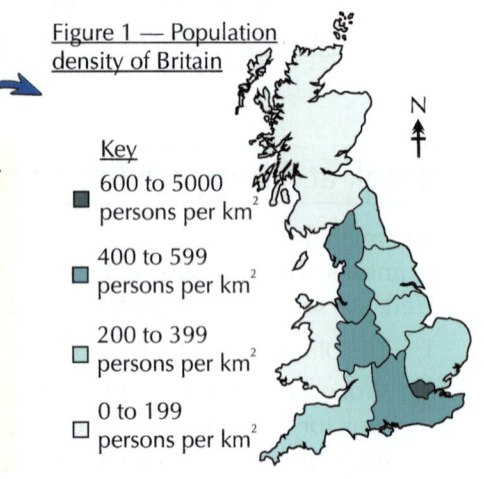

Key
- 600 to 5000 persons per km$^2$
- 400 to 599 persons per km$^2$
- 200 to 399 persons per km$^2$
- 0 to 199 persons per km$^2$

Q: Use Figure 1 to explain the pattern of population density in Britain.
A: The London area has a very high population density (600 to 5000 per km²). There are also areas of high population density (400 to 599 per km²) in the south east, Midlands and north west of England. These areas include major cities (e.g. Birmingham and Manchester). More people live in and around cities because there are better services and more job opportunities than in rural areas. Scotland and Wales have the lowest population densities in Britain (less than 199 per km²)...

## Describing Locations on Maps — Include Details

1) In your exam you could get a question like, 'describe the location of cities in ....'.
2) When you're asked about the location of something say where it is, what it's near and use compass points.
3) If you're asked to give a reason or explain, you need to describe the location first.

*You could be given two maps to use for one question — link information from the two maps together.*

Q: Use the maps to describe the location of the National Parks.

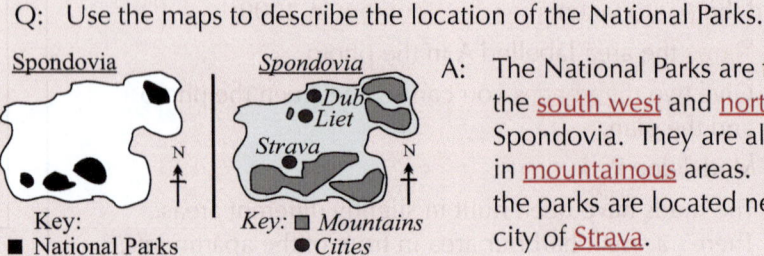

Spondovia — Key: ■ National Parks
Spondovia — Key: ■ Mountains ● Cities (Dub, Liet, Strava)

A: The National Parks are found in the south west and north east of Spondovia. They are all located in mountainous areas. Three of the parks are located near to the city of Strava.

## Learn the basics of reading and describing maps

It's really worth learning how to write detailed descriptions of distributions and locations — all the exam papers are likely to feature some kind of map, so read over this page carefully to make sure that you're well prepared.

Geographical Skills

# Maps

*These next few pages are all about **types of maps** that you might have to describe or interpret in the exam.*

## Dot Maps Show Distribution and Quantity Using Identical Symbols...

1) Dot maps use identical dots to show how something is distributed across an area.
2) Use the key to find out what quantity each dot represents.

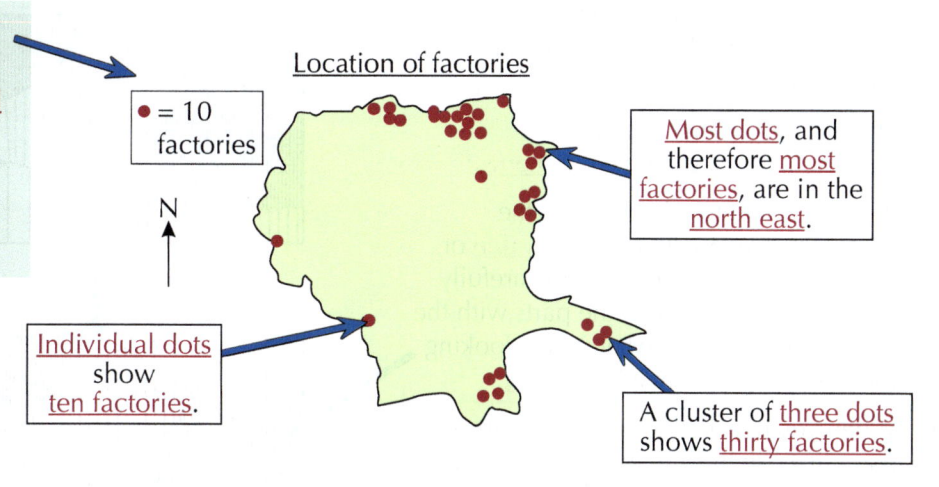

Location of factories

● = 10 factories

Most dots, and therefore most factories, are in the north east.

Individual dots show ten factories.

A cluster of three dots shows thirty factories.

## ...Proportional Symbol Maps use Symbols of Different Sizes

Car Parks in Drumshire

● 1
● 5
● 10

1) Proportional symbol maps use symbols of different sizes to represent different quantities.
2) A key shows the quantity each different sized symbol represents. The bigger the symbol, the larger the amount.
3) The symbols might be circles, squares, semi-circles or bars, but a larger symbol always means a larger amount.

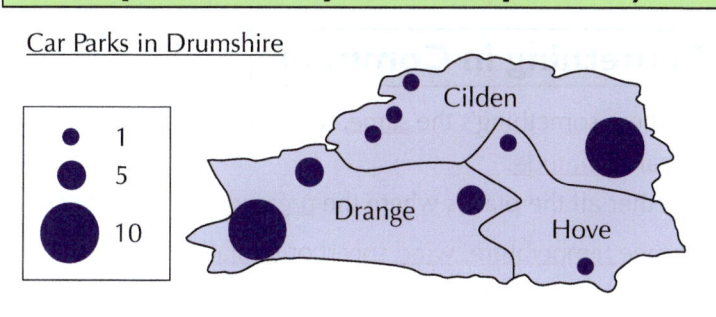

Q: Which area of Drumshire has the most car parks?
A: Drange, with 20.

## Thematic Maps show Information about a Theme

1) Thematic maps are used to show how a particular theme (e.g. weather, life expectancy, birth rate) varies across an area.
2) For example, this map shows how the average temperature varies across an area.
3) To read a thematic map you need to look carefully at the key to see what the colours or symbols stand for.

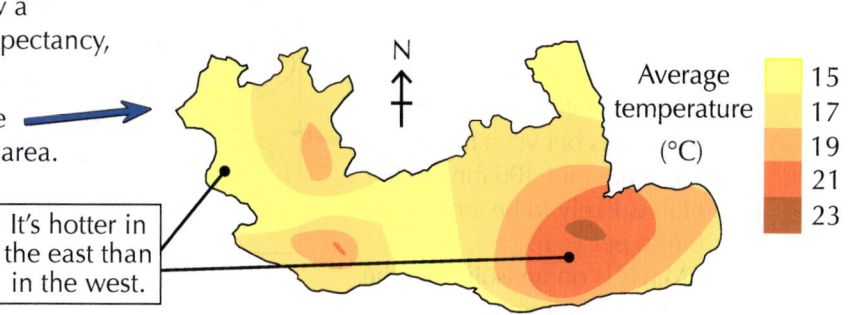

It's hotter in the east than in the west.

Average temperature (°C)
15
17
19
21
23

## Make sure you study the key for any map

Whether you've got identical dots, proportional symbols or different colours, the key to correctly interpreting the map is to understand what each symbol or colour means. The title helps here, but be sure to check the key carefully.

Geographical Skills

# Maps

*Choropleth maps* and *isolines* are useful for showing which areas are **similar** and which areas are **different**.

## Choropleth Maps show How Something Varies Between Different Areas

1) Choropleth maps show how something varies between different areas using colours or patterns.
2) The maps in exams often use cross-hatched lines and dot patterns.
3) If you're asked to talk about all the parts of the map with a certain value or characteristic, look at the map carefully and put a big tick on all the parts with the pattern that matches what you're looking for. This makes them all stand out.
4) When you're asked to complete part of a map, first use the key to work out what type of pattern you need. Then carefully draw on the pattern, e.g. using a ruler.

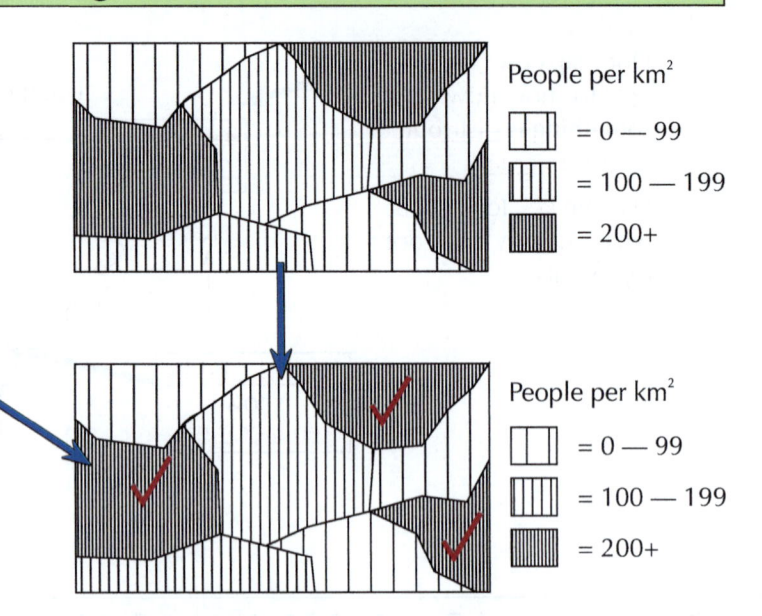

People per km²
- = 0 — 99
- = 100 — 199
- = 200+

People per km²
- = 0 — 99
- = 100 — 199
- = 200+

## Isolines on Maps Link up Places with Something in Common

1) Isolines are lines on a map linking up all the places where something's the same, for example:
   - Contour lines are isolines linking up places at the same altitude.
   - Isolines on a weather map (called isobars) link together all the places where the pressure's the same.
2) Isolines can be used to link up lots of things, e.g. average temperature, wind speed or rainfall.
3) Isolines are normally labelled with their value. The closer together the lines are, the steeper the gradient (how quickly the thing is changing) at that point.

### ① Reading Isoline Maps

1) Find the place you're interested in on the map and if it's on a line just read off the value.
2) If it's between two lines, you have to estimate the value.

Q: Find the average annual rainfall in Port Portia and on Mt. Mavis.
A: Port Portia is between the lines for 200 mm and 400 mm so the rainfall is likely to be around 300 mm per year.
Mt. Mavis is on an isoline so the rainfall is 1000 mm per year.

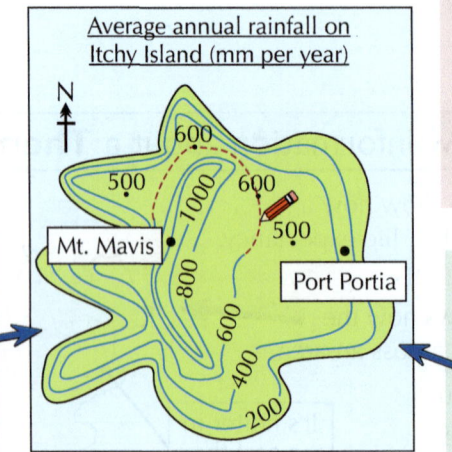

Average annual rainfall on Itchy Island (mm per year)

### ② Completing Isoline Maps

1) Drawing an isoline's like doing a dot-to-dot — you just join up all the dots with the same numbers.
2) Make sure you don't cross any other isolines though.

Q: Complete on the map the isoline showing an average rainfall of 600 mm per year.
A: See the red line on the map.

## Learn how to read choropleth maps and isolines

For a choropleth map you can simply use the key to find the information for a particular location, but remember that with isolines the answer isn't always a value written on the map — you might have to make an estimate.

Geographical Skills

# Maps

*Route maps* and *sphere of influence maps* are pretty straightforward to *read* and *draw*.

## Route Maps are Simplified Maps

1) Some maps are hard to read because they show too much detail.

2) Route maps get around this by just showing the most important features like roads and rail lines. They don't have correct distances or directions either, which makes them easier to read.

3) They're often used to show transport networks, e.g. the London tube map.

4) If you have to read a route map — dots are usually places and lines usually show routes between places. If two lines cross at a dot then it's usually a place where you can switch routes.

5) As always, don't forget to check out the key.

Q: How many different transport routes pass through Port Portia?
A: Three (coast bus, cable car and ferry).

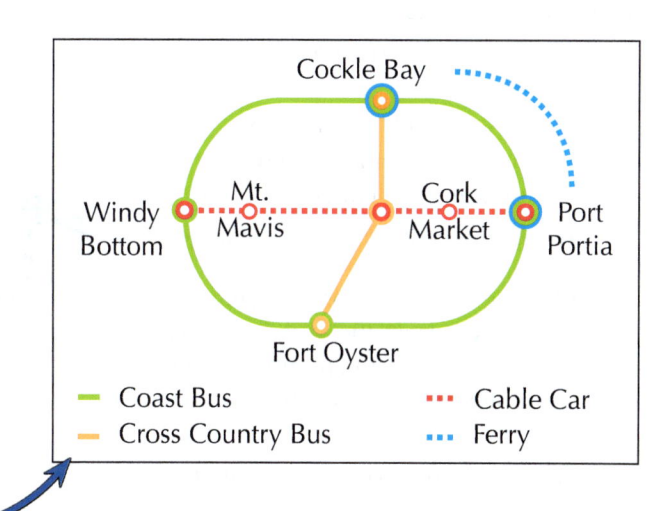

## Sphere of Influence Maps Show How Important Places Are

1) The sphere of influence of something is the area affected by it.

2) For example, the sphere of influence of a local shop could extend to just the few surrounding streets, if it's only people from the area who normally use it. But the sphere of influence of a supermarket could extend over a larger area because people are prepared to travel further to buy items they can't get at the local shop.

3) To draw a sphere of influence map, you need to know the maximum distance people are prepared to travel. You can then draw a circle whose outer edge lies at that distance from the thing you are interested in (i.e. the shop or supermarket in this example) in every direction.

Q: Where would people who live at point A normally shop?
A: At their local shop.

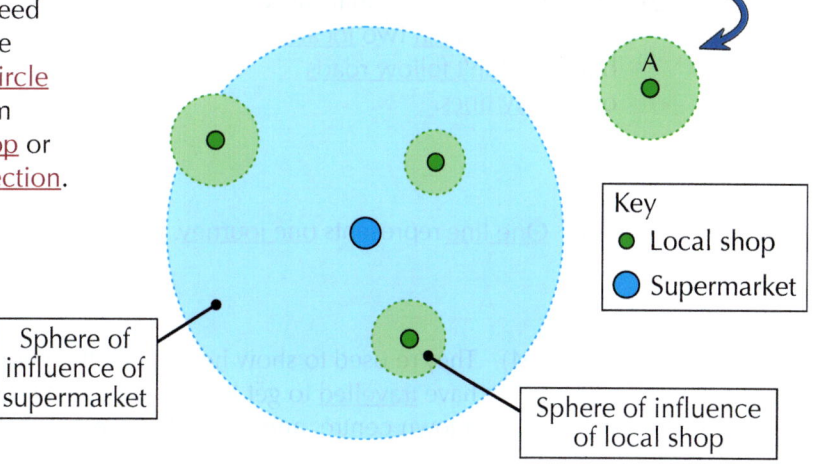

## People can use route maps to easily look at transport links

If you compare the London tube map to a real map of London, they won't match up — they're designed for different purposes. Route maps are good for showing transport networks, but don't show realistic distances between places.

Geographical Skills

# Maps

*You need to know how **lines** can be used on **maps** to show **movement**.*

## Flow Lines show Movement

1) Flow line maps have arrows on, showing how things move (or are moved) from one place to another.

2) They can also be proportional symbol maps — the width of the arrows show the quantity of things that are moving.

> Q: From which area do the greatest number of people entering the UK come from?
> A: USA, as this arrow is the largest.
>
> Q: The number of people entering the UK from the Middle East is roughly half the number of people entering from the USA. Draw an arrow on the map to show this.
> A: Make sure your arrow is going in the right direction and its size is appropriate (i.e. half the width of the USA arrow).

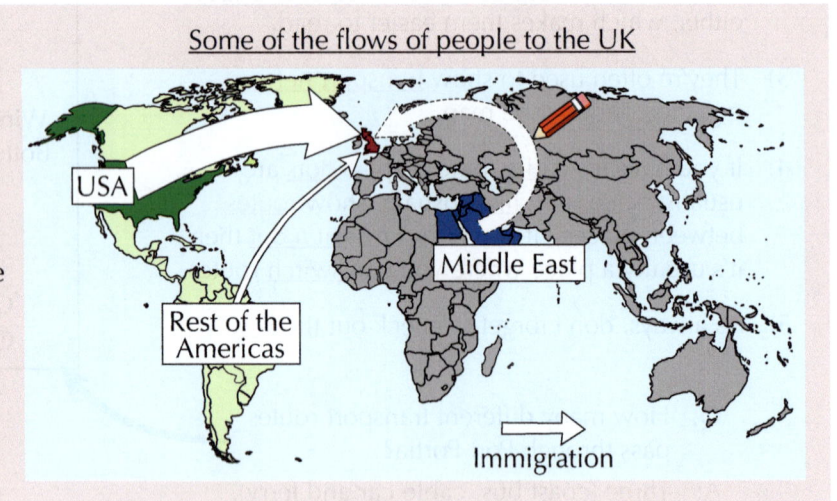

Some of the flows of people to the UK

## Desire Lines show Journeys

1) Desire lines are a type of flow line as they show movement too.

2) They're straight lines that show journeys between two locations, but they don't follow roads or railway lines.

3) One line represents one journey.

4) They're used to show how far all the people have travelled to get to a place, e.g. a shop or a town centre, and where they've come from.

Desire Lines showing journeys to Cheeseham

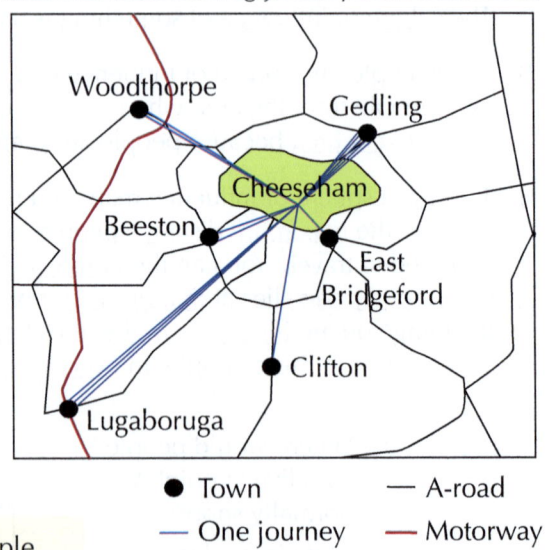

● Town — A-road
— One journey — Motorway

## Flow lines and desire lines can show movement of people or products

These are fairly straightforward. The width of a flow line can tell you how many people or things are moving between two locations. With desire lines, you can look at the number of lines to see how many journeys have been taken.

Geographical Skills

# Ordnance Survey Maps

*Next up, the dreaded **Ordnance Survey**® maps. Don't worry, they're easy once you know how to use them.*

## Learn These Common Symbols

Ordnance Survey (OS®) maps use lots of symbols. It's a good idea to learn some of the most common ones — like these:

Don't worry if you can't remember them all — you'll be given a key for each map.

- Motorway
- Main (A) road
- Secondary (B) road
- Bridge
- Railway
- County boundary
- National Park boundaries
- Building
- Bus station
- Footpaths
- Viewpoint
- Tourist information centre
- Parking
- Places of worship

## You have to be able to Understand Grid References

You need to be able to use four figure and six figure grid references for your exam.

**Q:** Give the four figure and six figure grid reference for the place of worship.

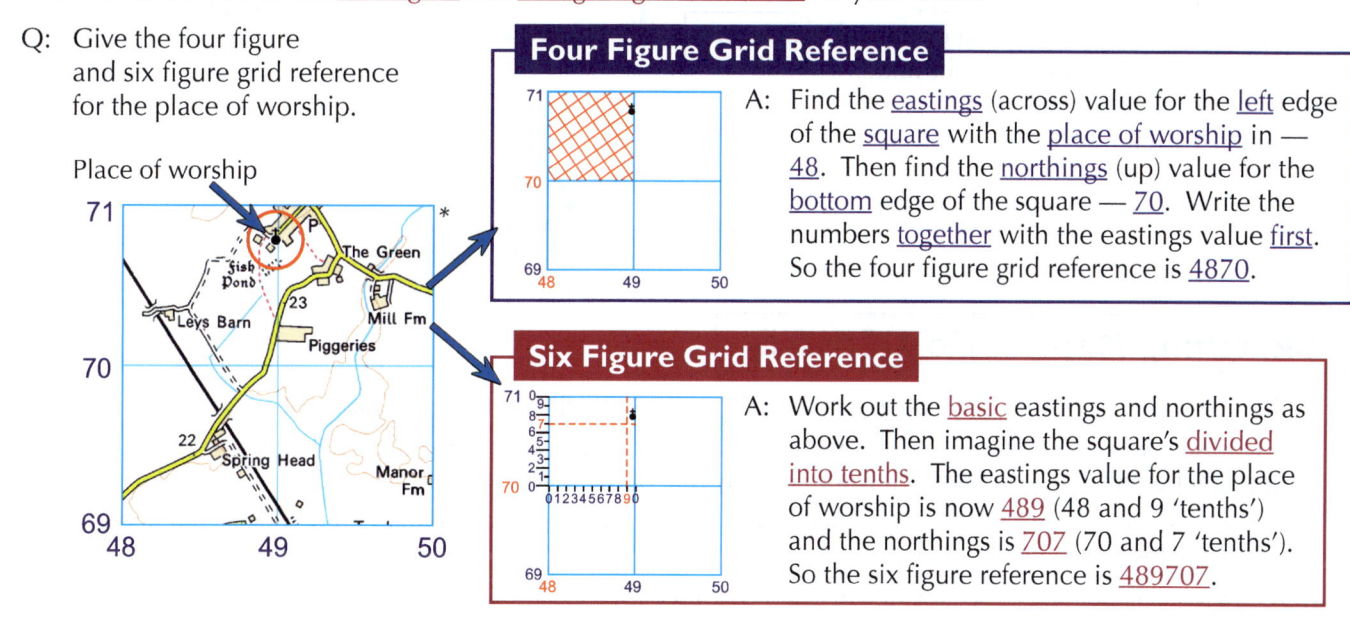

### Four Figure Grid Reference

**A:** Find the eastings (across) value for the left edge of the square with the place of worship in — 48. Then find the northings (up) value for the bottom edge of the square — 70. Write the numbers together with the eastings value first. So the four figure grid reference is 4870.

### Six Figure Grid Reference

**A:** Work out the basic eastings and northings as above. Then imagine the square's divided into tenths. The eastings value for the place of worship is now 489 (48 and 9 'tenths') and the northings is 707 (70 and 7 'tenths'). So the six figure reference is 489707.

## You need to Know your Compass Points

You've got to know the compass — for giving directions, saying which way a river's flowing, or knowing what they mean if they say 'look at the river in the NW of the map' in the exam. Read it out loud to yourself, going clockwise.

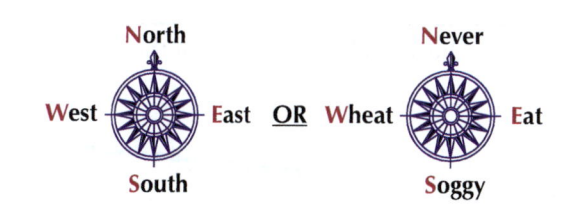

North, East, South, West **OR** Never, Eat, Soggy, Wheat

## You Might have to Work Out the Distance Between Two Places

To work out the distance between two places on a map, use a ruler to measure the distance in cm, then compare it to the scale to find the distance in km.

**Q:** What's the distance from the bridge (482703) to the church (489707)?

**A:** They're 2.2 cm apart on the map...

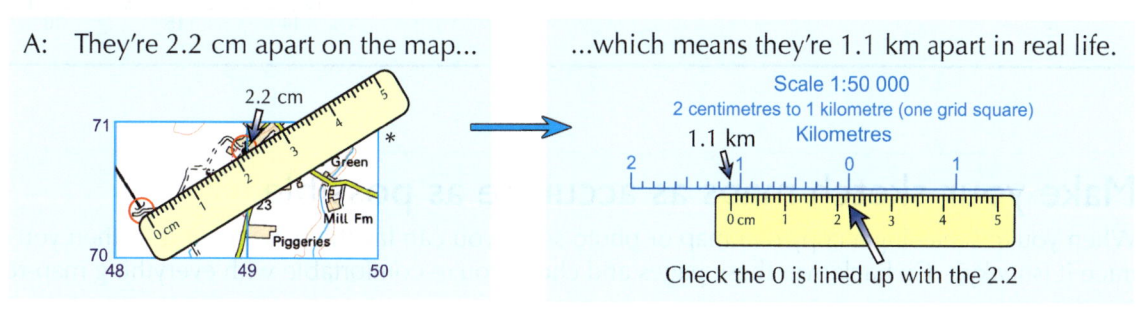

...which means they're 1.1 km apart in real life.

Scale 1:50 000
2 centimetres to 1 kilometre (one grid square)

Check the 0 is lined up with the 2.2

\* © Crown copyright 2023 OS 100034841

Geographical Skills

# Ordnance Survey Maps

## The **Relief** of an Area is Shown by **Contours** and **Spot Heights**

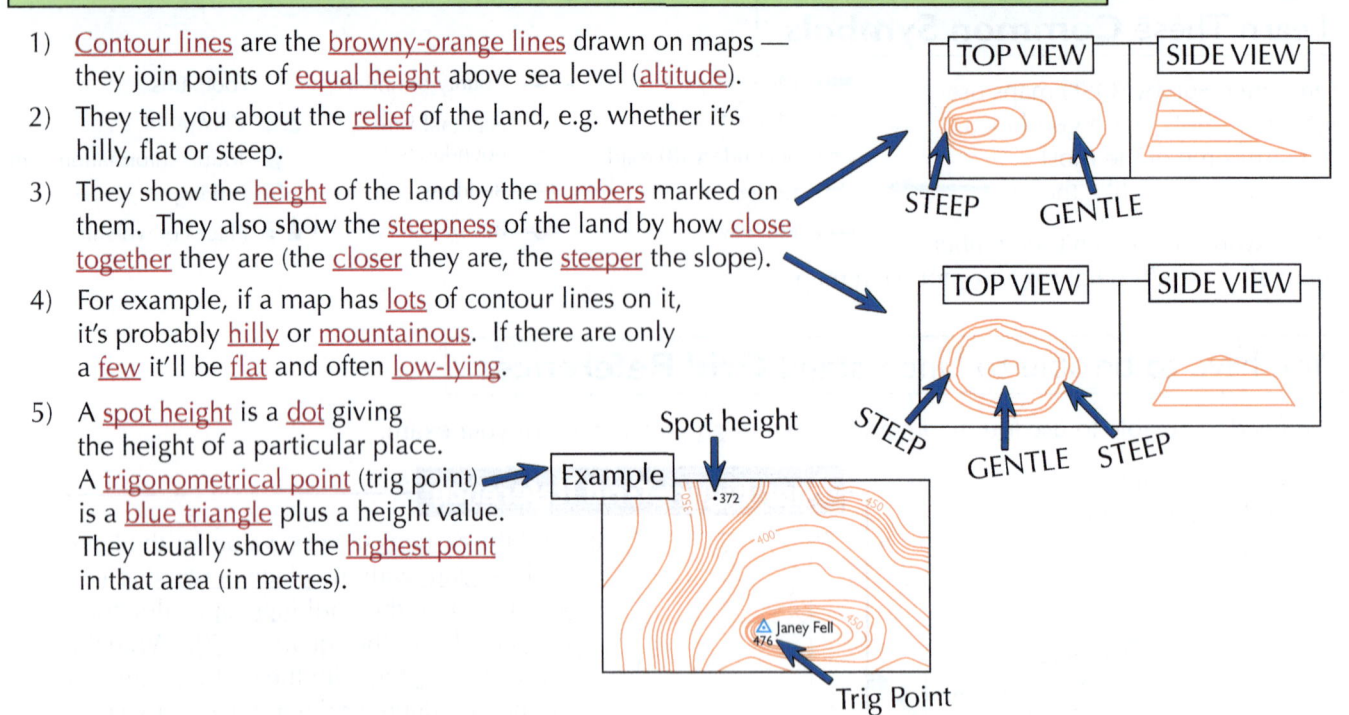

1) Contour lines are the browny-orange lines drawn on maps — they join points of equal height above sea level (altitude).
2) They tell you about the relief of the land, e.g. whether it's hilly, flat or steep.
3) They show the height of the land by the numbers marked on them. They also show the steepness of the land by how close together they are (the closer they are, the steeper the slope).
4) For example, if a map has lots of contour lines on it, it's probably hilly or mountainous. If there are only a few it'll be flat and often low-lying.
5) A spot height is a dot giving the height of a particular place. A trigonometrical point (trig point) is a blue triangle plus a height value. They usually show the highest point in that area (in metres).

## Sketching Maps — Do it Carefully

1) In the exam, they could give you a map or photograph and tell you to sketch part of it.
2) Make sure you figure out what bit they want you to sketch out, and double check you've got it right. It might be only part of a lake or a wood, or only one of the roads.
3) If you're sketching an OS® map, it's a good idea to copy the grid from the map onto your sketch paper — this helps you to copy the map accurately.
4) Draw your sketch in pencil so you can rub it out if it's wrong.
5) Look at how much time you have and how many marks it's worth to decide how much detail to add.

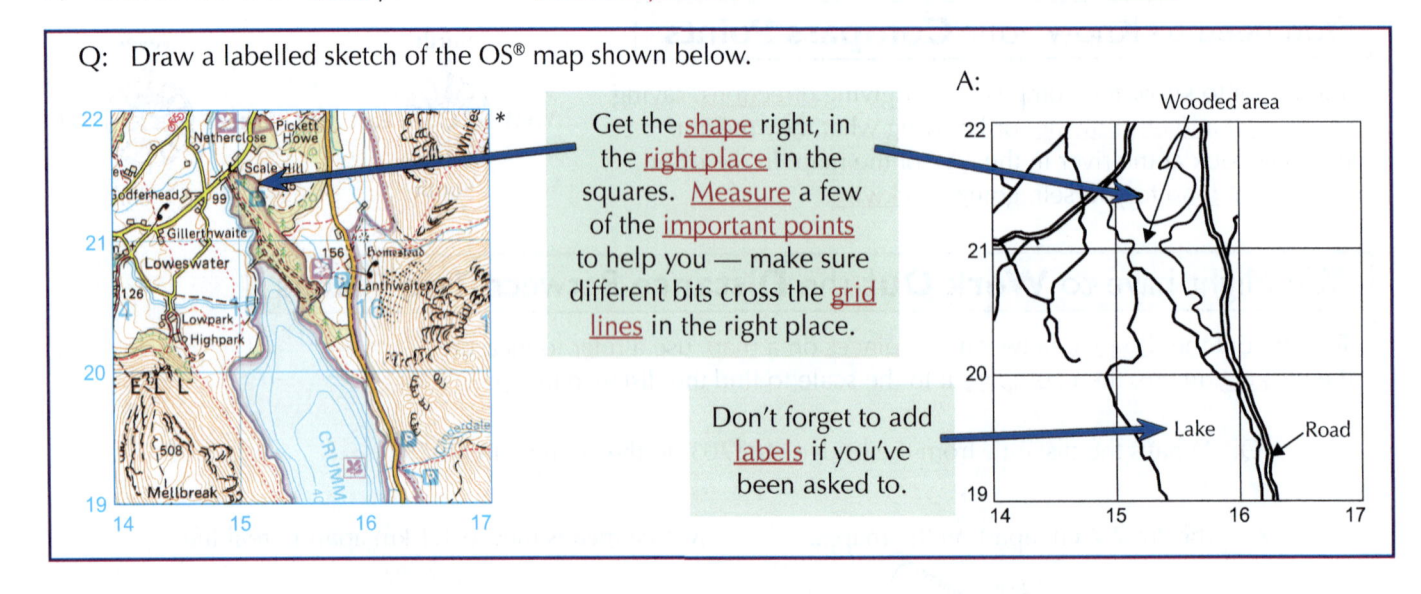

Q: Draw a labelled sketch of the OS® map shown below.

Get the shape right, in the right place in the squares. Measure a few of the important points to help you — make sure different bits cross the grid lines in the right place.

Don't forget to add labels if you've been asked to.

### EXAM TIP — Make your sketch maps as accurate as possible

When you're sketching a copy of a map or photo see if you can lay the paper over it — then you can trace it (sneaky). Go back over these pages and check you're comfortable with everything map-related.

Geographical Skills

*© Crown copyright 2023 OS 100034841

# Charts and Graphs

*Stand by for **charts** and **graphs**. Make sure you can **interpret** (read) and **construct** (draw) each of them...*

## Describing what Graphs Show — Include Figures from the Graph

When describing graphs make sure you mention:
1) The general pattern — when it's going up and down, and any peaks (highest bits) and troughs (lowest bits).
2) Any anomalies (odd results).
3) Specific data points.

Q: Use the graph to describe population change in Cheeseham.

A: The population halved between 1950 and 1960 from 40 thousand people to 20 thousand people. It then increased to 100 thousand by 1980, before falling slightly and staying steady at 90 thousand from 1990 to 2000.

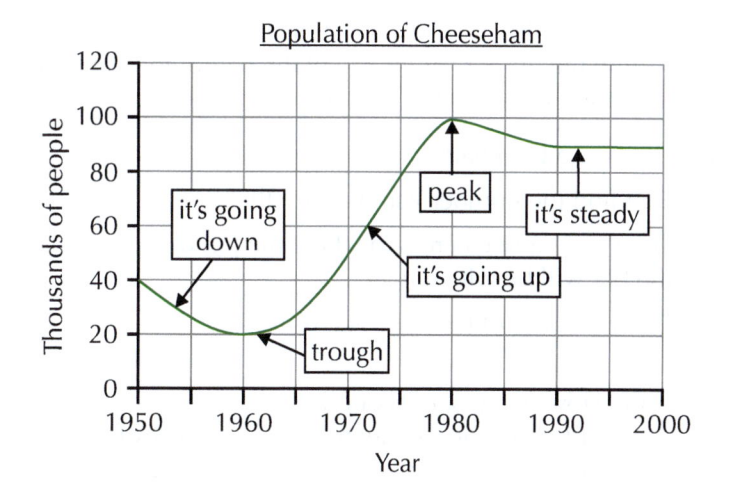

## Line Graphs — the Points are Joined by Lines

To read a line graph:
1) Read along the correct scale to find the value you want, e.g. 20 thousand tonnes or 1920.
2) Read across or up to the line you want, then read the value off the other scale.

To complete a line graph:
1) Find the value you want on both scales.
2) Make a mark (e.g. ×) at the point where the two values meet on the graph.
3) Using a ruler, join the mark you've made to the line that it should be connected to.

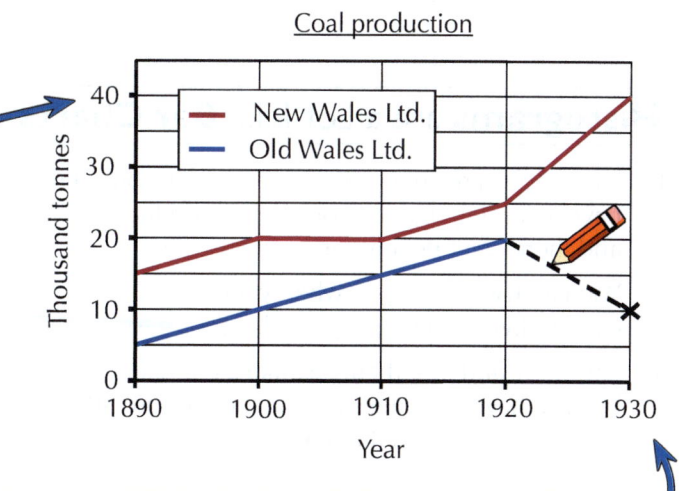

Q: Complete the graph to show that Old Wales Ltd. produced 10 thousand tonnes of coal in 1930.

A: Find 1930 on the bottom scale, and 10 thousand tonnes on the vertical scale. Make a mark where they meet, then join it to the blue line with a ruler.

## Mention the general pattern, any anomalies and specific data points

Remember what you need to include when describing a graph — it's not just useful for these line graphs, you'll need to mention these things when describing any of the charts and graphs featured on the next few pages.

Geographical Skills

# Charts and Graphs

*You're probably familiar with **bar charts** — they're quite simple really. **Histograms** are very similar.*

## Bar Charts — Draw the Bars Straight and Neat

*You might also see bar charts with horizontal bars.*

To read a bar chart:
1) Read along the bottom to find the bar you want.
2) To find out the value of a bar in a normal bar chart — go from the top of the bar across to the scale, and read off the number.
3) To find out the value of part of the bar in a divided bar chart — find the number at the top of the part of the bar you're interested in, and take away the number at the bottom of it.

To complete a bar chart:
1) First find the number you want on the vertical scale.
2) Then trace a line across to where the top of the bar will be with a ruler.
3) Draw in a bar of the right size using a ruler.

Oil production — Thousands of barrels per day (2014, 2015) — Hoxo Plc., Gnoxo Ltd., Froxo Inc. Line across from 350.

Q: How many barrels of oil did Hoxo Plc. produce per day in 2015?
A: 500 000 − 350 000 = 150 000 barrels per day

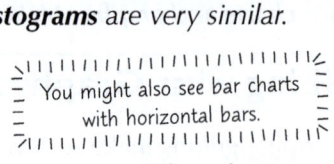

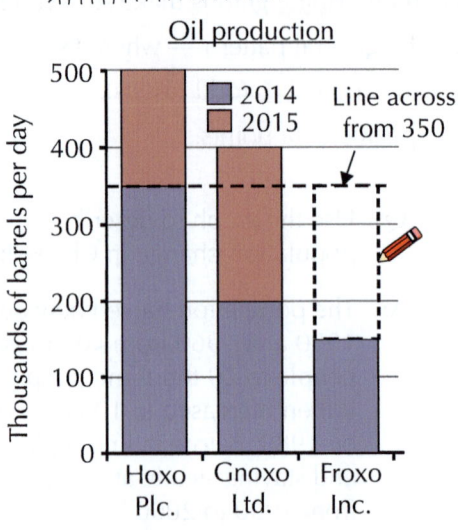

Q: Complete the chart to show that Froxo Inc. produced 200 000 barrels of oil per day in 2015.
A: 150 thousand (2014) + 200 thousand = 350 000 barrels. So draw the bar up to this point.

## Histograms are a Lot Like Bar Charts

1) Histograms are very similar to bar charts, but they have a continuous scale of numbers on the bottom and there can't be any gaps between the bars.
2) You can use histograms when your data can be divided into intervals, like this:
3) You draw and plot them just like a bar chart, but you have to make sure that the bars are all the correct width, as well as the correct height.

| Time | Cars |
|---|---|
| 0700-0800 | 334 |
| 0800-0900 | 387 |
| 0900-1000 | 209 |
| 1000-1100 | 121 |
| 1100-1200 | ? |

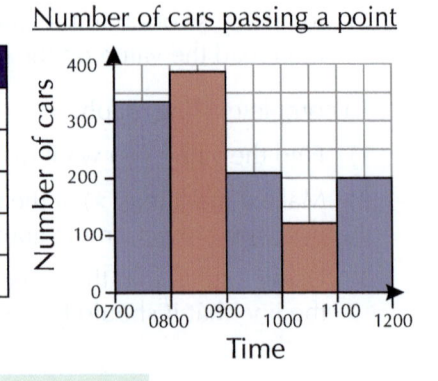

Number of cars passing a point

Q: How many cars were recorded between 1100 and 1200?
A: Trace a line from the top of the 1100-1200 bar and read the answer off — 200 cars.

## You're more likely to read a chart correctly if you use a ruler

Don't be put off by divided bar charts like the one above — they might look complicated, but they're really quite simple. Just make sure you don't read the value for the whole bar if you only need to know about one part of it.

Geographical Skills

# Charts and Graphs

*You might have seen **population pyramids** on p.110 — there's more of them here. Then it's on to **scatter graphs**.*

## Population Pyramids Show the Structure of a Population

1) Population pyramids are a bit like two bar charts on their sides.
2) It's way of showing the population of a country by age and gender.
3) The number of people goes on the horizontal axis, and the age groups go on the vertical axis. The left side is the male population and the right side is the female population.

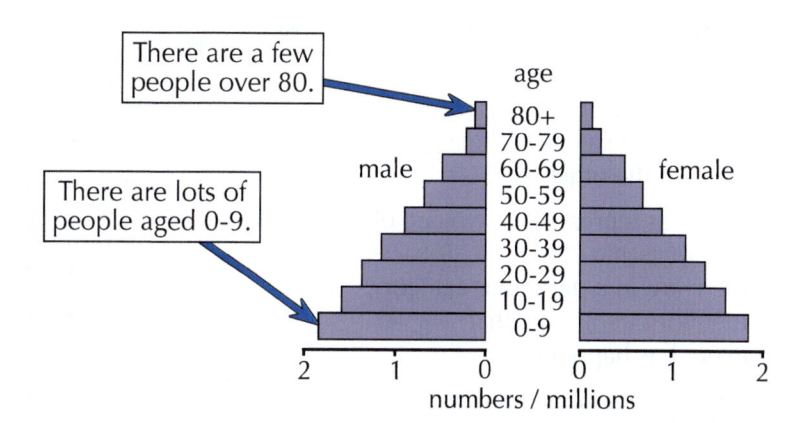

There are a few people over 80.

There are lots of people aged 0-9.

age: 80+, 70-79, 60-69, 50-59, 40-49, 30-39, 20-29, 10-19, 0-9
male / female
numbers / millions

## Scatter Graphs Show Relationships

Scatter graphs tell you how closely related two things are, e.g. altitude and air temperature. The fancy word for this is correlation. Strong correlation means the two things are closely related to each other. Weak correlation means they're not very closely related. The line of best fit is a line that goes roughly through the middle of the scatter of points and tells you about what type of correlation there is. Data can show three types of correlation:

1) Positive — as one thing increases the other increases.
2) Negative — as one thing increases the other decreases.
3) None — there's no relationship between the two things.

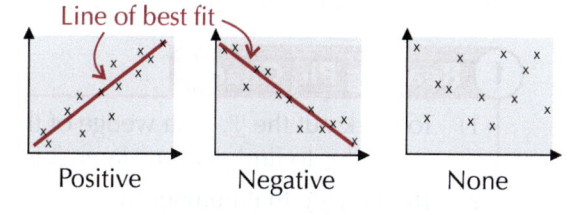

Positive / Negative / None

### 1 Reading Scatter Graphs

1) If you're asked to describe the relationship, look at the slope of the graph, e.g. if the line's moving upwards to the right it's a positive correlation. You also need to look at how close the points are to the line of best fit — the closer they are the stronger the correlation.
2) If you're asked to read off a specific point, just follow the rules for a line graph (see p.157).

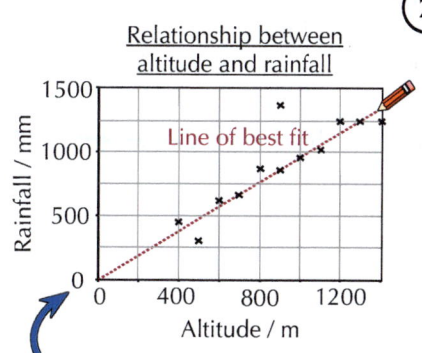

Relationship between altitude and rainfall
Rainfall / mm
Line of best fit
Altitude / m

### 2 Completing Scatter Graphs

1) You could be asked to draw a line of best fit — just draw it roughly through the middle of the scatter of points.
2) If you're asked to add a point — just follow the rules for adding a point to a line graph (see p.157).

Q: Describe the relationship shown by the scatter graph.
A: Altitude and rainfall show a strong, positive correlation — as altitude increases, so does the amount of rainfall.

- You can use your line of best fit to make predictions by reading off values from the graph.
- If you're confident your best fit line will continue, you can extend it beyond the data you have collected. This means you can make predictions outside the range of data you collected.

---

**EXAM TIP**

### Lines, bars and crosses should be neat and legible
If you're asked to read a value off a graph, or add some data to it, remember to read the scale carefully — it's easy to assume that each division is worth one, but sadly that's not always the case.

Geographical Skills

# Charts and Graphs

*Two more charts to learn about here — **dispersion diagrams** and **pie charts**.*

## Dispersion Diagrams Show the Frequency of Data

1) Dispersion diagrams are a bit like a cross between a tally chart and a bar chart.
2) The range of data that's measured goes on one axis. Frequency goes on the other axis.
3) Each dot represents one piece of information — the more dots there are in a particular category, the more frequently that event has happened.
4) The dispersion diagram on the right shows the percentage of household waste that's recycled for households in a particular village.

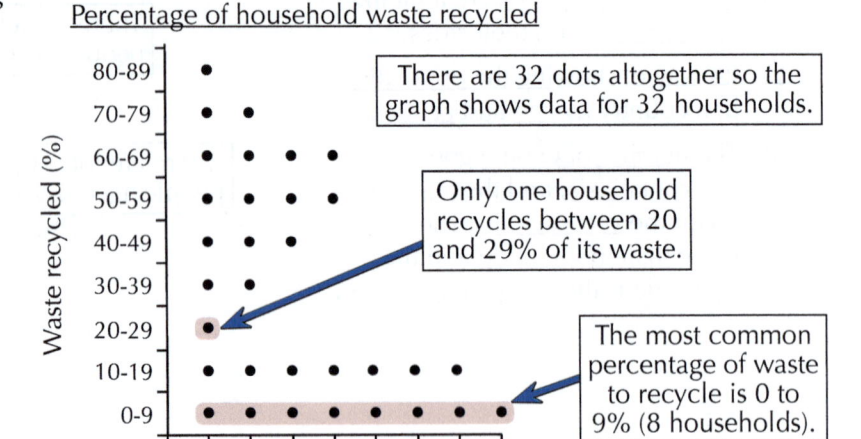

Percentage of household waste recycled

There are 32 dots altogether so the graph shows data for 32 households.

Only one household recycles between 20 and 29% of its waste.

The most common percentage of waste to recycle is 0 to 9% (8 households).

## Pie Charts Show Amounts or Percentages

The important thing to remember with pie charts is that the whole pie = 360°.

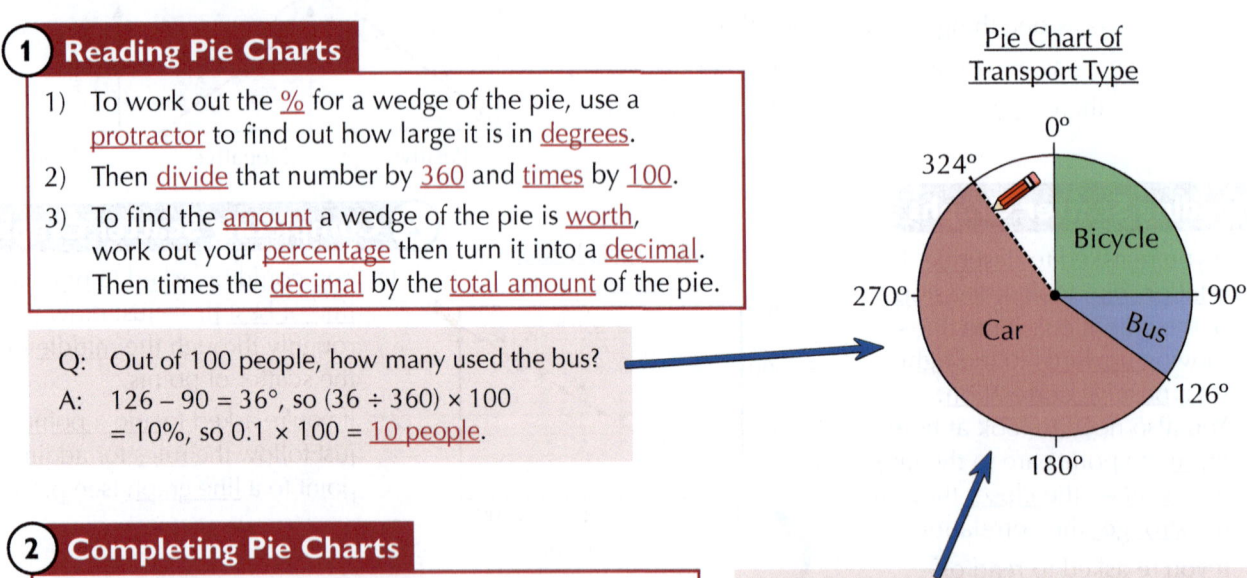

### ① Reading Pie Charts

1) To work out the % for a wedge of the pie, use a protractor to find out how large it is in degrees.
2) Then divide that number by 360 and times by 100.
3) To find the amount a wedge of the pie is worth, work out your percentage then turn it into a decimal. Then times the decimal by the total amount of the pie.

Q: Out of 100 people, how many used the bus?
A: 126 − 90 = 36°, so (36 ÷ 360) × 100 = 10%, so 0.1 × 100 = 10 people.

Pie Chart of Transport Type

### ② Completing Pie Charts

1) To draw on a new wedge that you know the % for, turn the % into a decimal and times it by 360. Then draw a wedge of that many degrees.

Q: Out of 100 people, 25% used a bicycle. Add this to the pie chart.
A: 25 ÷ 100 = 0.25, 0.25 × 360 = 90°.

2) To add a new wedge that you know the amount for, divide your amount by the total amount of the pie and times the answer by 360. Then draw on a wedge of that many degrees.

Q: Out of 100 people, 55 used a car. Add this to the pie chart.
A: 55 ÷ 100 = 0.55, 0.55 × 360 = 198° (198° + 126° = 324°).

---

### You'll need a protractor to draw a pie chart
Make sure you remember to convert any percentages into degrees before you draw a wedge of a pie chart.

*Geographical Skills*

# Charts and Graphs

*Here are the **last two** charts and graphs you need to know about — **radial graphs** and **cross-sections**.*

## Radial Graphs Often Show Directional Data

1) Radial graphs have axes that go round in a circle.
2) They often show directional data.
3) The most common radial diagram is a wind rose. The bars point in different directions to show which way the wind is blowing from. How far the bar reaches from the centre shows how often winds blow from that direction.

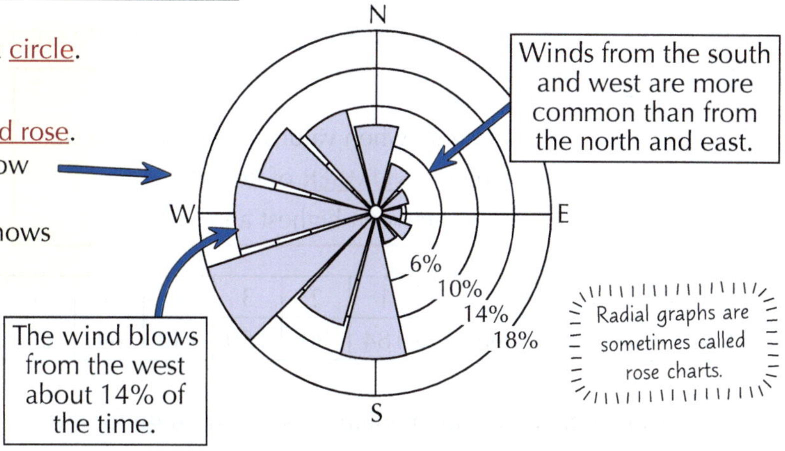

Winds from the south and west are more common than from the north and east.

The wind blows from the west about 14% of the time.

*Radial graphs are sometimes called rose charts.*

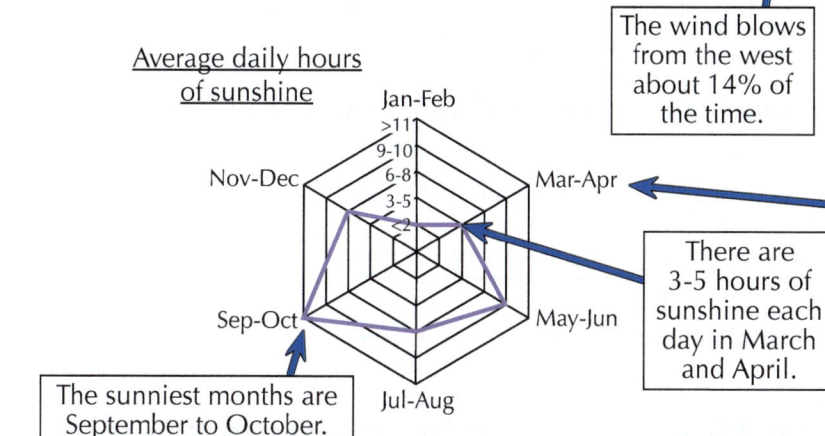

There are 3-5 hours of sunshine each day in March and April.

The sunniest months are September to October.

4) The points on the outside of the graph can also show other things, e.g. months of the year or ages.
5) The distance from the centre shows the size of the category, e.g. how many hours of sunshine there are in each two-month period.

## Cross-Sections show the Land from Sideways on

1) Cross-sections show what the landscape looks like if it's chopped down the middle and viewed from the side. 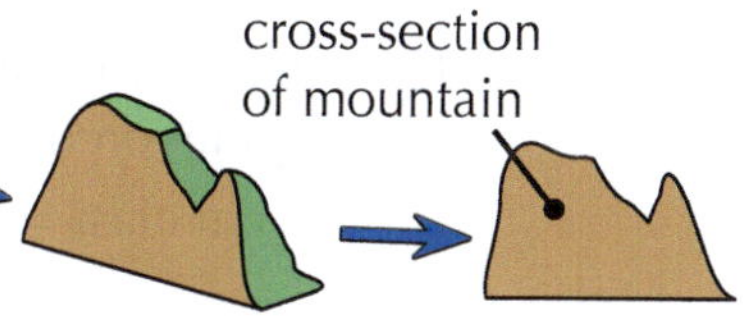
2) In geography, they're useful for showing things like the change in the height of the land, the shape of a river channel or the shape of a beach. They're often presented as a graph with height and distance shown along the x- and y-axes. E.g.:

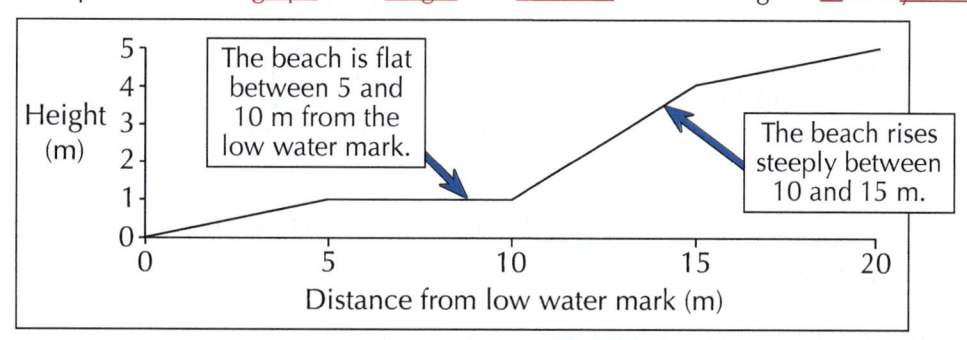

The beach is flat between 5 and 10 m from the low water mark.

The beach rises steeply between 10 and 15 m.

3) When you're drawing a cross-section graph, use the x-axis to plot the contour heights. Join all the points, then label the cross-section to show features of the landscape (e.g. valley sides, hilltops etc.). Don't forget to label both the horizontal and vertical scales (the x and y axes).
4) If you're interpreting a cross-section graph, make sure you look at both the horizontal and vertical scales carefully. Describe the general trends, e.g. the beach generally slopes upwards away from the sea, and then pick out the key features, e.g. where the land is steepest and where it is flatter.

## You might get asked about a radial graph or a cross-section in the exam

Before you move on, make sure you're happy with every type of graph and chart covered over the last few pages.

*Geographical Skills*

# Statistics

*You might be asked to do a bit of **maths** in the exam — it should all be **familiar** from your **maths lessons**.*

## Learn the Definitions for **Mode, Median, Mean** and **Range**

Mode, median and mean are measures of average and the range is how spread out the values are:

| MODE = MOST common | REMEMBER: |
|---|---|
| MEDIAN = MIDDLE value (when values are in order of size) | Mode = most (emphasise the 'mo' in each when you say them) |
| MEAN = TOTAL of items ÷ NUMBER of items | Median = mid (emphasise the m*d in each when you say them) |
| RANGE = DIFFERENCE between highest and lowest | Mean is just the average, but it's mean 'cos you have to work it out. |

| Sample | 1 | 2 | 3 | 4 | 5 | 6 | 7 |
|---|---|---|---|---|---|---|---|
| River discharge (cumecs) | 184 | 90 | 159 | 142 | 64 | 64 | 95 |

Q: Calculate the mean, median, mode and range for the river discharge data shown in the table above.

A: 
- The mode is the most common value = <u>64</u>.
- To find the median, put all the numbers in order and find the middle value:
  64, 64, 90, <u>95</u>, 142, 159, 184. So the median is <u>95</u>.
- Mean = $\frac{\text{total of items}}{\text{number of items}}$ = $\frac{184 + 90 + 159 + 142 + 64 + 64 + 95}{7}$ = $\frac{798}{7}$ = <u>114</u>
- The range is the difference between highest and lowest value, i.e. 184 − 64 = <u>120</u>

*When there are two middle numbers, the median is halfway between the two.*

## You Need to **Know** How to Find the **Modal Class** and **Interquartile Range**

If your data is grouped you might need to find the modal class. This is just the group with the most values in.

| Age | Number of people |
|---|---|
| 0-19 | 21 |
| 20-39 | 37 |
| 40-59 | 27 |
| 60+ | 15 |

Q: Find the modal class of the population data shown in the table.

A: Modal class = <u>20-39 years</u>

*Remember, the modal class will be the group — not how many items are in that group.*

As well as finding the median (the middle value in a list), you can also find the upper and lower quartiles — the values a quarter (25%) and three-quarters (75%) of the way through the ordered data.

Q: The number of shoppers in each shop in a village were counted. Find the median and the quartiles of the data set.

A: 2, 3, <u>6</u>, 6, 7, <u>9</u>, 13, 14, <u>17</u>, 22, 22

Lower quartile | Median | Upper quartile

The interquartile range is the difference between the upper quartile and the lower quartile. It contains the middle 50% of values.

Q: Find the interquartile range of the number of shoppers.

A: 17 − 6 = <u>11</u>

## You Need to be Able to **Calculate Percentages**

To give the amount X as a percentage of a sample Y, you need to divide X by Y and multiply by 100.

Q: This year, 35 out of the 270 houses in Foxley were burgled. Calculate the percentage of houses burgled in Foxley.

A: 35 ÷ 270 × 100 = <u>13%</u>

### EXAM TIP — Read the question carefully and check your answer

There are some easy marks up for grabs here as long as you calculate the right figure — don't miss out on them by working out the median rather than the mean, or typing the wrong number into your calculator.

Geographical Skills

# Statistics

*Almost at the end now — just a few more things to know about **percentages**, **percentiles** and **ratios**.*

## Make sure you can Work Out Percentage Change

Calculating percentage change lets you work out how much something has increased or decreased. You use this formula:

$$\text{Percentage change} = \frac{\text{final value} - \text{original value}}{\text{original value}} \times 100$$

A positive value shows an increase and a negative value shows a decrease.

Q: Last year in Foxley, only 24 houses were burgled, compared to 35 this year. Calculate the percentage change in burglaries in Foxley.

A: $\frac{35 - 24}{24} \times 100 = \underline{46\% \text{ increase}}$ in the number of burglaries in Foxley.

## Percentiles Tell You Where in Your Data Set a Data Point Lies

1) Percentiles are useful if you want to compare the value of one data point to the rest of your data.
2) To find a percentile, you rank your data from smallest to largest, then divide it into one hundred equal chunks. Each chunk is one percentile.
3) This means that each percentile represents one percent of the data, and so the value of a percentile tells you what percentage of the data has a value lower than the data points in that percentile.

   E.g. A stone is in the 90th percentile for weight in its section of the river bed. This means that 90% of the stones are lighter than it.

4) Percentiles can be used to give a more realistic idea of the spread of data than the range (see p.162) — by finding the range between the 10th and 90th percentiles in a data set (the middle 80% of the data), you can look at the spread of the data while ignoring any outlying results.

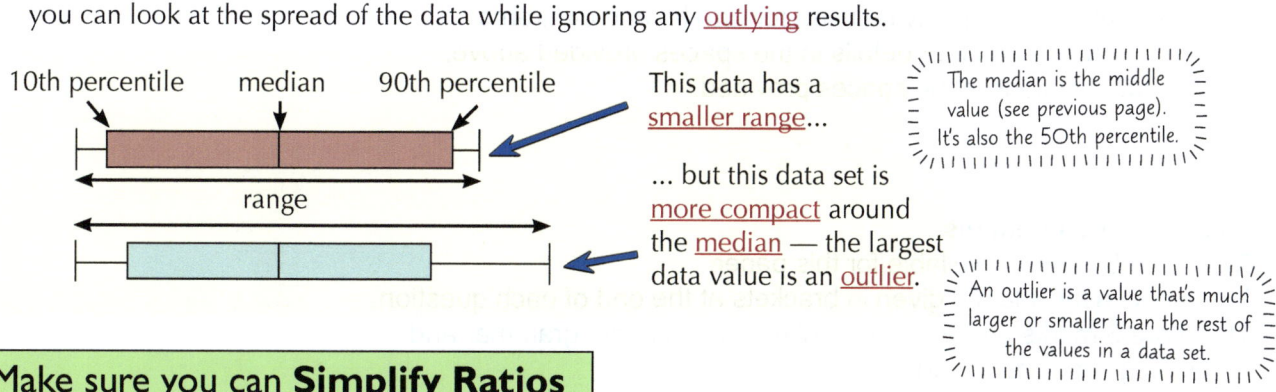

This data has a smaller range...

*The median is the middle value (see previous page). It's also the 50th percentile.*

... but this data set is more compact around the median — the largest data value is an outlier.

*An outlier is a value that's much larger or smaller than the rest of the values in a data set.*

## Make sure you can Simplify Ratios

A ratio shows how two amounts compare to each other — it's one way of showing a proportion.

Ratios are written like this ➡ 1:10. E.g. 'Droughts and storms occurred in the ratio 1:10.' This means that for every 1 drought, there were 10 storms.

You might also be asked to simplify a ratio — this just means writing it using the smallest numbers possible.

E.g. If you're asked to simplify the ratio 45:60, find the highest number that both sides can be divided by. 45 and 60 can both be divided by 15 — this gives the ratio 3:4.

Q: Write the ratio 72:48 in its simplest form.

A: 72 and 48 can both be divided by 24 to give 3:2.

## You might need to do these calculations in the exam

All this maths might seem a bit dull, but it could really come in handy — the examiners do expect you to know all this stuff about statistics, so it's definitely worth making sure you've got it all covered before going into the exam.

Geographical Skills

# Practice Exams

Once you've been through all the questions in this book, you should feel pretty confident about the exams. As final preparation, here is a mini set of **practice exams** to give you a taste of what the exams will be like. Each of your real exam papers will be longer than these, but they will follow a very similar structure.

*CGP* Practice Exam Paper
GCSE Geography

# GCSE Geography
## Paper 1: Our Natural World

In addition to this paper you should have:
- A pencil.
- A ruler.
- A calculator.

| Centre name |   |   |   |   |
|---|---|---|---|---|
| Centre number |   |   |   |   |
| Candidate number |   |   |   |   |

**Time allowed:**
- 57 minutes

| Surname |   |
|---|---|
| Other names |   |
| Candidate signature |   |

### Instructions to candidates
- Use black ink. A pencil may be used for graphs and diagrams.
- Write your name and other details in the spaces provided above.
- Answer **all** questions in the spaces provided.

### Information for candidates
- There are 53 marks available for this paper.
- The marks available are given in brackets at the end of each question.
- There are 3 marks available for spelling, punctuation, grammar and terminology in Question 5d).

### Advice to candidates
For multiple choice questions:
- Clearly shade the oval next to your chosen answer. For example: ●
- If you wish to change your answer, put a cross through your original answer. For example: ⊗
- If you wish to change your answer to one that you have previously crossed out, draw a circle around the answer. For example: ⊗

**For examiner's use**

| Q | Attempt Nº |   |   | Q | Attempt Nº |   |   |
|---|---|---|---|---|---|---|---|
|   | 1 | 2 | 3 |   | 1 | 2 | 3 |
| 1 |   |   |   | 4 |   |   |   |
| 2 |   |   |   | 5 |   |   |   |
| 3 |   |   |   |   |   |   |   |
|   |   |   |   | Total |   |   |   |

## Section A
Answer **all** the questions in this section.

### Global Hazards

**1** Study **Figure 1**, a map of climatic zones.

**Figure 1**

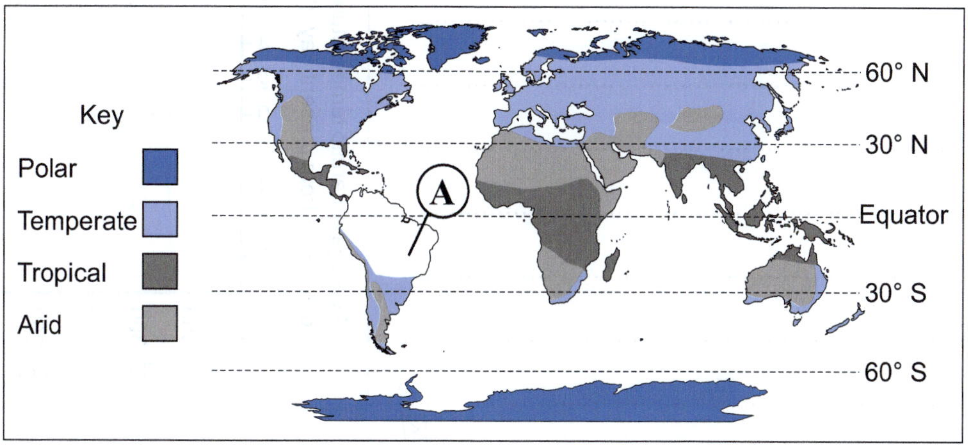

a) **Figure 1** is incomplete. Which climatic zone is found at the location labelled A in **Figure 1**?
Shade **one** oval only.

   A   Polar     ○
   B   Temperate ○
   C   Tropical  ○
   D   Arid      ○

[1]

b) Explain how global atmospheric circulation can cause extremely high temperatures in areas of high pressure.

...................................................................................................................................

...................................................................................................................................

...................................................................................................................................
[2]

c) Most tropical storms form near the equator. Describe the extreme weather conditions associated with tropical storms and explain how they are caused.

...................................................................................................................................

...................................................................................................................................

...................................................................................................................................

...................................................................................................................................

...................................................................................................................................

...................................................................................................................................

...................................................................................................................................

...................................................................................................................................
[6]

[Total 9 marks]

**Turn over ▶**

# Changing Climate

**2** Study **Figure 2**, a graph showing temperature changes during the Quaternary period.

a) i) Describe the general trends shown in **Figure 2**.

**Figure 2**

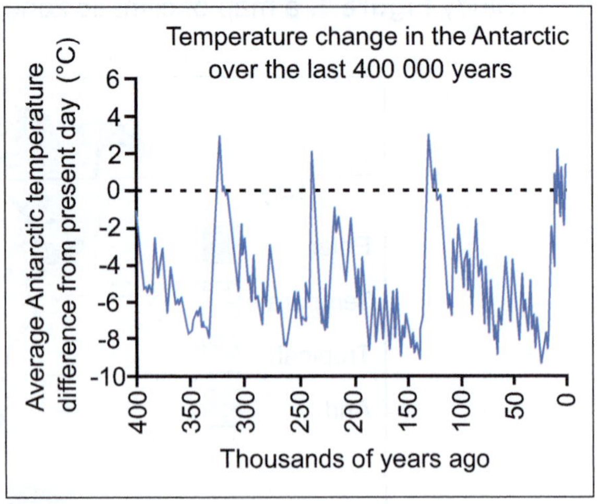

Temperature change in the Antarctic over the last 400 000 years

.................................................................

.................................................................

.................................................................

.................................................................

.................................................................

.................................................................

.................................................................
[2]

ii) The temperature changes shown in **Figure 2** were worked out from ice core records. Explain how ice cores provide evidence for past climate change.

..........................................................................................................................................

..........................................................................................................................................

..........................................................................................................................................
[2]

b) Study **Figure 3**, a photograph of a coal-fired power plant in South Africa.

**Figure 3**

Explain what impact this activity may have on climate change.

..........................................................................................................................................

..........................................................................................................................................

..........................................................................................................................................

..........................................................................................................................................

..........................................................................................................................................
[4]

[Total 8 marks]

## Distinctive Landscapes

**3** Study **Figure 4**, an Ordnance Survey® map of a coastal area in Devon.

**Figure 4**

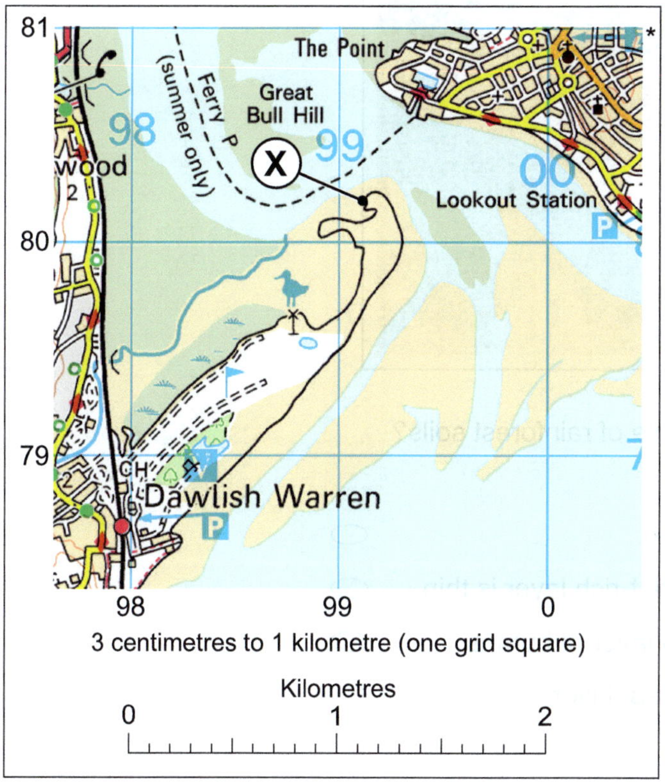

a) What is the six-figure grid reference for the end of the spit, marked X on **Figure 4**? Shade **one** oval only.

| | | |
|---|---|---|
| A | 992818 | ○ |
| B | 991802 | ○ |
| C | 090818 | ○ |
| D | 802991 | ○ |

[1]

b) Explain how constructive waves contribute to deposition on the coast.

..................................................................................................
..................................................................................................
..................................................................................................
..................................................................................................
..................................................................................................
..................................................................................................
..................................................................................................
..................................................................................................

[3]

c) Describe the erosional landforms in **one** coastal landscape you have studied, and explain how they were formed.

**Name of coastal landscape:** ........................................................................................

..................................................................................................
..................................................................................................
..................................................................................................
..................................................................................................
..................................................................................................
..................................................................................................
..................................................................................................
..................................................................................................
..................................................................................................

[6]

[Total 10 marks]

*© Crown copyright 2023 OS 100034841

**Turn over ▶**

## Sustaining Ecosystems

**4** Study **Figure 5**, a photograph showing exposed soil in an area of tropical rainforest.

**Figure 5**

a) Which statement best describes the soil profile of rainforest soils?
Shade **one** oval only.

| | | |
|---|---|---|
| A | Rainforest soils are shallow and infertile. | ○ |
| B | There is a thick leaf layer but the nutrient-rich layer is thin. | ○ |
| C | Rainforest soils are shallow with a thin layer of humus. | ○ |
| D | The deep soils are fertile, with a thick leaf layer. | ○ |

[1]

b) Explain how the climate affects the characteristics of the soils that form in tropical rainforests.

...........................................................................................................................................................

...........................................................................................................................................................

...........................................................................................................................................................

...........................................................................................................................................................

...........................................................................................................................................................

...........................................................................................................................................................

[4]

c) Explain how ecotourism can be part of a sustainable management strategy for a tropical rainforest.

...........................................................................................................................................................

...........................................................................................................................................................

...........................................................................................................................................................

...........................................................................................................................................................

...........................................................................................................................................................

...........................................................................................................................................................

[4]

[Total 9 marks]

## Section B: Physical Geography Fieldwork
Answer **all** the questions in this section.

**5** As part of a fieldwork enquiry, a student collected data on river velocity. He placed a float in the river and recorded the time taken for the float to travel 10 metres downstream. The results are shown in **Figure 6**.

**Figure 6**

| Sample | 1 | 2 | 3 | 4 | 5 | 6 | 7 | 8 |
|---|---|---|---|---|---|---|---|---|
| Time (s) | 315 | 255 | 278 | 310 | 947 | 302 | 279 | 297 |

a) Suggest **one** appropriate item that could be used as the float. Give **one** reason for your answer.

**Item:**......................................................................................................................
[1]

**Reason:** ................................................................................................................

..............................................................................................................................

..............................................................................................................................
[1]

b) The result for sample 5 is an anomaly.
Suggest **one** possible reason for this anomaly.

..............................................................................................................................

..............................................................................................................................

..............................................................................................................................
[2]

c) Excluding the anomaly, calculate the **mean** time taken for the float to travel 10 m.

..............................................................................................................................

..............................................................................................................................

Mean = ..................................... s
[2]

d) This question is about your fieldwork enquiry that involved the collection of physical geography data. To what extent did your results allow you to reach a valid conclusion to your original question?

*[8 + 3 SPaG]*
*[Total 17 marks]*

**END OF QUESTIONS**

# GCSE Geography
## Paper 2: People and Society

*CGP Practice Exam Paper GCSE Geography*

In addition to this paper you should have:
- A pencil.
- A ruler.
- A calculator.

Centre name

Centre number

Candidate number

**Time allowed:**
- 55 minutes

Surname

Other names

Candidate signature

**Instructions to candidates**
- Use black ink. A pencil may be used for graphs and diagrams.
- Write your name and other details in the spaces provided above.
- Answer **all** questions in the spaces provided.

**Information for candidates**
- There are 51 marks available for this paper.
- The marks available are given in brackets at the end of each question.
- There are 3 marks available for spelling, punctuation, grammar and terminology in Question 5c).

**Advice to candidates**
For multiple choice questions:
- Clearly shade the oval next to your chosen answer. For example: ●
- If you wish to change your answer, put a cross through your original answer. For example: ⊗
- If you wish to change your answer to one that you have previously crossed out, draw a circle around the answer. For example: ⊘

**For examiner's use**

| Q | Attempt Nº 1 | 2 | 3 | Q | Attempt Nº 1 | 2 | 3 |
|---|---|---|---|---|---|---|---|
| 1 | | | | 4 | | | |
| 2 | | | | 5 | | | |
| 3 | | | | | | | |
| | | | | Total | | | |

## Section A
Answer **all** the questions in this section.

### Urban Futures

**1** There are a number of challenges that affect life in LIDC and EDC cities.

a) i) Which of the following is **not** likely to be a challenge faced by a worker in the informal sector? Shade **one** oval only.

    **A** Working in dangerous conditions. ◯

    **B** Working long hours. ◯

    **C** Earning very little. ◯

    **D** Having to pay high taxes. ◯

[1]

ii) Describe **one** piece of evidence shown in **Figure 1** for challenges faced by many LIDC and EDC cities.

**Figure 1**

...................................................................................................................................................

[1]

b) Cities in advanced countries (ACs) also face a range of challenges.
Describe the challenges of transport provision in an AC city you have studied, and examine how these challenges affect life in the city.

...................................................................................................................................................

[6]

[Total 8 marks]

Turn over ▶

## Dynamic Development

**2** In 2014, Nicaragua had a 0.03% share of the world's total exports while the UK had a 2.66% share. Study **Figure 2**, which shows the types of goods exported by each country.

**Figure 2**

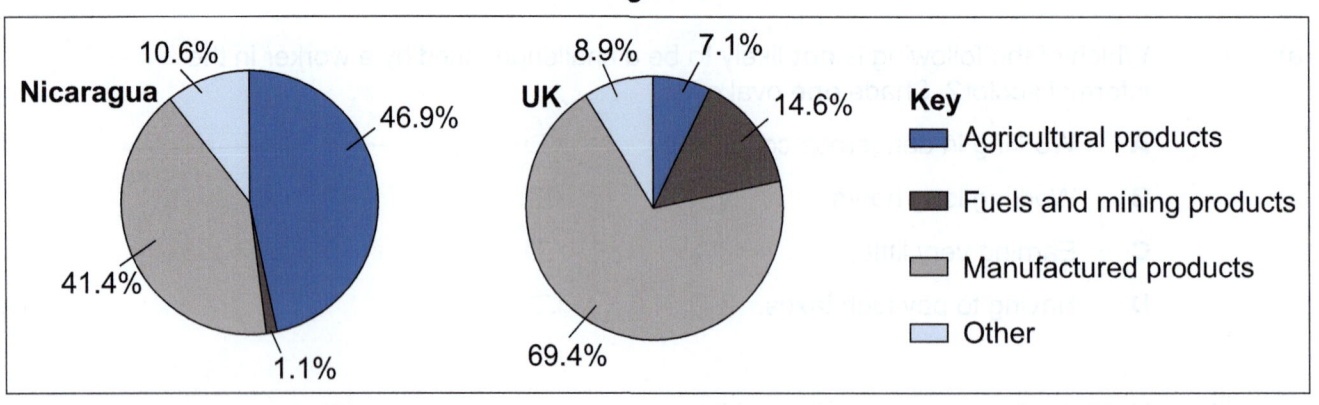

Nicaragua: 10.6%, 46.9%, 1.1%, 41.4%
UK: 8.9%, 7.1%, 14.6%, 69.4%

Key:
- Agricultural products
- Fuels and mining products
- Manufactured products
- Other

a) i) In 2014, what percentage of UK exports was not agricultural products, fuels or mining products?

.................................................................................................................................................. [1]

ii) Using **Figure 2**, suggest a reason why Nicaragua is less developed than the UK.

..................................................................................................................................................
..................................................................................................................................................
.................................................................................................................................................. [2]

b) For an LIDC you have studied, explain how political and social factors have affected the level of development.

..................................................................................................................................................
..................................................................................................................................................
..................................................................................................................................................
..................................................................................................................................................
..................................................................................................................................................
..................................................................................................................................................
..................................................................................................................................................
..................................................................................................................................................
..................................................................................................................................................
..................................................................................................................................................
.................................................................................................................................................. [6]

[Total 9 marks]

# UK in the 21st Century

**3** Study **Figure 3**, a table showing population change in the UK from 2001 and 2015.

a) i) Calculate the range of the net international migration values.

.................................................................
*[1]*

**Figure 3**

| | Internal growth (births – deaths) | Net international migration | Overall net change |
|---|---|---|---|
| 2001 | 74 300 | 153 200 | 227 500 |
| 2002 | 61 700 | 190 900 | 252 600 |
| 2003 | 76 700 | 194 200 | 270 900 |
| 2004 | 103 800 | 209 900 | 313 700 |
| 2005 | 127 000 | 336 000 | 463 000 |
| 2006 | 159 000 | 254 800 | 413 800 |
| 2007 | 187 100 | 304 900 | 492 000 |
| 2008 | 220 600 | 284 100 | 504 700 |
| 2009 | 216 700 | 220 100 | 436 800 |
| 2010 | 243 300 | 255 600 | 498 900 |
| 2011 | 255 200 | 270 500 | 525 700 |
| 2012 | 254 400 | 165 500 | 419 900 |
| 2013 | 212 100 | 188 500 | 400 600 |
| 2014 | 226 200 | 264 900 | 491 100 |
| 2015 | 171 800 | 341 400 | 513 200 |

ii) Calculate the percentage change in internal growth between 2011 and 2015.

.................................................................

.................................................................
*[1]*

b) The UK has an ageing population.

i) Which of the following is **NOT** a cause of the UK's ageing population? Shade **one** oval only.

A   Low birth rates.   ◯
B   Better healthcare.   ◯
C   Increased age of retirement.   ◯
D   Healthier lifestyles.   ◯

*[1]*

ii) Outline the possible responses to the UK's ageing population.

.................................................................................................................................

.................................................................................................................................

.................................................................................................................................

.................................................................................................................................
*[3]*

c) London is the capital city of the UK.
Study **Figure 4**, which shows part of London's financial district. London is an economic hub. Describe what an economic hub is.

**Figure 4**

.................................................................

.................................................................

.................................................................

.................................................................

.................................................................................................................................

.................................................................................................................................
*[2]*

*[Total 8 marks]*

**Turn over ▶**

# Resource Reliance

**4** Study **Figure 5**, which shows average daily calorie intake per person around the world.

**Figure 5**

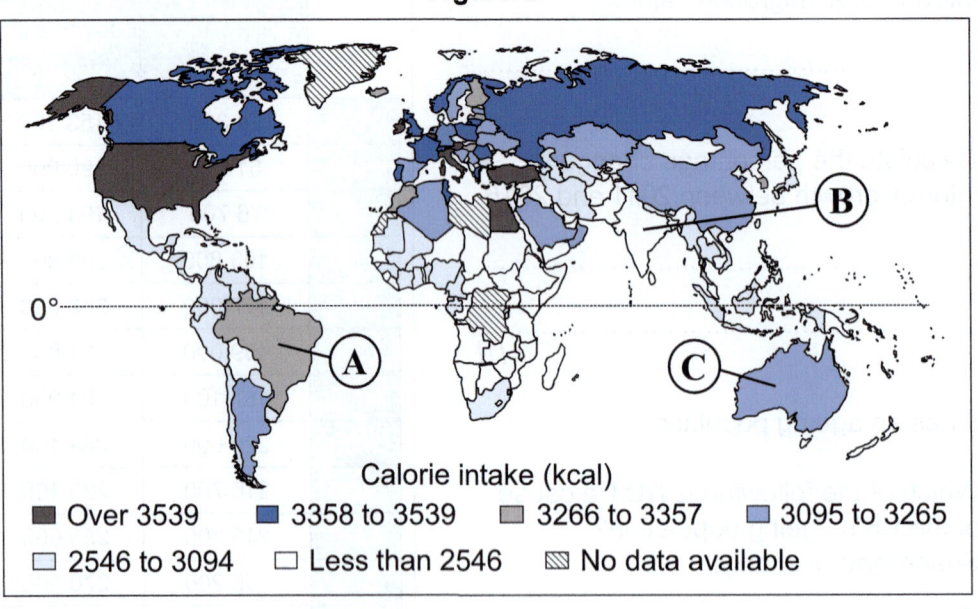

Calorie intake (kcal)
- Over 3539
- 3358 to 3539
- 3266 to 3357
- 3095 to 3265
- 2546 to 3094
- Less than 2546
- No data available

a) i) Which of the following statements about calorie intake is correct? Shade **one** oval only.

　A　Daily calorie intake is lower in Country A than in Country C.　○

　B　Daily calorie intake in Country B is 3095 to 3265 kcal.　○

　C　Daily calorie intake in Country A is 3266 to 3357 kcal.　○

　D　Daily calorie intake is highest in Country C.　○

[1]

ii) Which of the following statements best describes what the Global Hunger Index shows? Shade **one** oval only.

　A　The amount of food that people eat in different countries.　○

　B　How many people have access to food in different countries.　○

　C　How much food people can afford to buy in different countries.　○

　D　How many people are affected by lack of food in different countries.　○

[1]

b) For a country you have studied, compare the effectiveness of one past and one present attempt to increase food security at a national scale.

[8]

[Total 10 marks]

## Section B: Human Geography Fieldwork

Answer **all** the questions in this section.

**5** This question is about your fieldwork enquiry that involved the collection of **human geography** data.

a) Describe **one** primary data collection technique you used and explain why you used it.

**Primary data collection technique:** ......................................................................................

**Description and explanation:** ................................................................................................

..................................................................................................................................................

..................................................................................................................................................

..................................................................................................................................................

[3]

A group of students sent a questionnaire to a random selection of residents in twenty districts in Greaton. The results from one question for three of the districts are shown in **Figure 6**. **Figure 7** is a photo of a street in district Q and **Figure 8** is a map showing the percentage of people in each district from ethnic minority groups.

**Figure 6**

Q1 'To what extent has the city's character been influenced by ethnic diversity?'
(1 = not very much,
4 = very strongly)
Percentage of people giving each score in districts A, E and Q:

| | | District | | |
|---|---|---|---|---|
| | | A | E | Q |
| Score | 1 | 75 | 21 | 12 |
| | 2 | 10 | 7 | 2 |
| | 3 | 8 | 35 | 8 |
| | 4 | 7 | 37 | 78 |

**Figure 7**

**Figure 8**

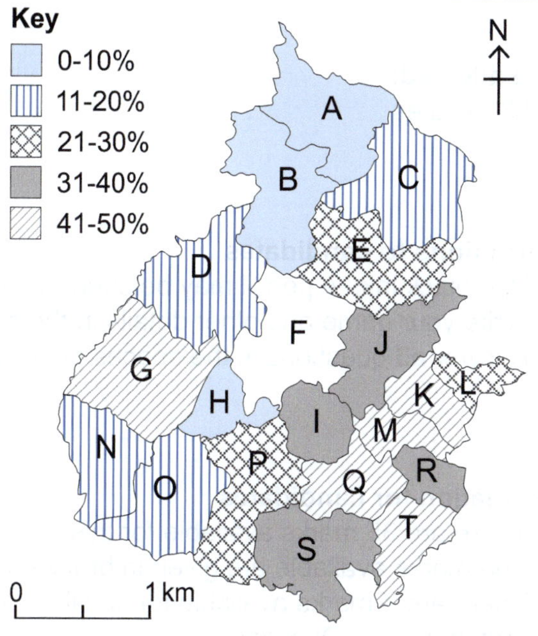

Key
- 0-10%
- 11-20%
- 21-30%
- 31-40%
- 41-50%

b) i) Complete **Figure 8** to show that the proportion of ethnic minority groups in district F is 17%.

[1]

ii) Suggest **one** other way in which the students could have presented the data shown in **Figure 8**.

..................................................................................................................................................

..................................................................................................................................................

[1]

c) The student's enquiry question was 'To what extent is ethnic diversity influencing the character of Greaton?' Using evidence from **Figures 6, 7** and **8**, write a conclusion to the investigation.

[8 + 3 SPaG]

[Total 16 marks]

**END OF QUESTIONS**

# GCSE Geography

## Paper 3: Geographical Exploration

**In addition to this paper you should have:**
- A pencil.
- A ruler.
- A calculator.

| Centre name |   |   |   |   |
|---|---|---|---|---|
| Centre number |   |   |   |   |
| Candidate number |   |   |   |   |

**Time allowed:**
- 53 minutes

| Surname |   |
|---|---|
| Other names |   |
| Candidate signature |   |

**Instructions to candidates**
- Use black ink. A pencil may be used for graphs and diagrams.
- Write your name and other details in the spaces provided above.
- Answer **all** questions in the spaces provided.

**Information for candidates**
- There are 35 marks available for this paper.
- The marks available are given in brackets at the end of each question.
- There are 3 marks available for spelling, punctuation, grammar and terminology in Question 4.

**For examiner's use**

| Q | Attempt Nº 1 | 2 | 3 | Q | Attempt Nº 1 | 2 | 3 |
|---|---|---|---|---|---|---|---|
| 1 |   |   |   | 4 |   |   |   |
| 2 |   |   |   |   |   |   |   |
| 3 |   |   |   |   |   |   |   |
|   |   |   |   | Total |   |   |   |

# Resource Booklet

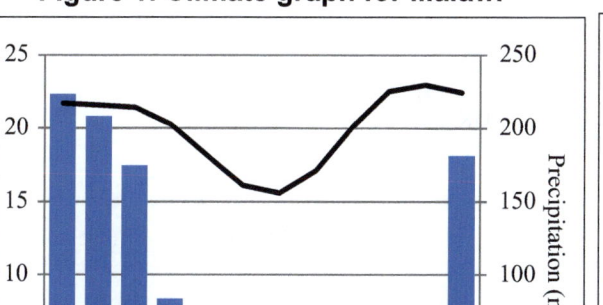

## Figure 1: Climate graph for Malawi

## Figure 2: World map

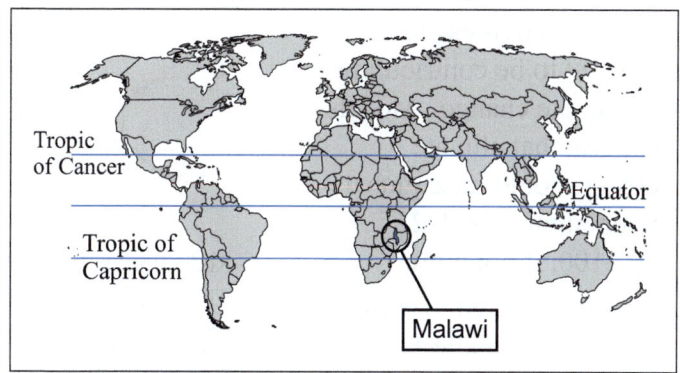

## Figure 3: Predicted changes in crop yields by 2050

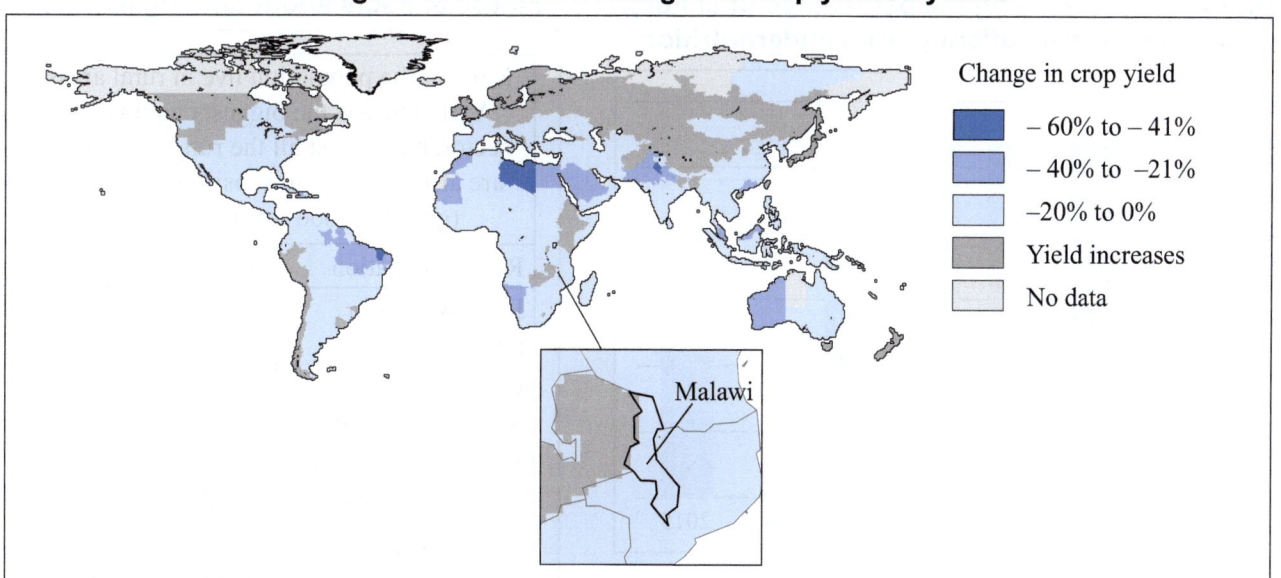

Change in crop yield:
- −60% to −41%
- −40% to −21%
- −20% to 0%
- Yield increases
- No data

## Figure 4: Population and development indicators for four countries

|  | Population (millions) | GNI per capita (US $) | HDI* | Global Hunger Index◆ | Access to safe water |
|---|---|---|---|---|---|
| UK | 65 | 43 350 | 0.907 | n/a | 100% |
| USA | 319 | 54 400 | 0.915 | n/a | 99% |
| Bangladesh | 159 | 1080 | 0.570 | 27.3 | 87% |
| Malawi | 17 | 360 | 0.445 | 27.3 | 90% |

* Human Development Index (HDI) is a number between 0 and 1. The closer to 1 the number is, the more developed a country is considered to be.

◆ Global Hunger Index is a number between 0 and 100 that measures hunger in EDCs and LIDCs. The scale ranks the severity of the problem from 'low' to 'extremely alarming' — scores from 20 to 34.9 indicate a 'serious' hunger problem.

Global Hunger Index values in Figure 4 source: von Grebmer et al. (2015).

**Turn over ▶**

### Figure 5: Effects of climate change

Human activities are thought to be contributing to climate change. Models suggest that climate change could raise global temperatures by 1-2 °C by 2100, if not more.

This is expected to cause precipitation patterns to change, with some areas seeing an increase in droughts and others seeing more frequent and extreme flooding.

### Figure 6: Areas predicted to have a reduced water supply by 2040

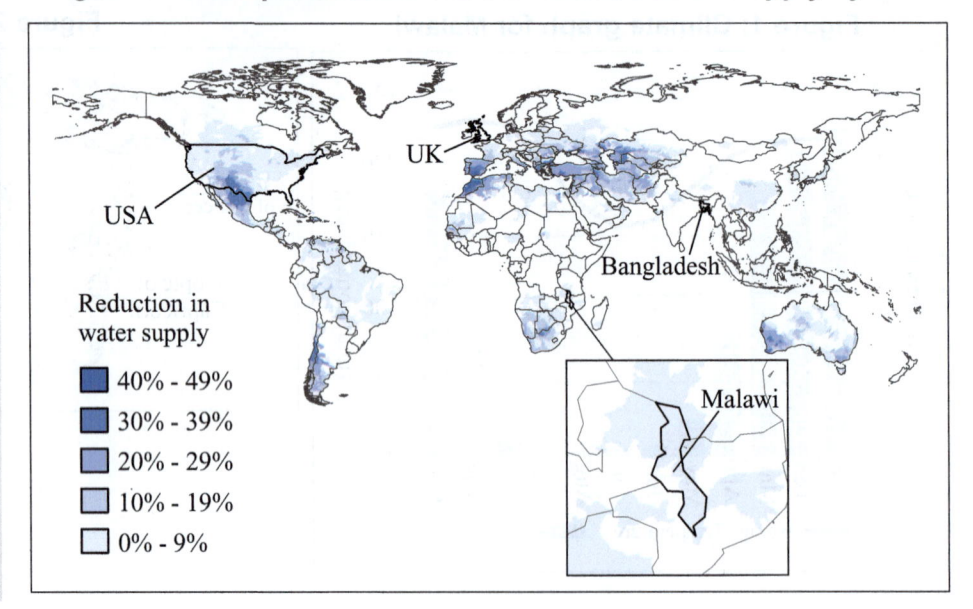

Reduction in water supply
- 40% - 49%
- 30% - 39%
- 20% - 29%
- 10% - 19%
- 0% - 9%

Labelled: USA, UK, Bangladesh, Malawi

### Figure 7: Graph showing the percentage of children under 5 in Malawi suffering from undernutrition

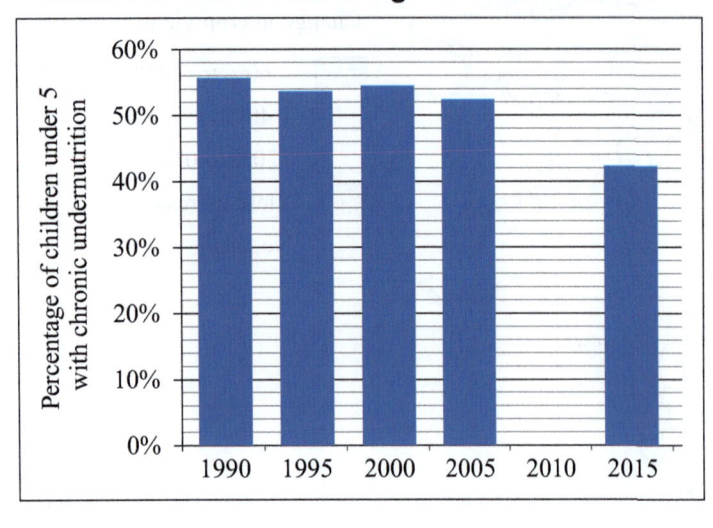

Bar chart, y-axis: Percentage of children under 5 with chronic undernutrition (0%–60%), x-axis years: 1990 (~56%), 1995 (~54%), 2000 (~55%), 2005 (~53%), 2015 (~42%).

### Figure 8: Facts about farming in Malawi

Most of the population live in rural areas. Agriculture is the biggest employment sector, but almost all the rural population are also involved in subsistence farming (growing food for personal use).

| | |
|---|---|
| Rural population | 80% |
| Employment in agriculture | 60% |
| Contribution of agriculture to GDP | 33% |
| People involved in subsistence farming | 90% of rural population |
| Natural vegetation | Savannah grasslands, deciduous forest |
| Main export crops | Tobacco, tea, sugarcane |
| Main subsistence crop | Maize |
| Farming methods | Slash and burn* used to clear land. Move on after 2-3 years, when land becomes unproductive. |

*Slash and burn is a technique where vegetation is cut down and burnt so that crops can be planted.*

Figure 7 source: von Grebmer et al. (2015).

**Figure 9: Comments on farming in Malawi**

*This summer, the rains were really heavy and my land flooded again. All my crops were destroyed.*
Subsistence farmer, southern Malawi

*The droughts meant that crop yields were much lower this year. Now food is so expensive, I can't afford to buy enough to keep my family healthy.*
City dweller, Lilongwe

*It's hard to grow food at the camp. The World Food Programme hands out the basics we need to keep going but there are about 23,000 people to feed.*
Refugee from war in Burundi, Dzaleka refugee camp, central Malawi

*We eat any fish I can't sell. It gives my children the nutrients they need to grow properly.*
Fisherman, Lake Malawi

**Figure 10: Examples of current food security projects in Malawi**

**Food banks**
The Hunger Project operates eight food banks distributed throughout Malawi. These have food stocks to ensure local communities have enough food all year round, even if they are affected by droughts or floods. Three of the food banks provide equipment so that farmers can process their crops and sell them for more money. Most also distribute fertiliser, so that farmers can increase their crop yields. However, the food banks currently reach less than 1% of the population.

**Subsidies**
In 2004, the government began offering subsidies to enable poor farmers to buy fertilisers and seed. This triggered a 'green revolution', massively increasing Malawi's maize production. However, the system collapsed because foreign donors pulled out and the government could no longer afford the subsidies. The government has continued to promote maize production over the diversification of crops.

**Permaculture**
Organisations such as the African Moringa and Permaculture Project are working with local communities to help them develop more reliable food supplies. For example, they are training local communities in permaculture principles. They also help local community groups develop products such as peanut butter to sell at a higher price. However, the project is in its early stages and needs funding to develop further.

**Turn over ▶**

**1** Study **Figures 1** and **2** on page 177, a graph of Malawi's climate and a map of the world.

Using **Figures 1** and **2**, describe the climate of Malawi and explain how this may be influenced by Malawi's location.

..................................................................................................................................................
..................................................................................................................................................
..................................................................................................................................................
..................................................................................................................................................
..................................................................................................................................................
..................................................................................................................................................
..................................................................................................................................................
..................................................................................................................................................

*[Total 6 marks]*

**2** Study **Figures 3**, **4** and **5** on pages 177-178, maps of predicted change in water supply and crop yield, and a table of development indicators.

a) Using **Figure 3**, state how Malawi's crop yields are predicted to change by 2050. Suggest **one** possible cause of this change.

..................................................................................................................................................
..................................................................................................................................................
..................................................................................................................................................

*[2]*

b) Using **Figure 3** and your own knowledge, suggest how changing crop yields might affect food security in Africa by 2050.

..................................................................................................................................................
..................................................................................................................................................
..................................................................................................................................................
..................................................................................................................................................

*[3]*

c) Which of the countries in **Figure 4** is the least developed? Justify your answer using evidence from **Figure 4**.

Least developed country: ......................................................................................................

..................................................................................................................................................
..................................................................................................................................................
..................................................................................................................................................

*[3]*

*[Total 8 marks]*

**3** Study **Figures 1**, **4, 7**, and **9** on pages 177-179. **Figures 7** and **9** show information about child nutrition and farming in Malawi.

a) In 2010, there were 2.5 million children aged under 5 years old in Malawi, of whom 1.2 million suffered from chronic undernutrition. Calculate this as a percentage and plot it on **Figure 7**.

...........................................................................................................................................................
[2]

b) Using evidence from **Figures 1**, **4** and **9**, suggest **two** reasons for the levels of undernutrition among children under 5 in Malawi shown in **Figure 7**.

...........................................................................................................................................................

...........................................................................................................................................................

...........................................................................................................................................................

...........................................................................................................................................................

...........................................................................................................................................................
[4]
[Total 6 marks]

**4** Study **all** of the information on pages 177-179.

Using information from pages 177-179 and your own knowledge, write a report on food security in Malawi and decide on a strategy to increase food security there.
In your report you need to:

1. Describe the current state of food security in Malawi including potential challenges for the country in the near future.

2. Suggest and justify a sustainable strategy to increase food security in Malawi.
[12 + 3 SPaG]
[Total 15 marks]

**END OF QUESTIONS**

# Answers

## Topic 1 — Global Hazards

### Page 7
1. a) *[1 mark]*
   b) *[1 mark]*
   c) A *[1 mark]*
   d) C *[1 mark]*

### Page 16
1. a) There were large areas affected by extreme drought around the equator, e.g. in central Africa *[1 mark]*. Extreme droughts also occurred around 23° S, e.g. in Australia and South America *[1 mark]* and north of 23° N, e.g. north Africa and the Middle East *[1 mark]*. There were smaller areas of extreme drought in areas of the far north, e.g. in North America and north east Asia *[1 mark]*.
   b) A drought is a long period (weeks, months or years) when rainfall is below average *[1 mark]*.
   c) C *[1 mark]*
2. This question is level marked. There are 3 extra marks available for spelling, punctuation and grammar.
   How to grade your answer:
   Level 0: There is no relevant information. *[0 marks]*
   Level 1: There is a basic description of the consequences of and responses to a drought or heat wave event. *[1-2 marks]*
   Level 2: There is a clear description of the consequences of and responses to a drought or heat wave event. *[3-5 marks]*
   Level 3: There is a detailed description of the consequences of and responses to a drought or heat wave event. *[6-8 marks]*
   Make sure your spelling, punctuation and grammar are consistently correct, that your meaning is clear and that you use a range of geographical terms correctly *[0-3 marks]*.
   Your answer should refer to one named drought or heat wave event. Here are some points your answer may include:
   - The effect of the drought or heat wave on people, including any injuries and deaths.
   - Damage to property and infrastructure.
   - The cost of the drought or heat wave.
   - How people and organisations responded during the drought or heat wave.
   - How people and organisations responded immediately after the drought or heat wave.
   - How people and organisations responded in the months and years after the drought or heat wave.
   - Answers may refer to the Millennium Drought in Australia. As a result of the drought, farmers lost income and livestock, vegetation loss and soil erosion increased, and wildfires affected 30 000 km² of land. In response, water allocations were reduced during the drought, the government gave families and businesses income support to help them survive, and cities like Sydney built new desalination plants to turn sea water into drinking water.

### Page 24
1. a) Plate boundary A is a constructive plate boundary *[1 mark]*. As the two plates move away from each other, magma rises from the mantle to fill the gap *[1 mark]*. The magma then cools, creating new crust *[1 mark]*.
   b) A conservative plate boundary *[1 mark]*.
   c) Plates could move sideways past each other *[1 mark]* or move in the same direction but at different speeds *[1 mark]*.
   d) A destructive plate boundary *[1 mark]*.
   e) In collision plate boundaries, both plates move towards each other but neither plate is forced down into the mantle *[1 mark]*. Both plates are folded and forced upwards *[1 mark]*.

## Topic 2 — Changing Climate

### Page 33
1. a) E.g. warmer weather, like that described in Figure 1, is likely to attract holiday-makers, so it could boost the UK's tourist industry *[1 mark]*. Climate change might make the growing season longer, which could increase crop productivity *[1 mark]*. It could also mean crops suited to warmer climates could be grown in the south of England *[1 mark]*.
   b) Any two from: e.g. increasing temperatures may mean that deaths from cold-related illnesses decrease *[1 mark]*, but more people could suffer from heat-related illnesses *[1 mark]*. / Sea level rise may cause more flooding in low-lying areas and on estuaries *[1 mark]*, which may damage people's homes and businesses *[1 mark]*. / Rainfall in some areas may increase, causing increased flooding *[1 mark]*. This could damage people's homes and businesses *[1 mark]*. / Drier summers may lead to decreased water availability *[1 mark]*, so people in dry or densely populated areas may experience water shortages *[1 mark]*.

## Topic 3 — Distinctive Landscapes

### Page 45
1. a) 10 km *[1 mark]*
   b) 0.8 m/s *[1 mark]*
   c) Between 20 and 30 km the river's velocity drops *[1 mark]*. When rivers slow down they deposit the material they are carrying *[1 mark]*.
   d) 

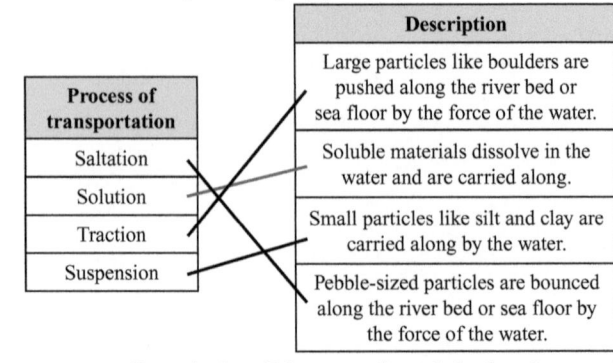

| Process of transportation | Description |
|---|---|
| Saltation | Large particles like boulders are pushed along the river bed or sea floor by the force of the water. |
| Solution | Soluble materials dissolve in the water and are carried along. |
| Traction | Small particles like silt and clay are carried along by the water. |
| Suspension | Pebble-sized particles are bounced along the river bed or sea floor by the force of the water. |

*[2 marks for all 3 correct, 1 mark for 1 or 2 correct]*

2   This question is level marked. There are 3 extra marks available for spelling, punctuation and grammar.
How to grade your answer:
Level 0:   There is no relevant information. *[0 marks]*
Level 1:   There is a basic description of some of the positive and negative impacts of human activity on a named coastal landscape. *[1-2 marks]*
Level 2:   There is a clear comparison of some of the positive and negative impacts of human activity on a named coastal landscape. *[3-5 marks]*
Level 3:   There is a detailed comparison of a range of positive and negative impacts of human activity on a named coastal landscape. The answer comes to a clear conclusion. *[6-8 marks]*

Make sure your spelling, punctuation and grammar are consistently correct, that your meaning is clear and that you use a range of geographical terms correctly *[0-3 marks]*.
Here are some points your answer may include:
- A description of the different types of human activity occurring in the area, e.g. coastal management, tourism and industry.
- An explanation of how these activities have impacted the coastal landscape, e.g. building sea defences may have reduced erosion in one area, but increased it in unprotected areas.
- An assessment of whether the impacts you described are generally positive or negative for the landscape.
- A conclusion that states whether the impacts of human activities on the coastal landscape have been generally positive or negative, backed up by the points in the body of your answer.
- Your answer could refer to the Dorset coast, where management, tourism and industry are all occurring. Some beaches (e.g. in Swanage Bay) have been replenished, which has decreased erosion in the immediate area. Tourists have eroded footpaths along the tops of cliffs. Quarrying of limestone has left large areas of rock exposed (e.g. on the Isle of Portland), which has increased weathering and erosion.

## Page 55
1 a) C *[1 mark]*
  b) 0.4 km *[1 mark]*
  c) Waterfall Y *[1 mark]*
*Remember that the steeper the gradient, the closer together the contour lines will be.*
  d) Waterfalls form where a river flows over an area of hard rock followed by an area of softer rock *[1 mark]*, so the Afon Merch must flow over rocks with alternating hardness *[1 mark]*.
  e) A gorge forms as a waterfall retreats up a river channel *[1 mark]*. The hard rock cap is undercut by erosion (abrasion) so it becomes unsupported and collapses *[1 mark]*. Over time, more undercutting causes more collapses, so the waterfall retreats, forming a steep-sided valley called a gorge *[1 mark]*.
  f) E.g. information about the geology of the area could be added *[1 mark]*.

# Topic 4 — Sustaining Ecosystems

## Page 63
1 a) Between about 50° north and south of the equator / between the tropics and at mid-latitudes *[1 mark]*.
  b) C *[1 mark]*.
  c) Grasslands consist mostly of grass and small plants *[1 mark]*. There may be a few scattered trees in grasslands between the tropics *[1 mark]*.
  d) E.g. plants get the nutrients they need to grow from the soil *[1 mark]*. The nutrients are returned to the soil through falling leaves and when the plants die and decompose *[1 mark]*.
2 Any two from: e.g. jerboas are quite small *[1 mark]* — many desert mammals are small so they can lose heat easily *[1 mark]*. / Jerboas are nocturnal *[1 mark]* — many desert animals are nocturnal so they can avoid the heat of the day *[1 mark]*. / Jerboas live in burrows *[1 mark]* — many desert animals live in burrows where temperatures are lower *[1 mark]*.

## Page 72
1 a) B *[1 mark]*
  b) Any one from: e.g. the extraction of metals from mined rocks produces lots of pollution *[1 mark]*, damaging ecosystems in the surrounding area *[1 mark]*. / There is a risk of oil spills *[1 mark]*, which are difficult to clean up and can harm habitats and kill wildlife *[1 mark]*. / Pipelines that are built to transport oil and gas *[1 mark]* can melt permafrost and interrupt the migration routes of caribou herds *[1 mark]*.
  c) Any two from: e.g. tourists may scare wildlife *[1 mark]*, which may interfere with breeding, e.g. if nesting birds abandon their young *[1 mark]*. / Tourists may trample on vegetation *[1 mark]*, which could threaten the survival of fragile species *[1 mark]*. / If tourism is unregulated there may be a lack of infrastructure *[1 mark]*. This can lead to pollution of waterways if, for example, sewage isn't treated properly *[1 mark]*. / Tourists can leave behind litter *[1 mark]*, which can kill or harm animals if they get trapped in it or eat it *[1 mark]*.
  d) This question is level marked. How to grade your answer:
Level 0:   There is no relevant information. *[0 marks]*
Level 1:   There is a basic description of the effect of scientific research. *[1-2 marks]*
Level 2:   There is a clear description of the effects of scientific research and an attempt to assess the extent to which they are positive. *[3-4 marks]*
Level 3:   There is a detailed description of the effects of scientific research and a clear assessment of the extent to which they are positive. *[5-6 marks]*

Here are some points your answer may include:
- A description of the positive effects of research in polar environments on ecosystems. E.g. its importance in understanding and acting on global issues such as climate change.
- A description of any negative effects of research in polar environments on ecosystems. E.g. rubbish, sewage and abandoned equipment from research stations and ships causing pollution, damaging habitats and harming wildlife.
- Any other relevant information, e.g. awareness of the effect of pollution on ecosystems, due to the research of scientists, has meant that research organisations now try to limit the release of harmful substances.
- A conclusion which examines the evidence and provides an overall judgement about the extent to which the effects are positive.

## Topic 5 — Urban Futures

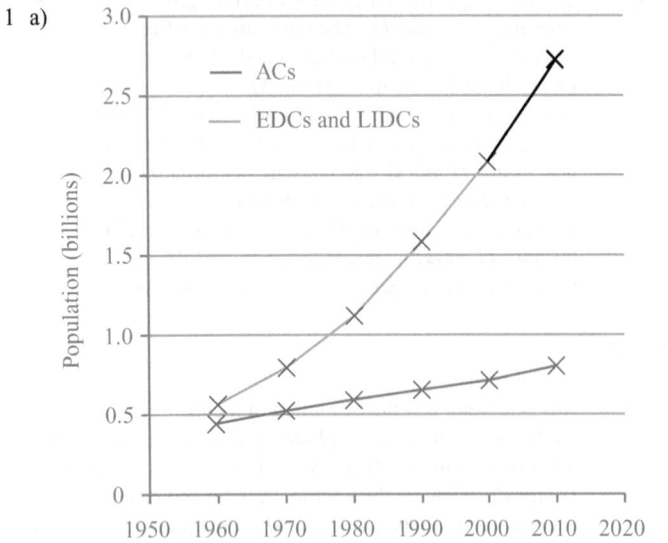

### Page 81
1 a) [Graph showing Population (billions) vs Year from 1950 to 2020, with two lines: ACs and EDCs and LIDCs. ACs line rises from ~0.45 in 1960 to ~0.8 in 2010. EDCs and LIDCs line rises from ~0.55 in 1960 to ~2.72 in 2010.] *[1 mark]*

b) $\dfrac{2.72 - 0.56}{0.56} \times 100$
= **386%** (to nearest whole number) *[1 mark]*

c) This question is level marked. How to grade your answer:
- Level 0: There is no relevant information. *[0 marks]*
- Level 1: There are a few points about the rate of urbanisation in either richer or poorer countries. *[1-2 marks]*
- Level 2: There is a clear explanation of the rate of urbanisation in richer and poorer countries. *[3-4 marks]*
- Level 3: There is a detailed explanation of the rate of urbanisation in richer and poorer countries. *[5-6 marks]*

Here are some points your answer may include:
- Urbanisation happened earlier in richer countries than in poorer countries, e.g. during the industrial revolution, so most of the population now already live in urban areas. This means that there are fewer people moving into cities in richer countries than in poorer countries.
- Good transport and communication networks mean that people in richer countries can live in rural areas and commute to cities, or work from home. This means that many people in richer countries are moving away from cities.
- Deindustrialisation in cities in richer countries caused an increase in unemployment. People desiring a better quality of life moved away from overcrowded cities to rural areas, meaning that urban population growth slowed.
- A lower proportion of the population in poorer countries currently live in urban areas, so there are more people living in rural areas who might move to cities.
- Many people in poorer countries are moving to cities to get a better quality of life, e.g. access to better health care, jobs and education. This causes rapid urban growth in poorer countries.

d) E.g. waste disposal services may not be able to keep pace with the growth, so rubbish may not all be collected or it may end up in big rubbish heaps *[1 mark]*. This can damage the environment, especially if the waste is toxic *[1 mark]*. Sewage systems may not be able to cope with the increased number of people, so sewage and toxic chemicals can get into rivers *[1 mark]*, which can harm wildlife *[1 mark]*.

*You could also have mentioned the higher number of vehicles on the roads, and the air pollution and greenhouse gas emissions that they cause.*

### Page 89
1 a) The population steadily increased from 2004 to 2014 *[1 mark]*.

b) The population is increasing so there is a high demand for houses *[1 mark]*. However, the number of houses built has slightly decreased on average over the same period *[1 mark]*. House prices have also increased, making it harder for poorer people to buy their own home *[1 mark]*.

c) Your answer will vary depending on the city you have chosen. E.g. London has significant financial inequality — it is home to the richest and the poorest people in the UK *[1 mark]*. In some poorer areas, e.g. Newham, around 25% of the population live in poverty, meaning that they struggle to afford rent, food, fuel etc. *[1 mark]*. In these areas, unhealthy lifestyles, e.g. drinking, smoking and poor diet, are more common than in wealthier areas *[1 mark]*. This has led to poorer health among less-wealthy residents, e.g. life expectancy is about 5 years lower in poorer areas than in wealthier areas *[1 mark]*.

d) Your answer will vary depending on the city you have chosen. E.g. In London, the Mayor's Transport Strategy aims to improve the city's transport network and make it more sustainable by easing congesting and reducing air pollution *[1 mark]*. For example, congestion charges aim to discourage drivers from entering the city centre, in order to decrease the amount of congestion and air pollution that are caused by vehicles *[1 mark]*. Rail services are being improved, e.g. more trains are being run every hour and each train has more carriages, to reduce overcrowding *[1 mark]*. Bikes are available to hire at numerous locations using self-service machines, to encourage cycling *[1 mark]*.

## Topic 6 — Dynamic Development

### Page 97
1 a) E.g. Libya has a very dry climate — more than 90% of the country is desert or semi-desert *[1 mark]*. This probably means that it can't grow much food *[1 mark]*. With fewer crops to sell, people have less money to spend on goods and services *[1 mark]*. The government will also receive less money from taxes (on food sold and bought), so has less to spend on developing the country, e.g. improving health care and education *[1 mark]*.

b) Any two from: e.g. lack of natural resources, such as coal, oil or metal ores *[1 mark]* means countries make less money because they have fewer products to sell *[1 mark]*. / Landlocked countries can struggle to develop *[1 mark]* because it can be harder and more expensive to transport goods into and out of the country *[1 mark]*. / Countries with lots of natural hazards may struggle to develop *[1 mark]*, because they have to spend a lot of money rebuilding after disasters occur instead of investing in development *[1 mark]*.

c) E.g. conflict is likely to have decreased Libya's level of development *[1 mark]*. This is because damage is done to infrastructure and property, such as the building in Figure 1 *[1 mark]*, and money is spent on arms and fighting instead of development *[1 mark]*. Conflict can also decrease foreign investment, e.g. oil companies started to leave Libya after the outbreak of violence, so there is less money coming into the country *[1 mark]*.

### Page 107
1 a) C *[1 mark]*

*The aid is long-term because it is to help with Ghana's development and is not in response to an emergency. It is top-down because the money is being given to the Ghanaian Government, not directly to the local people.*

Answers

b) Advantage: e.g. helps to improve the level of development of the recipient country (by improving health, education and agriculture) *[1 mark]*.
Disadvantage: e.g. the aid may not reach the poorest people *[1 mark]* / aid may be lost through corruption *[1 mark]*.

c) Advantage: e.g. helps provide immediate disaster relief in recipient countries *[1 mark]*.
Disadvantage: e.g. often doesn't help with long-term recovery efforts *[1 mark]* / doesn't help improve overall level of development *[1 mark]*.

d) This question is level marked. There are 3 extra marks available for spelling, punctuation and grammar.
How to grade your answer:
Level 0: There is no relevant information. *[0 marks]*
Level 1: There is a basic description of one top-down and/or one bottom-up development strategy. *[1-2 marks]*
Level 2: There is a clear description of one top-down and one bottom-up development strategy, with a good attempt to evaluate their success. *[3-5 marks]*
Level 3: There is a detailed description of one top-down and one bottom-up development strategy, with a thorough evaluation of their success. *[6-8 marks]*

Make sure your spelling, punctuation and grammar are consistently correct, that your meaning is clear and that you use a range of geographical terms correctly *[0-3 marks]*.
Your answer must outline the benefits and problems of both a top-down and a bottom-up development strategy in a named LIDC, and come to a clear conclusion about how successful they have been.
Here are some points your answer may include:
- A brief overview of the level of development of your chosen country, and why development strategies may be needed.
- A brief outline of a top-down development strategy that has been used in your chosen country, e.g. the construction of a dam for hydroelectric power or an irrigation scheme.
- A description of the benefits that the top-down development strategy has brought, e.g. improving the economy or helping with long-term development.
- A description of any problems that the development has caused, or ways in which it hasn't been successful, e.g.:
  - if the country borrowed money to fund the project, repaying it may keep the country in poverty,
  - the project may not benefit those in rural or remote locations, increasing inequality,
  - corruption in the government may mean that the money given hasn't all been used for the project it was intended for.
- A brief description of a 'bottom-up' development strategy that has been used in your chosen LIDC.
- A description of the benefits that the bottom-up development strategy has brought, e.g.:
  - that local people have a say in how the money is used and can get what they need,
  - that the projects employ local people, so they earn money and learn new skills.
- A description of any problems that the development has caused, e.g.:
  - the project was small-scale so it didn't benefit everyone in the community,
  - different organisations didn't work together well so the project was inefficient.
- A conclusion summarising the success of each project.

- Your answer could refer to development projects in the Democratic Republic of the Congo. One example of a top-down development strategy is the proposed construction of the Grand Inga Dam on the Congo River, which could provide cheap, reliable energy for the whole country, but will result in flooding of a huge area and relocation of the people who live there. One example of a bottom-up strategy is a community project funded by Comic Relief, which aims to improve rural schools and increase the number of children in education. This will increase education levels, which will help people find better-paid jobs, but it only focuses on some schools, so not everyone will benefit.

# Topic 7 — UK in the 21st Century

## Page 115

1 a) UK Population — 2001 *[1 mark]*
b) 30-39 years *[1 mark]*
c) 7.8 million (accept 7.6-8 million) *[1 mark]*
d) The UK population got older between 2001 and 2015 *[1 mark]*. In 2001, the highest number of people were aged 30-39, but by 2015 the highest number of people were aged 40-49 *[1 mark]*. However, there was also an increase in the number of people aged 20-29 between 2001 and 2015 *[1 mark]*.

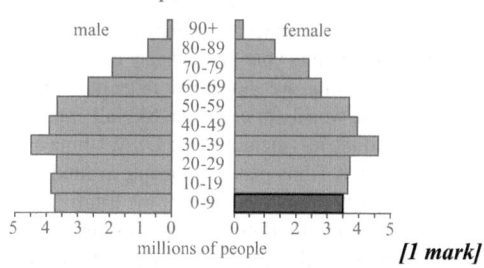

2 This question is level marked. How to grade your answer:
Level 0: There is no relevant information. *[0 marks]*
Level 1: There is a basic description of how population structure and ethnic diversity have changed in a named location since 2001. *[1-2 marks]*
Level 2: There is a clear description of how population structure and ethnic diversity have changed in a named location since 2001. *[3-4 marks]*
Level 3: There is a detailed description of how population structure and ethnic diversity have changed in a named location since 2001. *[5-6 marks]*

Here are some points your answer may include:
- How population in your chosen area has changed since 2001 (e.g. whether it has increased or decreased).
- How population structure has changed over the same period (e.g. whether the population is generally older or younger now than in 2001 and which age groups have seen the biggest changes).
- How ethnic diversity in your chosen location has changed since 2001 (e.g. whether it has increased or decreased, and which ethnic groups have seen the greatest change in numbers).
- Your answer could refer to London, where the population has increased rapidly since 2001, with the highest growth in the 40-49 age group. Over the same period, ethnic diversity in London has increased, and around 55% of the population are not white British (compared to 40% in 2001), with big increases in the number of people from Poland, Romania, Africa and Asia.

## Page 123

1  a)  US $146.1 million *[1 mark]*
   b)  14.3% (accept 14%) *[1 mark]*
      (158.4 ÷ 1110) × 100 = 14.3%
   c)  E.g. films such as the 'Harry Potter' series give people a positive impression of the UK as an attractive, interesting place, which encourages people to visit *[1 mark]*. / Media exports give people overseas a greater understanding of UK culture, so they may visit to experience it for themselves *[1 mark]*.
   d)  This question is level marked. How to grade your answer:
      Level 0:  There is no relevant information. *[0 marks]*
      Level 1:  There are a few basic points about the effect of UK films on people in other countries. *[1-2 marks]*
      Level 2:  There is a clear explanation of the effect of UK films on people around the world, and how this effect is achieved. *[3-4 marks]*
      Level 3:  There is a detailed explanation of the effect of UK films on people around the world, and how this effect is achieved. *[5-6 marks]*
      Here are some points your answer may include:
      - Some UK films are shown in a large number of countries around the world, for example 'Skyfall' was shown in lots of countries, including the USA, China and Russia.
      - Viewing UK films may give people around the world a better understanding of the English language and of UK customs and values.
      - Films might influence people's perceptions of the UK, for example, parts of the 'Harry Potter' films are shot in scenic locations, as shown in Figure 2, so people will have a positive impression of the UK.
      - The amount of money generated by exporting UK films, e.g. 'Skyfall' made over US $1 billion at the box office, some of which remained in the UK. This strengthens the UK's economic influence.
      - People may copy clothes and hairstyles from films, so UK films can have a global influence on fashion.

## Topic 8 — Resource Reliance

### Page 132

1  a)  E.g. most of the countries that produced less than 2.8 million tonnes of cereals are in Africa and the Middle East *[1 mark]*. There are several countries that produced less than 2.8 million tonnes of cereals in South America, and some smaller countries in Europe and Asia *[1 mark]*.
   *You may also have mentioned that there is a belt of countries producing less than 2.8 million tonnes of cereal running down the centre of Africa from north to south.*
   b)  Any one from: e.g. Angola has higher levels of poverty than the USA *[1 mark]*, which means that farmers may not be able to afford pesticides or fertilisers *[1 mark]*. / The USA may be able to afford better technology, e.g. mechanised farm equipment, than Angola *[1 mark]*, which can increase the amount of food that can be grown by making the process more efficient *[1 mark]*. / Angola may experience more conflict than the USA *[1 mark]*, which may affect the amount of farming land that is available and safe to use to produce food *[1 mark]*.
   c)  Food security is when people have access to enough nutritious food to stay healthy and active *[1 mark]*.
   d)  E.g. countries with climates that are too cold or have too little rainfall can't grow much food, so they are more likely to be food insecure *[1 mark]*. Extreme weather events (e.g. floods and droughts) can destroy crops, so countries that are prone to extreme weather are more likely to be food insecure *[1 mark]*. Pests can increase a country's food insecurity, e.g. rats or locusts can reduce yields by consuming crops *[1 mark]*. Diseases can also reduce yields and increase food insecurity by killing crops and animals *[1 mark]*.
   *You might also have mentioned factors such as geology and water stress, e.g. in countries that have impermeable rocks, groundwater stores can be limited, so it may be difficult to irrigate crops during dry periods.*

### Page 140

1  a)  The area of land used to grow organic crops generally increased from about 100 000 ha in 1999 to 190 000 ha in 2015 *[1 mark]*. However, the area used for organic crop production decreased slightly between 2004 and 2006 *[1 mark]*.
   b)  E.g. organic farming uses natural fertilisers, e.g. manure, instead of chemical fertilisers to return nutrients to the soil *[1 mark]*. Not using chemical fertilisers helps to protect natural ecosystems, making organic farming more environmentally sustainable *[1 mark]*.
   *You might have written about not using artificial pesticides instead — pesticides can be harmful to organisms, so not using them helps to preserve biodiversity.*
   c)  C *[1 mark]*
   *Intensifying farming means producing as much food as possible in as small an area as possible. It usually requires large quantities of chemicals, such as fertilisers and pesticides, to maximise crop yields.*
   d)  This question is level marked. How to grade your answer:
      Level 0:  There is no relevant information. *[0 marks]*
      Level 1:  There is a basic description of at least one technological development that increases food production. *[1-2 marks]*
      Level 2:  There is a clear description of at least two technological developments that increase food production, and a basic attempt to assess their sustainability. *[3-4 marks]*
      Level 3:  There is a detailed description of at least two technological developments that increase food production, and a clear attempt to assess their sustainability. *[5-6 marks]*
      Here are some points your answer may include:
      - A brief description of each technological development, e.g. what it is and how it increases food production.
      - A discussion of the ways in which each method is sustainable. This may include social sustainability (e.g. how it increases food security), economic sustainability (e.g. how it may increase the wealth of countries in which it is used), and environmental sustainability (e.g. how it can help to protect the environment and limit interference in natural ecosystems).
      - A discussion of any ways in which each method is not sustainable. This may include problems with social sustainability (e.g. high cost of the food produced meaning that not everyone can afford it), economic sustainability (e.g. high set-up or running costs meaning that profits are limited) and environmental sustainability (e.g. damage to the environment).
      - A conclusion that sums up the extent to which the technological developments are sustainable, based on the points in the body of your answer.

- Your answer could refer to GM crops and hydroponics. GM crops can be designed to have higher yields, higher nutritional values etc., so they can increase food security. They often require fewer artificial chemicals, which increases their economic and environmental sustainability. However, because fewer varieties of crops are planted, they can also decrease biodiversity. Hydroponics allows plants to be grown in closely monitored nutrient solutions. This maximises crop yields, so can increase food security. It uses less resources than conventional farming, which increases its environmental sustainability. However, food grown using hydroponics can be expensive, which limits its social sustainability because not everyone can afford it.

# Fieldwork

## Page 147

1 a) Your answer should include a description of the technique(s) you used and a reason why each technique used was appropriate for your investigation. E.g. I used land use maps to show the distribution of industrial buildings in the town *[1 mark]*. This helped me show how the industrial centres are linked to the major transport routes *[1 mark]*. I also used pie charts to show the proportion of people travelling by different methods of transport at two major industrial centres *[1 mark]*. This helped me to easily compare the two data sets *[1 mark]*. Here are some other points your answer may include:
- Maps, e.g. dot maps, can be used to show the variation and distribution of the variable you were investigating.
- Land use maps can show the proportion of an area that is devoted to a particular land use. Annotations can be used to explain interesting features.
- Scatter graphs can be used to show the correlation between two variables.
- Dispersion graphs can show the variation in a data set.
- Field sketches or photographs can be used to show particular features and add qualitative evidence to quantitative data.
- Desire line maps can be used to show journeys made and distances travelled.

*Your answer should be specific to your enquiry — you don't need to include all the information that's given here, just expand on the parts that are relevant to your investigation.*

b) You need to write about how your data collection methods could have been made more reliable and more accurate. Any one from: e.g. I could have repeated the environmental survey more times *[1 mark]*, at different times of day and on different days of the week *[1 mark]*. / I could have conducted a pilot questionnaire *[1 mark]*, so that my questions provided enough detail to answer my original question *[1 mark]*. / I could have used a more representative sample *[1 mark]*, to help make my results applicable to the wider population.

2 a) Any two from: e.g. the ranging poles may not have been held straight, affecting the angles recorded *[1 mark]*. / The ranging poles may sink into the sand, affecting the angles recorded *[1 mark]*. / It can be difficult to take accurate readings with a clinometer *[1 mark]*. / It might be difficult to identify the low water mark *[1 mark]*. / The tide will be going in or out during the data collection, changing the point where measuring starts unless all profiles are taken at the same time by different groups *[1 mark]*. / The 5 m interval could include a break of slope, so the results wouldn't show the true profile *[1 mark]*.

b) E.g. more cross profiles could have been measured *[1 mark]* at equal intervals along the beach *[1 mark]*.

# Practice Paper 1: Our Natural World

## Pages 165-169

1 a) C *[1 mark]*

b) In high pressure areas there are few clouds, due to the sinking air *[1 mark]*. This means there is little to block the Sun's energy, which causes high temperatures *[1 mark]*.

c) This question is level marked. How to grade your answer:
- Level 0: There is no relevant information. *[0 marks]*
- Level 1: There is a basic description of the extreme weather conditions associated with tropical storms. *[1-2 marks]*
- Level 2: There is a clear description of the extreme weather conditions associated with tropical storms and a clear explanation of how they are caused. *[3-4 marks]*
- Level 3: There is a detailed description of the extreme weather conditions associated with tropical storms and a detailed explanation of how they are caused. *[5-6 marks]*

Here are some points your answer may include:
- Tropical storms can have extreme wind speeds of more than 250 kilometres per hour. These winds are strong enough to damage or destroy buildings and plants, and cause loose objects (e.g. bins) to be picked up and transported.
- Strong winds in a tropical storm are caused by an area of very low pressure at the centre of the storm that creates a big pressure difference to the surrounding area.
- Extremely high amounts of precipitation can fall rapidly in tropical storms.
- High amounts of precipitation are caused by large amounts of warm, moist air being sucked towards the centre of the storm due to the difference in pressure. As this happens, the air rises, cools and condenses, causing rain.

2 a) i) Temperature has changed in cycles of approximately 100 000 years *[1 mark]*. The temperature difference ranges between -9 °C and +3 °C from the present day *[1 mark]*.

ii) Ice sheets are made up of layers of ice, with one new layer formed each year *[1 mark]*. By analysing the gases trapped in the layers of ice, scientists can tell what the temperature was in each year *[1 mark]*.

b) Burning coal (a fossil fuel) releases carbon dioxide ($CO_2$), into the atmosphere, so coal-fired power plants increase the concentration of greenhouse gases in the atmosphere *[1 mark]*. Greenhouse gases absorb outgoing heat, so less is lost to space — this is called the greenhouse effect *[1 mark]*. Increasing the amount of greenhouse gas in the atmosphere enhances the greenhouse effect *[1 mark]*. This means that more heat is trapped and the planet warms up, leading to climate change *[1 mark]*.

3 a) B *[1 mark]*

b) Constructive waves have a powerful swash which carries material up the beach *[1 mark]*. Their backwash is weaker, so doesn't take a lot of material back down the beach *[1 mark]*. This means that, overall, constructive waves contribute to deposition because they move beach material inland *[1 mark]*.

Answers

c) This question is level marked. How to grade your answer:
Level 0: There is no relevant information. *[0 marks]*
Level 1: There is a basic description of erosional landforms in a named coastal landscape. *[1-2 marks]*
Level 2: There is a clear description of erosional landforms in a named coastal landscape and a brief explanation of how they were formed. *[3-4 marks]*
Level 3: There is a detailed description of erosional landforms in a named coastal landscape and a clear explanation of how they were formed. *[5-6 marks]*

Here are some points your answer may include:
- Named examples of specific erosional landforms (e.g. caves, arches and stacks), with an explanation of how they formed.
- A brief description of the geology in the area, and how this has helped create different landforms (e.g. headlands and bays).
- The erosional processes that are currently occurring in the area, and how the landscape is changing.
- Your answer could refer to the Dorset coast, which is made from alternating bands of hard rock (e.g. limestone and chalk) and soft rock (e.g. clay). These rocks have been eroded at different rates, leading to a range of coastal landforms, including bays (such as Lulworth Cove), arches (such as Durdle Door) and stacks (such as Old Harry).

4 a) B *[1 mark]*
*Soils in tropical rainforests are deep but there is only a thin fertile layer because nutrients are rapidly reabsorbed by the dense vegetation. However, there is a thick leaf layer because the trees drop their leaves all year round.*

b) E.g. the hot, wet climate provides the ideal conditions for rapid chemical weathering *[1 mark]*. This means that deep soils form over time as the bedrock is weathered *[1 mark]*. Fallen leaves decay quickly in the hot, moist climate, so there is a nutrient-rich surface layer of soil *[1 mark]*. Heavy rain washes nutrients away, so the lower levels of soil aren't very fertile *[1 mark]*.
*You may also have mentioned that there are no distinct seasons, so trees drop their leaves all year round, which forms a thick leaf layer.*

c) E.g. sustainable management strategies balance development with the protection of the environment, so that people today can get what they need without preventing future generations getting what they need *[1 mark]*. Ecotourism minimises damage to the environment, e.g. tourists visit in small groups and often take part in activities to raise awareness of conservation issues *[1 mark]*. Ecotourism also benefits local people by giving them reliable employment, which helps economic development of the area *[1 mark]*. Ecotourism can help to conserve the rainforest as the money generated can be invested in education projects to promote conservation in the local community *[1 mark]*.

5 a) E.g. **Item:** dog biscuit/orange *[1 mark]*
**Reason:** any one from: e.g. they float so you can take measurements from them *[1 mark]*. / They don't have much surface area above the water, so they are less likely to be affected by wind *[1 mark]*. / They biodegrade so the investigation won't harm the environment if the floats aren't caught *[1 mark]*.

b) E.g. the float got caught on something, e.g. a rock as it passed downstream *[1 mark]* so it took much longer for the float to reach the end of the timed section *[1 mark]*.

c) $\frac{315 + 255 + 278 + 310 + 302 + 279 + 297}{7} = \frac{2036}{7}$ *[1 mark]*
Mean = **291** s (to the nearest second) *[1 mark]*
*You may have written your answer to more significant figures — you'll still get a mark as long as it rounds to 291 s.*

d) This question is level marked. There are 3 extra marks available for spelling, punctuation and grammar.
How to grade your answer:
Level 0: There is no relevant information. *[0 marks]*
Level 1: There is a basic evaluation of the results, but little or no attempt to form a judgement on their effectiveness in providing a conclusion. *[1-2 marks]*
Level 2: There is a clear evaluation of the results of the enquiry and an attempt to make a judgement about their effectiveness in reaching a valid conclusion. *[3-5 marks]*
Level 3: There is a detailed evaluation of the results of the enquiry and a clear judgement about their effectiveness in reaching a valid conclusion. *[6-8 marks]*

Make sure your spelling, punctuation and grammar are consistently correct, that your meaning is clear and that you use a range of geographical terms correctly *[0-3 marks]*.
Here are some points your answer may include:
- A description of the results obtained in the investigation.
- The conclusions that could be drawn from the results obtained.
- Whether the conclusions drawn answer the original question of the enquiry.
- Any limitations that may have affected the reliability or accuracy of the results obtained, including the size of the samples used.
- An overall judgement as to whether or not the results enabled valid conclusions to be drawn.

## Practice Paper 2: People and Society

### Pages 171-175

1 a) i) D *[1 mark]*
*Informal sector jobs aren't taxed — they aren't formal jobs so are not regulated by the government.*
ii) E.g. housing in squatter settlements like that shown in Figure 1 is often badly built and overcrowded *[1 mark]*.

b) This question is level marked. How to grade your answer:
Level 0: There is no relevant information. *[0 marks]*
Level 1: There are a few points about the challenge of transport provision in a named AC city. *[1-2 marks]*
Level 2: There is a clear description of the challenges of transport provision in a named AC city, and a discussion of how these challenges have affected life there. *[3-4 marks]*
Level 3: There is a detailed description of the challenges of transport provision in a named AC city, and a detailed discussion of how these challenges have affected life there. *[5-6 marks]*

Your answer must focus on a named city in an AC.
Here are some points your answer may include:
- A brief overview of the city's transport system, e.g. road and rail networks.
- A description of the challenges the city faces in transport provision, such as increasing population and lack of funding.
- A discussion of how these challenges affect life in the city, e.g. congestion on the roads, overcrowding on trains and increased air pollution.

- Your answer could refer to London, which has a good transport system, including frequent buses and the Underground, but is experiencing difficulties in transport provision due to the rising population and increasing number of commuters. This has led to congestion on the roads, with average daytime traffic speeds in central London of only 8 miles per hour, and overcrowding on underground and overground trains, with delays due to overcrowding on Underground services more than doubling between 2013 and 2015.

2 a) i) 78.3% *[1 mark]*

*Manufactured and other products are left. 69.4 + 8.9 = 78.3.*

  ii) Nicaragua's largest exports are agricultural products (which are primary products), and manufactured goods make up less of its exports than in the UK *[1 mark]*. Primary products don't generate as much money as manufactured goods, which means there is less money to spend on development in Nicaragua *[1 mark]*.

  b) This question is level marked. How to grade your answer:
  Level 0: There is no relevant information. *[0 marks]*
  Level 1: There is a basic description of how one or two political and/or social factors have affected development in a named country. *[1-2 marks]*
  Level 2: There is a clear explanation of how both political and social factors have affected development in a named country. *[3-4 marks]*
  Level 3: There is a detailed explanation of how both political and social factors have affected development in a named country. *[5-6 marks]*

Your answer should clearly link political and social factors to the level of development in a named LIDC. Here are some points your answer may include:
- A brief description of the level of development in your chosen LIDC.
- An explanation of how political factors have influenced development in your chosen country, e.g. whether there has been conflict that has held back development, or corruption that has prevented aid reaching the people who need it.
- An explanation of how social factors have influenced development in your chosen country, e.g. whether there is tourism to the country, and whether it has helped development.
- Your answer could discuss the level of development in the Democratic Republic of the Congo, where conflict over political power and control of mineral ore resources, as well as political corruption, have severely hindered development. A recent government focus on improving health, education, access to clean water, etc. has helped to increase economic development in the country.

3 a) i) 188 200 *[1 mark]*

*Work out the range by subtracting the lowest value from the highest value, which here is 341 400 − 153 200.*

  ii) −32.7% (accept −33%) *[1 mark]*

*Work out percentage change by subtracting the original value from the final value, dividing the result by the original value, then multiplying by 100. So the calculation is ((171 800 − 255 200) ÷ 255 200) × 100.*

  b) i) C *[1 mark]*

*All of the other options either result in fewer young people, or in people living longer — both of these mean that the average age of the population increases.*

  ii) E.g. the UK government may need to raise taxes or cut spending in other areas in order to raise money to support older people *[1 mark]*. The government is raising the retirement age so that people work longer and don't claim a pension for as long *[1 mark]*. The government is also encouraging older people to save for their retirement, e.g. through 'pensioner bonds', so they are less dependent on state pensions or younger relatives *[1 mark]*.

  c) Economic hubs are places where economic activity is concentrated *[1 mark]*. They occur at a range of scales — e.g. they can be an entire region, a town or city, or a single street within a city *[1 mark]*.

4 a) i) C *[1 mark]*
   ii) D *[1 mark]*

*The Global Hunger Index shows how many people are suffering from hunger or illness caused by lack of food.*

  b) This question is level marked. How to grade your answer:
  Level 0: There is no relevant information. *[0 marks]*
  Level 1: There is a basic description of one past and/or one present attempt to increase food security at a national scale in a named country. *[1-2 marks]*
  Level 2: There is a clear comparison of one past and one present attempt to increase food security at a national scale in a named country. *[3-5 marks]*
  Level 3: There is a detailed comparison of one past and one present attempt to increase food security at a national scale in a named country. *[6-8 marks]*

Here are some points your answer may include:
- A brief introduction to food security issues in the country you have chosen.
- A description of one past scheme to increase food security, e.g. intensifying farming or the 'Green Revolution'.
- An evaluation of the scheme's effectiveness, e.g. to what extent it increased food security and any issues it caused (e.g. for the environment or people's health).
- A description of one present scheme to increase food security, e.g. GM crops or food production methods.
- An evaluation of the scheme's effectiveness, e.g. to what extent it is increasing food security and any issues it has caused (e.g. for the environment or people's health).
- A conclusion that compares the effectiveness of the two methods and reaches a decision about which was more successful.
- Your answer could refer to intensification of farming in the UK from the 1940s to the 1980s, which used mechanisation, higher yielding plants and large amounts of chemicals to increase food production. It decreased the UK's cereal imports from 70% to 20%, increasing food security. However, the use of monoculture meant that a high proportion of crops were harmed by drought in 1976, while the methods caused environmental problems such as water pollution and loss of biodiversity. Your second example could be the use of new technologies, such as hydroponics, that are currently being used in the UK. Hydroponics allows plants to be grown in a nutrient solution, sometimes in disused spaces such as old tunnels. It is increasing UK production of salad vegetables, and therefore increasing food security. However, the schemes can be expensive to set up and run, so the produce can be expensive. Some sites have been located in rural areas, damaging ecosystems.

5 a) The technique you describe should relate to human geography data that you collected yourself. You need to describe the technique and then explain why you used it, for example how it helped you to answer your original question and how it provided reliable and accurate data.

**Technique**: e.g. questionnaires / traffic counts / pedestrian counts / environmental surveys / land use mapping etc.

**Description and explanation**: e.g. I used an environmental survey, which involved giving a score out of 10 for a range of environmental factors, e.g. litter, at various different sites *[1 mark]*. The survey enabled me to identify areas that were experiencing environmental challenges so that I could assess the impact of urban sprawl on the rural-urban fringe *[1 mark]*. The score sheet I used in the survey meant that the results were numerical, so the data could be easily compared between sites *[1 mark]*.

b) i)

[1 mark]

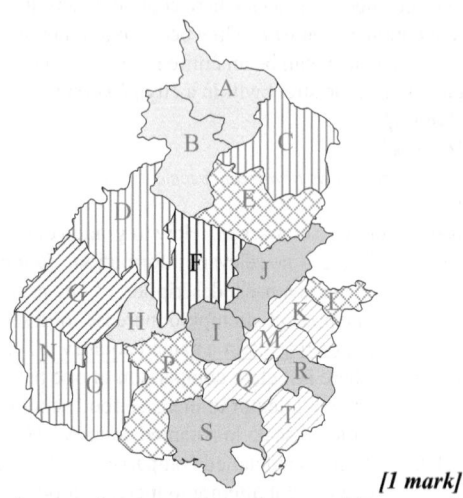

ii) Any one from: e.g. the students could have used a dot map, using identical symbols to show the distribution of people from ethnic minorities within the city *[1 mark]*. / Proportional symbols could have been used to show the relative number of people from ethnic minority groups in different areas *[1 mark]*.

c) This question is level marked. There are 3 extra marks available for spelling, punctuation and grammar.
How to grade your answer:
Level 0: There is no relevant information. *[0 marks]*
Level 1: There is a basic analysis of the evidence leading to a basic conclusion. *[1-2 marks]*
Level 2: There is a clear analysis of the evidence leading to a clear conclusion. *[3-5 marks]*
Level 3: There is a detailed analysis of the evidence leading to a detailed conclusion. *[6-8 marks]*
Make sure your spelling, punctuation and grammar are consistently correct, that your meaning is clear and that you use a range of geographical terms correctly *[0-3 marks]*.
Here are some points your answer may include:
- From the figures it can be concluded that ethnic diversity is having a strong influence on the character of Greaton.
- However, the influence varies across the districts, with a stronger influence where there are higher proportions of ethnic minority groups in the population.
- Figure 6 shows that in district A, where ethnic minorities make up 0-10% of the population (Figure 8), 75% of people felt that ethnic diversity wasn't having much impact on the city's character.
- In district Q, which has a much higher proportion of ethnic minorities (41-50%), 78% felt that there was a strong influence on the city's character.
- Figure 7 provides further evidence of the influence of ethnic diversity on the city's character. In the photo, an Indian restaurant, a shop selling Halal foods and a sign advertising Indian vegetables can be seen.

## Practice Paper 3: Geographical Exploration

### Page 180-181

1 This question is level marked. How to grade your answer:
Level 0: There is no relevant information. *[0 marks]*
Level 1: There is a basic description of Malawi's climate. *[1-2 marks]*
Level 2: There is a clear description of Malawi's climate and a basic explanation of how its location may have affected the climate. *[3-4 marks]*
Level 3: There is a detailed description of Malawi's climate and a clear explanation of how its location may have affected the climate. *[5-6 marks]*
Here are some points your answer may include:
- A summary of how temperature changes through the year in Malawi. E.g. it's hot all year round — the average temperature varies between 16 °C and 23 °C, but it is warmest from October to March.
- A summary of how precipitation varies, e.g. there's lots of precipitation from December to March, but almost no precipitation from June to October.
- A brief description of Malawi's location, e.g. Malawi is located in the southern hemisphere between the equator and the Tropic of Capricorn.
- An explanation for the temperatures and precipitation experienced. E.g. temperatures are hot all year round because Malawi is near to the equator. Malawi is between the low pressure belt at the equator and the high pressure belt at 30° S. Rainfall is high in low pressure belts and low in high pressure belts, which may explain why Malawi's monthly rainfall varies from almost nothing to over 200 mm over the year.

*Make sure you include information from the figures in your answer, for example, temperatures in specific months.*

2 a) Malawi's crop yields are expected to reduce by up to 20% *[1 mark]*. This may be caused by the reduction in water supply of up to 9% predicted for most of Malawi *[1 mark]*.

b) Most parts of Africa are expected to experience decreases in crop yields *[1 mark]*. This means that there will be less food available in Africa, so food security will decrease *[1 mark]*. The lack of crops to sell will limit income, inhibiting ability to import food from elsewhere and therefore decreasing food security further *[1 mark]*.

c) Least developed country: Malawi. Malawi has the lowest GNI per capita out of the four countries, so is the poorest country *[1 mark]*. It also has the lowest HDI score, which means that levels of social development, e.g. life expectancy and education level are also low *[1 mark]*. Bangladesh has a slightly higher percentage of people without access to safe water but Malawi scores significantly worse than Bangladesh on the other development indicators *[1 mark]*.

3 a) 48% *[1 mark]*

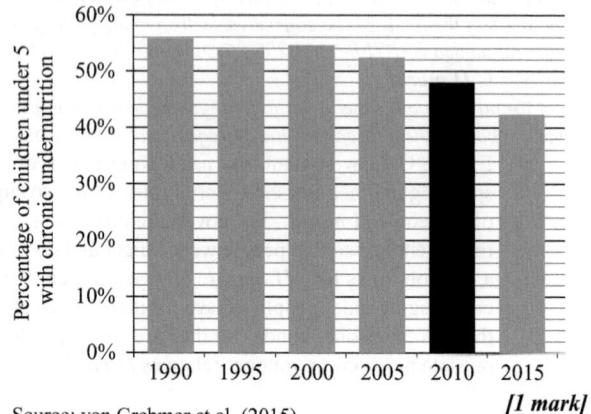

Source: von Grebmer et al. (2015)

*[1 mark]*

Answers

b) Any two from: e.g. Figure 1 shows that Malawi has a hot climate and very little rain between May and October *[1 mark]*. This may make it hard to produce food all year round, so children under 5 may not be getting enough to eat *[1 mark]*. / Figure 9 shows that there can be extreme events, such as droughts and floods *[1 mark]*. These can lead to crop failures so families may not be able to provide enough food for their children *[1 mark]*. / Figures 4 and 9 show that a lot of people in Malawi are very poor *[1 mark]*. This means that they may not be able to buy enough food to feed their children *[1 mark]*. / Figure 4 shows that Malawi is a poor country with a low level of development *[1 mark]*, so the government may not be able to import food from other countries if crops in Malawi fail, meaning children might not be able to get enough to eat *[1 mark]*.

4 This question is level marked. There are 3 extra marks available for spelling, punctuation and grammar.
How to grade your answer:
Level 0: There is no relevant information. *[0 marks]*
Level 1: There is a basic description of the state of food security in Malawi and a suggestion for a strategy that could increase food security. *[1-3 marks]*
Level 2: There is a basic description of the state of food security in Malawi and a suggestion for a strategy that could increase food security. The answer gives a simple justification using at least one figure and other knowledge. *[4-6 marks]*
Level 3: There is a clear description of the state of food security in Malawi and a suggestion for a strategy that could increase food security. The answer gives an adequate justification using several figures and other knowledge. *[7-9 marks]*
Level 4: There is a detailed description of the state of food security in Malawi and a suggestion for a strategy that could increase food security. The answer gives a detailed justification using several figures and other knowledge. *[10-12 marks]*

Make sure your spelling, punctuation and grammar are consistently correct, that your meaning is clear and that you use a range of geographical terms correctly *[0-3 marks]*.
You must use your own knowledge and information from pages 177-179 to suggest and justify a strategy to improve food security in Malawi. You will need to outline the advantages of your chosen strategy and provide evidence to support your choice.
Here are some points your answer may include:
- A brief description of the level of food security in Malawi, using evidence from the figures. E.g. Malawi currently has a high level of food insecurity. Its score on the World Hunger Index is 27.3, which indicates a 'serious' hunger problem, and 42% of children under 5 suffered from chronic undernutrition in 2015. Most of the population work in agriculture, many as subsistence farmers. But the country is vulnerable to natural disasters like droughts and heavy rainfall, which can destroy crops.
- An outline of the challenges for food security facing Malawi in the near future, e.g. water supply is expected to reduce by up to 9% by 2040 and crop yields are expected to decrease by up to 20% by 2050. This is likely to decrease food security in Malawi further.
- A proposal of a strategy that Malawi could use to increase food security, e.g. that Malawi should invest in permaculture projects along with community-run food banks.
- Your proposed strategy needs to be backed up with evidence from the figures and your own knowledge. E.g. permaculture and food banks are both small-scale approaches, so people don't need to rely on the government or large-scale organisations. This means it's less likely there will be problems with corruption or having to pay back large loans. A high proportion of Malawians are subsistence farmers (Figure 8), so already have access to land to grow crops. Permaculture also provides an environmentally friendly and low-maintenance way of producing food that recreates natural ecosystems. This should limit soil erosion from heavy rainfall and ensure that the land remains productive. Permaculture encourages a range of crop types, reducing the country's dependence on maize, which should help to improve nutrition among children (Figure 7). Although permaculture offers a long-term solution to the problem of food security, short-term solutions are also needed because of the problems with floods and droughts (Figures 5 and 9). Community-run food banks would ensure a reliable source of food for individuals affected by natural disasters and the poorest people in communities, improving food security for everyone.

*You may have decided on a different strategy — that's fine, as long as you can justify your choice.*

# Acknowledgements

Data used to construct graph on page 8: NOAA 2016; Vecchi and Knutson, 2011.

Map on page 10: Aqueduct Global Maps 2.1 Indicators. Constructing Decision-Relevant Global Water Risk Indicators by Francis Gassert, Paul Reig, Tien Shiao, Matt Luck, Research Scientist, ISciences LLC and Matt Landis Research Scientist, ISciences LLC - April 2015; water supply map on page 178: Luck, M., M. Landis, F. Gassert. 2015. "Aqueduct Water Stress Projections: Decadal projections of water supply and demand using CMIP5 GCMs." Washington, DC: World Resources Institute.
Both licensed under CC BY 4.0 https://creativecommons.org/licenses/by/4.0/

Map on page 11 contains OS data © Crown copyright and database right 2023.

Satellite image on page 12: Jeff Schmaltz, MODIS Rapid Response Team, NASA/GSFC.

Photograph of flood defences on page 12: U.S. Army Corps of Engineers.

Photograph on *p.13* (Haweswater) © John Douglas/ *p.27* (scientist analysing ice core) © NASA/Lora Koenig/ *p.40* (Old Harry) © Raymond Knapman/ *p.40* (Lulworth Cove) © Nick MacNeill/ *p.40* (Chesil Beach) © Eugene Birchall/ *p.40* (Swanage Bay) © Peter Trimming/ *p.42* (landslides) © Robin Webster/ *p.43* (sea wall) © David Dixon/ *p.43* (groynes) © N Chadwick/ *p.43* (beach replenishment) © Maurice D Budden/ *p.50* (Hell Gill Force) © Roger Templeman/ *p.50* (gorge) © Ian Greig/ *p.50* (Eden at Salkeld) © Greg Fitchett/ *p.50* (Eden floodplain) © Rose and Trev Clough/ *p.50* (v-shaped valley) © Mick Garratt/ *p.51* (landslide) © Stephen Craven/ *p.52* (sandstone cliffs) © Andy Waddington/ *p.52* (Great Asby Scar) © Peter Standing/ *p.53* (reservoir) © Rose and Trev Clough/ *p.53* (River Eden) © Andy Connor/ *p.54* (River Wampool) © Simon Ledingham/ *p.83* (Chinatown) © Colin Smith/ *p.97* (damaged building in Libya) © Al Jazeera English/ *p.118* (wetlands) © Steve Sheppard/ *p.121* (Chinatown, Liverpool) © Alan Walker/ *p.121* (London Road, Sheffield) © Basher Eyre/*p.123* (film set) © Jake Watson/ *p.126* (tractor) © Walter Baxter/ *p.138* (greenhouse) © David Anstiss/*p.145* (river fieldwork) © Robbie Livingstone/*p.173* (central London) © Colin Smith/*p.175* (street) © Stephen McKay. Licensed for re-use under the Creative Commons Attribution-Share Alike 2.0 Generic Licence. https://creativecommons.org/licenses/by-sa/2.0/

Map of drought risk on page 16 © UCL Global Drought Monitor/Ben Lloyd Hughes

Photograph of Nepal earthquake damage on page 19 © Rajan Journalist. Licensed under CC BY 4.0.
https://creativecommons.org/licenses/by-sa/4.0/deed.en

Short term climate graphs on pages 26 and 32 adapted from Morice, C.P., J.J. Kennedy, N.A. Rayner, J.P. Winn, E. Hogan, R.E. Killick, R.J.H. Dunn, T.J. Osborn, P.D. Jones and I.R. Simpson (in press) An updated assessment of near-surface temperature change from 1850: the HadCRUT5 dataset. Journal of Geophysical Research (Atmospheres) doi:10.1029/2019JD032361. HadCRUT5 data were obtained from http://www.metoffice.gov.uk/hadobs/hadcrut5 on [23.03.2023] and are © British Crown Copyright, Met Office [2020], provided under an Open Government License, http://www.nationalarchives.gov.uk/doc/open-government-licence/version/3/

Climate predictions on page 31 from Adapting to climate change UK Climate Projections, 2009; migration graph on page 112; 2013 population pyramid on page 112; 1964 average number of children per family on page 113; map of over-65s on page 113; working hours figures on page 116; statistics regarding media industries on page 120; calorie intake data, graph of wheat yield and UK produce-growing data on page 136 all contain public sector information licensed under the Open Government Licence v3.0. http://www.nationalarchives.gov.uk/doc/open-government-licence/version/3/

Sea level rise data on page 31 from Lowe, J. A., Howard, T. P., Pardaens, A., Tinker, J., Holt, J., Wakelin, S., Milne, G., Leake, J., Wolf, J., Horsburgh, K., Reeder, T., Jenkins, G., Ridley, J., Dye, S., Bradley, S. (2009), UK Climate Projections science report: Marine and coastal projections. Met Office Hadley Centre, Exeter, UK.

Figure 1 sea level rise graph on page 32 adapted from Climate Change 2001: The Scientific Basis. Contribution of Working Group I to the Third Assessment Report of the Intergovernmental Panel on Climate Change. Figure 5. Cambridge University Press.

Topographic map of the United Kingdom on page 35 by Captain Blood licensed under the Creative Commons Attribution-Share Alike 3.0 Unported license. https://creativecommons.org/licenses/by-sa/3.0/deed.en

Map extracts on pages 55, 155, 156 and 167 reproduced with permission by Ordnance Survey® © Crown copyright 2023 OS 100034841.

Population table on page 80 adapted from United Nations, Department of Economic and Social Affairs, Population Division (2014). World Urbanization Prospects: The 2014 Revision, Highlights (ST/ESA/SER.A/352).

Data on page 81: The World Bank: Urban population - Low & middle income. Source: World Bank staff estimates based on the United Nations Population Division's World Urbanization Prospects: 2018 Revision. Licensed under CC BY 4.0. https://creativecommons.org/licenses/by/4.0/

Photo of Makoko slum on page 87 © Heinrich-Böll-Stiftung. Licensed under CC BY 2.0.
https://creativecommons.org/licenses/by-sa/2.0/deed.en

Migration graph on page 88 adapted from data from the Office for National Statistics licensed under the Open Government Licence v.3.0.
https://www.nationalarchives.gov.uk/doc/open-government-licence/version/3/

Population graph on page 89; house prices line in housing graph on page 89; map of UK population density on page 109; 2001 population pyramids on pages 110, 112 and 115; ethnicity graph on page 112; map of UK regional population density on page 114 Source: Office for National Statistics licensed under the Open Government Licence v3.0. https://www.nationalarchives.gov.uk/doc/open-government-licence/version/3/

Graph of housing completions on page 89 licensed under the terms of the Open Parliament Licence
https://www.parliament.uk/site-information/copyright-parliament/open-parliament-licence/

# Acknowledgements

Development statistics on page 92 from 2015 Human Development Report, United Nations Development Programme from hdr.undp.org. Licensed under CC BY 3.0 IGO (https://creativecommons.org/licenses/by/3.0/igo/)

Statistics on page 96 (except GNI and HDI); data used to calculate GDP change on page 97; UK birth/death rates on page 111; population, employment and GDP data in Figure 8 on page 178 from The World Factbook 2013-14. Washington, DC: Central Intelligence Agency, 2023.

GNI per capita values on page 96, data in table on page 101 and data in table on page 177 (except HDI and Global Hunger Index): Source: The World Bank: GNI per capita, Atlas method (current US$). Source: World Bank national accounts data, and OECD National Accounts data files. Licensed under CC BY 4.0. https://creativecommons.org/licenses/by/4.0/

HDI values on page 96 from 2015 Human Development Report, United Nations Development Programme. Licensed under CC BY 3.0 IGO https://creativecommons.org/licenses/by/3.0/igo/

Development statistics on page 101 from 2015 Human Development Report, United Nations Development Programme. Licensed under CC BY 3.0 IGO https://creativecommons.org/licenses/by/3.0/igo/

Statistics on page 101 (education, vaccinations, water) from Unicef. Licensed under CC BY 3.0 IGO https://creativecommons.org/licenses/by-nc/3.0/igo/

Poverty statistics (undernutrition and death rates) on page 103: Source: Global Sustainable Development Goal Indicators Database © United Nations

Poverty statistics on page 103 from The World Bank: Countries / Democratic republic of Congo - Overview. © World Bank. Licensed under the Creative Commons Attribution 3.0 (CC BY 3.0 IGO) https://creativecommons.org/licenses/by/3.0/igo/

Import/Export data on page 104 and UK birth/death rates on page 114: The World Factbook 2021. Washington, DC: Central Intelligence Agency, 2023.

Data to construct map on page 106 from The World Bank: Country and Lending Groups. Licensed under CC BY 3.0 IGO (https://creativecommons.org/licenses/by/3.0/igo/)

Information used in article on page 107 from Department for International Development. Licensed under the Open Government Licence v3.0. https://www.nationalarchives.gov.uk/doc/

Data used to compile the UK average rainfall map on pages 109 and 114 from the Manchester Metropolitan University.

Land use map on page 109 based on: Cole, B.; King, S.; Ogutu, B.; Palmer, D.; Smith, G.; Balzter, H. (2015). Corine land cover 2012 for the UK, Jersey and Guernsey. NERC Environmental Information Data Centre. http://doi.org/10.5285/32533dd6-7c1b-43e1-b892-e80d61a5ea1d. This resource is made available under the terms of the Open Government Licence.

2015 population pyramid on pages 110 and 115 constructed using data from Population Division, World Population Prospects, the 2015 revision, by Department of Economic and Social Affairs. © United Nations 2023. Accessed 23.06.2016. Reprinted with the permission of the United Nations.

Data used to create graphs of employment sectors on pages 116 and 122: Welsh Government - Statistics © Crown Copyright 2015.

Table and total takings in question 1b) on page 123 source: The Numbers®, http://www.the-numbers.com/movie/Skyfall#tab=international

Calorie intake map on page 130 and 174 © Food and Agriculture Organization of the United Nations. FAOSTAT. World food supply 2011 - 2015 http://www.fao.org/faostat/en/#data/FBS/visualize. Accessed 09.09.2016

Map of World Hunger Index on page 130, data of Bangladesh and Malawi's GHI scores and Prevalence of Stunting in Children under Five Years on pages 177 & 178 from Global Hunger Index 2014. von Grebmer, K., A. Saltzman, E. Birol, D. Wiesmann, N.Prasai, S. Yin, Y.Yohannes, P. Menon, J. Thompson, and A. Sonntag. 2014. 2014 Global Hunger Index: The Challenge of Hidden Hunger. Bonn, Germany; Washington, D.C.; Dublin, Ireland: Deutsche Welthungerhilfe: International Food Policy Research Institute; Concern Worldwide. Adapted and reproduced with permission from the International Food Policy Research Institute www.ifpri.org.

Cereal production map on page 132 © Food and Agriculture Organization of the United Nations. FAOSTAT. Cereal production quantities by country 2012 -2014 http://www.fao.org/faostat/en/#data/QC/visualiz. Accessed 23.07.2018.

Photo of tomatoes grown on rockwool by Goldlocki. Licensed under CC BY 3.0 https://creativecommons.org/licenses/by-sa/3.0/deed.en

Data used to construct graph on page 140 from Eurostat © European Union, 1995-2016 https://creativecommons.org/licenses/by/4.0/

Data used to construct the population density of the UK map on page 150 and the flow map of immigration on page 154 - Source: Office for National Statistics licensed under the Open Government Licence v3.0. http://www.nationalarchives.gov.uk/doc/open-government-licence/version/3/

Data used to construct pie charts on page 172 © World Trade Organisation 2023.

Data used to construct table on page 173: Office for National Statistics licensed under the Open Government Licence v3.0. http://www.nationalarchives.gov.uk/doc/open-government-licence/version/3/

Change in crop yields map on page 177: The World Bank: Change in Agriculture Yields: Climate Change Knowledge Portal. Licensed under CC BY 4.0. https://creativecommons.org/licenses/by/4.0/legalcode

HDI values on page 177 provided by the UNDP. Licensed under CC BY 3.0 IGO. http://creativecommons.org/licenses/by/3.0/igo/legalcode

# Index

## A
abrasion 36
accuracy 145
Advanced Countries (ACs) 74, 92
ageing population 113
agriculture 126, 133, 135, 137, 138
  in tropical rainforests 66
aid 95, 99, 105
allotments 135
Amazon rainforest 67
analysing data 144
Antarctica 68-70
Antarctic Treaty 70
anticyclones 10, 13
arches 38
Arctic 68
atmospheric pressure belts 2-4
attrition 36
averages 162

## B
bar charts 158
bays 38
beaches 39
biological weathering 36
biosphere reserves 67
birth rates 91
Boscastle 11
Boserup's theory 130
bottom-up aid 99, 105
building design
  (tectonic hazards) 22
built landscapes 35

## C
caves 38
charts 157-161
chemical weathering 36
Chesil Beach 40
choropleth maps 152
climate change 26-29
  causes 28, 29
  evidence 26, 27
  global impacts 30
  impacts on the UK 31
climatic zones 3
coastal landscapes 38-43
coastal management 43
collision plate boundaries 18, 19
command words 148

commercial fishing 126
compass points 155
conclusions 144
conflict (UK's role) 119
conservative plate boundaries 18, 19
constructive plate boundaries 18-20
continental crust 17
contour lines 156
convection currents 17
coral reefs 58, 61
core (of the Earth) 17
correlation 159
counter-urbanisation 78
cross-sections 161
crust (of the Earth) 17
cyclones 5, 8

## D
death rates 91
debt
  effects on development 94
  relief 99
decision-making exercise 142
deforestation 29, 66, 127
deindustrialisation 77
Democratic Republic of the Congo
  (DRC) 101-105
Demographic Transition Model
  (DTM) 111
deposition 37
  along coasts 37, 39
  along rivers 37, 48, 49
depressions 10
desire lines 154
destructive plate boundaries 18-20
development 91-105
  economic 91, 98
  factors affecting 93-95
  measuring 91
  uneven 92
diaries (evidence for
  climate change) 27
dispersion diagrams 160
Dorset coast 40-43
dot maps 151
droughts 10, 14
  Millennium Drought,
    Australia 14
Durdle Door 40

## E
earthquakes 19
  building design 22
  early warning systems 22
  focus 19
  Kashmir, Pakistan 21
  prediction 22
economic development 91, 98
  effect on resource demand 125
economic hubs 117
  South Wales 118
economy (of the UK) 116
ecosystems 57-61
  global distribution 58
ecotourism 67
Eden basin 50-53
El Niño 9
Emerging and Developing
  Countries (EDCs) 74, 92
employment sectors 116
enhanced greenhouse effect 29
erosion 36
  coastal 36, 38
  river 36, 46-48
ethical consumerism 134
ethnic diversity
  in London 112
  in the UK 121
European Heat Wave 13
evaluations 145
exam structure 1
extreme weather 4-9
  climate change 30, 31
  droughts 10, 14
  El Niño and La Niña 9
  flash flooding 11
  heat waves 13
  in Australia 5, 14
  in the UK 5, 11, 13
  tropical storms 8, 12

## F
fair trade 134
farming 126, 129, 133, 137
fieldwork 143-145
fishing 69, 126
flash flooding 11
floodplains 49
flow line maps 154

# Index

food
  access  130
  banks  137
  consumption  130, 134
  increasing production
      133, 135, 137
  insecurity  129
  security  129
  small-scale production  135
  supply  125
  UK food security  136-138
  waste  134
fossil fuels  127
freeze-thaw weathering  36

## G

genetically modified (GM) crops
    133
geographical enquiries  143
geographical exploration  142
geomorphic processes  36, 37
glaciated landscapes  35
global atmospheric circulation  2-4
Global Hunger Index  130
gorges  47
graphs  157-161
grasslands  58, 61
greenhouse effect  29
greenhouse gases  29
grid references  155
Gross Domestic Product (GDP)  91
Gross National Income (GNI)  91
Group of Seven (G7)  119

## H

headlands  38
heat waves  13
  European Heat Wave  13
high pressure weather systems  10
histograms  158
hot deserts  58, 59
hotspots  20
Human Development Index (HDI)
    91
hurricanes  8, 12
  Katrina  12
hydraulic action  36
hydroponics  133, 138

## I

ice cores  27
infant mortality rates  91
informal sector jobs  87
intensive farming  133, 137

interdependence  57, 65, 68
  in polar environments  68
  in tropical rainforests  65
internal growth (of population)  75
international organisations  119
interquartile range (IQR)  162
isolines  152

## K

Kashmir earthquake  21

## L

Lagos  85-87
land use (in the UK)  109
La Niña  9
latitude  150
levees  49
life expectancy  91
line graphs  157
lines of best fit  159
literacy rates  91
logging  66
London  82-84, 112
longitude  150
longshore drift  39
lower course (of rivers)  46
Low-Income Developing
    Countries (LIDCs)  74, 92
lowland landscapes  35
Lulworth Cove  40

## M

magma  18
Malthus's theory  130
mantle  17
maps  150-156
  OS® maps  155, 156
mass movement  36
meanders  48
mechanical weathering  36
mechanisation of farming  126
megacities  74
migration  75
  to Lagos  85
  to London  82
  to the UK  112
Milankovitch cycles  28
Millennium Development Goals  98
  in the DRC  103
mineral extraction
  in polar environments  69
  in tropical rainforests  66

mining  127
mitigation
  (of tectonic hazards)  22
modal class  162

## N

natural increase (population)  75
natural landscapes  35
North Atlantic Treaty
    Organisation (NATO)  119
nutrient cycle
  (in tropical rainforests)  64

## O

oceanic crust  17
Ordnance Survey (OS®) maps
    155, 156
organic farming  133
ox-bow lakes  48

## P

paintings (evidence for
    climate change)  27
percentages  162
percentiles  163
permaculture  135
pie charts  160
plate boundaries  18-20
polar environments  58, 59, 68-70
  Antarctic Treaty  70
  characteristics  59, 68
  distribution  58
  human impacts  69
  interdependence  68
  Svalbard  70
politics
  effect on development  94
  in the DRC  101
  in the UK  116
population
  change in the UK  110-113
  effect on resources  109, 125, 130
  pyramids  110, 112, 159
prediction (tectonic hazards)  22
primary products  100
proportional symbol maps  151
pull factors  75
push factors  75

# Index

## Q
quartiles 162
Quaternary period 26

## R
radial graphs 161
rainforests (tropical) 58, 60, 64-67
ratios 163
reliability (of data) 145
reservoirs 128
resources 125
re-urbanisation 79
river basin management 53
river landscapes 46-53
Rostow's model 98
route maps 153
rural-urban migration 75
Russia-Ukraine conflict 119

## S
saltation 37
scatter graphs 159
sea ice positions 27
sea level rise 30, 31
seasonal food 134, 136
slides (mass movement) 36
slumps (mass movement) 36
slums 87
soil profiles
  (in tropical rainforests) 65
solution
  erosion 36
  transportation 37
South Wales 118
sphere of influence maps 153
spits 39
squatter settlements 76, 87
stacks 38
statistics 162, 163
suburbanisation 77
sunspots 28
suspension 37
sustainability
  and food security 133-138
  in cities 84, 87
  in polar environments 70
  in tropical rainforests 67
  of development 98, 103
  of forestry 67
Svalbard 70
Swanage Bay 40

## T
tectonic plates 17
temperate forests 58, 60
temperature data
  (evidence for climate change) 27
thematic maps 151
top-down aid 99, 105
tourism
  ecotourism 67
  effect on ecosystems 66, 67, 69
  effect on development 95
traction 37
trade
  effect on development 95, 100
  in the DRC 104
traffic congestion 76
trans-national companies
    (TNCs) 100
  in the DRC 105
transportation 37
tropical rainforests 58, 60, 64-67
  Amazon 67
  characteristics 60
  distribution 58
  goods and services 66
  human impacts 66
  interdependence 65
  soil 65
  water and nutrient cycles 64
tropical storms 5, 8, 12
  Hurricane Katrina 12
typhoons 8

## U
UK
  economic hubs 117, 118
  economy 116
  extreme weather 5
  food security 136-138
  impacts of climate change 31
  land use 109
  media exports 120
  multiculturalism 121
  population change 110-113
  population density 109
  rainfall 109
  relief (of landscape) 35
  working hours 116
Ukraine 119
United Nations (UN) 119
upland landscapes 35
upper course (of rivers) 46, 47
urban gardens 135
urbanisation 74-76
urban sprawl 85

## V
validity (of data) 145
volcanoes 20
  as a cause of climate change 28
  building design 22
  prediction 22
V-shaped valleys 47

## W
waste management 87
water cycle
  (in tropical rainforests) 64
waterfalls 47
water transfers 128
ways of life in cities 83, 86
weather hazards 8-14
weathering 36
whaling 69
wind roses 161
world cities 74
world hunger index 130